Film Diplomacy

Film Diplomacy

A Media History of
Turkey—US Relations

AYŞEHAN JÜLİDE ETEM

Columbia

University

Press

New York

Columbia University Press
Publishers Since 1893
New York   Chichester, West Sussex
cup.columbia.edu

Copyright © 2026 Columbia University Press
All rights reserved

Cataloging-in-Publication Data is available from the Library of Congress.

ISBN 9780231219990 (hardback)
ISBN 9780231220002 (trade paperback)
ISBN 9780231563017 (EPUB)
ISBN 9780231566216 (PDF)
LCCN 2025037930

Cover design: Elliott S. Cairns
Cover image: Educational Information Network of Turkey, Photograph Archive of the Ministry of National Education of Turkey, General Directorate of Innovation and Educational Technologies

GPSR Authorized Representative: Easy Access System Europe,
Mustamäe tee 50, 10621 Tallinn, Estonia, gpsr.requests@easproject.com

Contents

Introduction 1

1 From Ottoman Shadows to Global Stage: The Rise of Film in Turkey 39

2 Beyond the Contract: How Missionaries Forged Nontheatrical Havens 59

3 US Government Film Programming in Turkey 101

4 The Educational Film Center of Turkey 137

5 Audience Reception Research 179

Epilogue 211

Acknowledgments 217
Notes 221
Bibliography 261
Index 283

Film Diplomacy

Introduction

Turkey: Middle East Bridgeland (Otto Lang, 1961; hereafter *Bridgeland*), an American educational film, opens with a map of the world. From this global perspective, the focus gradually narrows, centering on Turkey and its pivotal role as a bridge between cultures and continents (figure 0.1). The film follows the journey of Mike Adams, a blond American boy, and Ahmet Yılmaz, an olive-toned boy from Adana, as they traverse Turkey's historical landscapes using modern transportation (figure 0.2). The juxtaposition of cultural heritage and rapid infrastructural development—the latter strengthened by American assistance—structures the film's narrative. "With the help of American know-how and modern road equipment," Ahmet explains, "a network of highways is being built, and today we travel on paved roads on modern buses." The film thus positions the United States as a benevolent force, instrumental in Turkey's transformation.[1] Western-style clothing and secular classrooms further reinforce the image of a nation remade through modernization.

This narrative of a modern nation converges with a civilizational iconography during a visit to the ancient amphitheater at Pergamum (figure 0.3). Ahmet describes the site as a "religious, cultural, and [commercial] center" where "gladiators [once] fought to the death for the glory of the Roman emperor." The boys reenact a gladiatorial contest, transforming imperial memory into playful performance. Their mock combat

FIGURE 0.1 Opening map of Turkey from *Turkey: Middle East Bridgeland* (1961).

Source: Indiana University Libraries, Moving Image Archive.

FIGURE 0.2 Mike and Ahmet on a modern ship in *Turkey: Middle East Bridgeland*.

Source: Indiana University Libraries, Moving Image Archive.

FIGURE 0.3 Mike and Ahmet in the ancient amphitheater at Pergamum in *Turkey: Middle East Bridgeland*.

Source: Indiana University Libraries, Moving Image Archive.

does more than animate history; it aligns Turkey's modern youth with a Greco-Roman legacy, framing the Turkish landscape as a dormant archive of Western greatness. Positioned alongside scenes of paved roads and secular classrooms, the sequence suggests that modernization—facilitated by US aid—is not an external imposition but the recovery of a rightful civilizational inheritance. The film presents Turkey as a former center of greatness reawakened through American partnership.

The film concludes with a symbolic exchange of gifts: Ahmet presents Mike with a photo album of Turkey, and Mike gives Ahmet his camera. Ahmet declares, "We have become the best of friends," indicating the broader diplomatic narrative: The boys' friendship mirrors the growing relationship between the United States and Turkey (figure 0.4). Produced for pedagogical use through United World Films' World Neighbors series and guided by consultants from the University of Wisconsin and Iowa State

FIGURE 0.4 Mike and Ahmet shaking hands in *Turkey: Middle East Bridgeland*.

Source: Indiana University Libraries, Moving Image Archive.

University, *Bridgeland* functions as a strategic film. It frames development not only as technical advancement but also as cultural alignment—subtly promoting a narrative of bilateral amity under the banner of modernization, progress, and civilization.

This film offers a compelling entry point into the phenomenon of film diplomacy, a strategic communication process that employs films to foster international relations, shape public opinion, and influence policy objectives. Unlike conventional analyses that focus on propaganda or cultural exchange, film diplomacy foregrounds the life cycle of a film. It examines how films are produced or reedited with specific national and geopolitical intentions, how they circulate through both national and transnational networks, where and how they are exhibited, and how audiences interpret them—each phase representing a potential site of diplomatic intervention. Rather than relying solely on the notion of soft power—"the ability to obtain preferred outcomes by attraction rather than coercion or payment"[2]—this framework attends to the physical infrastructures—understood, following media scholar Lisa Parks, as "material sites and objects"[3]—through which film operates as a strategic tool of influence. States and cultural institutions have deployed films like *Bridgeland* not only to foster amity or incite antagonism but also to shape alliances, manage public sentiment, and mediate stereotypes. Such films inform audiences about national dynamics while navigating intersections of race, religion, class, nationality, and gender. As the *Bridgeland* example illustrates, film functions as a subtle yet potent mechanism for reinforcing ideological narratives and aligning public perceptions with geopolitical imperatives.

By uncovering the multifaceted ways in which film serves as a tool for shaping perceptions, I develop the conceptual framework of film diplomacy to identify and analyze key stakeholders, their interests, and target audiences. In doing so, I address a significant gap in the existing historiography: The US-Turkey educational film partnership has been largely overlooked in both Cold War media studies and the history of diplomacy. The study of this film network offers a new way of understanding US engagement with Turkey—a country geographically bordered during the Cold War by Europe, the Middle East, and the Soviet Union—whose leadership and populace were intensely interested in the American way of life. Drawing on Michel Foucault's concept of governmentality—the strategic management of populations through institutional and discursive practices[4]—I examine how audiovisual technologies functioned as tools for enacting racialized visions of development, shaping subjects through the lens of whiteness, and aligning Turkish identity with Western-centric ideals of secularism and modernity. By identifying film diplomacy as an outcome of both foreign policy and domestic public relations between Turkey and the United States, I show how government-sponsored films were used to build relationships and implement policy on the ground. Given the complexity of international relationships and the prevalence of institutional media practices in the mid-twentieth century, this perspective provides a new lens through which to see how countries enact diplomacy as a multilayered process of negotiation to promote development and security.

By analyzing archival materials from three continents and over a dozen libraries, I show how film—especially nonfiction and nontheatrical genres—played a pivotal role in fostering closer ties between nations. Specifically, I identify and analyze the Educational Film Center in Turkey and engage with a wide array of previously unexamined and in some cases recently declassified archival documents to demonstrate the need for a new history of film that centers on the influence of government and institutional power. I argue that film was a pivotal medium for advancing institutional agendas within the framework of a modernization project fundamentally rooted in racialized assumptions. Within this context, educational films emerged as strategic tools, intended to address infrastructural challenges, disseminate public service messages, wage information campaigns, promote policy objectives, and shape social practices in Turkey and US-Turkey relations between 1930 and 1986. The versatile nature of educational films made them a key tool for institutional agents, enabling divergent applications and messages tailored to specific audiences. The establishment of an infrastructure centered around educational films in the 1950s laid the groundwork for transnational agents to use film as a medium for envisioning and negotiating the optimal relationship between the United States and Turkey. In other words, the iterative process of production, exhibition, distribution, and audience reception proved instrumental in honing a film's central message: Stakeholders on both sides could sharpen the film's focus through edits and contextual framing and introduce nuanced layers of meaning through translations, voice-overs, and targeted discussions. Ultimately, educational films played a vital role in strengthening diplomatic relations as part of a modernization initiative, harnessing the medium's capacity to accommodate and advance different institutional agendas under a unifying ideological banner. Educational films functioned as racialized technologies of modernization. The film reels, projectors, and mobile cinema units deployed across Turkey were not only pedagogical instruments; they were also tools of ideological persuasion, embedded with racialized assumptions about progress. For American officials and their Turkish partners, audiovisual technology symbolized modernity: Its presence signaled development, and its content prescribed what that development should look like.

Building on this framework, it is crucial to explore how the narratives embedded within these films intersected with ideological constructs of race and identity. I demonstrate that US actors and Turkish elites not only operated with a pro-American ideological framework of development and national unity but also fundamentally centered their efforts on whiteness. Drawing on critical race theory and whiteness studies, I approach whiteness as an institutionalized mode of governance—an invisible regime of power and norms that shaped the modernization project. In other words, I examine whiteness as an ideological lens that guided both American and Turkish modernization efforts, indicating how race operated not only on the screen but also within the broader dynamics of global politics and policy. In this context, whiteness functions as an "unmarked norm"[5]— an invisible benchmark of civilization, progress, and benevolence against which all others are measured. Western, white cultural values are equated with virtue and modernity, whereas nonwhite or not-yet-white bodies are positioned as needing development or uplift.

These mechanisms frame nonwhite nations as dependent on Western knowledge and resources, thus implicitly resisting the critiques of race that inform, for instance, the Non-Aligned Movement and the Afro-Asian Peoples Solidarity Group.[6] This process contributes to a Cold War logic that positions the United States and its allies as indispensable to the development of the so-called Third World nations, thus undermining the autonomy that solidarity movements sought to foster by challenging paternalistic interventions of Western powers. In this transnational communication network, whiteness was a critical element of the ideological infrastructure sustaining US global dominance. By situating the US-Turkey film network within a critique of how race, media, and diplomacy intersect, I link Turkishness to global whiteness, with Turkish whiteness embodying an affiliation with a civilization that embraces modernity and a Western identity. This alignment reflects not only a desire for acceptance within the international community but also a strategic maneuver to assert Turkey's position as a modern state. My conceptualization of whiteness as a performative, exclusionary, evolving, and institutionalized construct within Turkey and US-Turkey relations underscores these complex dynamics.

By integrating national and transnational perspectives, I scrutinize the production, distribution, exhibition, and reception of educational films to illuminate how these films served as strategic instruments for both American and Turkish actors, shaping bilateral relations and advancing a range of social, political, economic, and cultural objectives. Beyond a close textual and visual analysis of films, I identify the agency of key actors in shaping film programs under the influence of national and foreign policies. I employ critical discourse analysis to broaden our understanding of the institutional mechanisms, their agents, and their tools at work across these contexts. Through an investigation of the pre–Cold War and Cold War periods, I elucidate the tensions and collaborations among stakeholders and the subsequent impact on film content, infrastructure, and audience reception.

Building on this foundation, I explore four primary research questions. The first line of inquiry pertains to the medium of film and analyzes the discursive strategies employed within educational films. Specifically, I investigate the evolution and reception of film content over exhibition space and time in relation to shifting political and cultural contexts by exploring questions such as these: What arguments did the films convey, and how did they relate to the ideology of the time and place? How and why did the content of these films evolve over time? How were these films connected to policy efforts? Second, I focus on the role of institutional agents to find answers to the following question: Who exerted influence, and whose interests did the films promote? The third area of inquiry concerns the audiences, as I analyze reception surveys to explore a set of questions: Who were the intended audiences? Who were the interviewers and sponsors of the audience reception surveys? What were the audiences' responses to the films, and how did the researchers evaluate them? In what ways did the reactions and interests of audiences affect strategies? Finally, I examine the broader context: How did the national and international context affect, complicate, or support the production, exhibition, distribution, and reception of educational films?

To situate these inquiries, I consider the early years of the Republic of Turkey (1923–), when embracing modernity became synonymous with adopting a secular state identity. This shift implicitly aligned Turkey with whiteness and, by extension, with the United States. Educational films emerged as a key medium through which these connections were cultivated and reinforced. These nontheatrical and nonfiction films comprised a divergent array of productions that imparted ideas, facts, skills, morals, and social conduct in various contexts.[7] They usually were less than thirty minutes long in their original 16 mm or 35 mm format and were exhibited at schools, hospitals, public spaces, prisons, factories, churches, theaters, and festivals. A multitude of producers, including government agencies, religious organizations, philanthropic bodies, Hollywood studios, and commercial enterprises, contributed to their creation. In return, educational films, as a geopolitical phenomenon, facilitated the construction and maintenance of communication infrastructures worldwide, involving government bodies, organizations, humanitarian networks, and creative industries.

In 1930, an educational film network emerged out of the activities of the American Board of Commissioners for Foreign Missions (ABCFM), a Protestant missionary organization. The group's work extended to collaborative efforts with the Turkish Ministry of Health in 1937 and the US State Department in 1950. The 1952 partnership of the Ministry of National Education in Turkey (MNET); the United Nations Educational, Scientific, and Cultural Organization (UNESCO); and the US Information Service (USIS) led to a significant step in the development of educational films: the establishment of a comprehensive communication infrastructure. This collective effort operated under the banner of the Educational Film Center (EFC) in Ankara and remained active until 1986. My analysis focuses on the educational films produced, exhibited, and distributed between 1930 and 1986, with particular emphasis on the 1950s, a pivotal period in US-Turkey relations when Turkey was on the path to becoming a "little America."[8] For the Turkish elite, the United States became the epitome of civilized society, characterized by democratic values, economic prosperity, technological advancement, and cultural influence. Turkey's "little America" aspiration was historically rooted in a discourse of civilization and modernization tied to whiteness.[9]

The mid-twentieth century was a crucial time in Turkey's history, marked by its pursuit of modernization and alignment with Western powers, which fostered the emergence of an educational film culture shaped by domestic and international influences. In the early 1950s, commercial entities such as *Film ve Öğretim* (Film and education magazine); Mataş (distributor of media equipment); Bell and Howell–Gaumont (British licensed manufacturer and distributor of American Bell & Howell designs); and Teknik Kitabevi (Technical Bookstore) played a role in promoting educational films and related technologies in Turkey. Magazine writers prompted the government of Turkey to initiate an educational film revolution and encouraged teachers to use educational films in their classrooms. At times independently and at other times in cooperation with missionaries or American government agents, Turkish educators screened these films in schools, libraries, and open public spaces as well as Halk Evleri (People's Houses), which served as cultural and community centers.[10] The ABCFM, EFC, USIS, and Teknik Kitabevi maintained separate film libraries to preserve, distribute, and exhibit these materials. An examination of Turkey's educational film culture demonstrates the involvement of several key institutional agents, including Şinasi Barutçu, an award-winning Turkish painter, photographer, teacher, director of the EFC, and USIS-sponsored author; Adolphe Hübl, a UNESCO agent from Austria; Monteagle Stearns, a USIS film affairs officer; Sadun Katipoğlu, director of USIS-Turkey Cinema Services; Mahmut Özdeniz, the owner and editor of *Film ve Öğretim*; and Paul Nilson, an ABCFM missionary. The transmission channels within this network carried multidirectional flows; they mutually influenced one another as they disseminated information and propaganda that served both national and transnational purposes. Specifically, educational films were used by ABCFM missionaries to propagate Christian values and by US government agents to transmit anticommunist rhetoric and collaborate with Turkish officials to foster nationalism, all within the framework of modernization.

Another influential factor in the use of educational films originates from research projects conducted by American agents about the film industry and audience reception in Turkey. Notably, figures such as Eugene M. Hinkle, the second secretary of the American embassy in Ankara, and Daniel Lerner, an economist and social scientist, conducted crucial studies. In 1933, Hinkle's report for the US State Department's Near Eastern Affairs Division evaluated Turkey's foreign film policy, emphasizing the absence of import restrictions for American films in the country.[11] He referred to educational films as "practically unknown" and "a medium of propaganda" that would address challenges such as high illiteracy rates and national defense issues.[12] In support of this view, he referred to Nilson's observations that suggested educational films were a means for the United States to enter Turkish schools and foster government cooperation.[13] Unbeknownst to them, their vision of developing visual education as "a library of loan films in a center like Ankara" would eventually manifest in the establishment of the EFC.

Initially, the EFC functioned as a distributor of American films that promoted US models of education, governance, agriculture, and military structure. Over time, however, it evolved into a producer of nonfiction films about, by, and for the people of Turkey. This shift marked the emergence of a national educational film culture aimed at audiences that included rural populations, schoolchildren, and the general public. The EFC produced thousands of films on subjects such as health, history, geography, the sciences, the economy, the arts, the military, and technical information. These films modeled the practical steps and behaviors that aligned with the goals of the modernization project. In this sense, they were different from Hollywood films, which created desires and prompted audiences to dream. Educational films, by contrast, taught audiences in Turkey how to use tractors to improve the national economy, collaborate with Americans to fight communism, love the Turkish nation, and embrace new national policies like the population control law, which supported responsible family planning and reproductive health.

While these teachings were instrumental in cultivating productive, free-market-oriented, nationalist citizens, they were not without their drawbacks. American educational films, such as *Bridgeland*, often employed paternalistic and infantilizing tropes and reinforced a hierarchical relationship between the United States and its allies. They often portrayed non-Western nations as immature entities requiring external guidance, echoing the racist rhetoric of Cold War modernization theory. This strategy, as the historian Naoko Shibusawa argues, was employed by Western powers to justify their dominance over and interventionist policies toward nonwhite peoples.[14] In other words, American educational films reinforced the idea of US exceptionalism and global leadership. These films were part of the strategic deployment and control of knowledge, reinforcing Western hegemony.[15] By casting non-Western nations as immature and in need of development, these films showed the West as "superior" and perpetuated power imbalances.

This paternalistic framework also manifested in the context of Turkish educational films, where different pitfalls emerged. These EFC films served as a tool the state could use to promote a uniform and unified national identity, inculcating values of patriotism and unquestioning loyalty. They advanced a monolithic vision of Turkish identity as modern, white, Sunni Muslim, and Istanbul Turkish–speaking. By systematically erasing the histories of the diverse linguistic, religious, racial, and ethnic groups—such as Arabs, Armenians, Assyrians, Blacks, Circassians, Christians, Georgians, Greeks, Jews, Kurds, Laz, Shia Muslims, and Zazas—these films reinforced the notion of a homogeneous Turkish identity aligned with the state's vision of modernization. The notion of modernization became a path for these "nonexisting" people to become "Turkish," further consolidating the dominant ideological norms. This exclusionary approach, a hallmark of whiteness, rendered differences illegible within the national frame and upheld a normative identity tied to whiteness, heterosexuality, and able-bodiedness.

While these films did not explicitly reference the discursive categories of "white Turk" and "black Turk," their representational logic echoed the hierarchies embedded in these social constructs. In Turkish public discourse, the white Turk label typically refers to a secular, urban, educated, bilingual, and socioeconomically privileged Sunni Muslim.[16] By contrast, the metaphor of the black Turk evokes veiled, devout, rural, less privileged, monolingual citizens—often linked to communities excluded from dominant narratives of national identity. These terms, rooted in the intersections of religion, class, geography, and language, help illuminate the ideological terrain these films navigated. By privileging traits associated with the white Turk, educational films endorsed a vision of national belonging that implicitly regulated linguistic, religious, and ethnic differences. Rather than confronting diversity, these films absorbed it into a normative model of citizenship—one in which a population had to be managed, corrected, regulated, or rendered invisible. In this way, educational film functioned not simply as a reflection of national ideology but also as a constitutive technology of visual governance. It helped discipline audiences into a racialized and exclusionary vision of Turkish modernity—serving not only the foreign policy goals of film diplomacy but also the aims of a domestic campaign to consolidate a homogenized national identity.

Defining Film Diplomacy

Diplomacy, a dynamic process for navigating complex power structures, manifests in distinct forms beyond state-to-state interaction. Scholars have identified various subcategories of public diplomacy, such as cultural diplomacy, health diplomacy, and science diplomacy, each employing targeted strategies to achieve policy objectives.[17] While the influence of public diplomacy in shaping opinion and securing ideological consensus during the Cold War has been well documented,[18] the role of film as a material and institutional infrastructure for diplomacy remains undertheorized.

Historians and media scholars have made important inroads. Andrei Kozovoi analyzes how Soviet film diplomacy leveraged cinema as a "forefront" for promoting cultural exchange and "peaceful coexistence" between the United States and the USSR.[19] Hadi Gharabaghi's examination of the Syracuse Audiovisual Mission in Iran demonstrates the interplay among documentary production, legal discourse, and policymaking within the context of Cold War diplomacy.[20] These studies, alongside

Sangjoon Lee's work on the development of Asian film cultures and industries during the 1950s and 1960s, illuminate the multipurpose use of film as a diplomatic instrument.[21] Mila Turajlić examines the strategic use of film diplomacy in Yugoslavia's Cold War foreign policy.[22] By analyzing a network of cinematic collaboration between Yugoslavia and nonaligned African nations, she reveals how film functioned as a tool of diplomacy to balance ideological convictions by fostering alliances and downplaying socialist rhetoric. Additionally, through a partnership with the National Archives, Mark Williams has spearheaded innovative scholarship on film and the activities of the US Information Agency.[23] Yet despite this growing body of scholarship,[24] the term *film diplomacy* remains underdefined—often used descriptively rather than conceptually.

In this book, I address that gap by offering a historically grounded, theoretically informed definition of film diplomacy as a multiscalar infrastructure of governance—one that operates through production, circulation, and reception to support both geopolitical and national agendas. Rather than treating film as a passive vehicle of soft power, I conceptualize film diplomacy as an active process embedded in the governance of both domestic and foreign populations. Film diplomacy constitutes a technology of rule: It constitutes a system embedded in efforts to govern populations by modeling desirable behaviors and signaling that access to modernity, citizenship, and the political, economic, and social rewards of development depends on compliance with national norms and transnational agendas. In doing so, I provide a framework for understanding film as a technology of power used to regulate conduct and shape perception.[25]

Film diplomacy, as a form of public diplomacy, transcends the dichotomy between the two dominant schools of thought in public diplomacy, which advocate for either influencing attitudes and opinions through persuasion and propaganda or fostering lasting understanding through information and cultural exchange.[26] Film diplomacy weaves together narratives, information, and cultural connections, often modeling through personal encounters. For the communication scholar R. S. Zaharna, the holistic logic in public diplomacy emphasizes individuals navigating complex, interconnected relationships within a dynamic social universe.[27] Similarly, another communication scholar, Nancy Snow, argues that public diplomacy goes beyond government-to-government messages, encompassing both direct and indirect efforts by individuals, groups, and networks to shape foreign public opinion and influence policy decisions.[28] Building on Nicholas Cull's five activities of public diplomacy—listening, advocacy, cultural diplomacy, exchange, and international broadcasting—film resists neat classification, instead blending these categories.[29] As Cull observes, film's capacity to operate simultaneously across these domains underscores its strategic ambiguity and ideological reach. Understanding this layered function is key to analyzing film diplomacy, especially as it includes state-to-state communication (e.g., United States to Turkey), religious-organization-to-citizen interaction (e.g., missionaries to Turks or Americans), and state-to-citizen engagement (e.g., within Turkey).

Film diplomacy, therefore, functions as a complex form of public diplomacy that operates across social, cultural, and political domains. It facilitates mediated encounters and shapes public perception through the orchestration of curated foreign and domestic materials—strategically mobilized to cultivate support for both international and national policy agendas.

By navigating a dynamic network, film diplomacy operates not just across geographical borders but also within the intricate media ecology of each target audience. This engagement echoes Snow's emphasis on "measuring the communication context" surrounding actions,[30] acknowledging that effectiveness hinges on cultural resonance and audience reception. Film, with its narrative power and ability to evoke empathy, is uniquely suited to navigating these complexities. By weaving stories that resonate across cultures and engage audiences within their existing media ecosystems, film diplomacy provides a potent pathway for shaping attitudes, influencing policy agendas, and ultimately fostering lasting understanding.

I define film diplomacy as a communication process in which transnational agents accept, reject, adopt, and adapt films in order to build public relations, implement policies, and develop infrastructures. A holistic approach to film diplomacy integrates four key, interlinked domains: production (including sponsorship), exhibition, distribution, and reception of films. Production refers to the creation of films to present information or policy and to persuade audiences about a particular message. Exhibition entails presenting information or policy to a local or foreign public through films, film projectors, and mobile film units. Distribution is the orchestrated process that includes the formation and maintenance of film libraries to disseminate the intended messages to achieve policy goals. Reception involves the systematic collection, analysis, and transmission of information on films from and about a public, subsequently influencing policy. Film diplomacy refers to the efforts of institutions to communicate with both local and foreign publics to build relationships on global, transnational, and national scales to promote their influence, culture, values, and interests. By grounding film diplomacy in specific institutional settings and funding regimes, this definition illuminates how agents navigate legal frameworks and forge unexpected collaborations, even amidst divergent ideological stances.

Film Diplomacy as a Framework

The conceptual framework of film diplomacy operates across three interconnected levels, each distinguished by its tier of strategic intent, sophistication, and collaboration. The case of missionaries using film in Turkey exemplifies the rudimentary paradigm of this phenomenon. At the first level, missionaries, lacking a formal strategy or comprehensive deliberation, approach the task of influencing public attitudes through film in an ad hoc manner. Often this involves showcasing foreign solutions to local problems, such as agricultural practices or educational models, subtly aligning the community with the implicit agenda of the missionary society and, by extension, the foreign power it represents. This level is characterized by improvisation and limited understanding of local contexts, at times leading to unintended consequences.

Moving to the second level, a more sophisticated approach emerges, exemplified by the systematic engagement of players like the USIS during the Cold War. Here, film becomes a strategic tool, carefully selected, translated, and distributed through established channels to reach specific audiences with tailored messages. Public preparation is no longer incidental but a deliberate objective, achieved through film screenings coupled with magazines, books, cultural programs, surveys, and reports, all aiming to cultivate pro-American sentiment and align Turkish public opinion with US foreign policy goals.

Finally, the third level presents a heightened level of complexity in the form of collaborative models, such as the one established between Turkey and the United States. Here, both nations participate in film diplomacy, driven by intricate agendas that are both intertwined and distinct.

Turkey might seek to showcase its national identity and modernization efforts, while the United States might aim to maintain strategic partnerships and influence regional politics. This level requires navigating competing agendas, grappling with questions of whiteness, and maintaining mutual trust, all within a framework of streamlined bureaucratic processes. Each level builds upon the previous one, revealing a trajectory from improvised, individual-led efforts, to structured state strategies, to collaborative models that reflect complex, intertwined objectives.

Nontheatrical Film and Media

Building upon the growing body of scholarship in nontheatrical film and media studies, I examine the rich terrain of educational films within the context of Turkey and US-Turkey relations. In recent years, scholarly interest in nonfiction and nontheatrical forms has surged, offering new perspectives on cultural histories.[31] Recent monographs demonstrate a vast array of approaches for excavating new social, cultural, and institutional histories.[32] These studies collectively challenge traditional cinematic narratives, offering fresh perspectives on the medium's relationship to power, identity, nations, and everyday life.

In *Film Diplomacy*, I contribute to this literature by foregrounding nonfiction and nontheatrical cinema, particularly work that interrogates cinema's pedagogical, institutional, and governmental functions. At the same time, I move beyond the confines of Yeşilçam (Green Pine, ca. 1950–1990), often described as Turkey's counterpart to classical Hollywood, to analyze how educational films operated outside the commercial feature film industry. While books by Turkish film critics like Nijat Özön, Giovanni Scognamillo, and Rekin Teksoy, as well as those by scholars such as Savas Arslan and Gonul Donmez-Colin, have provided an important understanding of cinema in Turkey, their primary focus on fiction films has left a gap in the historiography.[33] Scholars have often ignored the study of the nontheatrical sector, as it has been "the domain of the anonymous, the uncelebrated, and the amateur."[34] In this book, I construct an alternative history of film that illuminates power dynamics, racial constructions, and the complex interplay among sponsors, films, and audiences, thus explaining the significance of these otherwise marginalized nontheatrical media.

The term *nontheatrical film* encompasses a wide range of formats and genres, including small-gauge film (works in formats like 16 mm and 8 mm), amateur film (noncommercial works like home movies), sponsored film, and useful film.[35] While these films were primarily shown in schools, factories, galleries, and even asylums, they also appeared in movie theaters, which complicates their classification.[36] In fact, in Turkey, the 1937 Öğretici ve Teknik Filmler Kanunu (the Law of Educational and Technical Films, Law 3122) required movie theaters to screen educational films before any feature, merging theatrical and nontheatrical exhibition practices.[37]

The cinema studies scholar Jacqueline Najuma Stewart critically examines how the classification of multiple film practices under the nontheatrical label served "the pedagogical, ideological, and financial interests" of those who adopted it as a category.[38] According to Stewart, this category reflects similar power dynamics, as it offers a terrain in which to explore how racial identities and inequalities manifest in cinematic contexts. She emphasizes that although many types of nontheatrical films are often associated with a commitment to a "social usefulness" such as education, they are not immune to the limitations of dominant racial ideologies.[39]

This is particularly evident in films like *Bridgeland*, which employs common strategies of mid-twentieth-century educational films—such as maps, expert consultants, and voice-over—but sets itself apart by giving Ahmet a voice as the narrator. This choice ostensibly lends the film a sense of authenticity, yet it raises important concerns. Ahmet does not speak in Turkish, he speaks in English, indicating that the film's primary audience was English-speaking. Furthermore, Ahmet's narration of Turkish history appears to be scripted by the film's educational consultants, suggesting that his agency and voice, though central to the film's framing, are ultimately controlled by external authorities. This mediated viewpoint is embedded in the racial and ideological frameworks of the Cold War. It underscores the subtle power dynamics of US Cold War media, where not-yet-white voices were included but shaped to serve US ideological and geopolitical agendas. However, even when nontheatrical films attempt to give voice to nonwhite subjects, Stewart contends, their form remains designed to facilitate the interpretation and response of viewers in ways that align with dominant narratives.[40] *Bridgeland* exemplifies this tension, as it merges the educational ambitions of the nontheatrical genre with the ideological imperatives of Cold War liberalism—promoting US-led modernization, secular nationalism, and capitalist development—and the racial imperatives that positioned whiteness as the civilizational norm and benchmark of progress.

Stewart also highlights that nontheatrical films create more opportunities for "audience interaction." While fan cultures play a significant role in the history of theatrical cinema, movie theaters are inherently designed for passive viewing, where the focus is on the screen rather than social engagement.[41] The arrangement of theater seating, along with established norms that discourage conversation during and after screenings, reinforces this dynamic. In contrast, nontheatrical films are specifically crafted to provoke discussion and foster participation.

The practice of fostering audience interaction is evident in educational films about Turkey. For example, in *Families of the World: Turkey* (Journal Films, 1976), the voice-over prompts viewers to compare American values and families with the Turkish ones seen on the screen. The cover of its 16 mm film container features questions to help teachers prompt classroom dialogue.[42] These questions invite students to examine the roles of religion, attitudes toward modernization, and gender dynamics in Turkish society, encouraging them to reflect on how these factors compare with their own experiences. This approach underscores the educational function of these films while also reinforcing a framework that positions Turkey as an object of analysis through an American lens, where progress and alignment with Western values are central themes.

Education and Propaganda

In the early twentieth century, Turkish elites, under the leadership of Mustafa Kemal Atatürk, first president of the Republic of Turkey, sought to modernize the nation through educational reform. Viewing the United States as a model, they invited the renowned educator John Dewey to assess the Turkish school system and offer recommendations for establishing a secular public education system. Dewey, conceptualizing education as a dynamic force for societal growth, advocated decentralized decision-making and the embrace of Turkey's pluralistic character to foster democratic citizenship.[43] However, Atatürk and his government envisioned a centralized, homogenous nation and sought to utilize education as a tool to achieve this goal. This divergence between Dewey's democratic ideal and Atatürk's nationalist vision reflects the tension between education as a means of social progress and as a potential instrument of state power.

The US government has a history of utilizing film as an educational tool for developing public relations and maintaining democratic governance. The film historian Richard Dyer MacCann characterizes the government's engagement with nonfiction filmmaking as a "moral responsibility for action."[44] This conception intertwines with the ideas of Walter Lippmann, whose work significantly influenced the trajectory of American government-sponsored films. He contended that the public is ill-equipped to engage in democratic processes due to factors such as time constraints, distance from events, and cognitive biases. MacCann concurs, arguing that documentary films can bridge the gap between policymakers and the public. He views the documentary's persuasive force as being "at the beck and call of ambitious bureaucrats."[45] For MacCann, the methods for making sponsored films are not important; what matters is that the content of the communication with the public contributes to a robust democracy and addresses the public's issues.

Historians of the Cold War have long grappled with defining propaganda, often resorting to the term *information* to describe government-sponsored messaging. For instance, Maria Fritsche equates propaganda with the dissemination of information aimed at influencing public opinion.[46] This departs from the term's often pejorative connotations associated with manipulation and deception. Recognizing the euphemistic use of "information" by US policymakers to distance domestic propaganda from its totalitarian applications, Fritsche emphasizes the persuasive intent of the sponsor's message, rather than its veracity, as a defining characteristic of propaganda.[47]

Building upon these philosophical foundations, I conceptualize propaganda and education as interconnected constructs serving distinct yet complementary goals. In the Cold War era, the USIS emerged as a pivotal actor within the transnational communication network underpinning US-Turkey relations. Simultaneously operating as a propaganda apparatus and a public diplomacy institution, it presented its public-facing activities in Turkey as educational. While it was no secret that the USIS was a propaganda agency, its emphasis on education proved instrumental in establishing a tenable equilibrium between its overt and covert objectives.

Within this dynamic, film functioned as a strategic tool capable of stimulating critical examination of domestic challenges among both the public and government officials. In this manner, American propaganda was subtly transformed into a catalyst for a self-reflexive moment of education.

While the US government sought to influence public opinion in Turkey through various channels and programs, it was simultaneously engaged in a process of learning about Turkish society through data collection, surveys, and research. This reciprocal process highlights the role of Turkish people in educating American agents.

In the transnational context of US-Turkey relations, educational materials and methods were employed by both sides to serve propagandistic goals: for the United States, to promote liberal capitalism, anticommunism, and the American way of life; for Turkey, to legitimize its modernization project, reinforce secular nationalism, and assert its status as a Western-aligned yet self-defined regional power. By centering whiteness, promoting modernization as a particular state ideology, and excluding or downplaying dissenting perspectives, these materials functioned as tools for managing public opinion. Educational film, in this context, became a vehicle for shaping the worldview of both populations, justifying certain actions and policies, and reinforcing dominant narratives. The implicit propaganda embedded in these educational films was designed to reinforce the state ideology and suppress alternative viewpoints. The theory of modernization, often used to justify the policies of Western nations in the Global South, is itself a form of "political propaganda" that presents Western-style development as the inevitable and "superior" path for all societies.[48] This ideological framework was used to justify the promotion of Western values, institutions, and technologies through education, often at the expense of indigenous and marginalized communities. Turkey exemplifies this dynamic, serving as a Cold War laboratory for modernization under American influence.

Turkey's Modernization: A Cold War Laboratory

Turkey's modernization process, initiated in the late Ottoman era (1839–1922) through institutional reforms, predates the arrival of American experts by nearly two centuries.[49] For the political scientist Ayşe Kadıoğlu, it was "cosmetic Westernization," a phenomenon embraced by Ottoman elites that made modernization possible by resorting to Western codes of conduct, but it was "usually portrayed as ridiculous for being artificial and phony."[50] She juxtaposes the elites' preoccupation with a superficial embrace of Westernization with an enduring association with civilization.[51] Specifically, the elite wanted to embrace the science and technology of the West, which resulted in an ostracization of spiritual-religious elements.[52] The modernization efforts dating back to the nineteenth-century Ottoman Empire served as a source for American development projects during the Cold War,[53] which were further fortified by Atatürk's modernization reforms and then Turkey's transition to a multiparty system.

The establishment of a secular nation-state under Atatürk's leadership in 1923 was a key milestone in Turkey's modernization. This process included the secularization of the state through the abolition of the caliphate and the separation of religion and state, the democratization of institutions, the liberalization of the economy, the advancement of women's rights, and the adoption of the Latin alphabet.[54] Through his initiatives, Atatürk became the first leader to employ the term *modernization* to delineate a political and economic strategy as well as a process of establishing a nation.[55] In 1950, Turkey cemented its status as a modern nation when its first fair multiparty election took place, resulting in the victory of the Democrat Party, under Adnan Menderes, the first democratically elected prime minister of Turkey.[56] Menderes was supportive of a liberal free-market economy and agriculture-based modernization,[57] embraced American foreign policies such as the Marshall Plan to boost the Turkish economy, and aligned his vision for Turkey with American modernization efforts.[58]

Following the election of Menderes, Turkey became a laboratory in which to test the American theory that the Middle East would be modernized by following the modern, democratic, and progressive ideals of the West. By calling it modernization theory, American social scientists and government officials aimed to reduce the fears of "Christianization," "Americanization," or "Westernization" and to ensure support for US Cold War foreign policy. Modernization theory emphasized the idea that non-Western countries could achieve modernity by going through the same stages of growth as the United States, which aligned with Atatürk's approach to Westernization.[59]

The underlying message behind modernization was that by adopting an American way of life, the people in the Middle East would develop their nations, accelerate the growth of democracy, and build market-based capitalist economies. The ideology of modernization provided a conceptual framework for collaboration between American officials at various institutions (including the US State Department, USIS, Central Intelligence Agency, and Joint US Military Mission for Aid to Turkey) and Turkish agents to achieve their objectives, which at times overlapped and at others diverged. Indeed, the modernization discourse of the Cold War era in US-Turkey relations relied on malleability to exert significant influence in American foreign policy.[60]

In his book *The Passing of Traditional Society*, Daniel Lerner developed a modernization theory that suggested mass media could help audiences develop empathy, which he considered to be "the capacity to see oneself in the other fellow's situation," by imagining themselves living in a modernized society.[61] Similar to the sociologist Gunnar Myrdal, who argued that whites had to help Blacks improve their social conditions,[62] Lerner concluded that whites had to help "backward" people in the Middle East change their "Oriental mentality."[63] He considered Turkey to be the most impressive example of modernization in the region, citing its steady evolution set in motion by Atatürk's behavioral and institutional innovations.[64] Lerner was impressed by Atatürk's ability to transform institutions and people by inciting communication revolutions, such as by establishing People's Houses and Köy Enstitüleri (Village Institutes), which played an important role in teaching nationalist secular culture, increasing literacy, and encouraging the growth of the media.[65]

Lerner's book became a classic resource in modernization literature for its examination of Turkey's transformation and its validation of the theoretical expectations of modernization literature.[66] It portrayed Turkey's adoption of Western norms, styles, and institutions as evidence of modernity's viability in a predominantly Muslim context. Turkey's "model ally" status and archetypal role in modernization theory were partly motivated by a desire to discredit alternative ideologies like pan-Arabism, political Islam, and socialism.[67] The promotion of Turkey as a model for other Middle Eastern countries was particularly appealing to those advocating Islamic moderation and neoliberal policies.[68]

Yet this emphasis on Turkey's modernization also obscured its undemocratic actions, such as Nazi sympathy, extreme nationalism, and racial as well as ethnic discrimination.[69] In the late 1960s, many critics from the Global South argued that Turkey's modernization had little to celebrate, and by the 1970s, modernization had become a derogatory term, and works like Lerner's were criticized for their methodological flaws.[70] After Turkey's 1980 coup, there was a shift among the elite away from a hypersecular perspective. Islam reemerged as a central force in Turkish politics, serving as a counterbalance to the threat of communism and challenging some of the secularist foundations of the Kemalist modernization project.[71]

This evolving notion of modernization, particularly with its ties to science and technology, found an outlet in film, a medium that became a vital tool for public education in both the United States and Turkey. American educational films often portrayed Turkey as a bridge between the East and the West. These films, echoing the binary of "modern" versus "traditional" in Lerner's theory, framed Turkey's transformation into a democratic and secular society as evidence of modernization's success while acknowledging ongoing challenges. However, they also hinted at the complex nature of Turkish identity, which sought balance between Western advancements and Eastern cultural roots, particularly Islam.[72] This tension—between modernization and tradition—created a palpable anxiety, as Turkey grappled with the task of adopting Western technologies while preserving its cultural foundations. This duality of admiration for and resistance to Western influence fueled internal conflicts within Turkish nationalism.[73]

Educational films visualized and materialized this junction, merging Western and Eastern practices into a distinct Turkish identity that met the agendas of institutional stakeholders. By the late 1960s and early 1970s, both American and Turkish educational films began to focus more on religion, foreshadowing the shift in the 1980s toward a less hypersecular perspective. Turkish films, such as *Elif'in Çilesi* (The suffering of Elif, Ayhan Eyikan, 1966) and *Altın Bilezik* (Golden bracelet, Engin Gülen, 1968), emphasized religion as a fundamental aspect of national identity. Meanwhile, American films like the USIS-produced Nasreddin Hoja (one of the most emblematic folk humorist figures from Southwest Asia and North Africa) series linked communism with atheism and positioned Islam as compatible with capitalism. This strategy aimed to strengthen Turkey's ties to the West and distance it from the Soviet Union.

Race as a Conceptual Tool

The historian Nell Irvin Painter, in her analysis of race, focuses on the term *Caucasian* in challenging the notion of "pure racial ancestry." She traces the term's origins, indicating its fabricated nature, and underscores the interconnectedness of civilizations, such as the Egyptians and Persians, which profoundly influenced Greek culture. Painter also explores how myth and reality influenced Greek perceptions of the Caucasus—a region spanning modern-day Armenia, Azerbaijan, Georgia, Iran, Russia, and Turkey.[74] She critiques the eighteenth-century work of the German physical anthropologist Johann Friedrich Blumenbach, who used *Caucasian* based on flawed racial classifications that linked physical traits, like skull shape, skin color, and facial features, to geography.[75] Blumenbach's hierarchical system placed white people at the top, followed by yellow- or olive-skinned people, bronze-skinned people, and finally black people.[76] Painter contends that these types of arbitrary and absurd classifications—rooted in myth, geography, and aesthetic judgments—led to the creation of the term *Caucasian* and reinforced racial hierarchies.

Similarly, the American studies scholar Matthew Frye Jacobson asserts that "Caucasians are made and not born," reinforcing the idea that race is socially constructed rather than biologically determined.[77] He describes race as a "public fiction," a learned concept perpetuated through narratives embedded in literature, films, and other media. In his study of European immigrant history, he stresses that race is fluid and shaped by historical contexts.

This fluidity of racial categorization is evident in a 1909 legal case in which a Turk appeared before the US Circuit Court in Cincinnati seeking naturalization as a white person in order to gain American citizenship.[78] The *New York Times* article "Is the Turk a White Man?" explored this legal debate, describing Turks as originally belonging to the "yellow or Mongolian race" but gradually intermingling with Caucasian groups as they migrated westward.[79] It described Turks as descendants of Arabs, Albanians, Greeks, Kurds, Slavs, and individuals of mixed ancestry, particularly foreign enslaved girls. Despite referring to the Turks as "a cruel and massacring people," it concluded that they were "Europeans" and could potentially be classified as "white." Yet, the judge in Cincinnati argued that Turks were descendants of "Asiatic Mongols" and therefore fell outside the racial categories legally permitted for naturalization.[80] The same year, however, a Massachusetts judge concluded that Armenians from Asiatic Turkey were "white persons," reasoning that, as Christians rather than Mohammedans, their faith had a civilizational proximity that aligned with "Europe" and thus legitimized their naturalization.[81]

The sociologist Murat Ergin observes that in the decades following the legal case in Cincinnati, Turkish elites recognized the significance of race for their modernization project and initiated a scientifically driven effort to affirm Turks' whiteness. This effort was framed within a discourse that positioned Turkey as "the cradle of Western civilization" and Turks as the originators of "human language" and "white racial stock."[82] In her examination of racial discourses in Turkey, the historian Elise K. Burton notes that the Turkish history thesis posited that Turks were part of the European race, originating in Central Asia, and that they were the founders of ancient civilizations worldwide.[83] She also indicates that human genetics research in Turkey supported this thesis and contributed to the nationalist narrative.[84]

The Turkish government funded researchers to conduct eugenics research to support the idea that Turks were the origin of the white race. Atatürk's stepdaughter, Afet Inan, received government backing for research through which she aimed to prove that Turks were white and not of a yellow race or Mongolian origin. In 1935, when she went to Geneva to earn a doctorate in sociology under the supervision of the Swiss anthropologist Eugène Pittard, she used this "opportunity to educate Europeans about the true character of the Turks."[85] In her dissertation, Inan analyzed data collected by the 1937 Turkish Anthropometric Survey on almost sixty thousand citizens that "aimed to support the claims of the Turkish History Thesis with regard to the Turks' essential racial type and their historical identity as simultaneously migrants from Central Asia, the original inhabitants of Anatolia, and the ancestors of European civilization." A team of physicians, nurses, and physical education teachers collected information about citizens' "cephalic, nasal, and scalic indices; height; and the colors of eyes, hair and skin."[86] Inan then interpreted these data to prove that Turks are biologically white and the origin of the white civilization, paving the way for the Turkish citizen's reinvention. However, her research on eugenics disregarded the diverse groups within Turkey, selectively focusing on proving that Turkish people were white while overlooking the country's rich internal diversity. Her investment in eugenics under the sentiment of nationalism demonstrates how race played a role in determining who would be included and excluded in Turkey's modernization project.[87]

Modernization sought to redefine national identity and progress through the lens of racial categorization and exclusion. Social scientists like Lerner, who were developing modernization as a theory after the World War II, did not believe in biological differences between "races." However, many social scientists embraced the idea that there were cultural differences justified by the "social science" of surveys, fieldwork, and development communication. Moreover, the white Turk ideology promoted a culturally racist position against nonwhite Turks by attributing Turkey's exclusion from Europe to "other Turks," whose socioeconomic differences, clothing, lifestyle, and media consumption were seen as "cultural deficits" and markers of backwardness.[88] This framing reinforced a sense of cultural superiority among white Turks. Inan's research to prove that Turks were white indicates that the West convinced many that to be modern is to be white.

Modernity is racialized insofar as it is constructed through distinctions between "*Europeanness* and *non-Europeanness*."[89] The construction of race in the United States often diverges from its portrayal in European metropolitan centers and is further accentuated by the American fascination with and reinterpretation of Europeanness, resulting in a unique representation of whiteness with its own peculiar characteristics. Discourses around Turkey exemplify this tension, as they are built on this binary opposition of European/Western versus Middle Eastern. Despite never having been colonized, Turkey is situated within a "wholly racialized world,"[90] and the persistent question of whether Turkey is European or Middle Eastern reflects the racialized nature of any categorization of the country.

This transnational racialization extends to film, as films made in and about Turkey have reinforced these racial ideologies. As Savas Arslan argues, cinema is "a result of exchanges [of resources and experiences], interactions and co-productions on various scales involving filmmakers from both the Western and non-Western world, and by practices that do not align with unitary nationalisms."[91] Most Yeşilçam films were remakes, adaptations, or spin-offs of American productions, exemplifying a transnational hybridity that unsettles binary distinctions between imitation and originality, center and periphery, and Turkishness and Americanness.[92] This hybridity also refracts global racial ideologies, filtering them through localized cinematic forms.

Whiteness as a Transnational Technology of Racialization

As a transnational process of racialization, whiteness reinforces social hierarchies by mobilizing ideals of virtue and moral superiority. This framework elevates whiteness not only as a visual norm but also as a civilizational logic that structures the moral and epistemic conditions of modern life.[93] In educational films—especially in the context of US-Turkey relations—whiteness becomes ideologically embedded by equating Western values with virtue and progress. These films rarely function as overt propaganda; instead, they rely on subtle strategies such as framing, narration, and visual juxtaposition. *God of Creation* (Moody Institute of Science, 1945), frequently screened by Nilson, exemplifies how film aesthetics and Christian theology were interwoven to project divine order as aligned with Western rationality. Accompanied by Nilson's Turkish-language recitation of Psalms, the film uses scientific imagery and religious awe to align Protestant Christianity with modernity, coding whiteness as moral clarity, technological sophistication, and epistemic authority. Similarly, the USIS-sponsored Nasreddin Hoja films recast a culturally iconic figure as a moral agent of Western alignment. By replacing Hoja's subversive wit with didactic parables endorsing anticommunism, religious moderation, and US alliance, the films reframed tradition within a framework of whiteness—embracing Islam only when subordinated to Western ideals of reason and order. Through curated dialogue and voice-over narration, US influence was rendered morally imperative—positioning whiteness as the ethical precondition of national development.

In this book, I extend my investigation beyond sponsorship structures and exhibition practices to examine the representational and ideological labor of film as a racialized technology of modernization. Drawing on Richard Dyer's foundational work, I treat whiteness as a mechanism of power that operates through both visible and invisible properties[94]—embedded in audiovisual design to shape how modernity was imagined and internalized. In the Turkish context, I build on scholars such as Murat Ergin and Sedef Arat-Koç, who demonstrate that Turkish national identity has long been constructed through distinctions from racialized Others (particularly Arabs) and through proximity to the West and Europe.[95] Barış Ünlü extends this line of thought and considers whiteness as a conceptual tool for analyzing the historical constitution of Turkishness, including its institutional foundations and everyday operationalization.[96] These dynamics have shaped not only the content of educational films but also their function as ideological instruments—mediating political aspirations while projecting a homogenized vision of national modernity.

Secularism played a central role in this racialized project.[97] Enforced through strict regulations on religious expression in media, it was more than a state doctrine; it became a performative standard of civilizational belonging within a Eurocentric order. Within this framework, whiteness emerged as a normative ideal—ethical, aesthetic, and epistemic—while religious Muslims, particularly those who visibly practiced Islam, were positioned at the margins of modern Turkish identity. Some Islamists, in turn, articulated their marginalization by identifying themselves as the *zenciler* (blacks) of Turkey[98]—highlighting how race operates not just through skin color but also through layered hierarchies of religion, class, and geography. Here, religion functions as a *technology of race*—a mechanism for governing national inclusion and exclusion.[99] To be seen as modern, one had to perform a secular identity modeled on Euro-American ideals.

This racial regime did not simply reproduce global hierarchies; it recalibrated them for domestic governance, projecting whiteness as both the gateway to and the reward for national progress. The convergence of secularization, developmentalism, and film diplomacy embedded eugenic logics into Turkey's modernization discourse. This process was further reinforced through cinematic pedagogy, which instructed viewers in a vision of national identity aligned with secularism, Westernization, and racial homogeneity.

Turkish educational films were containers of a pedagogy of whiteness. Drawing on Henry Giroux, I consider whiteness as a pedagogical force that shapes how individuals come to understand themselves and others through dominant racial frameworks.[100] In the Turkish context, this pedagogy is evident in the systemic marginalization of Afro-Turks. Blackness remains largely unrecognized in national discourse, and the history of African enslavement during the Ottoman Empire is often omitted from official narratives.[101] Estimates of the Afro-Turk population vary dramatically—from five thousand to eight hundred thousand—underscoring both the lack of demographic accountability and the state's disavowal of this community.[102] Everyday language further shows this exclusion: Racialized terms such as *zenci* and *arap* (Arab) circulate without reflection on their derogatory implications, cementing whiteness as the unmarked ideal and Afro-Turks as outside the boundaries of modern Turkish identity.

This combination of marginalization and cultural amnesia aligns with the conceptualization by Ed Guerrero, a cinema and Africana studies scholar, of Blackness as a fluid and relational construct, shaped by social struggles and the historical exigencies of whiteness. While whiteness dominates and excludes, as seen in the erasure of Afro-Turk identity, he highlights how Blackness is further constrained by the material demands of the film industry, which prioritizes economic gain over human, aesthetic, or philosophical concerns.[103] In Turkey, Blackness is not only marginalized but also caricatured and reduced to servitude through harmful stereotypes perpetuated in media. In the Yeşilçam era, Turkish films portrayed characters such as Arap Bacı, Bacı Kalfa, and Dadı in blackface,[104] exoticizing and marginalizing Afro-Turks while denying them authentic representation. Furthermore, in Turkish educational films, Black people are absent, rendering them invisible.

Film diplomacy amplified these dynamics as an effective mechanism for promoting a respectable, progressive, and civilized image of Turkey to both domestic and international audiences. As an ambivalent and malleable ideology, whiteness shaped both the logic and the aesthetics of this transnational project, structuring how Turkey was to be seen by the world—and how it came to see itself. This process unfolded not only through symbolic narratives but also through material investments in people, institutions, and infrastructure. Film diplomacy required more than rhetorical gestures; it depended on shared incentives and practical collaborations. The United States, for example, provided economic aid, educational support, and technological resources—offering mobile film units, curated film libraries, educational media, and instructional guides. It trained Turkish filmmakers, educators, and civil servants while also funding the development of local institutions capable of sustaining these modernizing efforts, including media centers and military bases. Researchers and experts were dispatched to study audience behavior and ensure ideological alignment, and Turkish officials, in turn, welcomed these initiatives in exchange for resources, international legitimacy, and integration into global networks. These reciprocal transactions were central to the function of film diplomacy. They allowed both parties to pursue their own goals—strategic for the United States, developmental for Turkey—while embedding whiteness as a shared horizon of aspiration, performance, and governance.

Methodology and Data Selection

Encompassing half a century of history, this book is based on my extensive primary research at archives and libraries in Turkey and the United States. The primary dataset draws on documents from the Milli Kütüphane (National Library) in Ankara, Turkey, and the National Archives and Records Administration (NARA) in College Park, Maryland, and on material archived at the Indiana University Libraries Moving Image Archive, the Houghton Library at Harvard University, and the Rare Book and Manuscript Library at Columbia University. In addition to conducting research in archival collections, I consulted digitized research materials from the American Research Institute in Turkey, the Foreign Relations of the United States series, the Foreign Affairs Oral History Collection, UNESCO, the Media History Digital Library, and the Audio-Visual Archives of the International Federation of Red Cross and Red Crescent Societies. I also accessed films through online platforms, particularly YouTube and Internet Archive. The archival holdings contain a broad spectrum of documents such as reports, memoranda, telegrams, personal correspondence, country studies, audience surveys, opinion polls, films, and film scripts. They also include a substantial volume of previously unexamined materials, augmented by a smaller but significant set of recently declassified documents from the records of the USIS at NARA. While these records offer a rich range of information, they predominantly reflect the American perspective. To mitigate any bias, I conducted a critical analysis of the materials, informed by secondary sources, to uncover power dynamics and ideological undercurrents. The lens of whiteness served as a heuristic device and proved instrumental in illuminating power dynamics within the films and their broader context.

Locating primary sources within archives and libraries in Turkey was challenging. From the Milli Kütüphane in Ankara, I compiled a collection of film catalogs, technical reports, and magazines. The digital platform of MNET's Educational Information Network (EIN, Eğitim Bilişim Ağı) yielded additional primary materials, including films and photographs. While the EFC generated a corpus of at least three thousand films, I examined a subset of this collection. I found and examined approximately one-third of the total output through film catalogs. From this pool, I identified, watched, and analyzed eighty-six films through EIN and cross-referenced them with catalogs from the USIS and EFC. I encountered other obstacles in doing archival research due to inconsistent preservation practices and inadequate cataloging. A Turkish archivist attributed the scarcity of educational films to the recycling of film stock for its silver content. Furthermore, EIN's use of *nostalji* (nostalgia) instead of *ögretici filmler* (educational films) in its database hindered my research. Despite these challenges, the eighty-six films from the EIN constitute a manageable and representative sample from the EFC's extensive output of educational films.

Film selection was primarily determined by archival accessibility. Similar to the EFC, the USIS distributed thousands of films in Turkey. The Smith-Mundt Act of 1948 (also known as the US Information and Educational Exchange Act) prohibited public access to USIS films within the United States and, therefore, restricted academic studies on the subject. Despite the relaxation of these restrictions, accessing films through NARA continues to be a complex and resource-intensive endeavor, even with standardized preservation practices. While NARA's recent digitization efforts have provided partial access to certain film series, such as the twenty-four-film Nasreddin Hoja series (1952–1974), comprehensive access remains limited. Employing a qualitative methodology, I selected and contextualized key films through a rigorous examination of legal, government, and policy documents as well as pertinent secondary literature.

The combination and variety of these archives, coupled with the unique access to previously unexamined materials, helped me understand the interplay among film, power, and international relations within the context of US-Turkey relations and the landscape of film diplomacy. I hope this contribution will help reshape historical narratives, unveil hidden power dynamics, and offer valuable insights into the global influence of film.

In addition to recovering underexplored archival materials, in this book I contribute a conceptual framework grounded in interdisciplinary analysis. By bridging cinema and media studies, diplomacy studies, Cold War studies, national and transnational history, critical whiteness studies, and reception studies, I bring together distinct but complementary frameworks to illuminate the cultural and ideological work of educational films. The archival findings—especially those relating to film production, distribution, exhibition, and reception—anchor these theoretical inquiries in material practice and institutional dynamics. Through this synthesis, I explore how encounters between Americans and Turks were mediated and structured by film diplomacy and how these interactions shaped racialized hierarchies, national imaginaries, and modernization discourses. Ultimately, this cultural and social history establishes a model for understanding film diplomacy as a framework—one that can inform future scholarship across transnational contexts and historical periods.

Chapter Overviews

Throughout the book, I focus on a set of institutional agents and their film-related interactions, examining how these agents navigate and contribute to infrastructural networks. Lee Grieveson, a media historian who studies cinema as an institution, emphasizes that it is used "to support . . . the infrastructures of circulation central to capitalist modernity; and to build and strengthen ties."[105] Hatim El-Hibri, a media and film scholar, highlights the incompleteness of infrastructures and views them as sets of relations.[106] Indeed, educational films put modernization into practice and created opportunities for agents from different institutions to collaborate in transnational settings and to serve their divergent goals in and for Turkey. Among these agents, missionaries justified their use of film to promote Christian values by relying on a discourse of modernization, while USIS agents used film to sell economic policies and programs to Turkey when they presented strategies for modernization. Turkish officials and teachers from the MNET used films to contribute to nationalism and modernization efforts. These agents formed networks of collaboration and used modernization efforts to suit their different end goals. They also shared whiteness as a core, yet invisible, system of practices. In each chapter, I spotlight these institutional actors and show how their engagement with film diplomacy contributed to the entwined projects of modernization.

In chapter 1, I offer a transnational and critical historiography of cinema in Turkey, situating its emergence and development within global circuits of power, race, and representation. I begin by challenging nationalist origin myths of Turkish cinema and instead foregrounding the hybrid, multinational, and multireligious contributions that shaped early cinematic culture in the late Ottoman Empire and early Turkish republic. Drawing on examples ranging from shadow puppetry and non-Muslim exhibition networks to missionary archives and Cold War propaganda, I demonstrate that film in Turkey was never merely a national affair but was always already embedded in transnational contexts. I show how cinema became a key site for the negotiation of Turkish modernity, where whiteness was not only performed but also operationalized as a structure of international legibility.

Through examples including state responses to foreign films, US-Turkey collaborations such as *The Reception of the US Ambassador Joseph C. Grew by Atatürk on the Forest Farm* (Fox Films Inc., 1930), and the marginalization of Arabness in educational films like *The Middle East: Change—Turkey and Saudi Arabia* (Encyclopaedia Britannica, 1984), I present film diplomacy as a racialized strategy of visual governance. I also discuss how, during the Korean War, Turkish media and American films transformed the "Terrible Turk" stereotype into an image of a heroic Western ally, casting Chinese soldiers as racialized enemies and positioning Turkish troops as embodiments of modern, militarized whiteness. Such visual interventions reimagined Turkey's place in the world, positioning it as a Western-oriented, secular nation (often achieved by pointedly downplaying or disavowing Ottoman and Arab affiliations) to secure geopolitical recognition within a global order structured by Eurocentric hierarchies. Ultimately, I demonstrate how cinema operated not simply as entertainment or cultural output but also as a strategic medium through which national identity was staged, international belonging was claimed, and civilizational value was negotiated.

In chapter 2, I examine the work of ABCFM missionaries in Turkey between 1930 and 1953. The ABCFM (1810–1961) became the most prominent and influential foreign missionary society of the nineteenth century, embarking on a mission to reclaim the biblical lands by spreading the Christian faith among its Muslim, Christian, and Jewish populations.[107] Missionaries embraced "the white supremacist ideology of the West"[108] and considered themselves natural leaders with privileged citizenship.[109] This approach "resulted in the normalization of Christianity and its conflation with whiteness in American national identity."[110] Whiteness is consistent with the capacity to achieve economic prosperity, drive innovation, establish a civilization, and, in the Turkish context, construct and maintain a philanthropic network.[111] Indeed, missionaries developed a network in Turkey as they built schools, hospitals, and libraries; filmed public spaces and landscapes; and exhibited films about education, agriculture, health, and religion. Although censorship regulations restricted religious content, nontheatrical films were largely ignored, and the Turkish government imposed no specific regulations on missionary film exhibitions.

Drawing on Ünlü's framework linking whiteness to the "Turkishness contract" (a contract of privileges), I demonstrate how missionaries used films and projectors to align with Turkish modernization ideals. This alignment leveraged the selective perception inherent in the Turkishness contract, leading officials to overlook religious undertones in missionary exhibitions and forgo censorship. Missionaries put film diplomacy into action in schools, hospitals, prisons, and churches. In prisons and churches, they rendered Christianity visible during their film exhibitions, but in hospitals and particularly schools, they created an optical illusion of secularism: Their whiteness and technological modernity lent them legitimacy in the eyes of Turkish officials, allowing Christian content to circulate. This illusion was occasionally challenged—as evidenced by a legal case over missionary activity in schools—but the broader effect was to blur the line between secular service and religious influence. American missionaries used their malleable whiteness to renegotiate their place in a secularizing Turkish society. Rather than achieving mass conversions, however, the missionaries' real impact lay in the infrastructural and institutional legacy they established through educational and medical services. *Film diplomacy* illustrates how these efforts not only advanced US prestige in Turkey but also solidified institutional development as the missionaries' lasting contribution, far outweighing their initial goal of religious conversion.

The missionary film program paved the way for both the Turkish and the American governments to utilize nontheatrical films as a tool of diplomacy and public engagement. In chapter 2, I demonstrate how the missionaries used film to offer information about health and agriculture, spread Christian values, and, in some instances, show acceptance of Muslims in ABCFM-sponsored schools and hospitals in Turkey. Missionaries also used films to develop institutional prestige, increase donations from Americans, and recruit Christians to work abroad. Their efforts intertwined with larger American economic, geopolitical, and diplomatic interests. Collaboration with the USIS film officer Monteagle Stearns illustrates how missionary film programs paved the way for continued US influence by shaping the perception of American education, laying the foundation for the USIS's film diplomacy, and establishing an early communication network between the United States and Turkey. Furthermore, the ABCFM's collaboration with Turkish ministries helped missionaries integrate their main goal of spreading Christianity into a discourse of modernization. While these entities had different primary goals, their collaboration through the use of film influenced and shaped the cultural, religious, educational, and geopolitical landscape of Turkey.

In chapter 3, I examine US government film programming in Turkey, focusing on the activities of the USIS, the largest international distributor of American nontheatrical films during the Cold War. It strategically mobilized film as a diplomatic technology to promote American values, counter Soviet influence, and secure Turkey's alignment with the Western bloc. These efforts extended beyond rhetoric; they involved the construction of media infrastructures, enforcement of censorship regimes, and formation of collaborative institutions designed to shape public opinion and manage ideological affinities. Drawing on archival materials and films such as the Nasreddin Hoja series, I show how the USIS blended education and propaganda to portray democracy, scientific progress, and religious freedom as central to American modernity. I also analyze how the USIS sought to reconcile Islam with American democratic values in order to counter Soviet atheism and garner support in Muslim-majority nations. Films such as *Washington Cami* (*The Washington Mosque*, 1957, produced by Craven Film Corporation for USIS) and *Washington'da İslam Etüdleri Merkezinin Açılışı* (*The Opening of the Islamic Center of Washington*, 1957)[112] staged religious freedom as an act of regulated visibility, selectively framing Islam as conditionally compatible with the US ideals of progress and democracy. This strategy—endorsed in Turkish media coverage and bolstered by symbolic gestures like President Eisenhower's respectful conduct at a mosque—indicates how the USIS used religion as both a cultural bridge and a geopolitical instrument. A similar logic shaped its civil rights film campaign, in which documentaries such as *Nine from Little Rock* (Charles Guggenheim, 1964) framed racial progress as part of a self-legitimating narrative of American democracy. Yet in both domains—religion and race—strategic inclusion was carefully managed to uphold the normative order of whiteness. Muslims and African Americans were rendered visible only when their stories could be mobilized to manage the United States' reputation abroad. This racialized diplomacy obscured the structural inequities that persisted at home and abroad, allowing the USIS to project a sanitized vision of democracy that emphasized symbolic gestures over systemic transformation.

In this chapter, I also trace the USIS's partnerships with Turkish ministries in building an educational film infrastructure—culminating in the creation of the EFC—and in using mobile cinema units to distribute films across the country. These programs operated within legal frameworks such as Turkey's tax exemptions for educational films and the US Smith-Mundt Act, which barred USIS films from domestic circulation to avoid accusations of government propaganda targeting US citizens. This legal and institutional architecture shows the contradictions between professed democratic ideals and the authoritarian practices of media control. I further highlight how American officials and Turkish collaborators negotiated the aesthetics and narratives of modernization through feedback loops, including revisions to Marshall Plan films like *Köy Traktörü* (*Village Tractor*, Clifford Hornby, 1951 and 1953). By foregrounding the careers of key figures—Monteagle Stearns, Sadun Katipoğlu, and Suha Arın—I demonstrate that film diplomacy was not a one-directional imposition of ideology but a dynamic field shaped by individual agency and transnational collaboration. Essentially, I reframe USIS film diplomacy as a racialized and technocratic system of influence that blurred the lines between education and propaganda to advance US geopolitical interests through curated narratives of modernization.

By examining the rise of an educational film revolution in Turkey in chapter 4, I reframe film diplomacy as a mode of internal governance. I trace how the EFC was established in 1952 through collaborations with the USIS and UNESCO and how it evolved—later as the Educational Film, Radio, and Television Center—into a central state institution tasked with producing, distributing, and exhibiting thousands of educational films, filmstrips, and audiovisual broadcasts across the country. Drawing on parliamentary debates, UNESCO reports, USIS archives, and Turkish periodicals such as *Film ve Öğretim*, I reconstruct the institutional, ideological, and transnational foundations of Turkey's educational media infrastructure. Through analysis of state-sponsored documentaries like *Depremde Kızılay* (Red Crescent in earthquake, Cahit Ünsalan, 1964), *Mardin* (Zeki Şahin, 1975), and *Ana Kucağı* (Orphanage, or Mom's lap, Nurcan Karagöz, 1977), I demonstrate how the Turkish state mobilized film not only as a pedagogical device but also as a biopolitical and ideological technology for managing populations, shaping public perspective, and normalizing exclusion. Educational films regulated visibility and audibility, advancing a homogenized model of Turkishness that was Sunni Muslim, Istanbul Turkish-speaking, and aligned with ideals of whiteness. These films functioned as tools of regulation, erasing linguistic, racial, ethnic, and religious differences in order to construct a centralized, secular vision of the nation.

Turkey's educational film project was entangled with Cold War geopolitics and US-led modernization initiatives. Turkish officials and media agents selectively accepted, modified, or rejected foreign films based on their ideological alignment and cultural appropriateness and gradually shifted toward producing domestic content that advanced nationalist goals. Adapting documentary models developed in the West to serve national objectives, educational cinema emerged as a strategic tool through which the Turkish state negotiated ideological contradictions—particularly those involving race, ethnicity, religion, and class. Ultimately, I demonstrate that film diplomacy in Turkey was a form of internal visual governance that aestheticized care, performed state legitimacy, and operationalized whiteness as the invisible standard of national belonging.

In chapter 5, I examine how US government–sponsored audience reception research in Cold War Turkey positioned educational film as a strategic instrument for aligning public opinion with American geopolitical interests. Drawing on archives from Columbia University's Bureau of Applied Social Research, the Economic Cooperation Administration, and the USIS, I argue that these studies were structured by a racialized epistemology that equated modernization with whiteness. Expanding on Miriam Hansen's formulation of classical cinema as vernacular modernism[113] and drawing forward Charles Acland and Haidee Wasson's notion of useful cinema as an institutional disposition,[114] I deploy the term *useful modernization* to describe the ideological work performed by educational films. These films framed American developmental ideals as universally applicable while disregarding the material asymmetries. Disseminated through mobile cinema units and national institutions, they targeted Turkish audiences with content on agriculture, democracy, education, and industrial growth—casting American capitalism as a model for national progress.

I interrogate the methodological foundations and ideological assumptions of audience research conducted by figures such as Daniel Lerner, whose categorization of traditional, transitional, and modern Turks encoded a civilizational hierarchy grounded in whiteness. While researchers interpreted Turkish viewers' responses as evidence of "cultural deficiency" audience interviews, in fact, reflected critical awareness of structural constraints, particularly around economic disparity and limited infrastructure. These findings were not simply misunderstood—they were selectively interpreted or strategically distorted to affirm US ideological objectives, reducing complex viewer perspectives to evidence supporting modernization theory.

For instance, films such as *Poultry Raising* (Vocational Guidance Films, 1946), and *The Rural Co-Op* (Pare Lorentz, 1947) elicited pragmatic and materially grounded reactions from Turkish audiences, yet these were dismissed by American analysts as signs of underdevelopment or apathy. Such misreadings were not incidental; they constituted a recurring pattern in which reception research was mobilized to legitimize US foreign policy and development agendas. Film diplomacy, in this context, functioned as a feedback mechanism; circulating ideological narratives while extracting audience data to refine strategies of influence. By analyzing how responses were shaped, misread, and repurposed, I show how whiteness operated not only as an invisible standard of evaluation but also as a governing logic for managing Cold War cultural encounters.

In the epilogue, I note that film diplomacy is recursive and continually reshaped through evolving infrastructures and persisting into contemporary geopolitical practice. By tracing the transnational and transhistorical network of films between the United States and Turkey, I show how film diplomacy operated as a dynamic infrastructure to shape public opinion, implement agendas, and govern populations. From missionary efforts to US information programs and Turkish state initiatives, film emerged as a strategic medium for aligning Turkish national identity with Western norms. This alignment was anchored in whiteness, imagined as both the condition and the reward of modernity and geopolitical belonging. Whiteness functioned as an institutionalized mode of governance embedded in the production, distribution, exhibition, and reception of films. It structured transnational and domestic relations through a pedagogy of selective visibility and audibility, orchestrating an aspirational affinity with a modern way of being. Educational films thus served as technologies of statecraft, reframing development as a mode of managing social difference and repositioning diplomacy as a mechanism for alignment.

1

From Ottoman Shadows to Global Stage

The Rise of Film in Turkey

> *Attempting to promote international understanding in the belief that it will help to prevent war is an act of faith . . . using films for this purpose is again an act of faith based on little experience and less tested evidence. But so urgent is the pressure of world affairs that I believe all methods should be directed to this one end and that each of us must use the means most familiar and best suited to our individual abilities. SO, I USE FILMS.*
>
> —Helen E. Coppen, "What Can School Films Do for Peace?"

Film has long held the power to shape public opinion and influence international relations, a potential that has captivated policymakers and scholars alike. The medium's capacity to reach vast audiences and evoke responses has made it an alluring tool for shaping narratives and advancing national interests. As the educator Helen E. Coppen observed in 1950, the use of film to foster international understanding has often been based more on a belief in its effectiveness than on empirical evidence. Yet it is precisely this "act of faith" that transformed film into a strategic medium for managing geopolitical perception during the Cold War.

In this chapter, I conceptualize film diplomacy as a negotiation of international recognition: a strategic process through which states seek to manage their image abroad, define their national identity, and secure their admission into the civilizational order of the modern world. Focusing on Turkey, I examine how cinema became a contested site of ideological production: A transnational medium where whiteness was performed, modernization staged, and imperial memory reconfigured. From Ottoman-era shadow plays and early exhibition circuits to documentaries and Cold War propaganda, the cinema of Turkey consistently operated within global circuits of power. Rather than serving merely as entertainment or instruction, it functioned as a diplomatic and ideological tool—projecting a vision of Turkey as Western oriented and modern while disavowing affinities with the Arab world. In doing so, film became instrumental in recoding Turkey's geopolitical identity for both domestic and international audiences.

Ottoman and Early Republican Cinema

Historical accounts of the origins of cinema suggest that film in Turkey has long been a transnational and global cultural phenomenon. In 1923, *Sinema Postası*, the republic's first film magazine—founded by the poet and novelist Nâzım Hikmet—published an article provocatively titled "Who Invented Cinema?"[1] Challenging the Eurocentric claim that cinema was invented by the French Lumière brothers or the American Thomas Edison, Hikmet proposed a more global genealogy, linking cinema to Chinese shadow theater and the Ottoman tradition of Karagöz puppetry.[2] He noted that Karagöz either imitated or was imitated by Chinese shadow puppetry and suggested that theater practices in the sixteenth-century Ottoman Empire provided the beginning of cinema-like experiences. Both shadow puppetry and cinema use projected images to tell a story or convey a message. In shadow puppetry, the images are created by manipulating cut-out figures behind a screen, while in cinema the images are captured on film or digitally and exhibited on a screen. Both media also manipulate light and shadow to create the illusion of movement and depth. To build on Hikmet's thesis and elaborate this transnational dimension, cinema has always been a product of global influences. The sinologist Fan Pen Chen has determined that "Chinese [audiences] were probably not among the first to enjoy shadow shows"; rather, shadow puppetry "arrived in China either through Central Asia or via sea routes to the ports of eastern China." Multidirectional influences potentially existed among the earliest shadow theaters in India, Indonesia, Southeast Asia, Egypt, China, Europe, and Turkey.[3]

In a vein similar to that of Hikmet, some film scholars attribute the origins of Turkish cinema to the Ottoman Empire. For example, the film scholar Asuman Suner locates the origins of Turkish cinema in the Ottoman sultan's private screenings of this technology in 1890.[4] Historians of Turkish cinema such as Nijat Özön believe that the first national film was the documentary *Ayastefanos'taki Rus Abidesi'nin Yıkılışı* (The demolition of the Russian monument at San Stefano, or *Ayastefanos*, 1914) made by Fuat Uzkınay, an Ottoman citizen and army officer with a passion for cinematography.[5] However, the film historians Nezih Erdoğan and Deniz Göktürk question whether this film ever existed.[6]

Conducting historical research to find an answer, the film scholar Dilek Kaya Mutlu has examined how Turkish film history remembered and represented the demolition of the Russian monument at San Stefano following the Russo-Turkish War of 1877–1878. She argues that the monument, which was seen by the Ottomans as a symbol of "shame" and "defeat," was later "reframed and embedded in a narrative of national (Turkish) heroism and the birth of a national (Turkish) cinema."[7] She questions whether the footage of the monument's demolition, shot by Fuat Uzkınay (a Turkish man), should even be considered a "Turkish film."[8] Kaya Mutlu found evidence that an Austrian company oversaw the filming of the demolition; a representative named Mordo was told that only a Turk could shoot the footage, so he enlisted Fuad Bey (Fuat Uzkınay) to shoot it.[9] Based on this historical account, she states that it is not possible to conclude that the footage was shot by a Turkish film company or that its shooting was arranged and led by the Ottoman military or government. For Kaya Mutlu, it is likely that a foreign film company wanted to independently record the demolition, and, therefore, the film, if it existed, is more precisely understood as a "foreign film" that was later claimed as a "founding myth or origin story" for Turkish cinema.[10] These considerations complicate the transnational origins of Turkish cinema and suggest that for a film to be Turkish, it has to be made by a Turkish (or in this case, an Ottoman) person or entity. Here, the assumption is that this Turk is a Muslim.

Kaya Mutlu is critical of Turkish film scholars who have ignored the work of non-Muslim Ottoman citizens as part of film history. She explains that documentaries existed in the Ottoman Empire before *Ayastefanos*, but many have been erased from Turkish cinema history because the filmmakers were either unidentified or not Muslim Turks.[11] She uses the example of documentary footage of Sultan Mehmed V's visit to Monastir and Salonika in 1911 and notes that it was shot by two brothers, Yanaki Manaki and Milton Manaki. Because these filmmakers were non-Muslim Ottoman citizens of Greek origin, historians found it "inappropriate" to attribute the beginning of Turkish cinema to them. Yet the details about the Manaki brothers and the Austrian company overseeing Fuad Bey speak powerfully to the transnational and global dimension of the cinema of Turkey. They reveal how the idea of national cinema can diminish our understanding of filmmaking, as it generates grounds for determining who and what get to be considered "national" (in this case, Turkish).

To move beyond the restricted boundaries of national cinema, I consider the multiple dimensions of identity and the transnationality of film's production, exhibition, sponsorship, and reception practices. Nationality is a complex phenomenon, and Ottomans were multinational. As scholars have already noted, non-Muslim multinationals made films and established exhibition spaces. For instance, a Polish Jew from Romania, Sigmund Weinberg, opened a movie theater in Pera in 1908, during the Ottoman Empire era.[12] Jewish and Christian entrepreneurs, in fact, operated many theaters during this period. While non-Muslim filmmakers and multinational exhibition networks defined the cinematic landscape of the late Ottoman period, the early years of the Republic of Turkey marked a shift toward national authorship, Muslim representation, and films that explicitly articulated Turkishness—as the following section on early republican cinema demonstrates.

Celluloid Seeds: How Early Film Nurtured the Potential of Education

Before the rise of educational films in Turkey, the renowned actor and director Muhsin Ertuğrul played a significant role in shaping a national cinema culture. He motivated the entrepreneurial brothers Kemal Seden and Sakir Seden to establish the first private film production firm, Kemal Film Studio, in 1922.[13] They produced Ertuğrul's silent film *Nur Baba* (The Bosphorus mystery, 1922), an adaptation of Yakup Kadri Karaosmanoğlu's novel on Bektashism, an Islamic Sufi mystic order. Six months prior to the establishment of the republic, the studio released Ertuğrul's *Ateşten Gömlek* (Shirt of flame, 1923). Inspired by Halide Edib Adivar's memoir of the Turkish War of Independence, the film featured the first Muslim actresses, Bedia Muvahhit and Neyyire Neyir, and celebrated the making of the modern nation-state.[14] It was also regarded as the first national film of Turkey.[15] Another film, *Sözde Kizlar* (The would-be girls, 1924), an adaptation of Peyami Sefa's novel about Mebrure's relocation after her father's disappearance amid the Greco-Turkish conflicts, offered a critique of moral erosion imputed to Westernization, elucidated through the representation of female characters.

In 1925, Ertuğrul went to the Soviet Union at the invitation of Anatoly Lunacharsky, the commissar responsible for the Ministry of Education. While there, he worked with the USSR State Committee for Cinematography (Goskino) and the All-Ukrainian Photo Cinema Administration (VUFKU),[16] and he met with the pioneering film director and theorist Sergei Eisenstein, the theater practitioner Konstantin Stanislavsky, and the theater director Vsevolod Meyerhold. After making *Tamilla* (1925), *Five Minutes* (1926), and *Spartakus* (1926) in the Soviet Union, Ertuğrul went back to Turkey and created one of his most successful films, *Bir Millet Uyanıyor* (A nation is awakening, 1932). This adaptation of Nizamettin Nazif Tepedelenlioğlu's novel was advertised as the first sound film in Turkish. It emphasized a patriotic sentiment encapsulated in the voice-over's declaration that Turkey belongs to the Turks ("Türkiye Türklerindir"), echoing a famous pronouncement by President Mustafa Kemal Atatürk.

While nationalistic sentiments were on the upswing, the silver screens of Turkey were also receptive to films from the United States, Germany, France, England, and Italy, a variety of which found their way into the country. In 1930, movie houses in Turkey presented at least 143 feature films, of which more than 53 were talkies or sound films.[17] Fueled by the arrival of sound technology and the influx of foreign films, exhibition spaces underwent a swift metamorphosis, transforming into technological and cultural interfaces mirroring the modernization project. The cinematic landscape expanded further in 1932, with the release of approximately 166 feature talkies, of which 75 were in French, 41 in English, and 30 in German. Additionally, the lineup included one or two films each in Greek, Italian, Polish, Russian, Spanish, and Turkish. Notably, musical comedies emerged as a favorite among Turkish audiences.[18] Some of the most popular films included *Love Parade* (Ernst Lubitsch, 1929), *Paramount Parade* (Edmund Goulding et al., 1930), *Der Blaue Engel* (*Blue Angel*, Josef von Sternberg, 1930) and *Le Roi de Resquilleurs* (The king of the gate crashers, Pierre Colombier, 1930).

While these foreign films primarily appealed to urban elites with knowledge of French, English, or German, their themes captivated broader audiences. A pattern emerged, emphasizing themes of wealth, love, and sexuality. According to a 1932 report, based on a one-month survey sample, 81.4 percent of the films exhibited in Turkey emphasized wealthy characters.[19] The narrative often centered around the success of the main characters in their romantic relationships, with love themes occupying the storyline in 77.8 percent of the films. Moreover, a backdrop of opulence characterized 74 percent of the films, and there was a notable focus on intricate love relationships in 70.4 percent. Suggestive clothing exposure was observed in approximately 66.6 percent of the films, while 37 percent featured elements of provocative dancing. Yet a mere 18 percent of the films had content related to religious, economic, political, industrial, commercial, or social issues. The films portraying modern life's commercial aspects accounted for 7.4 percent, while 3.3 percent of them represented agricultural life or ranching. The high exposure to subjects like wealth, love, and sexuality had an impact on audiences, shaping their expectations for and perceptions of societal ideals.

Illustrating the impact of these cinematic portrayals, a fifteen-year-old schoolgirl's reflection in the early 1930s encapsulated the allure and disillusionment induced by the silver screens in Istanbul:

> My greatest ambition is to be a movie star. Sometimes I am kept awake by a fascinating film and sometimes dream of it. I often play at making believe I am acting a part in the movies and have learned to make the *glad eye* like Dolores Del Rio, the smile of Lily Damita and showing my legs like Marlene Dietrich. Unfortunately, I am too poor to dress like the stars but from lovemaking in the movies, I have learned how to vamp boys as well as how to make them jealous of each other. Yes, the movies dissatisfy me greatly with my present life. If I was in the movies, the hard work would be compensated by my becoming a famous star with crowds to worship me and lots of money, men, beautiful jewels, dresses, automobiles, and houses.[20]

This adolescent fantasy of cinematic stardom—beginning with an identification with Dolores Del Rio, the first brown female star in Hollywood—offers insight into the influence of cinema and the motivations for attempts to control it. The film scholar Priscilla Peña Ovalle argues that Del Rio's Mexican heritage and popularity during Prohibition and the Great Depression challenged American representations of whiteness and Blackness within the Hollywood system.[21] Her musicals, released between the introduction of the Motion Picture Production Code (or Hays Code) in 1930 and its official enactment in 1934, illuminate how race, gender, and sexuality were policed and performed on screen.[22]

The Hays Code's emergence, spurred by anxieties around film's moral influence that were voiced by religious groups, underscores the power attributed to the medium. It also raises a question: How did other entities, such as missionary organizations and government agencies, seek to harness this power for their own purposes? Educational films emerged as one such response. Unlike commercial cinema, these films focused on public health, economic productivity, and social welfare. They modeled ideal behaviors, valorized specific occupations, and reinforced hierarchical social structures aligned with dominant ideologies of nationalism and modernization.

Film Diplomacy and Its Emergence in Turkey's Transnational Relations

In the early years of the republic, the Turkish government's intervention to influence films that other nations made about Turkey speaks to the transnational and global dimensions of film diplomacy and to its relation to propaganda, censorship, and state-sponsored advocacy. As the historians Ebru Boyar and Kate Fleet demonstrate, the Turkish government intervened in films about Turkey made by Bulgaria, Yugoslavia, Serbia, Germany, France, Britain, and the USSR—suggesting the global reach of film diplomacy.

Initially, these interventions focused on films that had already been completed and distributed. For example, in 1926, Turkey's Ministry of Internal Affairs banned *Yakub'un Kuyusu* (*Le Puits de Jacob* / A daughter of Israel, Edouard Jose, 1925), a French film showing the rape of a Jewish cabaret dancer in Istanbul, interrupted by a foreign journalist. For the Turkish ministry, this film was "Jewish propaganda" and "harmful to Turkish national feelings" as well as to "public morality."[23] While this act of suppression is an instance of censorship,[24] it also exemplifies film diplomacy in practice: Turkish officials communicated their objections to their French counterparts and attempted to prevent the film's circulation as a means of safeguarding national reputation. The absence of successful negotiation between the two states led to the film's brief exhibition at Melek Sineması in 1926 and its subsequent banning by Turkish authorities[25]—illustrating how diplomatic breakdowns over representation became part of the contest over who had the authority to shape Turkey's image on the global stage.

A similar pattern unfolded in response to the Bulgarian film *Buntat na Robite* (The slaves' revolt, Vassil Gendov, 1933), which the Turkish Foreign Ministry denounced as "an attack on the Turkish state and national identity."[26] The film, centered on Bulgaria's struggle for independence and the execution of its national hero Vasil Levski by Ottoman authorities, was condemned by Turkish officials for portraying Ottoman rule as an "imagined tyranny." Turkish diplomats lodged a protest with the Bulgarian government and demanded an official explanation. In response, Bulgarian authorities insisted that the film depicted fictionalized events from the Ottoman era and therefore did not pertain to the modern Turkish republic.[27] This justification, however, failed to satisfy Turkish officials, who—despite efforts to disavow the Ottoman past in official narratives—remained invested in how that Ottoman legacy was represented abroad. A similar case unfolded in 1934, when the Turkish embassy in Belgrade attempted to halt screenings of *The Balkan War*, a film about Serbia's military victory over the Ottoman Empire during the 1912–1913 conflict.[28] The film was viewed by Turkish officials as harmful to the national image, yet their efforts to block its exhibition were unsuccessful.

By contrast, from 1935 onward, Turkish officials sought to prevent the very production of films they deemed threatening to the nation's image, an escalation in the practice of film diplomacy. In 1935, the Turkish embassy in Belgrade successfully intervened to halt a film project being developed by the company Film Culturel and a French director known as Bernard, which aimed to depict the Serbian past "under Turkish rule."[29] The Turkish ambassador appealed directly to the Yugoslavian prime minister, who took the Turkish concerns seriously and responded favorably by terminating the production. That same year Turkish officials contacted the German Ministry of Propaganda to protest plans for a film centered on Sultan Abdulhamid II, citing concerns over how the late Ottoman period would be represented.[30] The German authorities complied and abandoned the project.

These cases illustrate both the varying degree of success and the evolving tactics of film diplomacy; from reactive censorship of completed films to proactive suppression of new productions. Through diplomatic pressure and strategic negotiation, Turkish officials worked to impose a vision of the nation as modern, progressive, and discontinuous with its imperial past. These instances of transnational coordination underscore the mechanics of film diplomacy—not simply as a matter of cultural outreach but also as a tool to assert representational sovereignty and manage perception on the global stage.

The Soviet Union capitalized on the Turkish government's appeals for films that could promote a rebranded national image—requests driven by Turkey's limited resources for producing its own state-sponsored media content. Film became a medium through which the Soviet Union and Turkey could, despite their different ideological orientations, temporarily align their interests. This collaboration yielded two documentary productions: *Ankara—Serdtse Turtsii* (Ankara—the heart of Turkey, Sergei Iosifovich Yutkevich, 1934) and *Idet novaia Turtsiia* (The new Turkey on the move, Esfir' Il'inichna Shub, 1935), both centered on the republic's capital city and its industry.[31] While these films promoted a vision of Soviet modernity in a transnational context, their aim was to influence Turkish public opinion in favor of communism.

Although the Soviet filmmakers sought to distance themselves from Western-centric models of development and emphasize anti-imperialist solidarity through their portrayal of Turkey, these documentaries ultimately reproduced orientalist tropes—rendering Turkey legible through exoticism and cultural otherness.[32] What enabled these projects to move forward was their presentation of a "Turkish reality in an acceptable form"—a framing that satisfied both Soviet ideological objectives and Turkish diplomatic sensitivities, as evidenced by the favorable reception among Turkish officials.[33] This case exemplifies how film diplomacy can facilitate cooperation across ideological divides, allowing conflicting regimes to find common ground through the negotiation.

These efforts to negotiate representations of the republic extended to confrontations with racialized stereotypes in Western and regional media. Race science, embedded in early twentieth-century geopolitics, operated as a tool of foreign relations—underpinned by the belief that civilizational conflict stemmed from racial difference.[34] Within this framework, Turkish nationalists were compelled to assert their whiteness to secure diplomatic recognition and to position the republic as a legitimate modern state. From the mid-1920s onward, films produced in the United States, Soviet Union, France, Germany, Serbia, Yugoslavia, and Bulgaria reflect the Turkish government's persistent attempts to monitor and shape the representation of the nation. These interventions consistently targeted a central obstacle: the "Terrible Turk" stereotype—originating during the period of the Ottoman Empire (1299–1923), reinforced by graphic accounts of the Armenian genocide (1915–1916), and inherited by the republic—which circulated globally in the guise of the "exotic" figure.[35]

In the United States, Christian missionary organizations invoked the image of the brutal, authoritarian Turk to raise funds for projects aimed at civilizing and protecting non-Muslim populations in Turkey.[36] At the same time, American industrial agents used the orientalist figure of the mysterious Turk to market commodities such as tobacco, dates, and carpets.[37] While distinct in form, both iterations of the stereotype reinforced the racialized "otherness" of Ottoman Muslims and served imperial and commercial agendas in the Middle East to support American foreign policy.[38]

The Turkish government's sustained efforts to counter racialized narratives—through diplomatic protests, censorship campaigns, and representational interventions—demonstrate its agency in shaping both national image and geopolitical perception. These actions were not merely reactive; they were part of a proactive strategy to dismantle the racist logics embedded in the Terrible Turk stereotype, assert Turkey's alignment with whiteness, and reframe the republic as a modern, Western-oriented nation. Film, in this context, became a critical site of ideological struggle—a medium through which Turkish officials attempted to recalibrate the racial optics of global spectatorship and renegotiate the terms on which Turkey could be seen, known, and legitimized in the international order. These efforts to displace visual regimes reveal how the state sought not only to manage its representation abroad but also to reconfigure its racial and civilizational positioning within a global hierarchy structured by imperial memory and Eurocentric modernity.

Much like the Russian monument at San Stefano—which was reimagined from a symbol that represented a shameful defeat into one that celebrated national cinema and heroic renewal—the Terrible Turk stereotype underwent a strategic transformation. Originally rooted in orientalist discourse and propaganda, this figure was recast from a barbaric villain into a valiant defender of national sovereignty and, increasingly, a champion of democratic values. In 1923, however, that transformation was far from complete; the Harvard historian Albert Bushnell Hart notoriously described the Turkish people as the "Near Eastern Ku Klux Klan."[39] His comparison of Turks to the white supremacist hate group employed the Terrible Turk stereotype in response to the Armenian genocide (1915–1916) of the Ottoman Empire era. This stereotype enabled many to vilify Turks as violent, uncivilized, and racially inferior. Such representations circulated widely, shaping public opinion and reinforcing racialized hierarchies that positioned the Turkish nation outside the moral and political boundaries of Western modernity.

Films that drew on or perpetuated this stereotype sparked transnational crises throughout the twentieth century. Perhaps the most infamous example is *Midnight Express* (Alan Parker, 1978), with its racist representation of Turkey that incited widespread international backlash and Turkish diplomatic protest.[40] Beginning in the mid-1920s, Turkish officials regularly intervened to protest and ban such films, issuing warnings to foreign governments about the risks of inciting anti-Turkish sentiment. These efforts were not limited to censorship; they laid the groundwork for transnational networks of communication, negotiation, and strategic image making. This process exemplifies what I term *film diplomacy*: a global practice through which states seek to influence their representation in cinematic media, manage political fallout, and reshape public perception.

In the context of increasing anti-Turkish narratives, state actors more often collaborated to counter negative imagery through coordinated media campaigns. The US State Department, American diplomats in Turkey, and Turkish government officials partnered to intervene in global media flows, seeking to rehabilitate Turkey's image and align it more closely with the ideals of modernization, partnership, and democratic reform. These campaigns illustrate the high diplomatic stakes of visual culture and the ways cinema became a contested site for negotiating national legitimacy on the global stage.

In an effort to foster global perceptions of Turkey as a modern and Western-oriented republic, Joseph C. Grew, US ambassador to Turkey from 1927 to 1932, advocated a public relations campaign and persuaded

President Atatürk to participate in a film.⁴¹ Through Grew's arrangements with Fox Movietone News, a leading producer of sound newsreels that covered cultural, political, and celebrity events around the world, *The Reception of the US Ambassador Joseph C. Grew by Atatürk on the Forest Farm* (1930; hereafter *Reception*) was made to promote a modern image of the newly established republic.⁴² Grew made a concerted effort to bolster relations between the two nations. His goal was to shift the American public's perception of Turkey from the racist Terrible Turk stereotype to that of a Western ally undergoing modernization.

In *Reception*, whiteness functions as an ideological structure through which Turkey is visually and symbolically positioned within European civilization. The film begins with a diplomatic meeting between Atatürk and Grew, which functions as an event celebrating US-Turkish cooperation. An elegantly dressed and well-spoken farmer named Tahsin Bey briefs Atatürk and his adopted daughter, Afet Inan, on the advancements made at the farm, emphasizing their forestry activities, use of Fordson tractors, and other agricultural developments.⁴³ The film served US interests by promoting its national products and demonstrating how tractors increased productivity, whereas it served Turkey's interest by promoting its modern image, illustrating its investment in agriculture and the national economy. *Reception* exemplifies film diplomacy as a process of negotiation by showing communication between institutional agents and their desire to influence public opinion and behavior as well as to develop a mutual understanding of the benefits of cooperation.

In the film, Inan wears a fox fur shawl, an accessory that was particularly in vogue in the 1930s in the West. Considered a sign of civilization, luxury, and glamour, it was worn by film stars, royalty, and wealthy individuals.⁴⁴ Unlike a chador or hijab, which viewers steeped in the orientalist Western imagination might expect Inan to wear, her fox fur reflects ideas about power and desire associated with luxury in the West and the iconography of Hollywood (even if the film's style counters this mode). Her outfit signals a desire to look modern and belong to the West and in this way to align with the new ideal Turkish woman. *Reception* carefully arranges the diplomatic encounter between transnational leaders so that Turkey is distanced from any form of representation that might suggest primitivism, a quality seen to be antithetical to Europeanness. That is, it asserts that Turkey belongs in Western civilization. Inan's presence enacts this belonging through whiteness—both in appearance and in comportment.

In this chapter, I use *whiteness* as a dynamic assemblage of symbolic and relational forms of power—a shifting structure of international legibility through which Turkish elites sought to secure their recognition, assert their modernity, and reconfigure their geopolitical standing within a global racial order. Inan's alignment with whiteness is not only symbolic but also intellectual. In the film, she delivers a speech aimed at American women. Speaking in Turkish, she congratulates American women for successfully obtaining their political rights. She further states that Turkish women are not content with their current rights, but she is optimistic that they will eventually have the right to vote and be elected to the Grand National Assembly. As a leading feminist and advocate for gender equality, Inan played a significant role in advancing women's rights in Turkey during the early twentieth century. Her efforts were instrumental in securing women the right to vote in Turkey in 1934. However, her national feelings (*milli hisleri*) were bruised when she read descriptions of Turks as barbarous (*barbar*) and a second-class race (*ikinci sınıf ırk*) in textbooks at a Christian missionary–founded school in Turkey, and in 1935, she turned to conducting eugenics research to help establish that Turks were white and European—thus contributing to efforts to modernize Turkey through a notion of racial belonging.[45] This suggests that it was possible in the 1930s for women's rights advocates to also advance eugenics. In addition, it underscores that whiteness, in this context, was not a stable identity but a strategic formation—mobilized in response to exclusion, insecurity, and the desire for international recognition. Within the framework of film diplomacy, whiteness did not operate silently in the background; it structured which nations were seen as modern, civilized, and worthy of inclusion within the Western-led global order.

Grew's 1930 initiative with *Reception* is one of the earliest instances of film diplomacy in the US-Turkey relationship. Similar efforts continued throughout this period. For instance, Charles H. Sherrill, the US ambassador to Turkey from 1932 to 1933, wrote *A Year's Embassy to Mustafa Kemal* (1934), a celebratory biography of Atatürk that highlights the progress achieved under his reforms.[46] Sherrill referred to Atatürk as a "liberator, regenerator, national hero, and world statesman" and held the "Turkish race" as "great" for producing such an outstanding figure.[47] This formulation depended on first positioning Turks as white to refer to their race as great. This kind of association helped construct a link between Turkishness and whiteness.[48]

The Korean War, the Cold War, and Media Militarism

The Korean War (1950–1953) provided a new geopolitical stage on which Turkey could solidify this racial and civilizational alignment. It marked Turkey's first postrepublic military engagement abroad and a critical opportunity to demonstrate its commitment to the West.[49] After initial hesitation, the Turkish media gave positive coverage to the government's decision to send soldiers to the Korean War on the grounds that this was needed for national security.[50] The war was pivotal in that it allowed Turkey to demonstrate loyalty to the West, particularly the United States, and to modernize its military in exchange for diplomatic recognition, investment, and aid. American training films, such as *Turkish Troops in Korea*, sponsored by the US Information Service, supported these efforts by highlighting the modernization of the Turkish military under American leadership. These films were popular among Turkish audiences and even inspired some to join the fight in Korea.

Importantly, the war also enabled state officials, media outlets, and cultural producers to rework the Terrible Turk stereotype from a figure of barbarism into an icon of fearless, disciplined military strength.[51] The US Joint Chiefs of Staff perpetuated the stereotype, although now using it as a fearless warrior. This rebranding bolstered Turkey's military potential in the fight against potential communist "enemies" like the Soviet Union and China. Moreover, it helped justify Turkey's entrance into the UN and NATO, which signaled its belonging in the West, a community that was predicated on whiteness. Consequently, the Turkish brigades received the US Distinguished Unit Citation for their service, an accolade that, in lauding soldiers for their heroic and warrior-like qualities, further legitimized the Terrible Turk stereotype.[52] By participating in the Korean War alongside American troops, Turkey was considered worthy of recognition, illustrating how whiteness functioned as a geopolitical currency of modernity and belonging within this alliance. In 1953, US Ambassador to Turkey George C. McGhee acknowledged that Turkey was a full and responsible member of the Western alliance, signaling that its collaboration in the Korean War had led to a significant shift in American attitudes toward the nation.[53]

Turkish media representations of the Korean War showcased themes such as the military, education, tourism, nationalism, and humanitarianism. Maps were published to educate the public about Korea's geography.

The Turkish government used Korean War films to enhance Turkey's image abroad as a modern nation that had a lot to offer to its Western allies. Turkish films like *Kore'den Geliyorum* (I am coming from Korea, 1951), which shows a Turkish veteran at Turkish historical sites, used the war to promote tourism. They were exhibited, for example, in the United States with the goal of attracting American tourists. Other Turkish media presented the war as an opportunity to travel to a faraway land and meet "exotic" Others while showing soldiers posing like tourists.[54] These media seldom reflected on the horrors of war, violence, and war crimes and instead affirmed the war's legitimacy by focusing on the greatness of Turkish soldiers and their nation. After the war ended, the newspaper *Hürriyet* released a cartoon depicting a globe saluting a Turkish soldier and his flag as thanks for aid and support during the war, reinforcing Turkey's sense of belonging to the West.[55] The Korean War allowed Turkey to prove itself as modern, white, and democratic.

To be accepted as a modern nation, Turkey had to perform whiteness and create an Other to win minds, hearts, and wars.[56] The representation of the Korean War in Turkish media illustrates how whiteness played a role in constructing China as the Other, creating space for the Turkish self to emerge as a Western leader. In some Turkish newspapers, cartoons represented Turks as brave warriors who protected their Western allies and maintained world peace. This created the "legend of the Turk," which provided a nationalist narrative that inspired pride in the heroic actions of Turkish soldiers.[57] A cartoon in the newspaper *Cumhuriyet* depicted China as a monster.[58] Another in *Hürriyet* showed a Turkish soldier overpowering Chinese soldiers and rescuing an American counterpart despite having been shot seventeen times; the Chinese soldiers fear their arrival more than that of an atomic bomb.[59] The cartoonists disparaged and vilified the Chinese soldiers and exaggerated the size and strength of the Turkish soldiers. These examples show how the Terrible Turk image evolved from Western hate speech into a heroic narrative that was used to control communism.

The Korean War also guaranteed the United States' commitment to Turkey's security. *The Incredible Turk* (Burton Benjamin, 1958) was a documentary film broadcast on the CBS television series *The Twentieth Century*. It relied on the voice-over of the American journalist Walter Cronkite, one of the most trusted men in the United States, to challenge the stereotype of the Terrible Turk, which he did by presenting Atatürk as an "Incredible Turk" and praising him for transforming Turkey from "an Eastern, authoritarian state to a democracy comparable to Western democracies."[60] The voices of Turkish people were conspicuously absent from the narrative. Choosing a white American male to tell the stories of silenced Others perpetuated the notion that not-yet-Western voices were unreliable.

The Incredible Turk reused footage from *Reception*, reframing the earlier diplomatic encounter between Grew and Atatürk to serve Cold War propaganda. Benjamin's film repurposed their images as part of a strategic effort to advance US foreign policy interests by portraying Turkey as a stable, modern ally in the fight against Soviet influence. Positioned as a response to national security concerns, it aimed to decrease communist influence and legitimize Turkey's role within the Western bloc. As the American studies scholar Perin Gürel has noted, the United States developed two main strategies to fight the spread of communism by the Soviet Union: modernization theory and the doctrine of containment. Both of these helped to improve Turkey's image in the West.[61] Introducing Atatürk as a "proto-hero of modernization theory" suggested that non-Western nations could become modern by following the same stages of growth as the United States.[62] Yet, as Gürel explains, it also downplayed "racial and religious differences" and "projected antidemocratic measures as intermediary necessities."[63] In this sense, the film reflects whiteness in its ideological construction, which allows certain groups to be admitted or rejected in order to maintain structures of privilege and marginalization.

Visualizing Modernity: The Educational Film and Its Others

The educational film *The Middle East: Change—Turkey and Saudi Arabia* (Encyclopaedia Britannica, 1984; hereafter *Change*) exemplifies how Cold War educational media constructed transnational racialization by juxtaposing Turkey and Saudi Arabia as civilizational opposites.[64] Produced as a pedagogical resource for high school and college students, the film employs maps, expert interviews, and audiovisual juxtapositions to construct a civilizational binary: Turkey is depicted as modern, secular, and aligned with the West, while Saudi Arabia is cast as its traditionalist, religiously fundamentalist counterpart. This contrast reflects the racialized logic of

Cold War media—positioning Turkey as the "exceptional" Muslim nation, rendered intelligible through its proximity to whiteness, and Saudi Arabia as the regressive Other against which that exceptionality is defined.

This audiovisual and ideological contrast draws on a much longer history of anti-Arab sentiment within Turkey's modernization discourse. Since the early republican period, efforts to Westernize and modernize Turkey have often relied on disidentification from the Arab world. Cultural debates over the quality of radio broadcasts, the influence of Egyptian cinema and arabesque music, and women's uses of headscarves were frequently framed through orientalist language that constructed Arabs as backward. Within this logic, Turkish national identity was articulated not only through alignment with Europe and secularism but also through the strategic rejection of Arabness as its racial and cultural foil.[65]

Change opens with fireworks and uses special effects to show the text *The Middle East* in multiple languages; then it cuts to a low-angle shot of an antenna and a satellite dish. These early visual cues associate modernization with technological connectivity—suggesting that the path to progress in the Middle East lies in access to communication infrastructures like radio, television, and satellite networks. The film's editing establishes a causal relationship between media technology and social transformation: Modernization is something to be transmitted, received, and staged through circuits of audiovisual mediation. In this framework, the ability to "receive" modernity is both a technical and a civilizational measure.

The narrative is anchored by the voice-over of Richard W. Bulliet, an American historian of Islam at Columbia University, who contextualizes twentieth-century transformations in the region. He characterizes Turkey as a "pro-Western, quasi-democratic, and religiously tolerant society," composed primarily of Turks with a small Kurdish minority (figure 1.1). Notably absent are any references to other ethnic or religious communities, such as Alevis, Armenians, or Syriacs—erasing the complexity of Turkey's demographic landscape. Bulliet contrasts Turkey's "Western way of life" with Saudi Arabia's adherence to an "ancient and traditional culture," emphasizing its governance according to Islamic fundamentalist principles and its identification with Sunni Islam (figure 1.2). Like many other educational films of the period, *Change* pairs expert commentary with animated maps and B-roll footage (supplementary shots) to render regional differences visually legible.

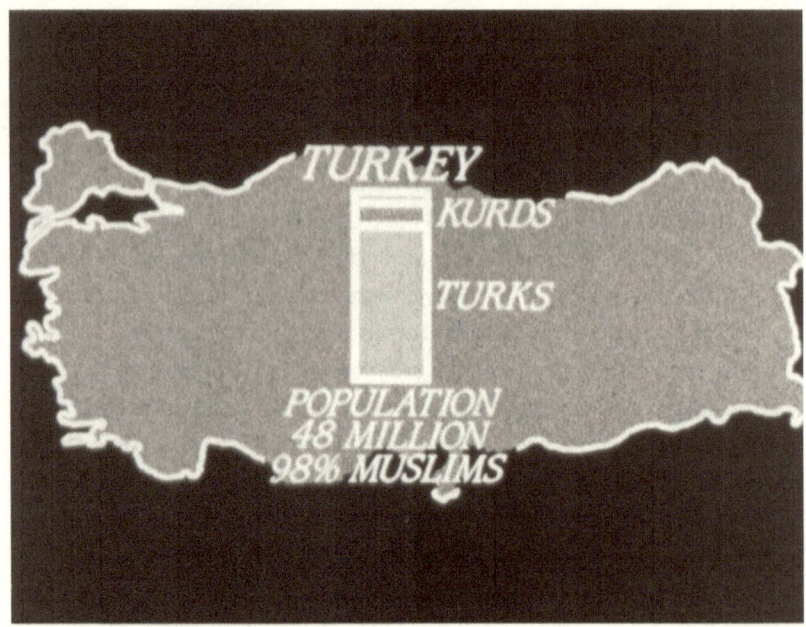

FIGURE 1.1 Map of Turkey in *Change* (1984).

Source: Indiana University Libraries, Moving Image Archive.

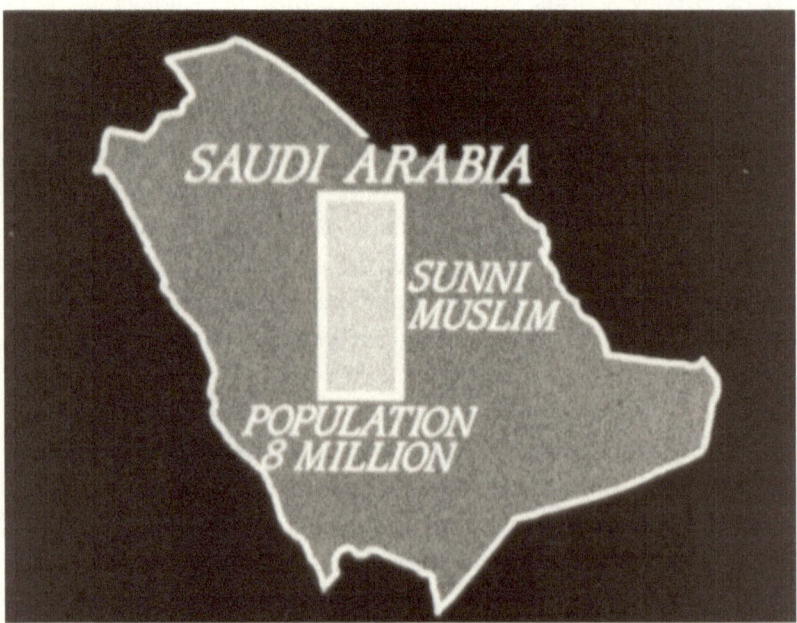

FIGURE 1.2 Map of Saudi Arabia in *Change*.

Source: Indiana University Libraries, Moving Image Archive.

A marked asymmetry emerges in the presentation of expert voices. Unlike most educational films about Turkey produced before the 1980s, *Change* includes a local expert, Dr. Ülkü Ü. Bates, a Turkish scholar of Islamic art. In contrast, the expert representing Saudi Arabia, Ahmad Al-Shanbary, is introduced simply as "someone who grew up in [Saudi Arabia]."[66] Both interviews take place in a Sheraton Hotel, itself a symbol of modernization in the Middle East.[67] Yet the juxtaposition between a credentialed Turkish academic and an unidentified Arab man—whose only qualification is lived experience—reinforces a racialized hierarchy of knowledge. Bates, Turkish, is visually and intellectually aligned with cosmopolitan modernity; Al-Shanbary, Arab and anonymous, stands in as a native informant.[68] This contrast reproduces a regional power differential between legally white, socially "modern" subjects and socially brown, culturally marked Others.[69]

This discursive strategy reflects a longer-standing effort by Turkish republican elites and their Western interlocutors (such as Eugène Pittard, Afet Inan's dissertation adviser) to differentiate Turks from Arabs as part of a racial taxonomy. In these frameworks, Arabs were cast as a separate race—enabling modernizers to position Turks as white and European.[70] This racial differentiation was not merely internal to Turkish nationalism; it was also strategically designed to render Turkey more relatable—and more useful—to American and European allies. By presenting Turkey as a secular, rational, and moderate Muslim nation, reformers sought to situate it as a bulwark against Islamic fundamentalism and as a reliable partner in regional governance. *Change* thus perpetuates a visual and ideological approach in which modernization is constructed relationally: Turkey's Western orientation is affirmed through the racialized othering of Saudi Arabia. In doing so, the film participates in a broader architecture of transnational whiteness, wherein racial legibility and geopolitical value are coconstituted. Whiteness here operates as a mediating structure of cultural proximity, political legibility, and civilizational worth.

As I have shown in this chapter, the rise of cinema in Turkey was never simply a national affair. From its transimperial roots in Ottoman shadow play and foreign exhibition networks to its deployment as a Cold War instrument of diplomacy and ideological struggle, film in Turkey has always been embedded within global circuits of power, race, and representation. Whether produced domestically or abroad, films about Turkey became contested sites where modernization was performed, whiteness was negotiated, and national identity was staged for international acceptance. Through film diplomacy, government officials sought to manage the nation's visual narrative—rejecting orientalist tropes like the Terrible Turk, embracing strategic alliances, and projecting Turkey as a secular, Western-oriented republic aligned with Euro-American ideals.

Yet this process was intended to recalibrate the terms through which Turkey could be seen, known, and legitimized in a world order structured by racial hierarchies and imperial memory. Cinema operated as a site of ideological struggle: It challenged geographical imaginaries that spatialized difference through discourses of civilization and race while asserting a vision of Turkey aligned with the Western world. From state-sponsored protests of foreign films to collaborative ventures like *Reception*, and from the visual strategies of *Change* to the racial logics that shaped them, the transnational history of cinema in Turkey shows how film functioned as a strategic medium for managing representation, contesting racial hierarchies, and repositioning the nation within global formations of modernity. Film diplomacy, then, operated as a racialized negotiation over who could be seen and understood and under what terms they could be admitted into the civilizational order of the modern world.

2
Beyond the Contract
How Missionaries Forged Nontheatrical Havens

In 1952, the Protestant missionary Paul Emanuel Nilson orchestrated a film screening in a prison in Kayseri, Turkey. Originally from Illinois, he had first arrived in Turkey in 1911. He represented the American Board of Commissioners for Foreign Missions (ABCFM), and he intended his event to provide "educational pictures" while conveying Christian values to the incarcerated individuals.[1] He opened the program with a Disney film featuring Donald Duck as an army pilot who found himself imprisoned.[2] The prisoners' laughter reverberated through the venue, signaling the transformative power of cinema within the prison walls. Nilson's program continued with *Lean Years*, a film sponsored by the United Nations Relief and Rehabilitation Administration that depicts the agency's efforts to aid those affected by hunger and poverty in war-torn Europe. By displaying the suffering of others, Nilson sought to instill empathy and solidarity among the prisoners. The final film, *God of Creation*, produced by the Moody Institute of Science in 1945, merged celestial wonders and vibrant blossoms with a religious discussion about God as the creator of the universe. Accompanied by Nilson's recitation of the book of Psalms in Turkish, amplified by a microphone, this film transformed the screening into a Christian event. The prisoners responded with resounding applause, and Nilson distributed twenty paperback books containing the Psalms to the prison schoolteacher, to be shared among the three hundred prisoners.

This use of film by Nilson reflects the broader strategy employed by ABCFM missionaries in Turkey during this period.

In this chapter, I use the framework of film diplomacy to examine the activities of ABCFM missionaries in Turkey between 1930 and 1953. Confronted with mounting challenges to traditional forms of missionary work, these missionaries turned to cinema as an alternative medium—one that allowed them to pursue their goals of proselytization, institutional legitimacy, and alignment with American geopolitical interests. At the same time, they had to navigate the complex interplay between their embedded ideology of whiteness and the secularizing political culture of the early Turkish Republic. Drawing on primary archival materials, I explore how missionaries sought to advance Christian values in a context where overt religious messaging risked state censure. Their strategic use of film—and the symbolic capital attached to American modernity— enabled them to gain a degree of social acceptance among a predominantly Muslim population.

Central to this process was what I describe as their malleable whiteness—a paradoxical flexibility that allowed missionaries to simultaneously embody modernity, neutrality, and spiritual authority. While this adaptability generated tensions between their religious commitments and the secular imperatives of the Turkish state, these tensions were not fixed. Through collaborations with local communities, Turkish educational institutions, and the US Information Service (USIS), missionaries engaged in ongoing negotiation, using discourses of modernization as a mediating force. Films became crucial tools in this process, enabling them to present Christianity not as a threat to secular progress but as a partner in national development. This strategic alignment with the modernization agenda of the Turkish Republic allowed missionaries a measure of operational space—though it often required subtle reframing of both religious and modernizing ideals to suit their objectives.

In 1953, Nilson organized another exhibition of *God of Creation*, this time at a church. The pews were packed, and the crowd was so immense that people stood patiently, spilling out onto the church grounds, eagerly awaiting their turn to witness the film. According to Nilson, those in the audience, predominantly Turkish Christians and members of Kurdish ethnic communities, were "hungry for the Gospel" and eager to learn about "the story of Jesus and . . . his way of Salvation."[3] In addition to screening the film, Nilson took the microphone and elaborated on marvels of creation that pointed to a living God who watches over, cares for, and loves humanity: "Beni sever, beni sever, Allah beni sever, Çiçekleri seven Allah, Beni dahi sever, . . . SENI sever, seni sever"; then he ended with "HE LOVES YOU, TOO."[4] For Nilson, the emotional atmosphere in the church was palpable, and both young and old were captivated by the stories, music, and visuals. After the exhibition, he wrote a letter to his friends, asserting that "the movie and projector and mi[c] are God's tools to help us."[5]

Film, alongside maps, photography, radio, and television, constituted a significant tool set employed by missionaries on a global scale. Scholars across various disciplines have investigated the different ways missionaries leveraged communication technologies to advance their objectives. For example, Joseph W. Ho, a historian, analyzes how portable photographic technologies shaped understandings of China's modernization and influenced US foreign policy.[6] The anthropologist and religion scholar Pamela E. Klassen explores the technological and theological role of radio in Protestant missionary work within the context of Canadian colonialism and Indigenous lands.[7] Lauren Turek, a scholar of diplomacy and American religious history, highlights the media savviness of missionaries, focusing on their innovative use of radio and television for broadcasting their messages and lobbying in the US Congress for protection of religious freedom in countries like the Soviet Union, Guatemala, and South Africa.[8] The understudied context of film-savvy missionaries in Turkey enriches this field of studies in two ways. First, Turkey holds a crucial place in Christianity as the geographical site of biblical events. Notably, the term *Christian* emerged in Antioch, where Saint Paul of Tarsus played a pivotal role in spreading Christianity. In addition, Constantinople served as the Eastern Church's center, and the seven churches of the Revelation were situated in Asia Minor—present-day Turkey.[9] American Protestant missionaries targeted both Muslims and Eastern Christians (e.g., members of the Orthodox, Armenian, and Syriac Churches), viewing them as degenerate, stagnant, and inferior.[10] By positioning themselves as liberators and leaders of these groups, missionaries aligned Protestantism with whiteness. The geopolitical context of Turkey's transition from an empire to a republic in 1923 adds further significance to this case of film-savvy missionary activity there.

Turkey emerged as a modern and secular nation not only through President Mustafa Kemal Atatürk's reforms (Atatürk inkılâpları) but also through implicit agreements among Muslims in the Ottoman Empire in 1915. Building upon Charles Mills's *The Racial Contract*, the sociologist Barış Ünlü defines the "Muslimness contract" as an unspoken yet widely acknowledged agreement that operated in opposition to the local Ottoman Christians and foreign Christians.[11] This framework consisted of two fundamental provisions and formed the cornerstone of societal dynamics in the last decades of the shrinking Ottoman Empire. The first clause dictates that a life of security and privilege in Anatolia hinges on adherence to being Muslim. The second provision forbids any divulgence of the truth regarding the treatment of non-Muslims, and it admonishes against any political involvement with or expressions of sympathy toward that marginalized group. Ünlü emphasizes that the Muslimness contract operated within a horizontal structure, in contrast to a hierarchical, top-down authority, as common feelings, expectations, and interests brought Muslims together. Muslims in the Black Sea, East Anatolia, and Aegean regions formed local congresses to organize resistance movements against the Christian populations, like Greeks and Armenians, in their regions. Their efforts laid the groundwork for Atatürk to successfully form the Grand National Assembly under a big Muslimness contract. Thus, the Turkish state emerged as a shield to protect the interests of the Muslims in Anatolia, who wanted to have a nation of their own.

Some Muslims were suspicious of the actions of those who did not share their identity. In 1947, a Muslim journalist criticized Christian missionaries and called on all religious magazines to embark on a series of publications exposing "the misguided and false nature of missionary beliefs" as well as emphasizing "the contradiction of these beliefs with human dignity and honor."[12] The following year the journalist Ömer Rıza Doğrul noted that missionaries began to distance themselves from their conventional titles and instead presented themselves as scholars specializing in religious sciences. This shift, he suggested, stemmed from their failed conversion efforts in Islamic countries. As the term *missionary* acquired an Islamophobic connotation, missionaries opted to change their image to find receptive audiences for their intended message.[13]

Film emerged as a strategic tool to mitigate risks, negotiate relations, and serve missionary agendas at a time when modernization and technological progress became secularized forms of religious missions. By focusing on missionaries' uses of films between 1930 and 1953, I identify their exhibition sites and audiences in Turkey. Then I contextualize these activities within Turkey's legal framework governing film exhibition and distribution. My analysis of the archival materials shows that film allowed missionaries to unlawfully function beyond the confines of censorship regulations, notably through exhibitions in nontheatrical sites such as prisons, churches, hospitals, and open spaces. Additionally, film importation laws allowed them to avoid taxes in some instances. These circumstances enabled missionaries to function like distributors of American films with their own privileges and backlashes. Operating within the racialized power dynamics of the early Turkish Republic, Protestant missionaries drew on the ideological power of whiteness to navigate legal ambiguities and establish a network of nontheatrical film exhibitions. These venues functioned as spaces for circumventing official censorship and promoting their own vision of modernization.

From Banned to Screened: Film Diplomacy and the Shifting Sands of Turkishness

A 1934 Turkish law prohibited the distribution of religious propaganda within the country,[14] and the Board of Censorship rejected films such as *The King of Kings* (Cecil B. DeMille, 1927), *The Miracle of the Bells* (Irving Pichel, 1948), and *The Silver Chalice* (Victor Saville, 1954) for propagating religion.[15] In a collaborative effort in 1953, Nilson and a local pastor, Kerim Bey, organized film screenings for *The King of Kings* and *God of Creation*. This exhibition drew a crowd of 140 to a church for a special service.[16] From Nilson's perspective, as the films played, a profound hush fell over the congregation, which was entranced by the portrayal of Jesus's life and teachings. Emotions ran high, and Nilson, seizing the moment, delivered a two-hour-and-fifteen-minute address in Turkish, speaking about love and God, that captivated the audience.

In Nilson's view, a Turkish police chief investigated his exhibitions for potential religious propaganda by questioning a Syrian Christian merchant named Thomas about the appropriateness of showing movies in a church setting. Thomas defended the films as educational and beneficial to children. When asked about future screenings, Thomas disclosed that Nilson planned to show the "science film" *God of Creation*. Intrigued, the police chief expressed a desire to attend the screening, and Thomas extended an invitation not only to him but also to his friends. Nilson believed he was under surveillance, and he immediately spotted the police chief at the church. Recognizing him as the same individual who had previously requested an old Turkish Bible, he wondered whether the police chief and his companions were attending the event out of genuine curiosity or for investigative purposes. Nonetheless, Nilson continued with the exhibition, and the police chief did not imposed any censorship restrictions, even though the film promoted Christian ideals.[17] This recounting suggests that, at least in some cases, nontheatrical film exhibitions operated outside the purview of censorship regulations. Turkish authorities did not enforce the 1934 law against missionaries who subverted regulations about religious propaganda.

I employ Ünlü's concept of Turkishness as a lens through which to interrogate the decision-making process of Turkish officials. Using whiteness studies, Ünlü traces the conceptual lineage of Turkishness to the Muslimness contract and subsequently characterizes the "Turkishness contract" as a modified iteration that emerged between 1924 and 1925 in the aftermath of the establishment of the Turkish Republic.[18] This historical contextualization serves as a foundation for understanding the evolution of Turkish national identity. Ünlü's formulation portrays Turkishness as a nuanced and often underestimated interplay between the ethnic identity of Turkish individuals and their cognitive perceptions, experiential realms, and acquired knowledge. It extends to the deliberate omissions in their sensory experiences—what they choose to overlook, neglect, or refrain from acknowledging. The integration of this concept into the analysis of the police chief's decision suggests that the act of not acknowledging religious propaganda during a nontheatrical film exhibition can be construed as an expression of Turkishness. Ünlü's framework posits that individuals of Turkish identity possess the agency to selectively perceive and engage with their surroundings. The choice of what to see, hear, acknowledge, or purposefully disregard becomes a manifestation of Turkishness. In this context, the discretionary ability to regulate sensory engagement and acknowledgment represents a privilege inherent to Turkish identity. This privilege, in turn, shapes the cognitive and emotional dimensions of how Turks discern and categorize phenomena, determining what is perceived as a potential threat and what is not.

The nontheatrical film exhibitions orchestrated by missionaries emerge as a noteworthy illustration of Turkishness and its manifestation in decision-making processes. Rather than being perceived as a threat, these exhibitions were characterized by an affirmative dimension, as missionaries purposefully employed film as a communication tool to establish connections with the Turkish public. Nilson, a prominent figure in this effort, was joined by fellow missionaries such as Mary Louise Lee Winkler and Raymond White. Winkler, a teacher and nurse, used film exhibitions to reach villagers, disseminate health-related information, and provide medical aid. Similarly, White's film activities attracted the attention of Monteagle Stearns, a US government agent responsible for the USIS activities in Turkey.[19] Collaborations between the missionaries and USIS staff facilitated film diplomacy, enabling both groups to communicate their messages to audiences and mediate local and foreign relations through film. Consequently, film exhibitions flourished and fostered transnational relations between the United States and Turkey.

Nilson was at the forefront of the Protestant missionaries' efforts to employ film. During his tenure in various missionary stations across Turkey, he witnessed the political transformation of the Ottoman Empire (1299–1923) into the Republic of Turkey (1923–). He was a pivotal figure because he recognized film's potential to support his agenda of reaching larger audiences and disseminating Christian values more broadly. Using mobile film units, Nilson journeyed to remote Turkish villages, where he received assistance from local teachers, students, and friends. Although the films he exhibited were originally produced for American audiences, they sparked interest among Turkish villagers through live and simultaneous translation to Turkish. His work attracted the attention of both the Turkish and the American governments, which were increasingly eager to use film as a strategic communication tool, and he emerged as a transnational agent who was capable of bridging the gap between the peoples of Turkey and the United States. This communication was as much a product of his curatorial and promotional labor as it was a characteristic of the films themselves.

Yet film screenings organized by missionaries did more than disseminate Christian values and foster connections with local communities. By showcasing Turkey and the necessity of missionary work, they encouraged financial support from various entities in the United States. They sponsored and produced silent films such as *Highlights of Village Life* (ABCFM likely late 1920s or early 1930s), *Beneath the Snows of Mount Argeaus* (ABCFM, 1931), and *Schoolmates at Scutare* (ABCFM, 1933) to demonstrate the positive reception of their work by the public. In these films, the audiences became the subjects. These ABCFM-sponsored films consequently served as promotional tools and enticed more Protestants to engage in missionary activities in Turkey.

During the transition to the Turkish Republic, which mandated secular education, missionaries recognized film's potential as an educational medium. What made film particularly appealing to missionaries, even before their educational and proselytizing efforts, was its ability to visually document and showcase missionary work across the globe—for example, through travel films, ethnographic studies, and documentaries.[20] Missionaries used film exhibitions as powerful conduits for building connections, bridging cultural gaps, and spreading Christian values in Turkey. They positioned their films as educational tools in order to enter various spaces (e.g., prisons, churches, and schools) and disseminate knowledge on subjects like agriculture, health, medicine, and science. Doing so allowed them to advance their agenda by introducing Turkish audiences to American Christian culture. Although most films avoided overt references to Christianity, the missionaries' presence within exhibition spaces, their active engagement with the public, and the distribution of Bibles clearly associated these educational films with the promotion of Christian ideals. In their use of film, missionaries navigated the evolving political landscape, strengthened their missionary work, and forged transnational relationships that transcended geographical and cultural boundaries.

Nilson attributed the Turkish government's interest in educational films to his persistent promotion of 16 mm film for educational purposes.[21] In a letter to American acquaintances, he noted that his efforts had begun to yield results, as Turkish institutions were starting to invest in film technologies. Despite limited funds, these institutions made small investments, and Nilson expressed gratitude for this on behalf of the ABCFM. These initial developments mark the emergence of film diplomacy and illustrate the willingness of agents to negotiate, establish feedback loops, mobilize films, disseminate ideas to the public, and mediate transnational networks. In Turkey, missionaries selected American educational films for screenings, but their approach lacked a systematic plan. They operated on an ad hoc basis, meaning they made decisions and adjustments as situations arose.

In 1937, the Turkish government passed Öğretici ve Teknik Filmler Hakkında Kanun (Law of Educational and Technical Films, or Law 3122).[22] This law eliminated import taxes on film products, which benefited missionaries who often had to purchase films from the United States. This early negotiation regarding films encouraged the importation of films, demonstrating how the government policy facilitated the mobilization of films by eliminating taxes.

From Smyrna to Screens: American Missionaries and Communication Networks

In the nineteenth century, the ABCFM had embarked on a global mission to spread the teachings of the Bible and establish missionary stations across the world. Its goal was to convert the world to Christianity and expand American Christians' understanding of the world beyond their own country.[23] The historian Emily Conroy-Krutz notes that American missionaries embraced Christian imperialism: That is, they spread Christianity worldwide by establishing an American empire akin to the British Empire to exert political power over others. To determine where to begin their evangelical efforts, they created a "hierarchy of heathenism," a ranking system that evaluated cultures and individuals according to their degree of civilization and helped missionaries determine their most receptive targets.[24] By fusing ideas about culture, race, and religion with geopolitical context, this hierarchy enabled missionaries to navigate space and pursue their mission of worldwide conversion.[25]

These missionaries strategically established communication hubs, employing a multifaceted approach that encompassed education, media, and health care to spread Christianity. In 1820, the missionaries Pliny Fisk and Levi Parsons embarked on a mission to Turkey, then part of the Ottoman Empire, with Smyrna as their destination. The city was ideal because it was a communication hub that connected all parts of the empire.[26] These missionaries sought to leverage Smyrna's connectivity in commercial and political networks to engage with diverse communities in the region. Their goal was to share the teachings of the Bible with "Jews, pagans, Mohammedans and Christians" in the Near East (what is now Turkey, Greece, Syria, and Lebanon). From Smyrna, the missionaries established stations that served as vital communication hubs and provided education, recreation, health care, and spiritual guidance. The ABCFM strategically positioned these stations among religious and ethnic groups such as Armenians, Assyrians, Jews, Greeks, Kurds, Alevis, and Yezidis. By 1860, the missionary presence had expanded to encompass three major regions in western, central, and eastern Turkey, and by 1880, the ABCFM had over a hundred churches and six thousand members in Turkey.[27] By the early twentieth century, a cohort of 179 missionaries managed a network of 450 educational institutions and 19 health centers.[28] One missionary attributed this success to education, written media (including the press, translations, and literary works), and health care, which were deemed the most successful methods to "permeate [the region] with Christianity."[29]

Sustaining its work through donations from millions of American churchgoers and government funding, the ABCFM wielded significant influence at the intersection of religious and government activities in the Near East.[30] Connections with prestigious American universities like Princeton, as well as influential families like the Rockefellers, the Morgans, and the Roosevelts, bolstered the board's impact and enabled advocates of America's foreign policy to shape the region.[31]

Near East Relief (NER) also served the Christians of the Ottoman Empire. After the 1915 Armenian genocide, NER raised $100 million (approximately $3 billion dollars today) to aid the Armenians.[32] A portion of the funds supported the production of films such as *Auction of Souls* (Oscar Apfel, 1919), *Alice in Hungerland* (director unknown, 1921), *Seeing Is Believing* (director and year unknown), and *Miracles in Ruins* (director and year unknown).[33] As an example, *Auction of Souls* depicted the harrowing experiences of Aurora Mardiganian, an Armenian survivor of the Ottoman soldiers' systematic killings. She was cast as herself and thus had to relive the trauma of rape, violence, and murder that she had endured to film these scenes. As the film scholar Anthony Slide noted, the production of the film led to Mardiganian's exploitation by the Hollywood film industry.[34]

While NER sponsored films to address the aftermath of genocide, domestically the Turkishness contract included a condition related to the genocide and expulsion of non-Muslims. Alongside the prohibition of resisting Turkification, a novel stipulation emerged: disseminating information about or engaging in politics concerning non-Muslims and Kurds who resisted the Turkification process was prohibited. The Turkishness contract played a pivotal role in shaping the history of modern Turkey and the lives of its residents, influencing their material, emotional, and epistemological worlds. Under this contract, every Turk or Turkified individual could potentially benefit from obeying the contract, active endorsement was not necessary. The key requirement was nonresistance and adherence to the contract, offering Turkified members the expectation of social mobility across various domains. Violating the contract, however, resulted in severe repercussions such as unemployment, imprisonment, or ostracism.[35]

Within this complex sociopolitical landscape, American Protestant missionaries in the Ottoman Empire and the early Turkish Republic operated through extensive communication networks and media infrastructures, employing tools such as formal schooling, medical dispensaries, translated texts, and strategically positioned mission stations. Using film as an integral medium, these missionaries facilitated cultural interactions, disseminated Christian values, and solidified American influence within diverse communities across the region.

The Double Exposure: Film, Faith, and Fear in the Missionaries' Modernization Project

During World War I (1914–1918) and the subsequent Turkish War of Independence (Kurtuluş Savaşı, 1919–1923), some ABCFM stations in Turkey were damaged, leading American leaders to consider withdrawing. However, the Conference of Lausanne in 1923 recognized the sovereignty of the Turkish Republic, bringing a renewed sense of hope. A missionary named Dr. James L. Barton noted that key Turkish negotiators, including Ismet Pasha, wanted American institutions to remain.[36] Turkish representatives acknowledged the importance of these institutions for Turkey's future and even hinted at potential collaborations in revising education laws.

Atatürk, the first president of Turkey, demonstrated his commitment to secular education by welcoming the renowned American philosopher and teacher John Dewey to assist in reforming education in the new nation.[37] Dewey's visit to Turkey in 1924 solidified his influence on

Turkish education. Recognizing the global impact of Dewey's ideas in Germany, Switzerland, France, and England, Turkish educators sought to align themselves with contemporary educational trends,[38] and Atatürk shared Dewey's vision of using education to modernize and unify society. Dewey provided a report to the Ministry of National Education of Turkey (MNET) that outlined recommendations for modernizing the educational system, including creating teacher training programs and constructing educational facilities. The ministry adopted these measures as a means to put education in Turkey on a modern, secular, and democratic path.[39] The different collaborations between American missionaries and Turkish leaders, along with Dewey's involvement, exemplified a unique interplay between religious missions and educational reform.

As secularization swept across Turkey in the 1920s, ABCFM missionaries operating in Turkey had to align their educational approach with the changing times. To meet this demand, they aimed to maintain secular classrooms while emphasizing moral and spiritual values derived from Christian principles. Rather than promoting religious ideology, they focused on presenting Christianity as a way of acting modern. By modeling Christian Protestant principles through their behavior, they tried to align with Turkey's secularization and modern nation-building efforts.

In their quest to innovate, missionaries introduced elements of the American educational system into Turkey. They established schools that emulated the US public school system in regions predominantly populated by Christian minorities and likened them to privately endowed seminaries, academies, and colleges that offered a "first-class private school course."[40] The international colleges (missionary schools) in Anatolia even conferred bachelor of arts degrees under Massachusetts charters, with their diplomas widely recognized by American universities for admission to postgraduate and professional courses. This assurance of educational quality extended beyond academics, as graduates of these institutions gained opportunities to further their education or pursue careers in the United States. In their pursuit of influence, missionaries in Turkey also embraced the film technologies popularized in American schools. Using tools like ViewLex slide and film projectors, they incorporated films into their educational programs.[41]

Yet missionaries also recognized film's potential as a tool for public engagement beyond formal education. They organized screenings in public spaces as a means of informing villagers. Nilson recounted villagers' reactions to an educational film exhibition in an open space in 1949, marveling at how the entire village had gathered in awe to witness the "living pictures" on the screen. He declared, "We made history that night, for it was the first movie of any kind ever seen there, and most of the people had never seen any movie before." He also described an incident where a film featuring a large snake caused approximately twenty women to flee in fear. He attributed their reaction to their naivete, implying that they could benefit from further exposure to education and reproduced the classic trope of the credulous spectator.[42]

It is possible that the women's astonishment stemmed not from a naive belief that they were under threat from an actual snake but rather from the visual transformation unfolding before their eyes. This parallels the analysis of Tom Gunning, a film historian, of *The Arrival of a Train* (Louis Lumière, Auguste Lumière, 1896), where he posits that the audience's shock derived from witnessing an unbelievable visual spectacle rather than a genuine threat.[43] Moreover, the poet and writer Ercüment Ekrem Talu attended the first film screenings (including *The Arrival of a Train*) around 1896 and 1897 in Istanbul at Sponeck Beerhouse, and his observations provide an understanding of the audiences' reactions.[44] He described how some in the audience feared the train derailing and potentially harming them, so they took precautionary measures by vacating their seats.[45] He also experienced some apprehension, but his curiosity prevailed, keeping him firmly seated.

Talu also noted that early film exhibitions spurred discussions among members of the public about cinematography, with divergent views emerging. Some viewed it as *günah* (sinful), leading to repentance, while others, embracing a more progressive stance, welcomed the advent of a new facet of *medeniyet* (civilization) in the nation.[46] These discussions suggest that audiences viewed film as a technological tool that carried dual implications, concurrently interpreted as a potential threat and a harbinger of civilization. Within this discourse, it is important to underline that civilization was the nineteenth-century version of modernization and was at the heart of the ABCFM's work from its beginnings in 1810. Given these accounts, the missionaries' goals were to educate and empower the local communities and simultaneously to further their religious and ideological agenda.

Beyond Conversion: Trust and Tension in Educational Encounters

Over his forty-six-year career in both the United States and Turkey, Nilson believed in his ability to effect transformative change. After graduating from Beloit College in Wisconsin, he embarked in 1911 on his mission to Turkey and until 1915 served as a missionary teacher in Tarsus, the hometown of Saint Paul. After studying at the Hartford Theological Seminary in Connecticut, he returned to Tarsus in 1920 and directed the ABCFM station there until 1924. During this time, he witnessed the Turkish War for Independence and the establishment of the Republic of Turkey, which influenced his understanding of the country and its people.

In 1924, the Turkish Republic secularized its educational landscape and abolished the caliphate, the Ministry of Religious Affairs, and religious schools (e.g., *madrasas*).[47] This step wrested control of public education from the hands of religious authorities and entrusted it to the MNET. Further solidifying this secular trajectory, the law for the unification of instruction (Tevhid-i Tedrisat), passed the same year, unified the educational institutions under a centralized administration. This radical act dismantled all religious instruction in state schools and introduced coeducation at the ministerial level.

When Minister of National Education Ismail Safa Bey reached out to John Dewey for advice on developing Turkey's education system, Dewey advocated progressive education, which prioritized socially engaging, lifelike learning experiences tailored to students' development and social setting.[48] Such an approach resonated with the governing elite's modernization vision. However, implementing Dewey's ideas presented challenges. For example, the term *progressive education* itself became a crucial barrier. Mistranslations and imprecise renditions made the core principles ambiguous. Educators often misunderstood the concept, viewing it as simply a "mature," "developed," or "improved" form of education[49] rather than grasping its essence of active engagement and experiential learning. Beyond these terminological issues, broader contextual challenges further complicated the implementation. Even when aspects of Dewey's recommendations, such as establishing Village Institutes, were adopted, their success was contested. This led critics to conclude that many foreign consultants misjudged the specific cultural and political dynamics in Turkey.[50]

Although Dewey advocated a flexible, student-centered pedagogy, his ideas were at odds with the state-controlled educational framework implemented by Turkish authorities. Dewey emphasized democratic localism, calling for decentralized education tailored to local conditions as a means to promote active participation and pluralism. In contrast, Turkish officials—driven by the desire to forge a modern, homogeneous, secular republic—prioritized centralized control and uniformity in education to consolidate national unity and state identity.[51] This divergence between Dewey's democratic ideals and Turkey's modernization agenda reflects the tensions between progressive education and nation-building imperatives. Although Dewey's vision initially resonated with the Turkish elite, it was ultimately reinterpreted within a framework of bureaucratic standardization and pedagogical uniformity.[52] This situation diluted Dewey's core principles, transforming his philosophy into a tool of statecraft rather than a vehicle for democratic empowerment. The resulting missed opportunity underscores the challenges of transplanting educational models across divergent political and cultural contexts. Dewey's case exemplifies a recurring pattern in modernization projects where educational reforms modeled on Western ideals often clash with local imperatives. His ideas, lost in translation, illuminate the limits of universalizing pedagogical frameworks and the complex negotiations involved in adapting foreign models to fit national development goals.

Similarly, Nilson's educational philosophy—shaped within a distinct framework—wrestled with the challenges of translating moral values across cultural and national boundaries. Drawing on his experiences in Turkey, Nilson initially approached the country as a blank slate on which to project his educational ideals. Yet he soon found that meaningful engagement required attunement to local perspectives and the careful negotiation of trust. Rather than advocating Christianity explicitly, he sought to promote the humanitarian dimensions of missionary work, believing that moral values could be more effectively conveyed through personal relationships than through institutional authority. This conviction led him to pursue graduate study at the University of Chicago, where he articulated his concept of moral education in his 1926 master's thesis. In this framework, moral education prioritized the cultivation of humane behavior over the doctrinal tenets of Christianity, emphasizing interpersonal bonds between American missionaries and Turkish students. Nilson wrote that "American teachers [became] advisors, playmates, and sharers with their Turkish students," underscoring his belief that such "personal relationships," rather than formal structures, were the foundation for mutual understanding.[53] His approach eschewed direct conversion in favor of modeling the ethical dimensions of the Christian way of life. To that end, he emphasized fostering personal interactions—both inside and outside the classroom—as a means of transmitting American educational ideals.

Nilson embodied his philosophy of moral education during his tenure at the missionary-founded Talas American College (TAC), putting his principles into practice through everyday interactions.[54] Presenting himself as a model Christian citizen and moral exemplar, he sought to build trust through informal encounters. On the first day of school in 1928, he played volleyball with students, recognizing the value of physical and recreational activities in cultivating bonds. For him, care for the human body was not merely a pedagogical concern but also a theological one: He regarded it as a "God-given gift," framing such activities as spiritually meaningful. Beyond TAC, he established relationships with students and teachers at the neighboring Turkish school in Zincedere. In one instance, boys from the Zincedere Teachers School visited TAC in the evening to listen to the radio, sing songs, and socialize while Nilson's wife played the school organ. Nilson later wrote, "We opened [the school] with the friendship and cooperation of the Turkish people."[55] For him, friendship and cooperation were not just social values but also strategic tools, instrumental in advancing the goals of the ABCFM.

Nilson managed to maintain relations with the public and the Turkish government by complying with national regulations requiring instruction in Turkish language, history, and geography. To meet these requirements, he hired a Turkish national named Setter Bey to teach geography and history in the Turkish language. However, unable to find a Turkish teacher to lead the language course, Nilson turned to the missionary Adelaide S. Dwight, who volunteered to teach Turkish. This unconventional arrangement caused some unease among the missionaries, as well as the students and their families, as they found it awkward to have an American instructing Turkish students in their native tongue. Despite this discomfort, the course satisfied state requirements by using textbooks distributed by the Cumhuriyet Halk Partisi (Republican People's Party).

Nilson's difficulty in finding a Turkish language teacher likely stemmed not only from practical challenges but also from a broader misreading of local cultural and political dynamics. Deep-seated suspicions toward missionaries—exacerbated by postgenocide propaganda that accused them of encouraging foreign intervention against Muslim Turks—contributed to an atmosphere of distrust.[56] Many local educators were reluctant to associate with missionary institutions for fear of political or social repercussions. This reluctance highlights Nilson's underestimation of the historical traumas and ideological tensions that shaped missionary-Muslim relations in the early Turkish Republic.

Winning Hearts and Minds: Sports, Health Care, and the Agenda of Nilson's Films

Nilson's efforts to build relationships with students and the broader public were documented in the ABCFM-sponsored films *Beneath the Snows of Mount Argeaus* and *Schoolmates at Scutare*. *Beneath the Snows of Mount Argeaus*, a black-and-white silent film, focuses on missionary activities at TAC and the adjacent American hospital in the Kayseri region.[57] The film's title pays tribute to Elnathan Gridley, the first missionary who explored the area. He died during an attempt to climb Erciyes Dağı (Mount Argeaus)—one of the highest peaks—and was buried there in 1827.[58] The film not only commemorates his legacy but also constructs a symbolic geography of missionary sacrifice and spiritual aspiration. It opens with a panoramic sweep of Mount Argeaus, visually linking physical elevation with moral and spiritual elevation.[59] The film then transitions to scenes of Turkish village life and presents three different narratives through the activities of Mehmet and Ali, two boys with typical Muslim names, as well as Nilson and the ABCFM doctor Wilson F. Dodd.

The camera pans through the village of Reshadiye on the eastern side of Argeaus, showing houses and a religious site, with particular attention given to a minaret of the local mosque. In the morning, Mehmet runs errands such as drawing a bucket of water from a well and carrying it back home before going to school. The intertitle indicates that Mehmet is on his way to "the American school," which is the missionary-sponsored TAC. The sequence incorporates scenes of ox-driven carts and metalworkers, subtly reinforcing the image of a traditional, premodern economy. These depictions not only document rural life but also create a visual contrast between local practices and the modernization associated with American missionary institutions.

The second narrative centers on Nilson at TAC, where his interactions with students—most notably, a scene in which boys help him repair a broken car—highlight themes of mutual assistance and community building. A volleyball match between Kayseri High School and TAC becomes a focal point for what might be called sports diplomacy, with intertitles noting the score: "Kayseri High School 9 and Talas American School 21."[60] This moment, highlighting the American school's superiority, implicitly links missionary presence with progress and success, suggesting that collaboration with American Christians can accelerate Turkey's modernization. The event is portrayed as a communal spectacle, drawing a crowd that includes Nilson's wife and children. These close-up shots foreground the nuclear Christian family as a model of moral and social order while simultaneously underscoring the missionaries' integration into village life. As a recruitment tool, the film promotes a vision of fulfilling, family-centered missionary work in a welcoming Turkish context.

The use of English intertitles suggests that the film was primarily intended for American audiences—particularly prospective missionaries—rather than local Turkish viewers. While many missionaries stationed in Turkey were fluent in Turkish, the English-language framing indicates the film's role in publicizing ABCFM efforts and encouraging further participation by US missionaries. Scenes of missionary teachers, nurses, and doctors offering services to local populations depict a harmonious relationship between Americans and Turks in the village.

A significant portion of the film documents the medical work of Dr. Dodd, who was born in Talas in 1893 to missionary parents and served in Turkey from 1922 to 1937.[61] The film shows Dodd caring for women and children, portraying moments of healing and recovery—such as a woman showing signs of improvement and a boy named Ali who barely avoids amputation. (See figures 2.1 through 2.4.) These depictions, along with the attentive presence of the nursing staff, exemplify the principles of medical diplomacy, wherein health care functions not only as aid but also as a means to build trust, foster goodwill, and fortify missionary legitimacy.[62]

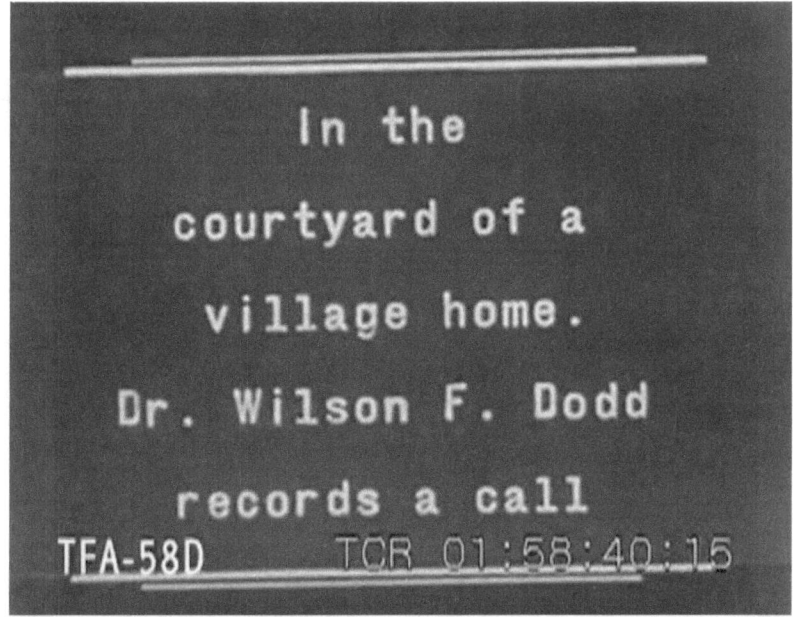

FIGURE 2.1 Dodd's name appears on an intertitle from *Beneath the Snows of Mount Argeaus* (1931).

Source: Travel Film Archive/GIW Photos.

FIGURE 2.2 American hospital in Turkey in *Beneath the Snows of Mount Argeaus*.

Source: Travel Film Archive/GIW Photos.

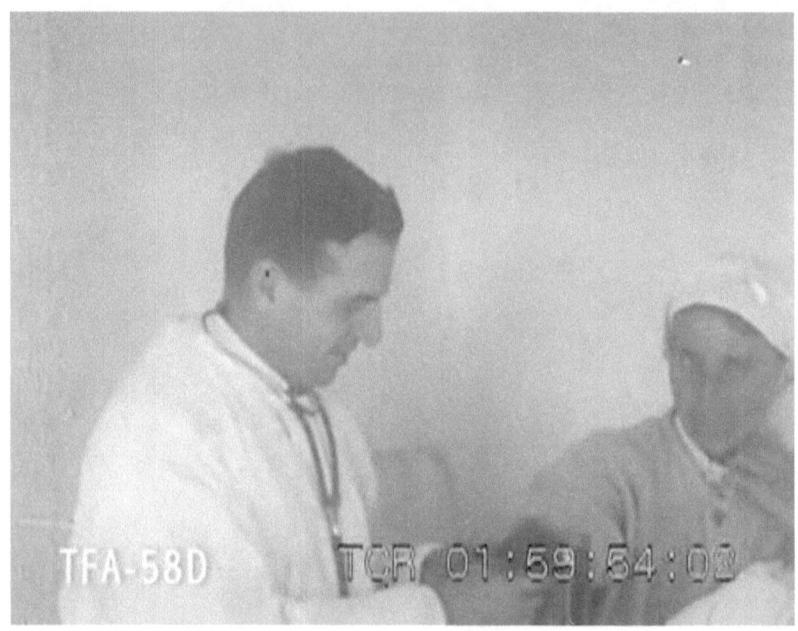

FIGURE 2.3 Dodd and a female patient in *Beneath the Snows of Mount Argeaus*.

Source: Travel Film Archive/GIW Photos.

FIGURE 2.4 Nurse, patient, and Dodd smiling in *Beneath the Snows of Mount Argeaus*.

Source: Travel Film Archive/GIW Photos.

The film thus reassures its audience that missionary intervention is both needed and welcomed, reinforcing the narrative that Turkey offers fertile ground for continued Christian service.

Beneath the Snows of Mount Argeaus serves as a visual articulation of Christian imperialism, advancing the idea that civilizational uplift—through education, medicine, and technological progress—prepares the ground for eventual Christianization. The film showcases agricultural labor, infrastructure projects, and mechanical technologies as evidence of developmental transformation. Meanwhile, scenes of Nilson's family promote an idealized white Christian domesticity. Importantly, the film also gestures toward a secular shift: Although Mehmet's journey begins at a mosque, there is no depiction of religious practice, such as Islamic prayer. Instead, the narrative privileges his transition to the American school, symbolically relocating the site of moral and intellectual authority from the mosque to the missionary classroom.

From Scandal to Screen: Missionaries' Film Diplomacy After a Public Crisis

Situating the ABCFM's films within the broader context of missionary activity in Turkey provides insights into the motivations behind their visual messaging and efforts to garner public support. A pivotal moment that reshaped the public perception of American missionaries occurred in 1928, when three American women were tried and convicted for allegedly attempting to convert Muslim students at the Bursa American College for Girls.[63] The trial, which led to the school's closure, became a national scandal that cast a long shadow over the legitimacy of all missionary work in Turkey. It raised serious concerns about the missionaries' ability—or willingness—to provide secular education in compliance with the Turkish Republic's strict separation of religion and state.

In response, ABCFM missionaries did not retreat from their goals but instead recalibrated their methods. The trial served as a catalyst for adopting more sophisticated forms of strategic communication, including the use of film as a medium to rehabilitate their public image and reframe their educational mission. Film enabled the missionaries to present themselves as modern, benevolent, and aligned with secular educational ideals, even while continuing to promote Christian values. Film as a diplomatic medium served to appeal simultaneously to Turkish officials and communities as well as to ABCFM supporters and prospective missionaries in the United States. A key example of this approach is the silent film *Schoolmates at Scutare*, which encapsulates the posttrial shift in missionary messaging and reflects an effort to align missionary work with the values of modern Turkish society.[64]

Schoolmates at Scutare is a black-and-white silent film that shows an all-female missionary-founded school as a space where students of diverse ethnicities, nationalities, and religions can coexist and practice their customs freely. Set in Scutare (Üsküdar), a municipality on the Anatolian side of Istanbul, the film centers on the friendship between two students—Mutena, of Arab background, and Polimnia, of Greek descent—both attending the American Academy for Girls, established by the ABCFM in 1876. The film opens with Polimnia's ferry ride across the Bosphorus and her ascent through the hills of Asia to the school. Upon her arrival, Mutena seeks permission from the school's white female principal to celebrate Şeker Bayramı (Sugar Feast or Ramadan Bayramı) with Polimnia. The intertitles explain, "The Month of Fasting ends today, and now I want Polimnia to spend the Festival vacation with me at my sister's home." The principal's approval positions the school as an inclusive institution. The two friends leave the school joyfully, and the film shifts to an image of a watchtower and a shot of a mosque—signaling the importance of the Ramadan celebration in the upcoming scenes. Şeker Bayramı unfolds in a sequence of warm domestic moments: Coffee is poured, sweets are shared, and conversation flows, portraying Muslim hospitality in an intimate and affirmative light. These scenes are intercut with shots of daily life in the town—horse-drawn carriages, crowds, and flipping calendar pages that visually marking the passage of time. The film then returns to the school, where Polimnia and Mutena prepare a meal and invite the principal to join them. This is followed by scenes of students typing, solving math problems on the blackboard, and participating in sports such as baseball and volleyball—activities that collectively showcase the school's modern, well-rounded curriculum and its emphasis on intellectual and physical development.

While *Schoolmates at Scutare* presents an image of an inclusive educational space, other historical evidence complicates this portrayal by suggesting that the school disavowed Turkish Muslim identity and promoted

American Christian values. In an interview, Semiha Malatyalıoğlu—a 1928 graduate who later served as the school's Turkish vice principal—said that as one of the three Muslim Turkish students at the school, she felt like a minority among non-Muslim students.[65] She voiced her frustrations about being unable to fully participate in religious holiday celebrations or wholeheartedly embrace the emerging Turkish nationalism during the transition from the Ottoman Empire to the Turkish Republic. The extent to which missionaries accepted Turkish Muslims warrants scrutiny, particularly given how few Turkish Muslim students attended the school. Malatyalıoğlu's recollections suggest that *Schoolmates at Scutare* distorts the school's treatment of students with different religious, ethnic, or national identities. It is challenging to discern whether the missionaries' claims were genuine, were fabricated, or conveyed a vision for the future. Certainly, though, the film exemplifies their effort to communicate that the American school accepted Turkish Muslim girls—a positive aspect intended to depict the missionary school as inclusive and accommodating toward religious diversity.

This effort to signal tolerance is part of the process of modernization and the operation of whiteness as a transnational racialization. Through the film, the missionaries framed their activities as compatible with secular ideals, subtly embedding Protestant values like respect, kindness, and discipline in the educational setting. This messaging reflects a strategic attempt not only to rebuild public trust but also to deploy religion as a technology of race to manage differences. Whiteness, in this context, functions as a legitimizing force, sustaining social hierarchies by associating progress, virtue, and modernity with American Protestantism. Within Turkey's secularizing environment, the film operates as a diplomatic tool designed to restore confidence in the missionaries and maintain their influence by highlighting inclusivity and cooperation.

Herman Kreider: An Architect of Film Diplomacy

Herman Harold Kreider played a pivotal role in building connections between Turks and missionaries in Turkey, although he was not a missionary. Rather, he worked for the ABCFM in various capacities from 1926 to 1940, serving as a treasurer, writer, film librarian, film exhibitor, and filmmaker. His passion for photography led him to become the official photographer of the ABCFM in Turkey, and he oversaw the cinematography in films such as *Schoolmates at Scutare*. Moreover, his contributions extended beyond film: He authored a Turkish-language textbook titled *First Lessons in Modern Turkish* in 1945, which was revised in 1954 under the title *Essentials of Modern Turkish*. The book was widely used by missionaries and others learning the Turkish language. Following his work for the ABCFM, Kreider served as the bursar of Robert College, an American missionary-founded institution, and of the American College for Girls in Arnavutköy until his retirement in 1965.[66]

Kreider combined his interest in learning Turkish with photography, as he aimed to communicate verbally and visually with people in Turkey. In 1927, he attended the ABCFM's Language School to acquire Turkish language skills.[67] During an ABCFM meeting that same year, he delivered a talk in Turkish on photography, showcasing his multifaceted abilities. Collaborating with a *National Geographic* photographer, he captured images of families, individuals, model classes, and special events in Turkey and, in 1928, exhibited these photographs, earning the reputation of the ABCFM's official photographer. A report stated, "Mr. Kreider's work has not been entirely with figures, with the legal aspects of the Mission; he has made a real place for himself as the official photographer of the Mission."[68]

Kreider was a key architect of the missionaries' film program, which aimed to influence activities, habits, and ideas in Turkey. Reports prepared by Nilson highlighted Kreider's responsibility for selecting and purchasing films for village film tours.[69] These screenings garnered the attention of the Turkish government, leading to a collaboration among the MNET, Ministry of Health, People's Houses, and the missionaries in 1936 that explored ways of enhancing the national investment in film technologies. The partnership between the Turkish government and missionaries commenced when Dr. Remzi, a doctor at the Ministry of Health, contacted Kreider in 1937, seeking assistance in procuring film materials for village work. This collaboration exemplifies film diplomacy, whereby institutional agents use films to foster cooperation to advance national and foreign agendas.

Kreider's role, however, extended beyond mere acquisition. He actively shaped the cinematic content distributed, directing films himself, such as *Tree* (year unknown) and *Turkish Playground* (year unknown). In addition, he oversaw a bureau dedicated to curating and distributing films to other stations. This agency transcended genre boundaries, prioritizing potential educational value rather than narrative form. Kreider's film selections and purchases included titles like *The Country Doctor* (D. W. Griffith, 1909), *Personal Hygiene for Young Men* (Bray Studios, 1924), *From Wheat to Bread* (Eastman Kodak Company, 1928), *Quality Milk* (C. A. Lindstrom, 1930), and *Baby's Bath and Toilet* (director and year of production unknown).[70] These films were about such subjects as agriculture, health, religion, and education, and they represented aspects of social development and ideological promotion inherent to film diplomacy.

This curatorial venture, featuring films that intertwined fiction and nonfiction over a generation, constituted an experiment in diplomatic communication. By embracing ad hoc solutions, genre-bending exhibitions, and a temporally expansive canvas, this curation offered a multifaceted lens through which to understand missionary engagement. The curatorial strategy also transcended mere archival preservation. It challenged traditional notions of structured planning and comprehensive deliberation in diplomatic outreach. The lack of a structured plan for using film allowed missionaries to respond organically to the specific needs and cultural contexts they encountered. The blending of fiction and nonfiction blurred the lines between didacticism and entertainment, potentially creating a more engaging and relatable experience for audiences. This curatorial strategy provided an opportunity to trace the evolution of missionary thought and practice over time. It highlighted the ongoing processes of negotiation and reinterpretation that characterized missionary engagement with target communities.

Teaching Beyond the Farm: Film for Strategic Cultivation of Agricultural Knowledge

During the transition from the Ottoman Empire to the Republic of Turkey in 1922 and 1923, American and Turkish agents collaborated to modernize agriculture. Correspondence between Ottoman Sultan Abdul Hamid and the American envoy, Minister Alexander Terrell, details this transformation.[71] The sultan agreed to pay American experts endorsed by the US Department of State for their guidance in overseeing agricultural programs in schools. A program established at the missionary-founded

Robert College in Istanbul supported the initiative, and a graduate of the college who specialized in agriculture at Cornell University later became the director of the newly established College of Agriculture program.[72] The objective was to obtain optimal harvest yields and develop livestock and dairy cows. Additional support for the program came from NER, which commissioned a survey of economic and social conditions in the region. The survey characterized the Near East region using racially coded words such as "backward," "primitive," "underutilized," and "underdeveloped" to describe its agriculture, transportation, and communication facilities.[73] In light of these observations, missionaries joined the NER program and provided sponsorship to plan the modernization operations.

Within this context, *Highlights of Village Life*, a silent film sponsored by the Near East Mission of the ABCFM, frames the Turkish landscape through the lens of Kreider, the film's cinematographer. The film opens with a shot of village houses, and a pan follows, capturing the landscape, where women work while nurturing their children.[74] Intertitles indicate that some villagers go to the city for market day, with an array of animals in motion. Men walk alongside camels laden with goods. A medium shot of the grain market shows a flurry of activity around an arch-adorned building, where grain is spread across the floor. An elder transfers grain from one basin to another, and tin cans for oil are filled and sealed, capturing the craftsmanship. During the lunch break, a man grills shish kabobs and sells them in bread. The setting transitions to a workshop, where the brisk business of crafting boxes for grape-sugar production unfolds. Next, a scene portrays a man and two women demonstrating their expertise at making *yufka* (bread) without relying on ovens, as the intertitles note (figures 2.5 and 2.6). The film captures other manual labor practices, offering glimpses of women washing clothes on stones, farmers collecting grapes, men pressing grapes to extract sugar, and villagers using animals to plow the soil. The film culminates in a celebratory moment, documenting a village wedding, where men and women dance to the rhythm of drums and flutes. As the day comes to a close, villagers depart with their camels against the backdrop of a setting sun—a closing image that romanticizes rural life while constructing the film's ethnographic and missionary gaze.

What is particularly striking about *Highlights of Village Life* is its emphasis on process. From the opening shot of houses to the final scene of villagers departing, the film unfolds a day—or perhaps a series of days—in the

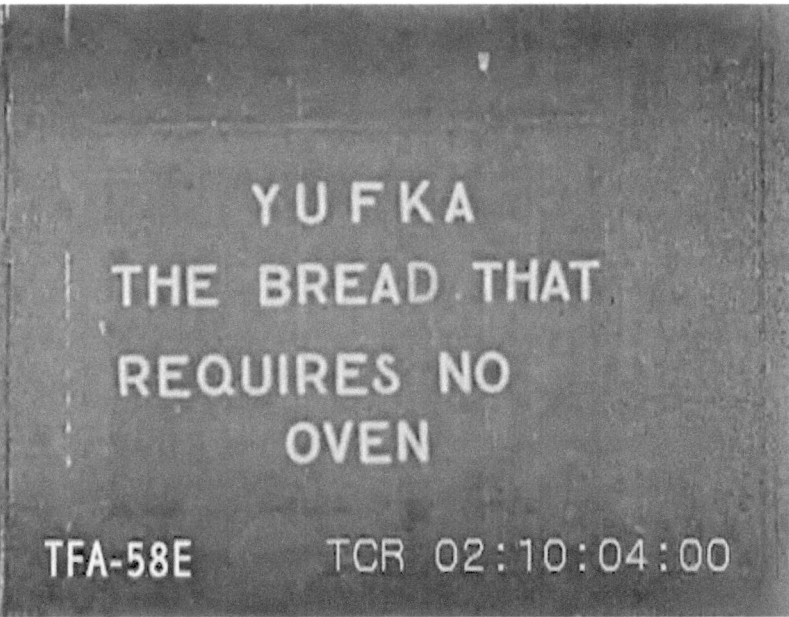

FIGURE 2.5 Intertitle mentioning the no-oven bread in *Highlights of Village Life* (1920s).

Source: Travel Film Archive/GIW Photos.

FIGURE 2.6 Men and women making *yufka* in a scene from *Highlights of Village Life*.

Source: Travel Film Archive/GIW Photos.

village and offers a continuous flow rather than static tableaux. This narrative strategy immerses the viewer in the rhythms of rural life, foregrounding not just what people do but also how they do it. The cinema scholar Salomé Aguilera Skvirsky defines the process genre as a form of representation that shows processes with a clear beginning, middle, and end.[75] Focusing on how things are made or done, it serves as a guide to artisanal and industrial production. Although it intersects with educational, industrial, and ethnographic films, the process genre extends beyond these categories by communicating labor practices through sequential steps.

By highlighting manual labor while omitting the presence of missionary aid, the film subtly constructs a narrative of lack—showing the village as industrious but economically stagnant, rooted in practices that are framed as inefficient. This representation functions to justify the missionary enterprise, positioning Western knowledge, technology, and values as the necessary catalysts for transformation. In doing so, the film invokes whiteness in a way that is not explicit but structural—as the unseen yet organizing logic behind the implied promise of modernization. The process genre here, then, serves not only as an observational mode but also as a racialized visual discourse that encodes development as a project of Protestant intervention.

Highlights of Village Life framed rural labor as inefficient and in need of transformation, and ABCFM missionaries recognized that engaging with agricultural development was essential to building local credibility and support. Lacking agricultural training, these missionaries turned to the film projector as a surrogate for technical proficiency. This technology, deployed in rural settings with portable reels, allowed them to bypass linguistic barriers and circumvent the need for direct, hands-on instruction. Films such as *Quality Milk* exemplify this strategy by using the process genre to guide viewers step by step through agricultural tasks. These visual narratives not only instructed audiences in modern farming techniques but also advanced ideological claims about efficiency, hygiene, and progress. By curating and projecting these representations, missionaries aligned themselves with scientific modernity and positioned film as a pedagogical tool capable of delivering expertise they themselves did not possess. In doing so, they extended their influence beyond religious instruction and into the secular domains of development and modernization—fields increasingly central to their mission in a secularizing Turkish Republic.

Quality Milk focused on agricultural practices developed in the United States and was part of the Educational Film Series sponsored by the US Department of Agriculture.[76] This silent film demonstrated "approved methods of dairying for high-quality production," as described in the Educational Film Catalog. Its final intertitles encouraged viewers to contact the department for instructional pamphlets covering a range of topics, including the production of clean milk, prevention of feed-related odors, sanitation of milking equipment, proper cooling of milk and cream, sterilization of farm utensils, and effective financial management. By guiding viewers through the entire dairy production process—from start to finish—the film exemplifies the process genre's educational logic. As Skvirsky argues, the process genre's sequential structure does more than transmit information; it performs ideological work by naturalizing particular forms of labor and organization.[77] In the case of Quality Milk, the step-by-step visualization of "best practices" positions American agricultural techniques not only as instructive but also as universally applicable. The film thus functions as more than a training tool: It serves as a medium through which American scientific agriculture is framed as the benchmark for modernization and rational progress.

From Sick Man to Muscular Nation: The Healing Gaze in Early Republican Turkey

In their efforts to spread Christianity in Turkey, missionaries identified medical services as a strategic avenue for building trust with the Turkish public and initiating conversations about faith. The medical missionary Thomas Spees Carrington observed that hospitals were an ideal environment for identifying non-Christian individuals seeking spiritual guidance. Nurses and doctors offered both physical healing and solace to burdened souls.[78] Patients often questioned Carrington about his decision to leave his home and to work in Turkey, opening the door for him to introduce them to the teachings of Christ.

Recognizing the value of medical encounters, missionaries extended this logic to the realm of public health education. They began incorporating films about the human body and hygiene into their outreach efforts, believing that visual instruction could foster similar openings for religious dialogue outside clinical settings. Missionary doctors such as Dr. Clark and Dr. Nute occasionally joined these film tours, offering basic medical care during visits to rural villages. They often drove cars, but when the trips were short, Dr. Nute rode on horseback. These health-oriented expeditions aimed to demonstrate "sympathy" and "loving care" in hopes of "mak[ing] friends" with local communities.[79] The underlying message was clear: While medicine could ease the body's pain, Christianity could offer solace to the soul.

This fusion of health and religion reflects a core Christian principle: that the body is the temple of the Holy Spirit and, as a divine gift, must be protected and preserved.[80] The religion-health binary at play underscores the tension between faith-based persuasion and scientific rationalism, with modern medicine functioning as a legitimizing framework through which spiritual care was rendered more acceptable.[81] This synthesis of medical knowledge and Christian doctrine found expression in the missionaries' use of films.

Missionaries integrated the rhetoric of health education with Christian values through silent films such as *Personal Hygiene for Young Men*, part of the Science of Life educational series sponsored by the US Public Health Service.[82] Originally intended for American audiences, the film educated men about sex, personal hygiene, and the dangers of venereal disease. The film opens with a shot of a man flexing his arm muscles, and intertitles proclaim that although muscular strength is visually impressive, other qualities such as "health, energy, alertness, endurance, and courage" hold greater value and can be attained through "faithful training." Then it cuts to images of US Presidents Theodore Roosevelt and Abraham Lincoln, positioning them as exemplars of disciplined masculinity in service to the nation. Subsequent scenes of men engaged in javelin throwing, horseback riding, mountain climbing, and rowing advance this narrative that with "faithful training," disciplined bodies lead to moral citizens. The concept of faithful training should be understood in relation to "muscular Christianity," the term used by the historian Cliff Putney for "a Christian commitment to health and manliness."[83] He notes that American Protestants at the turn of the twentieth century advocated for competitive sports and physical education to redefine ideals of Christian manhood.

When screened in Turkey, this vision of masculinity found unexpected synergy with Kemalist nationalism, which emphasized bodily discipline as essential to modern nation-building. The idea of strengthening men's bodies has been a concern in Turkey since at least the late nineteenth century, when Emperor Nicholas I of the Russian Empire and then the European states declared the Ottoman Empire to be the "Sick Man of Europe."[84] The Turkish government has since focused on curing this "sickness," with one remedy being instilling athleticism. The missionaries' exhibition of *Personal Hygiene for Young Men* in Turkey aligned with these national efforts, transmuting Christian muscularity into Turkish muscularity. This vision of bodily strength resonated with nationalist sentiments, frequently aligned with Kemalists (or adherents of Atatürk), and found expression in Atatürk's renowned proclamation: "Sağlam Kafa Sağlam Vücutta Bulunur" (a sound mind resides in a sound body). This axiom encapsulates the importance ascribed to physical fitness and intellectual capacity in the Turkish Republic's developmental project.

Mary Louise Lee Winkler: A Woman Missionary in a White Coat at a Film Exhibition

An often-overlooked group of individuals played a pivotal role in exhibiting educational health films in Turkey: women missionaries and female students. They not only facilitated the dissemination of information but also fostered connections through woman-to-woman interactions. These interactions proved instrumental in communicating practices associated with civilization, particularly when it came to caring for infants. One notable figure was a missionary known as Miss Blatter, who oversaw movie tours and health services in the Merzifun and Talas regions during the late 1930s.[85] She screened educational health films such *Baby's Bath and Toilet*, which aimed to teach local village women the art of bathing and caring for babies. But her contributions extended far beyond the screen. She used posters to advertise health talks, gave lectures, provided health services to sick people for free, and, along with her fellow women missionaries, collected and distributed much-needed clothes to those in need.

This commitment to health education was evident throughout the period under consideration in this book. In 1958, Mary Louise Lee Winkler, a missionary nurse at the Talas Nute Clinic, embarked on a journey to various villages in Turkey, carrying with her a series of health films.

Her screenings promoted public health in the Talas and Kayseri areas, and other missionary nurses and doctors accompanied Winkler to provide medical care. *What Is Disease?* (director and year of production unknown) and a film about tuberculosis[86] were typical fare in her programming. These health films not only aimed to raise awareness about patient care and preventive measures but also served as a catalyst for fostering personal relationships to uplift communities. Prior to her missionary service abroad, Winkler had taught in the United States. Her application to work for the ABCFM included a recommendation letter that highlighted her leadership abilities yet also emphasized the need for her to develop "diplomacy skills"—an essential quality for her work overseas.[87]

Photographs taken by the Turkish photographer Orhan Akdemir capture the essence of Winkler's mission and illustrate the impact of her film exhibitions on the local population. One image shows a young male student with tattered jacket helping Winkler use a film projector in a classroom (figure 2.7). Another image shows male villagers helping Winkler

FIGURE 2.7 Mary Winkler and children with a projector.

Source: Salt Research, American Board of Commissioners for Foreign Missions Archive. Courtesy of ARIT.

FIGURE 2.8 Mary Winkler and villagers next to a generator. Photographer: Orhan Akdemir.

Source: Salt Research, American Board of Commissioners for Foreign Missions Archive. Courtesy of ARIT.

start a generator so that they can bring a film about childcare to life in an open public space (figure 2.8). These visual records portray film as a tool of diplomacy that connected missionaries and Turkish villagers. Through these screenings, Winkler tried to respond to health-related concerns and cultivate connections with both children and adults.

Adapting a lens of whiteness helps to see how missionaries used film technologies (e.g., projectors and reels) to create an optical illusion of secularism. Whiteness, here, operates not only as a racial signifier but also as a proxy for neutrality, modernity, and universality. By aligning themselves with these connotations, missionaries aimed to present their interventions as scientific and secular. For example, the photograph of Winkler with children (figure 2.7) constructs a visual façade that suggests an absence of religious influence and fosters an appearance of a neutral environment. This photograph notably lacks any religious symbols, such as the Christian cross, crucifix, or Bible. Winkler wears what appears to

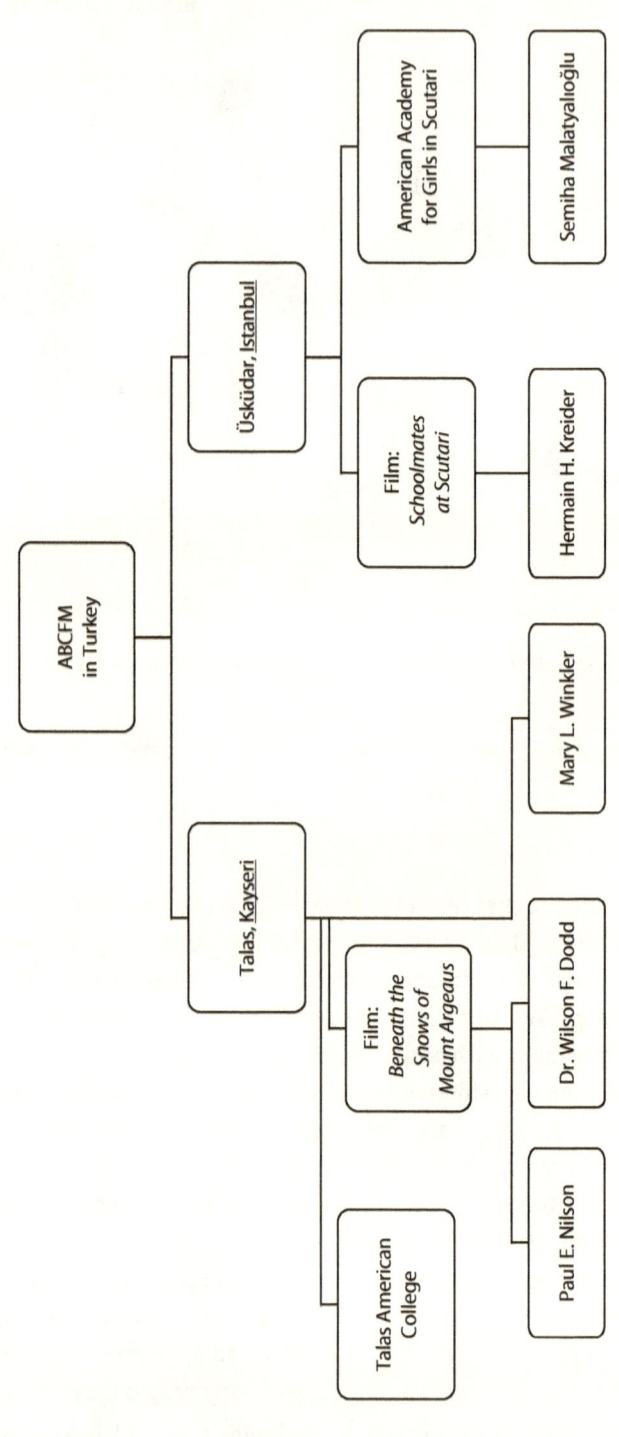

FIGURE 2.9 Notable locations, schools, films, and people in the ABCFM network in Turkey.

be a white lab coat, a garment nurses often choose in order to look professional and authoritative.[88] This sartorial choice creates, to some extent, a cognitive distance from her Christian missionary identity. The white coat functions as a scientific marker employed to navigate secular environments, such as classrooms, where overt religious influence might be met with skepticism. This visual cue might have helped to downplay Christian objectives and project an image of neutrality, particularly through the use of modern film technologies.

The Interplay of Religion, Science, and Film

The use of modern scientific tools to substantiate religious claims predates the advent of cinema, with roots in the emergence of biblical archaeology and photography.[89] By incorporating film into their tool kit, missionaries extended their reach across spatial and generational divides, projecting their religious vision in different settings like prisons and churches. They curated exhibitions showcasing Christianity through a strategic blend of Hollywood epics like Cecil B. DeMille's *The King of Kings* and didactic works like the Moody Institute of Science's *God of Creation*. This juxtaposition served not only to project their religious vision but also to ensure their work resonated with different audiences across generational lines. While films like *The King of Kings* were products of Hollywood, it was the missionaries' curatorial labor—their act of selecting, juxtaposing, and contextualizing—that truly activated the films' potential for religious engagement. This strategic labor of curation aligns with Terry Lindvall and Andrew Quicke's characterization of these films as works "of, by, and for the people of the church" that prioritize renewal, uplift, and propagation over high aesthetic values or economic profit.[90] Similarly, the media historian Heather Hendershot views Moody Institute of Science (MIS) films like *God of Creation* as "evangelical science films" that use "facts, rationality, and logic" to argue for God as the creator of the world.[91] However, she also raises concerns about these films' "soft-sell evangelism" and potential violation of secularism during their public school exhibitions in the United States.[92]

These films emerged amid Christian anxieties about evolution and Darwinism. To counter the threat posed by the Darwinists' view that nature did not have a divine designer, a pastor in California named Irwin A. Moon pioneered the concept of "sermons from science" in the 1930s.[93] These experiments offered religious interpretations of scientific phenomena, showcasing visible evidence of a divine plan of creation. In 1945, Moon partnered with the Moody Bible Institute to establish MIS, which produced "religiously motivated science and social studies films."[94] These films were made to bridge the gap between religion and science, portraying Christianity as a logical faith supported by scientific evidence.

God of Creation was one such film. In it, Moon directly addressed the audience, speaking from a study filled with books about the wonders of the solar system, plants, and animals as manifestations of God's creations. The film intertwined images of stars, oceans, and flowers with Moon's narration. Over a close-up of a bee on a flower, for example, Moon elucidates how the colors of flowers were designed to attract insects. In another sequence, the film employs micrographic time-lapse techniques to depict the process of germination, as Moon emphasizes the insignificance of humankind compared to God's immense power. The presence of the renowned physicist Albert Einstein at a screening of *God of Creation* in the chemistry auditorium of Princeton University added to the film's impact, leaving the audience in awe. After the screening, seventy attendees received copies of the Gospel of John.[95]

God of Creation served multiple purposes in the United States and was screened in science classrooms, in churches, and even at military training sites. Educators exhibited it in response to "communist educational trends" in the post–World War II era.[96] Fearing the influence of godlessness and communism, American officials promoted it as a tool for moral education. Military bases screened it to instill a sense of moral and religious duty in service members. The US Air Force and Department of Defense received numerous copies of MIS films during the 1950s, and *God of Creation* became mandatory viewing for all military personnel as part of the Character Guidance Program.[97] These efforts in moral and religious instruction served as "public relations programs" to reach parents of soldiers and promote American military training programs.[98] Even the Federal Bureau of Investigation endorsed the film, recognizing its potential to "bring people closer to God."[99]

Yet whereas *God of Creation* was exhibited in public spaces in the United States, Nilson primarily screened the film in churches throughout Turkey.

In the early 1950s, two copies of the film made their way to Diyarbakır, a southeastern city with a predominantly Kurdish population. Christian friends sent the first copy to Nilson's son Paul after he encountered it in Chicago during his furlough, while Nilson's daughter Dorothy purchased the second copy for $240, using donations she collected from fellow students at Wheaton College.[100] Nilson encouraged his Christian peers in the United States to contribute additional films so that he could develop a film library, and he urged his friends to share any Christian movies that touched their hearts for potential use in Turkey.

In a 1951 letter, Nilson declared the silent film *The King of Kings* to be the most significant donation sent by American Christians to Turkey.[101] This film depicted the life of Jesus of Nazareth and incorporated intertitles featuring quotes from the Bible, biblical stories, and hymns. It portrayed moments such as Jesus's acts of compassion, including healing a blind boy and helping a poor family; the Last Supper; and the Resurrection. Nilson believed the film was an exceptional storytelling tool for reaching the people of Turkey and conveying the Christian way of life. Other missionaries appreciated the film's quality and considered it capable of countering Hollywood's misrepresentations of Christianity, and this led to the distribution of translated versions in Turkish, Arabic, Hebrew, Hindustani, and Chinese to missionaries worldwide.[102] Through strategic curation, missionaries used *The King of Kings* as a potent tool for religious engagement. For instance, they talked about the religious content of the film to audiences, encouraging them to understand that emphasis by either distributing Bibles or hosting exhibitions in churches.

According to Nilson, *The King of Kings* was immensely popular during his church exhibitions in Turkey. In one instance, at the Syrian Church in Kilit, the exhibition drew such a large crowd that Nilson and his assistants struggled to make their way inside. Men and women occupied separate sections, with children sitting on the floor. After an introductory song and prayer in ancient Syriac, Nilson presented *The King of Kings*. He observed that the struggles faced by Mary Magdalene and Jesus on the screen resonated with the audience. He later wrote, "The crowd is united, their bodies packed close together, not even standing room, but the spirits of all of us seem united in one blessed union of sinful human beings drawing near to the purity, holiness, and power of Jesus."[103] Through these words, Nilson emphasized the film's ability to unite people physically and spiritually.

Nilson's exhibitions at churches not only united people but also ignited aspirations for a better future among young ethnic minorities. The screenings triggered gratitude, voluntary service offers, job inquiries, and requests for information on immigration to the United States. Some young Assyrian Turkish boys approached Nilson, expressing their gratitude for the film's screening. William Mathews, a Bible tutor, offered his assistance during the summer indicating his experience working with film projectors.[104] Others approached Nilson, sharing their dreams and hopes. For instance, a hungry boy sought job opportunities while two high school graduates inquired about the possibility of going to America. These questions, centered around employment, education, and immigration, revealed their desire to improve their socioeconomic conditions, which was perhaps more of a priority than religious awakening. While Nilson might not have been able to assist every individual, he used film as a diplomatic tool to develop a sense of unity and goodwill.

As his outreach expanded in southeastern Turkey, Nilson recognized that growing student enrollments presented an opportunity to reach broader audiences and support the nation's modernization efforts.[105] He partnered with six local teachers and transported films, projectors, curtains, and a portable generator in a car donated by Christian supporters in the United States. He created a map of their tour through villages like Çınar and Ergani, located in the Diyarbakır region, which had large Kurdish populations. In each village, his screening drew approximately six hundred attendees, including villagers, students, churchgoers, prisoners, and industrial workers.[106] The participation of local teachers helped validate the educational value of the films. Audience receptivity was likely influenced by both the novelty of the technology and the prestige of its American presenters.

Yet beneath the surface of these educational initiatives lay a geopolitical and economic agenda. Nilson's embrace of film as a pedagogical tool aligned with broader US state and corporate interests in the region. In a 1953 letter, he noted that American engineers had arrived in Diyarbakır to construct a large airport—an infrastructure project intended to enhance mobility, boost agricultural development, stimulate local economies, and reinforce military readiness.[107] An American oil company was also preparing to construct a refinery in the area. These construction projects served as mechanisms for exerting influence and securing access to strategic resources. For Nilson, they also symbolized a united front in the struggle against the USSR. Framed by Cold War imperatives, he interpreted these activities as both spiritual and political support for Turkey.

Missionaries' Collaborations with the US Information Service

Missionaries exhibited films and collaborated with the USIS in Mardin. According to Raymond White, who led the ABCFM station in Mardin, the USIS was planning to establish a headquarters for their mobile film unit around 1950. Indeed, Monteagle Stearns, the film officer from the American embassy in Ankara, visited the missionary station, underscoring the USIS's engagement in the region. The plan included establishing a permanent cinema team, contingent on budgetary considerations. The team's objective was to visit the numerous villages accessible by train during the summer months to hold outdoor screenings of films showing American life and activities. White used a USIS car to exhibit films such as *The Marshall Plan*, *The Southwestern States* (Erpi Classrooms Films Inc., 1942), and *Childhood of Jesus*, which received "deep interest" from Syrian Christians.[108]

The USIS's more immediate focus was education: training schoolteachers and students to operate film projectors. White noted that each school in the area had been invited to gather at the People's Houses to watch educational films. This implies that the missionaries and the USIS took a systematic approach in their collaboration to provide educational film screenings for students in the region.[109] This partnership not only reflects a structured approach to audiovisual pedagogy but also marks a formative moment in the evolution of film diplomacy in southeastern Turkey.

The efforts of missionaries to shape the Turkish public through film were critical to the Turkish government's educational film initiatives. In this chapter, I have underscored the instrumental role played by American Protestant missionaries in bringing attention to educational films long before they were officially institutionalized by Turkish ministries for use at schools and other spaces. I have further demonstrated that the missionaries' influence on educational film culture in Turkey was facilitated by their preexisting network of schools.

Nilson attributed the government's growing interest in films to his persistent advocacy for 16 mm educational cinema.[110] In a letter to his American friends, he expressed satisfaction that his efforts had begun to yield results and Turkish institutions had begun to invest in film technologies. On behalf of the ABCFM, Nilson thanked Turkish officials for increasing their investments and using film technologies to improve public welfare. His letter links the mobilization of nonfiction, nontheatrical, and educational films in Turkey in the 1950s to the missionary groundwork laid in the 1930s.

The Turkish government took concrete steps to institutionalize educational film by passing the Law of Educational and Technical Films in 1937, which removed import taxes on educational and technical films.[111] This legislation benefited missionaries, who often purchased films from the United States, and symbolized the republic's broader aim to modernize education in line with Western models. It also facilitated the importation of films and related technologies, easing barriers for distribution.

Still, missionary film efforts faced regulatory scrutiny. The Turkish Board of Censorship, tasked with overseeing imported content, banned films it deemed religious propaganda. While Nilson's personal letters suggest that he occasionally felt surveilled, he did not report any interruptions to his screenings. This suggests that the board primarily focused on commercially distributed films that were shown in movie theaters and ignored nontheatrical, community-based exhibitions organized by missionaries.

The missionaries' growing visibility also drew the attention of USIS agents who wanted to circulate films in Turkey and expand the reach of US foreign policy. Their objective was to leverage the missionaries' reputation and expand the distribution and exhibition of USIS films to amplify the impact of US influence in Turkey. Missionaries were a key force in laying the groundwork for the USIS in Turkey. A key example of this collaboration was the involvement of Monteagle Stearns, who later became motion picture officer at the US State Department and eventually an official diplomat. This relationship highlights how missionary film programs contributed to building a US-Turkey communication network. This network expanded further in 1952 when the USIS, in partnership with Turkey's MNET, founded the Educational Film Center.

Missionaries left a lasting imprint on Turkish perceptions of American education. Their schools—such as Üsküdar American Academy, Tarsus

American College, Robert College, and what is now Boğaziçi University—still operate today, albeit independently and without formal ties to the Congregationalist Church. These institutions, rooted in the educational infrastructure built by nineteenth- and twentieth-century missionaries, continue to convey prestige. Many Turkish students pursuing higher education in the United States are alumni of these schools.

American Protestant missionaries strategically employed film as a tool of communication to navigate the secularizing terrain of the early Turkish Republic. As figure 2.10 shows, the missionary van and generator function as tools that bind rural audiences to transnational networks, drawing villagers into a moment of looking—curious, wary, hopeful—where the infrastructure of showing meets the politics of being shown (figure 2.10). Film served as a multifaced medium, allowing missionaries move beyond traditional proselytizing and capitalize on legal reforms, circumvent censorship, foster relationships with local communities, and promote American values and missionary visions of modernization

FIGURE 2.10 Villagers around a generator and van in Talas. Photographer: Orhan Akdemir.

Source: Salt Research, American Board of Commissioners for Foreign Missions Archive. Courtesy of ARIT.

through nontheatrical screenings in churches, hospitals, schools, and public squares. With productions such as *Beneath the Snows of Mount Argeaus* and *Schoolmates at Scutare*, missionaries crafted their image as benevolent modernizers, using visual narratives to integrate health care, education, and community service into their religious outreach. Meanwhile, films like *Quality Milk*, *Personal Hygiene for Young Men*, *God of Creation*, and *The King of Kings* fostered religious engagement, conveyed public health knowledge, and performed ideological work by aligning scientific authority with Christian morality.

This strategic deployment of film aimed not only to build goodwill among diverse Turkish communities but also to counteract the growing nationalist suspicion of missionary activity amid the rise of the Turkish secular identity. Collaborations with Turkish educational authorities and US government entities further extended the influence of these film initiatives, positioning missionaries as intermediaries in efforts of diplomacy and development. Thus, understanding the use of film by American Protestant missionaries in Turkey illuminates not only the history of missionary activity in the region but also the complex ways the ABCFM adapted and even co-opted existing structures to advance its intertwined agendas of Christianization and modernization.

3
US Government Film Programming in Turkey

The 1949 film *Turkey*, sponsored by the US Department of Defense and the Department of the Army, offers an example of Cold War cinema mobilized to advance US foreign policy objectives.[1] Through a blend of pastoral and urban imagery, military scenes, and diplomatic encounters, the film constructs Turkey as both a vital barrier against Soviet expansion and a willing partner in the project of modernization. Early sequences—including a cut to a map featuring a semicircle of bricks that symbolizes Turkey as "the block between Russia and the Middle East" (figure 3.1)—frame the country's strategic significance. A male voice-over reinforces this geopolitical narrative, emphasizing Soviet ambitions to control the Turkish straits and casting Turkey's army of six hundred thousand as steadfast, though underequipped, in resisting communist encroachment.

At the heart of the film's message lies the theme of friendship. Through military aid, particularly as a result of the Truman Doctrine, the United States is represented as a key partner in Turkey's defense and modernization. Scenes featuring Edwin C. Wilson, US ambassador to Turkey (1945–1948), conferring with Turkish officials who peruse booklets titled *Shipping, Communications,* and *National Defense,* underscore a vision of modernization as a shared, strategic project. These visuals emphasize that US involvement is technical, advisory, and collaborative. Turkey emerges in

FIGURE 3.1 Map showing bricks around the northern border in *Turkey* (US Army, 1949).

Source: Records of the Office of the Chief Signal Officer, Record Group 111, National Archives and Records Administration, College Park, Maryland.

the film as both a regional stabilizer and an aspirational state aligning itself with the West. The film also confronts internal challenges by juxtaposing images of monumental state projects, such as the Anıtkabir (the mausoleum of Atatürk) with those of underdeveloped rural life. Through descriptions of farmers using antiquated tools and sparse schoolhouses, the voice-over frames these conditions as opportunities for reform and cooperation. Initiatives like the Village Institutes and agricultural cooperatives are presented as national efforts toward modernization, with American support cast as an accelerant.

Toward the end, the film turns to media and diplomacy. Exterior and interior shots of the headquarters of *Cumhuriyet* (1924–), Turkey's oldest secular newspaper, highlight the media's role in disseminating pro-Western policies and building public consensus. Even editors critical of domestic political interference, the voice-over notes, tended to align with the government on foreign affairs—further reinforcing Turkey's pro-Western orientation. The film continues by showing Turkey's aspirations for global friendship,

FIGURE 3.2 USIS office in Istanbul, shown in *Turkey*.

Source: Records of the Office of the Chief Signal Officer, Record Group 111, National Archives and Records Administration, College Park, Maryland.

exemplified by a diplomatic feast hosted for King Abdullah of Jordan. The final sequences culminate in footage of a building bearing signs for "U.S.I.S." (US Information Service) in Istanbul (figure 3.2). The film shows Turks reading books and magazines within this gateway to American culture, avidly seeking knowledge about the United States. This compelling footage, a rarity for its time, highlights the strategic use of media to cultivate positive perceptions of the United States abroad.

Using this example as a point of departure, in this chapter I examine the film activities of the US government in Turkey, with particular emphasis on USIS operations. Although the USIS was officially established as a State Department entity in 1953, archival evidence—such as the 1949 footage—testifies to its earlier presence.[2] Expanding on this case, I analyze how the USIS funded the Educational Film Center (EFC) and distributed a wide array of films aimed at shaping Turkish public opinion. I argue that the USIS strategically deployed film as a diplomatic instrument to promote American ideals, counter communist influence, and reinforce Turkey's

Western alignment. This approach—rooted in ideals of modernization and racialized notions of progress—blurred the lines between education and propaganda, raising critical ethical questions about the boundaries of film diplomacy. While it helped construct a media infrastructure in Turkey, the USIS actively engaged in censorship practices designed to manage and constrain public perceptions of the United States. Here, I interrogate the disjuncture between the USIS's rhetorical commitment to democracy and its authoritarian methods of information control, demonstrating the contradictions embedded in its Cold War film operations.[3]

Finally, I situate film diplomacy not merely as a top-down institutional strategy but also as a dynamic network shaped by individual agency. Figures such as the diplomat Monteagle Stearns, the public relations officer Sadun Katipoğlu, and the documentary filmmaker Suha Arın exemplify how personal trajectories intersected with broader state goals. Their contributions show that transnational media infrastructures were not only extensions of state power but also spaces where individual vision, creativity, and ambitions for education and modernization could take root. By foregrounding these actors, I frame film diplomacy as a site of negotiation and contestation during the Cold War.

USIS Films and the Promotion of American Ideals Worldwide

The USIS had an extensive film program in over eighty countries, with films in languages including Arabic, Bengali, Cantonese, French, Greek, Japanese, Persian, Portuguese, Serbo-Croat, Spanish, Turkish, Urdu, and Vietnamese.[4] After a committee selected films for their educational value, the USIS distributed them to countries, including Turkey, either duty free or at a reduced rate. It operated over 210 film libraries abroad, in both cities and remote rural areas. To reach global audiences, it dispatched over 6,000 sound projectors and approximately 350 mobile motion picture units for screening films. The USIS's mission encompassed disseminating information regarding the United States and portraying democratic capitalism as the American way of life.[5] To achieve these goals, it employed films and other media to explain US policy and American ideals to global audiences.

The USIS's film programs reached an extensive viewership, estimated at half a billion people annually.⁶ The films had distinctive characteristics that contributed to their global reach. They were delivered in multiple formats, including television broadcasts and screenings in theaters and information centers and through mobile units that reached remote regions. The USIS also took a multilingual approach, producing content in numerous languages and offering soundtracks in multiple languages to ensure accessibility and comprehension for different audiences. Its collaboration with private American firms and industries enabled it to acquire, translate, reproduce, and distribute educational, scientific, and cultural films. It also cooperated with national and local government agencies, civic organizations, religious groups, and educational institutions in foreign countries, involving them in programming, scheduling, and exhibition. Using theaters, television, and mobile units equipped with projectors and other technology, the USIS was able to exhibit films in commercial theaters, rural areas, and regions without reliable electricity, facilitating access for different communities. It also encouraged other nations to integrate their films into foreign educational systems, promising that they would support classroom learning and promote cross-cultural understanding in schools, colleges, and universities. Finally, it established information centers worldwide that served as cultural hubs. Through these efforts, USIS films played a central role in shaping global perceptions of the United States, fostering narratives of mutual understanding, development, and cooperation.

Importantly, not all films distributed by the USIS were produced by the agency itself. In fact, many were drawn from a wide array of US government and nongovernment sources. For example, the historian Mikael Nilsson studied how the USIS disseminated propaganda films in Sweden and noted that the US Office of Education sent a catalog of educational and instructional films from various government departments, including the Office of Education, Navy and War Departments, Department of Agriculture, and Public Health Service, to the Swedish legation.⁷ In other words, the USIS served as a distributor of a broader constellation of American government media. For clarity, my use of the term *USIS film* throughout this chapter includes not only films directly produced by the agency but also those it strategically selected, repurposed, and distributed through its international network. A film's presence in USIS catalogs and libraries renders it part of the agency's media arsenal.

One illustrative example is *Abraham Lincoln'un Hayatı* (Life of Abraham Lincoln), which appears in a Turkish-language USIS film catalog.[8] The listing includes neither year nor director, but archival evidence suggests it was likely D. W. Griffith's *Abraham Lincoln* (1930)—a film not produced by the USIS. Nevertheless, its inclusion in USIS materials in Turkey qualifies it as a USIS film. Its rebranding and strategic deployment underscore how the agency curated films to align with key themes—such as American leadership and democratic values—regardless of original authorship.

While many such films were imported, a smaller number were produced locally in Turkey under USIS direction. One notable example is *Sadiye: Bir Köy Ebesinin Hikayesi* (Sadiye: Village midwife, 1951), a film that advocated the training and deployment of government-certified midwives, emphasizing their role in improving maternal health and education in rural villages.[9] The film was the product of a contractual collaboration among the US State Department, the Turkish government, and Syracuse University. Robert W. Wagner, a professor of education and photography at Ohio State University, played a central role in its development.[10] Serving as both a USIS adviser and the director of motion pictures for the government of Turkey, Wagner was responsible for conducting the research and writing the script.[11] However, he was not in Turkey long enough to direct the film himself. As a result, the directing role went to Irvin Kershner—then a young filmmaker—who would later gain international recognition for films such as *The Hoodlum Priest* (1961), *S*P*Y*S* (1974), *Star Wars: Episode V—The Empire Strikes Back* (1980), and *RoboCop 2* (1990). Kershner's early involvement with the USIS exemplifies the fluid boundaries between state-sponsored media and commercial cinema. The porous relationship between USIS film production and the careers of filmmakers who would go on to work in Hollywood suggests an ideological continuity. This convergence served the aims of film diplomacy—deploying the cinematic form not simply to inform or educate but also to foster alignment and ideological affinity with the United States.

USIS films addressed a range of themes, including American society, the promotion of democracy, the celebration of scientific advancements, Soviet oppression, the importance of regional alliances, and the glorification of productivity and progress. Some were about communism, detailing events like the Cuban Missile Crisis, the Hungarian Revolution, and Soviet suppression in Latvia and Vietnam. Examples of these films include *Küba Bekliyor* (Cuba: A World Verdict, USIS, 1963), *Macaristan'da Hürriyet Savaşı* (Hungarian Fight for Freedom, USIS, 1957), *Letonyam Benim* (My Latvia, Albert Jekste, USIS, 1954), and *Vietnam'da Durum* (Vietnam, The Issues, USIS, 1966).[12] Other films emphasized the principles of American democracy, civil rights, historical leadership, and economic prosperity. Titles such as *Basın Hürriyeti* (Freedom of the press), *Başkan Eisenhower'ın Ikinci Yemin Merasimi* (The second inauguration ceremony of President Eisenhower), and *Büyüyen Amerika Pazarı* (Growing American market) celebrated the strength and stability of US governance and the vibrancy of its economy.[13]

Additionally, films like *Atom Çağı için Eğitim* (Education for the atomic age), *Fende İlerleme* (Scientific progress), *Feza Keşfi—Mercury Projesi* (Space exploration—Mercury Project), and *John Glenn Arz Etrafında* (John Glenn around the earth) showcased America's scientific advancements and space exploration, underlining the nation's role at the forefront of technological progress.[14] Cultural and social aspects of American life were also featured. Films such as *Amerikan Müziği* (American music), *Amerika'da Şehir Dışı Bölgeler Halkının Sanat Çalışmaları* (Artistic works of the rural population in America), *Çalışan Amerikan Kadınlar* (Working American women), and *California Üniversitesi* (University of California) offered representations of American music, arts, and education and women's participation in the workforce, highlighting values central to American identity.[15] Furthermore, films emphasizing international collaboration and regional alliances, including *Avrupayı Kalkındırma Programı İş Başında* (The European development program is underway), *Birleşmiş Milletler Teşkilatının Merkezi* (The headquarters of the United Nations Organization), and *Burası Avrupa* (This is Europe), underscored the significance of American-led productivity and cooperation within institutions such as NATO and the United Nations.[16]

Through these themes, USIS films aimed not only to cultivate appreciation for the United States among global audiences but also to shape public opinion, counter misinformation—particularly notable after events such as the Kennedy assassination—and foster dialogue and understanding.[17] In Turkey, the dissemination of these films was coordinated through the EFC, exemplifying a curated approach to managing and contextualizing foreign-produced materials and illustrating the strategic role of film diplomacy in advancing American interests abroad.

The USIS in Turkey: Shaping Perceptions During the Cold War

The USIS played a central role in advancing the United States' national strategy abroad during the Cold War, operating a vast global network that extended into hundreds of cities across multiple continents. In Turkey, it operated under the name Amerikan Birleşik Devletleri Haberler Servisi (US Information Agency/Service), with regional headquarters in Istanbul, Ankara, Izmir, and Adana.[18] In a period defined by psychological warfare, the USIS became a key instrument in bolstering Turkey's association with the Free World and promoting the American way of life as a model. To ensure broad reach across the country, it had a strategy of screening films in multiple venues such as public squares, schools, hospitals, universities, factories, and military units. By 1951, it had amassed a fleet of six vehicles and over four hundred film projectors, enabling mobile units to reach remote areas with film programming designed to educate and persuade.

The USIS aimed to disseminate, gather, and process information to secure Turkey's alignment with the West and prevent a turn toward communism. Its media arsenal was wide-ranging: Films, radio programs, music performances, television broadcasts, books, traveling art exhibitions, and public libraries were all mobilized to generate goodwill toward the United States and reinforce Turkey's position as a key anticommunist ally. Its media strategies were carefully tailored to different audiences. For example, it sponsored the quarterly magazine *Ufuk* (Horizon), which targeted intellectuals, journalists, and policy elites,[19] while its films reached schoolchildren, residents of rural communities with limited formal education, and members of the military. To improve these outreach efforts, US government agents conducted field research, interviews, and sociological analyses, experimenting with formats and messaging to identify the most effective ways to cultivate pro-American sentiment and support US foreign policy goals in the Middle East.

In addition, the USIS collaborated with commercial media companies to advance the US government's propaganda initiatives abroad, often framing these partnerships as mutually beneficial arrangements that combined ideological outreach with economic opportunity.[20] A mechanism established to support this strategy was the Information Media Guaranty (IMG) Program, which aimed to expand the export of American media—newspapers, magazines, and films—while generating significant revenue.

By the 1950s and 1960s, the IMG Program had yielded over $80 million in sales to overseas markets for US media companies.[21]

In Turkey, the USIS used the IMG Program both to import American media and to serve as the public relations arm of the American diplomatic mission. Turkey joined the IMG Program in 1956, amid a convergence of economic and political factors: the devaluation of the Turkish lira, the growing debts owed by Turkish film importers to American distributors, and the strategic value of Turkey as a Cold War propaganda front.[22] The lira's devaluation had sharply reduced foreign film imports, leaving Turkish distributors unable to meet their financial obligations to US firms. Concerned about losing its foothold in a key foreign market, the US government intervened. Under the IMG Program, Turkish importers paid their invoices in Turkish lira into a designated local account, which transferred those funds to the US government; Washington then converted an agreed annual portion of the lira proceeds into US dollars and paid participating American rights holders, while the Turkish government remitted any remaining dollar balance under the bilateral agreement. This arrangement was subject to annual renewal, with new quotas and terms renegotiated each year.[23] This restored the flow of American films without requiring importers to source scarce dollars up front, and it ensured US companies a predictable repatriation stream. By withholding dollar conversion from selected titles, USIA could impose a de facto distribution bar, not a legal ban, but an economic veto that kept prints out of Turkish theaters.

The primary rationale behind Turkey's inclusion in the IMG Program was to stabilize the film trade and preserve the dominance of American movies in the Turkish market. Yet the program also functioned as a tool of cultural control. The USIS could deny dollar conversion to films it deemed unrepresentative of American values, filtering Hollywood content to align with US strategic messaging abroad. Films that conflicted with the idealized image of American life were censored or withheld from distribution.[24] In this capacity, the USIS became an arbiter of cultural legitimacy, filtering Hollywood content to align with US strategic messaging abroad. Several Hollywood films were banned in Turkey under USIS oversight, including *Rebel Without a Cause* (Warner Brothers, Nicholas Ray, 1955), *Around the World in 80 Days* (United Artists, Michael Anderson, 1956), *Something of Value* (MGM, Richard Brooks, 1957), *The Garment Jungle* (Columbia Pictures, Vincent Sherman, 1957), and *A Hatful of Rain* (20th Century Fox, Fred Zinnemann, 1957).[25]

These censorship practices directly contradicted the USIS's stated mission of promoting democracy and freedom of expression.[26] Turkish critics, already battling domestic restrictions from the Turkish Board of Censorship, viewed the additional layer of American censorship as particularly pernicious.[27] The critic Semih Tugrul argued that USIS control over Hollywood films undermined the very principles of private enterprise and democratic practices that the United States claimed to uphold.[28] Turkish film writers expressed frustration at being denied access to what they considered some of Hollywood's most artistically and culturally significant works.[29] The film critic Nijat Özön even noted that American film companies themselves were increasingly exasperated by the USIS's restrictive practices in Turkey.[30] These critical interventions appear to have had some effect: The IMG Program was ultimately dismantled in 1962.[31]

Throughout the Cold War, the USIS deployed a range of 16 mm nonfiction films to craft ideological narratives, promote American democratic ideals, and highlight failures of communism. For instance, *Amerika'da Seçim Günü* (Election day in America) illustrated how American citizens elect public officials, while *J.F.K.'nin Seçimi* (*The Election of John F. Kennedy*,1960, produced by Hearst-Metrotone for USIS) detailed the presidential campaign, televised debates, and electoral process that brought John F. Kennedy to the presidency.[32] In contrast, films such as *Hürriyete Kaçış* (Escape to freedom) showed the struggles of individuals fleeing oppressive regimes in East Berlin and the People's Republic of China. Similarly, *Hürriyet Kıvılcımı* (Spark of freedom) was about anticommunist uprisings in Hungary, Poland, Korea, and Germany between 1945 and 1961.

The USIS also addressed internal contradictions in American democracy, particularly the country's racial inequalities. The 1957 Little Rock Crisis, in which a white mob blocked the entry of nine Black students into Central High School in Arkansas, quickly became an international embarrassment.[33] Secretary of State John Foster Dulles acknowledged its global repercussions, warning that "Little Rock was ruining American foreign policy" and urging the USIS to foreground media that showed racial progress.[34] In response, it launched a film campaign centered on civil rights and the federal government's commitment to racial justice under Presidents Kennedy, Johnson, and Nixon.[35]

This campaign included films such as *Yürüyüş* (*The March*, James Blue, 1963) and *Little Rock'dan Dokuz Kişi* (*Nine from Little Rock*, Charles Guggenheim,

1964).³⁶ These films were circulated in Turkey soon after their release and were strategically positioned to counter negative global perceptions by showcasing the United States as a nation capable of confronting its internal struggles. Yet by the early 1970s, USIS agents began deeming race-related films "irrelevant" to Turkish audiences, arguing that content focused on education and culture better resonated with local viewers.³⁷ While the USIS was responsive to shifting international contexts, its refusal to fully grapple with systemic racism reflected an ongoing reluctance to challenge the foundations of whiteness. In this way, it contributed to the reproduction of whiteness by selectively highlighting narratives of progress while obscuring the structural inequalities embedded in American life.

The USIS engaged in a parallel discourse that aimed to align Islam with American democracy. Through films and news stories, it highlighted religious freedom and the inclusion of Muslims in the United States and contrasted it with the repression of religion under communism. Films such as *Washington Cami* (*The Washington Mosque*, 1957, produced by Craven Film Corporation for USIS) and *Washington'da İslam Etüdleri Merkezinin Açılışı* (*The Opening of the Islamic Center of Washington*, 1957) were screened at USIS film stations in Turkey to emphasize that Islamic institutions could flourish within a democratic system.³⁸ *Washington Cami* documents President Dwight D. Eisenhower's speech at the dedication of the Islamic Center of Washington on June 28, 1957, where he addressed the global Muslim community.³⁹ Turkish newspapers such as *Milliyet* and *Cumhuriyet* covered the event, noting that Turkey had sent its famous *çini* tiles and artisans to contribute to the mosque's interior and observing with approval that both President Eisenhower and First Lady Mamie Eisenhower removed their shoes before entering—an act interpreted as a respectful acknowledgment of Muslim customs.⁴⁰

These efforts to represent Islam as compatible with American democratic values demonstrate the strategic malleability of whiteness in US diplomacy. In contexts where Muslim identity could be framed as politically useful—particularly in fostering anticommunist alliances—Muslims were symbolically embraced as partners. Yet this strategic inclusion did little to disrupt the racial and cultural hierarchies. The USIS's film diplomacy thus shows how narratives of freedom, progress, and inclusion were carefully curated to serve geopolitical objectives, often at the expense of a fuller reckoning with the contradictions they masked.

Finding a Balance in the Nexus of Laws, Education, and Propaganda

Laws and regulations in both Turkey and the United States played a crucial role in shaping the operations of film diplomacy, aligning its functions with each government's legal framework and policy decisions. In 1937, the Turkish government enacted Law 3122, commonly known as Öğretici ve Teknik Filmler Hakkında Kanun (Law on Educational and Technical Films), which eliminated import taxes on educational and technical films.[41] This legislation served as a financial incentive for the importation of educational content and associated media technologies, laying the groundwork for an influx of foreign audiovisual materials. In 1942, the US government began to certify select films as educational, aiming to streamline their tax-free importation into foreign nations like Turkey that granted preferential customs treatment to educational materials.[42] While the USIS established regulations for the certification of these materials, it also withheld certificates from films that it believed had the potential to be misinterpreted by foreign audiences, who presumably lacked sufficient understanding of the American cultural context.[43] This decision stemmed from the assumption that Turkish audiences required a deeper cultural knowledge to fully understand certain films—an assumption fundamentally shaped by the dynamics of whiteness, which governed not only who had access to particular kinds of knowledge but also what the conditions of that access were. The ambiguity built into these determinations highlights how whiteness operates as a selective filter, dictating which narratives are deemed appropriate for export and which are to be withheld, based on perceptions of legibility and alignment with US interests. Within this regulatory context, USIS films entered Turkey as educational films and received tax-free import privileges. At the same time, the Smith-Mundt Act of 1948 explicitly prohibited the domestic dissemination of USIS materials within the United States.[44] This prohibition was designed to prevent the perception that the federal government was engaging in propaganda on its own soil, effectively confirming congressional awareness of the propagandistic nature of the agency's content, even as it was promoted abroad under the guise of education and cultural exchange.

The contradictions at the heart of this system became particularly evident in the 1980s when a group of American filmmakers sued the USIS after the agency refused to classify their films as educational.⁴⁵ The plaintiffs argued that the denial violated their First Amendment right to freedom of speech. However, the court ruled against them, stating that their films were "attempting to influence opinion," reflected "a standpoint," and were, therefore, "anti-educational."⁴⁶ The irony, of course, is that USIS films themselves were overtly designed to shape public opinion. While these independent filmmakers may have diverged from the government's propagandistic goals, the judicial decision in favor of the agency underscores deeper structural biases—particularly in the mechanisms by which government-sanctioned narratives are privileged over dissenting or alternative viewpoints. This case highlights the complex interplay involving film, power, and politics, indicating that whiteness not only shapes access to information but also determines the criteria by which films are evaluated and deemed educational or subversive.

The USIS's Distribution of Marshall Plan Films in Turkey

USIS agents identified economic productivity as a topic that captivated audiences in Turkey. In response, the agency prioritized the distribution of films that showcased agricultural modernization and the economic benefits of US aid. Many of these were Marshall Plan films, designed to promote the successes of American economic assistance in Turkey. Notable examples include USIS-distributed films like *Marshall Plan at Work in Turkey* (James Hill, 1950), *Village Tractor* (Köy Traktörü, Clifford Hornby, 1951 and 1953), *Yusef and His Plough* (Yusuf ve Sabanı, Clifford Hornby, 1951), and *Turkish Harvest* (Clifford Hornby, 1952). These films shared a common objective: to show Turkey as a nation undergoing transformation, marked by increased agricultural productivity and alignment with Western development ideals.

To contextualize these films, Turkey was a frontline nation in the American Cold War strategy, given its geographical proximity to the USSR. President Harry S. Truman solidified Turkey's significance in 1947 by introducing the Truman Doctrine, which outlined a road map for American foreign policy and justified investment in Turkey (and Greece) to combat communist infiltration.⁴⁷ This doctrine aimed to protect against the spread of communism from the USSR and increase programs that disseminated information about the United States across the globe. As a result, Turkey received $100 million in military assistance in 1947.[48] Truman subsequently signed Public Law 472, known as the Economic Cooperation Act (ECA) of 1948, which implemented economic and financial measures designed to maintain favorable conditions abroad for the survival of free institutions while also ensuring the strength and stability of the United States.[49] Additionally, the ECA granted the United States the ability to distribute propaganda through various media and authorized exporters. In exchange, Turkey assumed the responsibility of promoting technical cooperation programs and endorsing the American agenda.

In 1948, the collaboration between the United States and Turkey expanded through the Marshall Plan, a US program proposed by Secretary of State George C. Marshall to rebuild postwar Europe's economy and promote the political and social stability needed for democracy to flourish. Because of its strategic location, Turkey received $225 million, alongside Greece, to develop its agricultural economy even though it had not participated in World War II.[50] The Marshall Plan strategists sponsored films that provided audiovisual instruction about modernizing and increasing agricultural productivity. Subsequently, Marshall Plan media operations shifted from the Economic Cooperation Administration (1948–1951) to the Mutual Security Agency (1952–1953) to the US Information Agency (USIA, 1953–1999).[51] The USIA, known abroad as the USIS, distributed Marshall Plan films, classifying them as both educational films and part of the USIS film collection.

Although the ECA granted the United States the authority to disseminate propaganda through films and mandated that Turkey promote them, the information being disseminated had to be approved by the Turkish government.[52] Indeed, interactions between American agents and the Turkish government regarding the Marshall Plan films reveal feedback loops that facilitated bidirectional communication. In 1951, the Ministry of Agriculture disapproved of the representation of Turkey in *Village Tractor* and *Yusef and His Plough* and demanded that these films show "Turkey as modern or beautiful or both."[53] This request showcases the ministry's desire to move away from presenting Turkey as traditional, antiquated, or obsolete. It also requested that the boy in *Village Tractor* be selected "for his ability" and "not for being the mayor's son."[54] This request highlights the ministry's intention to promote equal opportunities for all citizens and avoid endorsing a system based on nepotism. The US government agents took the criticism seriously and edited the 1953 version of *Village Tractor* to show that the boy who drove the tractor did so because he had attended a driving course sponsored by the Marshall Plan.[55] This feedback loop exemplifies film diplomacy as a means of acknowledging and responding to demands to facilitate the transmission of information in a transnational network.

The USIS's Film Collaboration with Military Forces

In addition to garnering civilian support, the USIS collaborated with military institutions to amplify its messaging through film. A notable example is *Tepkili Uçaklar Türk Semalarında* (Jets over Turkey, Harald Kubens, 1954), produced jointly by the USIS, the Turkish Air Force, the US Air Force Advisory Group in Turkey, and the Joint American Military Mission for Aid to Turkey (JAMMAT). The film documents the construction of an air base, the training of Turkish personnel, and the execution of aerial drills—visually reinforcing the modernization of Turkey's military in alignment with American Cold War objectives. This collaboration illustrates how film diplomacy functioned not only through content but also through institutional partnerships designed to communicate strategic goals to targeted audiences, especially within the military. Beyond film production, JAMMAT maintained a small theater in Turkey where military personnel screened films from the Army and Air Force Motion Picture Service five times a week.[56] These screenings highlighted military morale, training, and ideological alignment, further embedding audiovisual media into the machinery of US-Turkish military cooperation.

JAMMAT's presence dates back to 1947, when the US Congress approved financial aid to Turkey for its establishment in Ankara.[57] This prompted the construction of an air base located south of Ankara, beginning in 1951, with the objective of using it as an emergency staging and recovery site for bombers. After Turkey officially became a member of the NATO in 1952, the Turkish General Staff and the US Air Force signed a joint use agreement for the base, which was subsequently named Adana Air Base in 1954. Later known as Incirlik Air Base, its location made it strategically significant in countering the Soviet threat and responding to crises in the Middle East.

JAMMAT was responsible for distributing American military equipment and training foreign military personnel in Turkey.[58] Its primary goal was to modernize Turkey's military forces and establish a robust national defense system against the Soviet Union.[59] Through JAMMAT, the US Air Force offered aircraft to the Turkish Air Force and trained Turkish soldiers. Additionally, it contracted with American industrial firms to construct and improve Turkish air bases, further strengthening American influence in the country.[60] In these endeavors, film served as a strategic instrument to cultivate support, both domestically and regionally, for Turkey's military role within the Cold War context. JAMMAT's film distribution channels within Turkey reached specific military personnel and communities crucial to garnering support for both training initiatives and the US-Turkish alliance.

Other branches of the US government similarly produced films aimed at educating and orienting American military personnel stationed in Turkey. *Turkey: The Land of "In-Between"* (Armed Forces, 1952) is a film that characterizes Turkey as a crucial ally of the United States in the fight against communism.[61] In addition to informing viewers about Turkey's history, economy, industry, and role in NATO, the voice-over highlights Turkey's mandatory military service as a means of safeguarding the "free" world against Russian threats.

This framing was echoed in the 1953 pamphlet *A Pocket Guide to Turkey*, produced by the US Department of Defense's Office of Armed Forces Information and Education.[62] The guide provided American service members with a primer on Turkey's people, culture, and strategic significance. Like the earlier film *Turkey* (1949), the pamphlet stressed Turkey's geographical role as a crossroads between East and West and encouraged US troops to act as ambassadors of modernization and democratic values.[63] It also celebrated the reforms of Mustafa Kemal Atatürk as evidence of Turkey's progress toward becoming a modern, secular, and Western-aligned state while reinforcing the urgency of the US-Turkish alliance in resisting Soviet expansion.[64]

Films in this genre continued to be produced, sponsored, and circulated by various US institutions into the 1960s and 1970s. Films such as *Turkey: A Strategic Land and Its People* (Coronet Films, 1959), *Turkey: Emergence of a Modern Nation* (Encyclopaedia Britannica, 1963), and *Turkey: Crossroads of the Ancient World* (Centron Educational Films, 1973) reflected American interest in representing Turkey as a modernizing, cooperative ally. American universities such as Indiana University (with its growing Audio-Visual Center) circulated these films in schools and libraries under the category of educational films. Some of these films arrived with standardized evaluation forms that librarians and other evaluators completed to assess a films' instructional value and suitability for various audiences. This practice was part of the Educational Film Library Association' program (EFLA), through which the organization supported and coordinated the production, distribution, and use of 16 mm educational films for adult and academic audiences.

Establishing an Educational Media Infrastructure in Turkey

In a report about Turkey, Monteagle Stearns, an American film officer, asserted that US government agents went beyond the role of mere propagandists and that their films were more than vehicles for propaganda. He and his team developed a strategy to move past what they described as the "mechanical" and "impersonal" methods of foreign information services. Their strategy involved integrating American films into the Turkish curricula and building close relationships with Turkish educators and ministry officials.[65] Their vision positioned film as a tool with dual purposes: simultaneously educational and propagandistic.

To advance this goal, American agents in Turkey fostered transnational cooperation with a range of Turkish entities—including the Ministries of National Education, Health, Public Works, Agriculture, and National Defense; the office of the prime minister; and the Turkish Press Bureau (TPB). USIS agents considered this cooperation to be a milestone in the process of building a relationship between Americans and Turks through which to develop propaganda and information programming.[66] Thomas E. Flanagan, a public affairs officer, described the establishment of an interministerial committee as a landmark that demonstrated democracy in action. He envisioned this coordination as the foundation of a centralized media infrastructure, eventually formalized as the National Teaching Films Center, later known as the Educational Film Center.[67]

By 1952, the USIS launched an innovative media program that paired American and Turkish information officers to design and implement coordinated information campaigns. The US officers were tasked with establishing the foundational infrastructure for selecting, adapting, producing, and distributing media, and over time, the Turkish officials were expected to assume increasing responsibility for content development and production, a strategy that aimed to promote long-term sustainability and local ownership. The initiative culminated in efforts to build a Turkish-run media production and distribution system with technical, financial, and managerial support from the United States.

A key development in this collaboration was the creation of the EFC, jointly established by the USIS and the Turkish Ministry of National Education (MNET), with the support of the United Nations Educational, Scientific, and Cultural Organization.[68] The center operated as a communication hub that connected various Turkish ministries through centralized media coordination. In 1952, this effort led to the founding of thirteen regional film centers and nine mobile units designed to bring films to rural areas, with additional centers planned soon after.[69] The information officer Hugh A. Crumpler described this program in Turkey as "unique among USIS films program throughout the world."[70]

To support the expansion of this infrastructure and feature Turkish-language prints and magnetic recorder-projectors, the USIS requested approximately $125,000 from the State Department in 1953. Crumpler recommended that $90,000 of that budget be saved for purchasing raw stock and recording, printing, and other necessary equipment. Moreover, USIS agents wanted the equipment to be either developed by the US State Department or compiled by the director of the National Teaching Films Center (or the EFC of Turkey) in collaboration with the film officer and consultants designated by the department.[71] In other words, USIS agents wanted to use 72 percent of the requested budget to purchase American products to furnish the film production center in Turkey, highlighting the financial aspect of their operations. As a matter of fact, the EFC initially carried hundreds of American films.[72]

One of the agency's strategic goals was to produce films about Turkish subjects that aligned with American themes. Crumpler observed that "the Turks are most interested in Turks," citing *Turkish Troops in Korea* as one of the most popular titles in the USIS collection. The film described Turkish heroism during the Korean War, satisfying nationalist pride while reinforcing the US-Turkey alliance. Crumpler argued that such locally relevant content was the most effective means of fulfilling USIS's objectives.[73]

In the long run, building a production infrastructure was cheaper than having Americans produce films in and about Turkey. USIS agents estimated that producing USIS films would cost the government of Turkey much less because Turkish employees (rather than Americans) would provide the labor and services. Indeed, agents estimated that USIS films produced by Turkish commercial firms would cost approximately $3,000 per reel, whereas those produced by the State Department would cost between $10,000 and $15,000 per reel. Furthermore, USIS agents anticipated that as production facilities were established in Turkey, Turks would increasingly contribute to the cost of films and slowly take over the financial responsibility.[74] Accordingly, USIS agents wanted Turkish ministry personnel in Istanbul to learn how to install, operate, and maintain equipment within six months of the facilities' completion.

USIS agents planned to provide financial and technical support for establishing production facilities in Turkey. They anticipated that local funds or special allocations from the State Department could finance the Turkish personnel and that Turkish sound and laboratory engineers could work on a contractual basis for the US government. Consequently, American agents had managerial and financial control over the development of the media infrastructure in Turkey. USIS agents also recognized the importance of technical training for Turkish personnel across various production stages.[75] To facilitate this transition, an unnamed film officer was responsible for coordinating the installation of production equipment as well as for training writers, camera operators, directors, and editors. In addition, this process involved determining film subjects that would be of mutual interest to both the USIS and the Turkish ministry program. By deploying an American writer-director-editor for approximately a year and a camera operator for approximately six months, the USIS aimed to ensure the effective technical training of Turkish personnel and foster their expertise in film production.

The film production facilities in Turkey fell under the jurisdiction of the Interministerial Coordinating Committee on Visual Aids, established under a directive from the prime minister.[76] This committee divided authority over the facilities between the MNET and the TPB. The MNET served as the production agency for 16 mm films for all government groups, while the TPB functioned as the production agency for 35 mm films. Turkish authorities assured the US government that the ministries would assign qualified personnel and contribute to the cost of film operations from the national budget.

Still, some US officials expressed doubts about Turkey's capacity to sustain such an ambitious program. William E. Kugeman, the deputy public affairs officer at the US embassy in Ankara condescendingly remarked that "Turks ... cannot be given bigger chances to bite off more than they have the teeth to chew thoroughly and to easily digest."[77] This patronizing sentiment exemplifies the skepticism that sometimes accompanied American aid efforts, despite the goal of partnership.

USIS agents anticipated potential resistance from Turkish officials regarding the dominance of American content. Crumpler noted concerns that Turkish collaborators might question a media program centered largely on US themes—education, agriculture, economy, history, and military strength.[78] Indeed, the earliest accessible EFC film catalog listed hundreds of American films, signaling the ideological imprint of US media in Turkish public life.[79]

The USIS's mission in Turkey was guided by President Eisenhower's directives and rooted in the strategic communication practices of the Cold War. Its goals were threefold. A key goal was to promote understanding of US policies, institutions, and people. Another mission was to cultivate admiration for the American way of life.[80] Emphasizing mutual security and countering the influence of the Soviet Union were essential components of this approach. The third objective was to publicize the role of US aid in Turkey as a symbol of friendship, partnership, and prosperity to fortify Turkish public confidence in US programs.[81] These objectives were explicitly linked to larger geopolitical concerns, including Turkey's role as a stalwart member of NATO, the Baghdad Pact, the Balkan Alliance, and the United Nations.[82]

Yet USIS efforts were not without critique. Turkish citizens voiced frustration, with some arguing "The United States has encouraged us to develop our economic and military strength. We are now in desperate financial straits, and the United States turns a deaf ear to our appeals."[83] In response, the USIS redoubled its investment in media—particularly film—to reinforce America's image as a benevolent ally. Internal correspondence shows how strongly US officials relied on media infrastructure to perpetuate the image of the United States as a savior nation, using film to secure political loyalty, economic alignment, and ideological affinity.

The USIS Cinema Course and Mobile Film Program in Turkey

USIS agents relied on local networks of reporters, teachers, and community members to disseminate their messaging, positioning these individuals as essential intermediaries in advancing US foreign policy goals. By presenting propaganda in the form of educational content, the USIS sought to convince Turkish audiences that its exhibitions offered practical solutions to everyday challenges. Film, in particular, was embraced as a compelling medium for educational communication—one capable of reaching audiences across class, gender, and geography. This strategy earned favorable coverage in Turkish media, where the dual nature of the USIS's mission was both acknowledged and, at times, praised.

For example, in 1950, *Film ve Öğretim* (Film and education) published an article titled "Amerikan Haberler Bürosu Film Servisi Nasıl Çalışıyor?" (How does the USIS film unit work?), which highlighted the dual role of films as propaganda and education, commending the agency for its contributions in both domains. Accompanying the article was a photograph (figure 3.3) taken after a 16 mm cinema course organized by the USIS and attended by Monteagle Stearns and Sadun Katipoğlu, director of USIS-Turkey Cinema Services.[84] Katipoğlu explained that USIS films were regularly screened in schools, hospitals, universities, and military units, all equipped with 16 mm projectors and supported by mobile film units. The USIS film library included a wide range of subjects—current affairs, American social life, medicine, agriculture, science, industry, transportation, education, and travel—designed to inform while subtly promoting American values.

A year later *Film ve Öğretim* published a firsthand account by an unnamed reporter who described a USIS mobile cinema event in Kağıthane (figure 3.4). The screening was organized by Faruk Gürman, a schoolteacher from İzmir and manager of the USIS's mobile cinema services. Motivated by what the reporter described as "patriotism," Gürman traveled across Anatolia using mobile cinema as a teaching tool. He believed that these screenings had the transformative potential to educate rural populations and elevate national development through the power of moving images. The reporter observed the event's impact: Villagers were gathered in the town square, silently captivated by films that explained, for instance, how microbes cause disease. The reporter noted the unique

FIGURE 3.3 Stearns and Katipoğlu are among the participants in the USIS cinema course.

Source: "Amerikan Haberler Bürosu Film Servisi Nasıl Çalışıyor?," *Film ve Öğretim*, no. 1 (1950): 8. National Library of Turkey, Ankara.

FIGURE 3.4 People gathering at a USIS mobile cinema unit.

Source: "Amerikan Haberler Merkezinin Seyyar Sinemasında Bir Saat," *Film ve Öğretim*, no. 6–7 (1951): 6. National Library of Turkey, Ankara.

power of this audiovisual medium: In just one hour, the USIS mobile cinema succeeded in delivering public health information in a way that posters and printed materials often could not. He concluded that the mobile cinema was a "magical remedy," capable of addressing health, agricultural issues, and rural development where traditional methods had failed.[85]

Importantly, while praising the event's effectiveness, the reporter also recognized the USIS initiative as a form of "propaganda." He described the blending of education and propaganda as "the most practical method of achieving their objectives for Turkey."[86] The screening drew an estimated five hundred attendees—far more than any static display of posters in a coffeehouse might attract. Posters about farming tools, tax announcements, and military service obligations were typically ignored or only selectively read, and they were predominantly viewed by men. Coffeehouses, the usual venues for such materials, were largely male-dominated spaces, inaccessible to many women and children in rural communities.

In contrast, mobile cinema created an inclusive, communal setting in which entire families could engage with information collectively. Thus, USIS films not only extended the reach of American messaging but also functioned as a rare medium of egalitarian access in gendered social environments. Even as Turkish observers acknowledged the propagandistic function of these screenings, they recognized their effectiveness and accessibility. In this way, film diplomacy in rural Turkey blurred the boundaries between influence and instruction, persuasion and pedagogy—making cinema one of the USIS's most powerful tools of outreach.

The USIS's Hoja Film Series

Between 1952 and 1974, the USIS sponsored an unusual film series featuring Nasreddin Hoja, a Turkish folk culture figure known across the Middle East for his humorous pedagogical and moral analysis of society.[87] It strategically used Hoja to bridge cultural divides and embed pro-Western values through narratives centered on anticommunism, religion, modernization, and the blend of tradition with progress. Within the broader landscape of Turkish cinema, the Hoja figure was already well established. In 1940, Muhsin Ertuğrul partnered with Ipek Film to produce *Nasreddin Hoca Düğünde* (Nasreddin Hoja at the wedding), likely initiating a tradition of

Hoja-themed films in both national and transnational circuits.[88] The USIS versions were animated marionette films, the result of a collaboration between Mary Chase Marionettes and Trident Films. Marionettist Mary Chase contributed her puppetry expertise, while Trident Films, known for educational films on topics like missionary work and agricultural productivity, handled production.[89] Together, they created at least twenty-five films, including *The Heart of a Tyrant*, *The Emperor's Elephant*, *Hoja and the Woodcutter*, *Inshallah*, *Hoja Tries to Please All*, *The Inn Keeper's Bill*, and *Hoja Shares His Yogurt Dish*.[90] These films emphasized unity, cooperation, and modernization while maintaining traditional values. However, US diplomats quickly learned that reception did not always match intention. In Iraq, audience feedback collected by US embassy officials in 1953 described the films as propaganda, at times prompting viewers to throw stones at the screen.[91] This early backlash indicates the limits of film diplomacy in the wider region.

The films used Nasreddin Hoja as a cultural anchor to communicate ideological messages. Believed to have lived in the thirteenth century, Hoja is recognized across Eastern Europe and Asia. In the USIS films, he becomes a moral compass, offering relatable lessons that subtly reinforce anticommunist and pro-Western ideals. Supporting characters included Effendi, Burhan, and Hamid. Effendi, a wise sheik and narrator, replaces the traditional voice-over, lending authenticity and cultural familiarity. Burhan, Effendi's confidant, represents the receptive audience. He consistently aligns with Hoja's perspectives and looks up to him as a source of wisdom and guidance. Hamid, identified by his red scarf, symbolizes radicalized youth sympathetic to communism. He is represented as brash, disrespectful, and foolish—a cautionary figure who resists moral instruction and illustrates the dangers of leftist ideologies.

Set in a coffeehouse adorned with hookahs and nestled in a small village, the Hoja films unfurl in a world where Hoja, Effendi, Burhan, and Hamid all converse in English. The voice-over often points out that the story takes place in a village not far from the viewer's own home. The characters and voice-over employ terms such as *nation* but refrain from explicitly mentioning any specific countries besides the United States and communist countries. This omission of specific names strategically extends the films' influence and audiences, allowing them to transcend geographical boundaries. Imbued with the tradition of shadow puppetry, these films possess an allure reminiscent of the traditional Turkish shadow plays like Karagöz and Hacivat.

The Heart of a Tyrant opens with the "honorable sheik" Effendi and his companion Burhan seated in the coffeehouse (figures 3.5, 3.6, and 3.7).⁹² The camera follows Burhan as he approaches the doorway, witnessing a growing crowd and the restless Hamid. Burhan reports on the gathering in the square, where Hamid and others wield rocks and sticks. After a rock breaks the coffeehouse window, Hamid enters the scene, agitated, and warns of an impending riot at the government house (figure 3.8.). When Burhan questions Hamid's participation in violence, he attributes it to the government's "dishonesty and corruption" and claims that their country remains "backward." Effendi counters by highlighting the progress that the country's own labor and American aid have achieved, such as constructing roads, schools, and housing projects. He explicitly remarks

FIGURE 3.5 USIS sponsorship is credited in *The Heart of a Tyrant.*

Source: Motion Picture Films from the "Hoja" Program Series, 1952–1974, Record Group 306, Records of the US Information Agency, NAID: 140135766, Local ID: 306-HA-4, National Archives and Records Administration, College Park, Maryland.

FIGURE 3.6 Opening credits for *The Heart of a Tyrant* showing Hoja on his donkey.

Source: Motion Picture Films from the "Hoja" Program Series, 1952–1974, Record Group 306, Records of the US Information Agency.

FIGURE 3.7 Burhan, Effendi, and the coffeehouse owner in *The Heart of a Tyrant*.

Source: Motion Picture Films from the "Hoja" Program Series, 1952–1974, Record Group 306, Records of the US Information Agency.

FIGURE 3.8 Hamid in *The Heart of a Tyrant*.

Source: Motion Picture Films from the "Hoja" Program Series, 1952–1974, Record Group 306, Records of the US Information Agency.

on the United States' contributions in modernizing the country in which the characters live.

Dismissing the modernization efforts, Hamid exits the scene, prompting Effendi's remark that he has "the heart of a tyrant." Reminiscing, Effendi proceeds to recount a tale about Hoja and the tyrannical Emperor Tamerlane (also recognized as Tamburlaine and Timurlenk), known for violent acts like boiling a man in oil and cutting off slaves' heads.[93] Upon the emperor's return from a weeklong trip, he is unexpectedly cheerful. When Hoja inquires about the highlights of the journey, the emperor shares his amusement at witnessing violent incidents throughout the city. The scene cuts in and out to hand-drawn sketches of those violent scenes, overlayed with moans of agony. Effendi concludes with a moral lesson, emphasizing that individuals who fixate on the negatives, wrongs, and unfinished aspects of their country reveal their own inclination toward violence—the "heart of a tyrant." For Effendi, if such individuals gain unquestioning followers and attain power, they pose a threat to the very foundations of the country. By intertwining the story of the tyrannical ruler with that of a protester (Hamid), the film creates an unexpected parallel, aiming to dissuade individuals from fixating on negative events within their country.

A subtle yet powerful undercurrent of anticommunism lies at the heart of the USIS's animated marionette films. By highlighting the dangers and shortcomings of a "godless society," the films implicitly advocate preserving traditional values and religious faith, positioning them as essential elements for progress. *Inshallah*, for example, celebrates progress, religion, and the capacity of mankind to surpass the marvels of nature. The opening sequence features a soaring kite that captures the attention of the central character, Hamid, who wears a red scarf around his neck. This scene sets the stage for a discussion between Hamid and Burhan. As a devout Muslim with ingrained convictions about the value of religion, Burhan opposes Hamid's vision of constructing a society that is emancipated from religious constraints. Their spirited debate serves as a microcosm of the prevailing ideological conflicts within society. It also offers a counterpoint to the orientalist association of religiosity with backwardness.

Effendi weaves a tale about Hoja as the scene fades to Hoja walking with his ax on a hill. He sits down in the shade of a walnut tree and wonders why pumpkins do not grow on trees but walnuts do; then he realizes that pumpkins are too heavy for trees and that they would fall on him if they grew on branches. This leads to a religious epiphany: Hoja admits to his sin for questioning God and then praises Allah for his divine wisdom. A guard passes by on a donkey, demanding that Hoja guide him to a distant city. Objecting at first, Hoja realizes that this task must be his punishment for questioning God and accompanies the guard. The scene cuts to a rainy night at Hoja's house, where his wife worriedly awaits him. Hoja eventually makes it home, repeating "Inshallah" (God willing) with relief, as he has made it back to his wife. This story within a story illuminates the consequences of questioning divine wisdom and Hoja's subsequent journey of repentance and redemption. The film concludes by cutting back to Effendi, Burhan, and Hamid, who is still flying the kite. Hamid insists that the power of his man-made kite is mightier than God's bird. Effendi explains to Hamid that his kite flies only because it is attached to a tether and is reliant on the violent winds that lift it. Effendi proclaims that kites do not have freedom like birds and likens man-made creations to "violence and chains." The scene ends with Hamid losing control of the kite. As it tumbles away, the black bird continues to fly.

Inshallah promotes piety as vital to societal well-being and impiety as a looming threat. Hamid, who embodies communist ideology, references a godless society. His use of "comrades" to describe his progressive associates reinforces his connection to communist regimes like the Soviet Union. The film equates atheism with communism, casting belief in God as a direct counterforce to communist ideology. By representing Hamid as the antagonist, it functions as both religious and anticommunist propaganda, aligning spiritual devotion with political resistance. By incorporating Arabic phrases such as "Inshallah" and "Allahu Akbar," *Inshallah* invokes Islam as both a cultural and a moral cornerstone. It frames religious devotion as essential to national unity and progress and casts communism as a foreign threat to both. In doing so, it merges religion with a nationalist vision, positioning Islam as integral to the defense and identity of the nation.

While *Inshallah* grounds its ideological message in the moral authority of religion and the dangers of a godless society, *The Emperor's Elephant* turns its attention to the geopolitical terrain, where the preservation of national stability hinges on the strength of alliances. Where *Inshallah* emphasizes the internal unity of a nation rooted in spiritual devotion, *The Emperor's Elephant* frames external cooperation—particularly with the United States—as essential for a collective defense against communist aggression. Together, these films construct a twofold logic of Cold War propaganda: one that fuses religious and nationalist values at home and another that promotes international alliances as a bulwark against ideological and military threats abroad.

The Emperor's Elephant opens inside a coffeehouse, where Hamid voices vehement complaints about the government's alliances. To counter Hamid's perspective, Effendi regales him with a Nasreddin Hoja story aimed at dispelling his misconceptions. The scene cuts to a tale about an elephant owned by Emperor Tamerlane that instills fear and wreaks havoc on a village, trampling innocent people. The villagers eventually realize that hiding indoors is futile, and they unite to construct barriers to shield themselves from the menacing creature. The film addresses the imperative for a collective defense against common adversaries, conveying the necessity of forming an alliance with the United States to safeguard Turkey from potential threats posed by its Soviet neighbor. By emphasizing the benefits of unified action over solitary efforts, the film assuages concerns about the newfound alliance, presenting diplomacy as a valuable national asset rather than a liability. By adapting the tale, the USIS employs a familiar narrative framework so that the Western alliance does not evoke a sense of trepidation. Effendi's statement, "When people—or countries—make plans together for their mutual defense, each one of them is protected by the strength of all against the evils and dangers of the world," highlights the advantages derived from collaborative efforts and emphasizes the collective shield provided by alliances in the face of communist threats.

In the original Turkish tale, the narrative is different, positing that collective action rooted in free will is impracticable because of the unpredictability of the masses. In that version, the villagers agree to unite with Nasreddin Hoja in petitioning Tamerlane for assistance. However, Hoja finds himself isolated and disheartened in the denouement. Consequently, he astutely beseeches the emperor to dispatch additional elephants to the village, contending that the villagers have expressed elation regarding the one previously dispatched. The discrepancy between the Turkish the USIS versions of this tale supports the argument that modernization manifests as a shared theme with different operational nuances in the transnational network of institutions engaged in diplomacy.

The USIS's Nasreddin Hoja films are examples of film diplomacy, as they employ a cultural icon to advance strategic alliances while simultaneously shaping perceptions to further US interests. Yet by omitting the proper names of countries in the Middle East, which is predominantly populated by Muslims, the Hoja series generalizes the cultures, customs, and ways of life within these communities. This omission is indicative of how the films generate oversimplifications. In a letter discussing the films, a USIS agent raised concerns over the use of Turkish cultural stories for American propaganda and acknowledged potential objections from Middle Eastern and South Asian audiences, who might view the films as exploiting their cultural heritage.[94] This cautionary note indicates the ethical complexities within the communication network. The Hoja films showed the central character and the community as marionettes, controlled by strings from above. The use of the puppets thus opens the films up to an alternative reading—that the USIS assumed the role of the puppet master, orchestrating the manipulation of public opinion—pointing to the ethical dilemmas woven into these films, in which cultural figures became pawns in the pursuit of propaganda.

Soviet-era Russian films featuring Nasreddin Hoja present a striking counterpoint and further illuminate the ideological malleability of cultural figures. In films like *Nasreddin in Bukhara* (Yakov Protazonav, 1943), *The Adventures of Nasreddin* (Gabi Nabi Ganiyev, 1946), *Nasreddin v Hodzhente* (1959), *Nasreddin in Khujand* (Erazm Karamyan and Hamo Beck-Nazaryan, 1959), and *The Return of Hoja Nasreddin* (1989), Hoja remains a clever challenger of authority but aligns with Soviet values: antielitism, secularism, and revolutionary ideals.[95] These films represent the working class as morally superior, critique religious institutions, and expose capitalist hypocrisy. In these films, Soviet whiteness functions as a superpower identity—one that casts itself simultaneously as a liberator and a developer.[96] As noted earlier in my discussion of the USIS marionette films, Nasreddin Hoja proved to be a pliable screen figure for modernization narratives. The Soviet case shows that this flexibility persisted even under a radically different ideological program. That Hoja could serve pro-religious, anticommunist messaging in the US context and secular, revolutionary messaging in the Soviet one underscores the power of film diplomacy: on screen, Hoja could be mobilized to legitimize entirely opposing state projects.

The US films vilify atheism and uphold religion as a necessity (e.g., in the USIS Hoja films *Inshallah* and *Hoja and the Thief*), whereas the Soviet films do the opposite, depicting religion as a detriment that holds society back. The Soviet representation illustrates a capitalist society founded on hypocrisy and deceit, where religious undertones serve as a façade to mask the immorality of the ruling elites who subjugate the laboring class.[97] Gender is also a central site of ideological contrast. Soviet Hoja films frequently represent women as victims of patriarchal religious traditions—particularly within Islamic societies—casting them as harem-bound, sexualized subjects in need of liberation.[98] These representations function as orientalist critiques of religion and tradition and as justifications for Soviet interventionism framed as emancipation. In doing so, these films aim to teach local populations that their history, tradition, and religion should elicit feelings of shame, thereby encouraging them to align with the Soviet ideology.[99] The Soviet use of Hoja also aligns with internal minority policies in ethnically segregated Central Asia. By reconfiguring Hoja into a nonreligious, streetwise trickster—a charming rogue who critiques authority while embodying socialist virtues—Soviet filmmakers have transformed a culturally specific figure into a model for the idealized Soviet citizen.[100]

Soviet films featuring the Hoja character offer a starkly contrasting vision of modernization compared to their American counterparts. While both draw on a familiar oriental trickster figure to challenge authority, the Soviet films promote a pro-working-class, antireligious ideology that critiques Western capitalism and positions revolutionaries as agents of social progress. Religion is depicted as an instrument of elite oppression, with liberation tied to secularism and class struggle. In this context, Soviet whiteness operates as a civilizing force—a superpower identity that frames itself as both liberator and modernizer. By contrast, the American Hoja films present communism as a threat to Muslims in the Middle East, advancing a USIS-driven ideology in which Islam is seen as compatible with democracy—provided it adheres to a specific mold. The flexibility of whiteness in both contexts—cast alternately as secular and religious or revolutionary and reformist—underscores its instrumental role in Cold War film diplomacy. The Hoja figure thus becomes a site of ideological projection, repurposed to serve competing global agendas under the banner of modernization.

From USIS Operations to Careers in Diplomacy, Public Relations, and Film

To establish the US-Turkey communication network, a group of institutional agents forged their paths across diplomacy, public relations, and the film industry. Among these figures, Monteagle Stearns, Sadun Katipoğlu, and Suha Arın were instrumental in developing and navigating this transnational network. Stearns functioned as an architect whose career trajectory continued to influence foreign relations.[101] Katipoğlu, a pioneering woman in public relations, broke barriers in a male-dominated field. Arın, a visionary filmmaker, produced documentaries about social issues in Turkey. All three, through their unique roles, left legacies in the network's fabric and contributed to the fields of film, education, and diplomacy.

As the USIS film affairs officer, Stearns organized film exhibitions, built collaborations with MNET, and worked with American Protestant missionaries to bring films to Turkish audiences.[102] In addition to developing USIS film operations in Turkey, he oversaw the budget for the EFC. His work with film led him to become a career diplomat, affording him the opportunity to engage with every Turkish president from the 1950s through the 2000s, thereby highlighting the contemporary impact of the US-sponsored film program in bolstering foreign relations with Turkey. Spanning over four decades, Stearns's career in foreign service saw him navigate the complexities of global diplomacy as the US ambassador to Greece and Ivory Coast.[103] His trajectory demonstrates how Cold War media initiatives not only shaped cultural relations but also cultivated career diplomats with regional expertise.

The US-Turkey communication network also played a significant role in advancing women's careers in public diplomacy. During the early 1950s, Sadun Katipoğlu, a Turkish woman who had graduated from Istanbul's Robert College (a school founded by American Protestant missionaries), became director of USIS-Turkey Cinema Services. Her involvement with the USIS propelled her career trajectory, leading her to work as the director of the Turkish American University Association and the Alumnae Association for the American College for Girls (later known as the Robert College Alumni Association).[104] Throughout her career, she facilitated communication, welcomed international visitors, served as a translator, and garnered visibility and experience in public relations. In recognition of her outstanding representation of Turkey abroad, she became the first woman to receive a prize from the Public Relations Foundation of Turkey (Türk Tanıtma Vakfı).[105] Her career reflects the symbiotic connection between the USIS and the American Board of Commissioners for Foreign Missions in Turkey, which fostered an environment that empowered multilingual women to excel in the realms of public relations and communication.[106]

The US-Turkey communication network also left an important mark on the trajectory of acclaimed documentary filmmaker Suha Arın. After his time at the EFC, he received an invitation to work for Voice of America, an agency affiliated with the USIS, and left law school in Turkey to pursue film studies at Howard University in Washington, D.C., ultimately earning a degree in film directing in 1965. He then pursued a master's degree in mass communications, specializing in government and public information, at American University. While studying, Arın held positions as a projectionist and a sound recorder at the Capital Film Laboratory in Washington, D.C. From 1967 to 1973, he served as a translating speaker and interviewer at the Voice of America. When television broadcasting debuted in Turkey, Arın became a correspondent in Washington, D.C., for Turkish Radio and

Television (TRT). Acting as the communication bridge between the USIS and TRT, Arın prepared radio programs that catered to Turkish audiences. In addition to his radio responsibilities, between 1969 and 1973 he disseminated USIS news films to Turkish audiences and covered significant events such as the 1969 moon landing. His education and work experience in the United States shaped his films when he went back to Turkey, leading him to produce documentaries.

Beyond his pioneering work as a documentary filmmaker, Arın's legacy lies in his enduring impact on film education. Teaching at various universities for over forty years, he fostered a community of filmmakers and scholars, solidifying his position as a foundational figure in Turkish cinema. He produced a remarkable body of documentaries from 1964 to 2000, shaped by his commitment to documenting social issues and preserving Turkey's history.

Arın's documentaries addressed social justice and labor conditions. His first educational film, *Yayalar için Trafik Emniyeti* (Traffic safety for pedestrians, 1964), aimed to shape public behavior amid modernization and exemplified EFC's interest in public health and the national economy.[107] He later explored a range of pressing topics: *Gurur* (Pride, 1968), a television film supporting a Black organization called Pride; *Sessiz Emekçiler* (Silent toil, 1974), which exposed the struggles of forestry workers excluded from social security; *Kaygı Kuyuları* (Wells of worry, 1975), on perilous working conditions of miners in the Zonguldak coal mines; *Affın Ardından* (After the amnesty, 1974), on former prisoners who returned to incarcertation; *Bir Yuva Dağılıyor* (Turned out of their nest, 1975), on the upheaval experienced by orphans in Ankara; and *Tahtacı Fatma* (Fatma of the forest, 1979), which followed the dreams and struggles of young Fatma, a member of the nomadic Tahtacı subgroup of the Alevite community in the Toros Mountains.[108]

Arın dedicated significant energy to cultural preservation. Films such as *Midas'ın Dünyası* (The world of Midas, 1975), *Safranbolu'da Zaman* (Safranbolu: Reflections of time, 1976), *Urartu'nun İki Mevsimi* (Two seasons of Urartu, 1977), and *Likya'nın Sönmeyen Ateşi* (The eternal flame of Lycia, 1977) explored the country's ancient civilizations, archaeological landscape, and artistic heritage. His oeuvre also included influential figures like the composer Cemal Reşit Rey and founding President of the Turkish Republic of Northern Cyprus Rauf Denktaş.

Arın's films, imbued with themes of equality, democracy, liberalism, and social justice, undoubtedly resonated with Cold War liberal ideals. His films stand as a testament to his own artistic and intellectual agency, reflecting the collective creative spirit of his collaborators and the interplay of political, socioeconomic, and cultural forces within both Turkey and US-Turkish relations. As noted by the educator İlhan Özdil (founder of the Education Department at the Middle East Technical University and the undersecretary of technical education in Turkey), motion pictures during this period assumed a dualistic function, serving as both powerful tools for pedagogical dissemination and vehicles for ideological messaging. He captures this by stating that film acts as a multifaceted instrument, simultaneously capturing social realities as a documentary, conveying societal messages as propaganda, embodying the visual language of society, and contributing creatively to the fabric of social life.[109]

The US-Turkey communication network was not solely the product of bureaucratic directives; it was also created by the intertwined trajectories of individuals. Among these threads, Monteagle Stearns, Sadun Katipoğlu, and Suha Arın stand out, their careers highlighting the impact of individual agency on public and international relations. As a Cold War diplomat, Stearns built bridges through film and influenced leaders across the globe for decades. A pioneering woman in public relations and an alumna of a missionary-founded school in Turkey, Katipoğlu shattered barriers and served both national and international communities. Arın, a social justice documentarian shaped by experiences in the United States, became the father of documentary film in Turkey. Stearns, Katipoğlu, and Arın, each making unique contributions, stand as testaments to the power of individual agency and the impact of media infrastructures on their careers. Rather than a rigid structure, the network was a dynamic ecosystem, one animated by individual agency and transnational collaboration.

In summary, the USIS developed a sophisticated media infrastructure in Turkey, collaborating with ministries, missionaries, educators, and creatives to produce, distribute, and exhibit films. This process included establishing regional film centers, rebranding imported content, training Turkish personnel, and generating localized media that aligned with US foreign policy. While Americans retained control over funding and messaging, the long-term objective was to transfer operational responsibilities to Turkish institutions. The USIS's aims were to secure an alliance with

Turkey, cultivate pro-American sentiment, and promote aid initiatives. Its films framed the United States as a beacon of modernization and Turkey as a frontline ally in the Cold War.

Whether promoting economic productivity or using figures like Nasreddin Hoja to foster cooperation and anticommunism sentiments, USIS films were far more than educational tools. They were curated narratives crafted to shape Turkish perceptions of the United States. The USIS exerted control over what was seen and how it was interpreted, blurring the lines between education and propaganda. While presenting itself as a champion of democracy, the agency employed censorship and selective distribution to advance strategic objectives—raising questions about the boundaries of film diplomacy and traversing a minefield of ethical concerns.

4
The Educational Film Center of Turkey

While I showed film diplomacy as the strategic use of film to influence foreign publics in the previous chapter, I reframe it here as a domestic tool of governance. In the context of Turkish educational cinema, film diplomacy operated as both a transnational strategy and a technology of internal rule—a mechanism for managing difference, regulating visibility and audibility, and instilling ideological conformity under the guise of care, education, and modernization. I argue that the Turkish state used educational films not only to instruct but also to control—crafting a national audiovisual pedagogy that coded secularism, linguistic homogeneity, and whiteness as normative. This inward-facing mode of film diplomacy materialized through state-media infrastructures like the Educational Film Center (EFC), which operationalized modernization through audiovisual techniques aimed at managing citizens' bodies, beliefs, and behaviors. In this framework, film diplomacy becomes a form of governance through not only the circulation of cultural capital but also the production of normative subjecthood within Turkey's modernization project.

Produced by the EFC and cosponsored by the Ministry of Health (Sağlık Bakanlığı) and Social Assistance and the General Directorate of Human Population Planning (Nüfus Planlaması Genel Müdürlüğü), *Elif'in Çilesi* (The suffering of Elif, Ayhan Eyikan, 1966) features a mobile unit that brings government officials to a rural village to deliver information sessions on family planning. Narrated in standardized Istanbul Turkish by a male voice-over, the film presents the government official Cemil Bey addressing a group of men beneath a tree, holding up a certificate from the Directorate of Religious Affairs to affirm that contraception is permissible in Islam. Indoors in a classroom, Kamuran Hanım instructs a group of women on the dangers of unsafe abortion—citing tools like wire, knitting needles, and borage seed—while using chalkboard diagrams and visual aids to explain the safe use of oral contraceptives and intrauterine devices. Although she presents contraception as safe and accessible, she declares abortion a sin and insists that once pregnancy occurs, women are morally obligated to give birth.[1]

To reinforce this message, the film juxtaposes the fates of two couples—Elif and Mustafa, and Ayşe and Hasan (played by the actors Baykal Saran, Ilkay Saran, Elçin Şanal, and Oytun Şanal, respectively), some of whom speak in standardized Istanbul Turkish in the film. Elif, already exhausted from raising six children, begs her husband to consider contraception, but Mustafa insists that divine providence will suffice (figure 4.1). In contrast,

FIGURE 4.1 Mustafa and his family having dinner in *Elif'in Çilesi* (1966).

Source: Educational Information Network of Turkey, Photograph Archive of the Ministry of National Education of Turkey, General Directorate of Innovation and Educational Technologies.

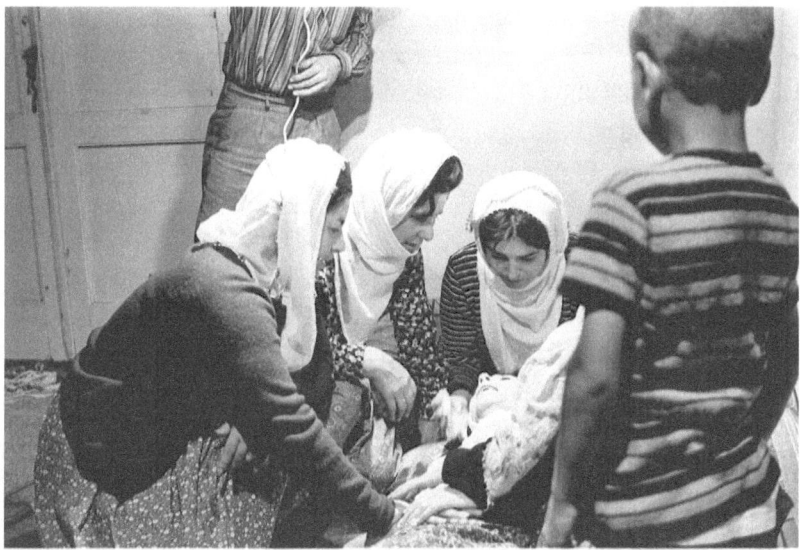

FIGURE 4.2 Elif lying down in pain, surrounded by women and a child in *Elif'in Çilesi*.

Source: Educational Information Network of Turkey, Photograph Archive of the Ministry of National Education of Turkey, General Directorate of Innovation and Educational Technologies.

Ayşe and Hasan agree to delay having another child until their daughter enters school, and Ayşe responsibly consults a doctor. When Elif becomes pregnant again and undergoes a dangerous abortion, she dies—a fate foreshadowed by the state's warnings (figure 4.2). Meanwhile, Ayşe's planned pregnancy affirms the film's central message: Responsible contraception, when practiced in accordance with state-sanctioned norms, protects both family and nation.

Combining public health education with moral instruction, *Elif'in Çilesi* exemplifies how mid-century Turkish educational cinema functioned as a tool of state ideology, advancing narratives of reproductive responsibility in service of modernization. Though framed as a pragmatic intervention, the film reveals biopolitical anxieties: By describing abortion as both sinful and deadly, it constructs reproductive autonomy as a threat to the social order and to economic stability.[2] *Elif'in Çilesi* enforces a state-sanctioned view—folding religious authority into the mechanism of population management, creating both a moral obligation and a patriotic duty.

Produced shortly after the passage of Turkey's 1965 population planning law, *Elif'in Çilesi* embodies the state's shift from pronatalist policies to controlled reproduction. This first population control law allowed the sale, distribution, and utilization of contraceptive methods and promoted family planning education.[3] Earlier laws criminalized abortion and restricted contraceptives to stimulate population growth: In 1926, Turkish criminal law banned abortion while the Public Health Law of 1930 criminalized the importation, production, and sale of contraceptives (excluding condoms).[4] These measures sought to stimulate demographic expansion in the early republican era. However, by the mid-twentieth century, rapid population growth had begun to strain economic and social infrastructures, prompting a new demographic policy focused on controlled reproduction. Educational films like *Elif'in Çilesi* thus became key tools for communicating this vision of national development to rural and urban publics.

Linked to these demographic shifts, *Elif'in Çilesi* illuminates the racialized and class-based dimensions of Turkish modernization. Influenced by European eugenic thought—particularly German models—Turkish policymakers and physicians promoted population control as a national improvement project. Turkish eugenicists, primarily composed of doctors educated in Europe, influenced the state's policies and public discourse.[5] They argued that human bodies were the nation's most valuable capital, and they advocated their management to increase national wealth.[6] In a move to alleviate economic burdens, the Turkish government embraced eugenics in two ways: It used incentives and competitions such as the Gürbüz Çocuk Yarışmaları (Sturdy Child Competitions) to encourage individuals who were considered genetically superior to procreate, and it limited reproduction by implementing measures such as premarital exams, birth control, and marriage restrictions for those with illnesses (e.g., syphilis, gonorrhea, leprosy, and tuberculosis) and disabilities.[7] Unlike Germany, Turkey did not resort to extreme measures like forced sterilization (outlawed in 1936). However, Turkish eugenicists admired Germany's authoritative racial hygiene policies, especially their emphasis on premarital health exams and education in hygiene, reproduction, and childcare.[8] They framed marriage and reproduction as patriotic duties essential to the nation's future,[9] but their endorsements were selective: They discouraged certain unions in the name of maintaining racial hygiene and reinforcing ideals of whiteness critical to the modernization project. *Elif'in Çilesi* and films like it demonstrate how educational cinema became entangled with ideologies of whiteness, modernization, and developmentalist governance. Rather than simply transmitting public health information, they functioned as technologies of governance, producing bodies disciplined by ideals of health, economic utility, and moral citizenship.

As I demonstrate in this chapter, *Elif'in Çilesi* is not an isolated case but part of a broader strategy in which educational films functioned as instruments of governance—controlling bodies, regulating difference, and advancing a homogenized vision of modernization aligned with secular, Sunni Muslim, and ethnically Turkish norms. Between 1952 and 1986, a network of institutions in Turkey produced thousands of educational films. At the center of this network was the EFC, a prominent institution responsible for creating, exhibiting, and disseminating media throughout the country (figure 4.3). In this chapter, I offer a history of the center and analyze how educational film became a tool for modernization efforts in Turkey. The EFC, later renamed the Educational Film, Radio, and Television Center of Turkey (EFRTC, Film-Radyo ve Televizyonla Eğitim Merkezi),

FIGURE 4.3 *Educational Film, Radio, and Television Center of Turkey*

Source: Educational Information Network of Turkey, Photograph Archive of the Ministry of National Education of Turkey, General Directorate of Innovation and Educational Technologies.

operated under the auspices of the Ministry of National Education of Turkey (MNET), forging collaborations with the US Information Service (USIS, Amerikan Haberler Merkezi or American News Center) and the United Nations Educational, Scientific, and Cultural Organization (UNESCO).[10] Alongside the EFC, commercial entities such as *Film ve Öğretim* (Film and education magazine), Mataş, Bell & Howell–Gaumont, and Teknik Kitabevi (Technical Bookstore) contributed to the circulation and promotion of educational films and related technologies.

I argue that educational films, while framed as instruments of care, education, and national unity, systematically erased minority languages, regional accents, non-Sunni religious expressions, and non-Turkish identities—positioning them not as part of the national fabric but as deficiencies to be corrected, assimilated, or effaced—enforcing a homogenized vision of citizenship within the audiovisual and ideological contours of state-led modernization. The EFC produced thousands of films across subjects ranging from agriculture and health to geography, history, economics, and military training. In this context, film diplomacy emerges not as a tool of foreign persuasion but as a domestic instrument of governance—determining who is seen, who is heard, and who is granted legibility within the ideological framework of the Turkish Republic.

In this chapter, I identify the key institutional agents who helped construct Turkey's educational film culture: Şinasi Barutçu, an award-winning Turkish painter, photographer, teacher, director of the EFC, and USIS-sponsored author; Adolphe Hübl, a UNESCO agent from Austria; Monteagle Stearns, a USIS film affairs officer; and Mahmut Özdeniz, the owner and editor of *Film ve Öğretim*. Through an analysis of their activities, I demonstrate how transmission channels within this network operated multidirectionally, mutually influencing one another as they circulated information and propaganda serving both national and transnational objectives. Educational films, shaped by these collaborations, functioned as strategic tools to advance Turkey's modernization project.

Initiated under the leadership of Mustafa Kemal Atatürk, Turkey's modernization campaign sought to transform the country into a modern, secular republic. These efforts are evident in reforms such as the adoption of the Latin alphabet to increase literacy, the democratization of institutions and the expansion of civil liberties, the liberalization of the economy to attract foreign investment, the secularization of the state through the abolition of the caliphate and the separation of religion and governance, and the advancement of women's rights, including suffrage and expanded access to education. Western models provided the basis for many of these reforms: For example, the French legal system served as the template for Turkey's administrative law governing public service, property, and economic enterprises.[11] While Atatürk's reforms expanded institutional access and facilitated economic development, they also entrenched exclusions along linguistic, ethnic, racial, sexual, and religious lines.[12] This contradiction between modernization's promise of national progress and its systematic exclusions was not an aberration but a foundational logic of Turkish modernization, one that film diplomacy helped to produce, perform, and legitimize.

Film Diplomacy and Commercial Interests: The Role of *Film ve Öğretim*

The entwinement of the Turkish government's modernization agenda with the publishing industry's promotion of educational technologies highlights the compatibility of film diplomacy with private commercial interests. This relationship underscores the appeal of US-led liberalism to Turkish elites during this period. As the state aimed to modernize its institutions and educate its citizenry, commercial sponsorship emerged as a pivotal force shaping educational media initiatives. These political, economic, and infrastructural considerations show a reconfiguration of the state's role: Modernization was no longer a purely governmental project but one increasingly intertwined with private actors eager to participate in and profit from the modernization narrative. Film diplomacy thus provided a strategic channel where national aspirations and commercial ambitions could align, facilitating the diffusion of educational technologies while reinforcing the notion that progress was best achieved through public-private collaboration.

One of the earliest and most visible expressions of this public-private convergence was the founding of *Film ve Öğretim*. Launched in December 1950, the magazine's inaugural issue offered a compelling exposition of its mission. The editorial emphasized cinema's modern potential as an educational tool capable of captivating audiences across sectors including medicine, forestry, engineering, and science.[13] While acknowledging the commercial success of entertainment films, the editorial's writers argued that cinema's educational advantages remained largely untapped, particularly in a country like Turkey, where low literacy rates hampered modernization. They presented cinema as a powerful instrument for enhancing public knowledge and advancing the state's reformist aims.

At the same time, the editorial's writers grounded their mission in an explicitly nationalist ethos. Fostering a profound love for the nation, they argued, required more than platonic affection; it demanded deep knowledge of Turkey's geography, history, and cultural wealth. They criticized the public's limited awareness of their own country's awe-inspiring wonders and attributed this gap to the commercial film industry's focus on entertainment over education. Advocating a shift away from capitalist profit-seeking toward a more civic-minded use of media, they envisioned a new model in which film agencies produced educational cinema in service of the public good.

This ambition for an educational transformation extended beyond content to the very structure of the film industry itself. The editorial writers proposed partnerships between professional filmmakers and emerging amateur talent, emphasizing that many educational filmmakers, including those affiliated with the EFC, began their careers with little to no prior experience. Figures such as Cahit Ünsalan, Suha Arın, and Şinasi Barutçu exemplified this trajectory: Recruited to the EFC without formal film training, they learned filmmaking through their production of educational films. When Suha Arın, for instance, was approached to direct *Yayalar için Trafik Emniyeti* (Traffic safety for pedestrians, 1964), he openly admitted his lack of directing experience but embraced the challenge.[14]

Although the inaugural editorial framed educational film as a vehicle for national uplift, a closer examination of the magazine's eleven issues indicates an entanglement of civic idealism with commercial imperatives. Even as the magazine championed educational films for public good, it was deeply enmeshed in commercial enterprise. It promoted educational media technologies, using film's association with modernization to advance private commercial interests.

This tension between public mission and commercial imperatives surfaced in 1951 when *Film ve Öğretim* published a critical article lamenting the government's failure to enforce Law 3122 (Öğretici ve Teknik Filmler Hakkında Kanun).[15] Originally passed in 1937, the law required movie theaters to screen educational films before their features.[16] The editorial writers, uncertain of the law's origins, called it a "magical law" and expressed frustration that the government did not strongly enforce it and that educational films were screened only at the whim of the theater operators.[17] Law 3122 was designed to integrate educational cinema into everyday civic life—positioning film as a central tool of public pedagogy and national development. Yet the government's unwillingness to enforce the law reveals a limited commitment to realizing these goals. Instead, the law functioned as a symbolic gesture—a performative expression of modernization designed to signal alignment with global norms of media governance and public enlightenment. This ambivalence underscores the gap between the aspirational rhetoric of modern educational reform and the institutional failures that undermined its consistent implementation. The regulatory vacuum also highlights how power over exhibition ultimately rested with private theater owners—who likely catered to audience preferences, as state-sponsored educational films were often viewed as overly didactic, propagandistic, and unappealing in a commercial entertainment setting.

In the absence of consistent state enforcement, commercial actors increasingly stepped in to shape the infrastructure of educational media—blurring the line between civic pedagogy and market imperatives and playing an influential role in circulating modernization discourses. Commercial partnerships became even more prominent through the magazine's alliances with local distributors. *Film ve Öğretim* operated as a strategic intermediary between commercial interests and state-driven modernization efforts. Owned and edited by Mahmut Özdeniz, it prominently featured products from Teknik Kitabevi (Technical Bookstore), a company specializing in technical books and educational films imported from Europe and the United States. Teknik Kitabevi operated a film library known as Teknik Kitabevi Film Servisi (Technical Bookstore Film Services) that rented and sold educational films—sourced from institutions such as Encyclopaedia Britannica Ltd.'s Film Division and United World Films—on subjects such as biology, physics, zoology, and geography. In addition, the company supplied mobile units, projectors, amplifiers, and related equipment. Its advertisements, which appeared regularly in *Film ve Öğretim*, emphasized the flexibility of film screenings in settings such as schools, homes, and clubs, further embedding commercial products into the discourse of modernization in Turkey.

Teknik Kitabevi imported films from Gaumont-British (G. B.) Equipments and used *Film ve Öğretim* to advertise Bell & Howell–Gaumont film equipment, solidifying its role as the primary distributor of audiovisual media for public sales locations in Turkey.[18] In 1950, Özdeniz, the magazine's editor, visited the renowned G. B. Film Library in London—then considered Europe's largest film archive.[19] His trip was sponsored by Mataş, a company based in Istanbul that served as the official representative for Bell & Howell–Gaumont in Turkey and also imported goods from the American company Hoover. Mataş's sponsorship extended beyond financial backing: It used *Film ve Öğretim* as a venue to promote its media equipment, particularly projectors and educational films produced by G. B. and Bell & Howell. Özdeniz's visit to the G. B. Film Library enabled Turkish readers to acquire insights into European film preservation and educational practices, reinforcing transnational connections vital to the development of Turkey's educational media infrastructure.

In 1951, the reciprocal nature of these collaborations was evident when Özdeniz and Sermet Baykurt, the manager of Mataş in Ankara, were visited by Mr. Allen, an enthusiastic young businessman working for the foreign services of the G. B. Film Library, whom Özdeniz had met during his trip to London.[20] During their meeting, Özdeniz sought to learn about the use of educational films in English schools and discovered that many schools screened films from the G. B. Film Library in their classrooms. This exchange of information highlighted the educational potential of films and the progressive practices employed in England. Recognizing the significance of educational films as a symbol of progress in the West, Turkish agents embarked on a mission to embrace the medium as part of their modernization agenda. In point of fact, MNET agents also met with Mr. Allen.[21] These encounters illustrate how private commercial interests, state modernization goals, and Western influence coalesced around the educational film sector.

Film ve Öğretim and other affiliated Turkish companies emerged in the wake of Atatürk's modernization reforms, which had influenced media operations within the publishing industry. One critical example is the 1928 alphabet reform, which replaced the Ottoman (Perso-Arabic) script with a Latin-based Turkish alphabet to make the language more accessible and to raise literacy rates. While the reform aligned with broader modernization goals, it created significant challenges for the publishing sector, which was forced to overhaul its "technological infrastructure to adjust the new lettering system."[22] This costly transition increased media producers' dependence on government support, thereby expanding the state's influence over media content.[23] Although it remains unclear whether *Film ve Öğretim* received direct financial backing from the government, the magazine advocated state investment in educational film, publishing articles that urged government agents to establish a national film institute.[24]

Film ve Öğretim urged the government to make strategic investments in infrastructure to harness the transformative potential of educational films for Turkish-language speakers.[25] It aimed to create a society of well-informed citizens and transform Turkey into a modern nation, and to this end, its writers explored educational film trends, state-of-the-art media technologies, and renowned film institutions from the United States, the United Kingdom, France, Switzerland, and the Netherlands. For example, they highlighted the instrumental role played by national documentary cultures such as those in the United Kingdom and the United States in educating mass audiences, attributing their achievements to institutions like the British Film Center and the American Film Center, respectively. By presenting these Western models, they underscored the urgent need for Turkey to establish its own film institute and library. Such institutions, they argued, would serve as the cornerstone for creating a vibrant film culture centered on education. The magazine's vision was clear: Through strategic investments in educational film infrastructure, Turkey could empower its citizens, tackle agricultural challenges, curb the spread of diseases, and propel the nation into a dynamic and progressive future.

Beyond textual promotion of educational film, *Film ve Öğretim* participated in the visual construction of modernization through its cover imagery. These images did more than advertise technology; they also projected a vision of national progress aligned with global models of audiovisual education, particularly those emanating from the United States. In this visual economy, film projectors, microphones, and classroom scenes symbolized Turkey's entry into a modern, technologically mediated world. At the same time, the covers' racial representations—emphasizing whiteness as normative and racialized figures as performers—evoke the ideological structures underpinning Turkey's modernization discourse.

Reflecting the ambition to modernize education through media, the magazine's cover images featured children alongside film projectors and microphones—symbols of global technological progress. Through these photographs, *Film ve Öğretim* promoted a vision of global culture infused with the promise that media technologies would modernize Turkey's educational landscape. However, these images lacked context, with no explanation of who these children were, where they were, and why they were photographed. Given Turkish publishers' tendency to incorporate content from American periodicals, it is likely that these images were sourced from American publications. In this way, *Film ve Öğretim*—alongside Hollywood films—served as a conduit for introducing Turkish audiences to American cultural ideals, including the narrative of the "American dream" that permeated the postwar period.

The cover of the magazine's inaugural issue exemplifies this visual rhetoric. It shows a classroom filled with students, their backs turned to the viewer and their gazes fixed on a film projected above a chalkboard (figure 4.4).[26] A beam of light from a projector illuminates the screen,

FIGURE 4.4 *Film ve Öğretim* cover, 1950.

Source: *Film ve Öğretim*, no. 1 (1950). National Library of Turkey, Ankara.

THE EDUCATIONAL FILM CENTER OF TURKEY 149

bathing the classroom in a glow that signals both wonder and technological authority. Overseeing the students is a male teacher. The students and teacher are shown without visible racial markers; this blankness constructs an implicit racelessness, positioning whiteness as the invisible norm of learning, progress, and modern citizenship.

Later covers introduce a different visual logic, featuring children of racially marked backgrounds engaged in performing roles. The third issue, published in February 1951, showcases a girl who appears to be East Asian standing beside a movie projector, microphone in hand, looking away from the camera (figure 4.5).[27] Another example appears on the combined sixth and seventh issue (May–June 1951), where a Black boy smiles while

FIGURE 4.5 *Film ve Öğretim* cover, February 1951.

Source: *Film ve Öğretim*, no. 3 (1951). National Library of Turkey, Ankara.

FIGURE 4.6 *Film ve Öğretim* cover, May–June 1951.

Source: *Film ve Öğretim*, no. 6–7 (1951). National Library of Turkey, Ankara.

holding a microphone and leaning toward a film projector (figure 4.6).[28] His gaze, also averted from the camera, suggests the realm of projected futures made possible through cinematic technology. Across these issues, nonwhite children are positioned as performers of modernization, while whiteness continues to operate as the unmarked standard of educational progress. Educational technologies are marketed not as neutral tools but as instruments for embedding global racial hierarchies within Turkey's modernization project.

This visual distinction between racially unmarked learners and racialized performers indicates a logic of representation structured by whiteness. By portraying nonwhite children as icons of technological promise—figures whose value emerges through visible, staged interaction with media— *Film ve Öğretim* reproduced global hierarchies that positioned whiteness as the invisible benchmark of modern subjecthood. In these images, whiteness signifies the normative condition of rational, autonomous citizenship, while racialized figures occupy the periphery of modernization—granted symbolic entry but denied full belonging. This representation mirrors Cold War development discourses, in which technological advancement is framed as a universal good, although access to its social and civic benefits remained racially coded. Thus, even as Turkish modernization projects celebrated audiovisual technologies as signs of national progress, they also internalized and reproduced global structures of racialization—rendering whiteness visible only in its invisibility and racialized subjects in their proximity to modernization.

At the heart of these representations lies the symbolic power of educational technologies—microphones, film projectors, and classroom films—as markers of global influence and authority. Microphones symbolize amplified power, enabling teachers or other figures of authority to transmit knowledge across distances and break down barriers of space and communication. This shift from oral to technologically mediated pedagogy reflects a transformation in educational practices. Film projectors and classroom films signify the movement from static, text-based learning to dynamic audiovisual instruction, offering multisensory experiences that both captivated students' attention and made complex concepts more accessible. These technologies, embedded within the magazine's visual and textual rhetoric, were central to the agenda *Film ve Öğretim* was promoting: to integrate media into educational spaces and position Turkey as a nation poised to join the global ranks of technologically advanced modern states.

Another image featured in *Film ve Öğretim* hints at Turkey's desire to project itself as a modern and Western-aligned nation during the Korean War. The magazine devoted a full page to *Kore'den Geliyorum* (I am coming from Korea, Nurullah Tilgen, 1951), a film showcasing the role of Turkish veterans in the conflict.[29] Produced by *Film ve Öğretim*, it was likely the first Turkish film in a series about the Korean War. Although the magazine provided few details about the film's narrative, it emphasized that the production had undergone laboratory and dubbing services in Turkey and would soon be screened nationwide. The accompanying photograph from the film set—a citizen shaking hands with a Turkish veteran (figure 4.7)—visually

FIGURE 4.7 Citizen shaking a veteran's hand in *Kore'den Geliyorum* (1951).

Source: "16mm Mevzulu Bir Film Cekiliyor," *Film ve Ogretim*, no. 10–11 (1951–1952): 7. National Library of Turkey, Ankara.

celebrates the veteran as a symbol of national pride, appealing to nationalist sentiments while eliding the brutal realities of war.

Turkish government agents used films like *Kore'den Geliyorum* to promote Turkey's image abroad, particularly in the United States. These Korean War films sought to challenge the lingering "Terrible Turk" stereotype and instead present Turkey as a modern, democratic, and heroic American ally. Participation in the Korean War—and its cinematic representation—became a critical means by which Turkish officials attempted to assert Turkey's status as a progressive nation aligned with Western ideals. These films thus played a strategic role in shaping the emerging communication networks between Turkey and the United States during the early Cold War.

The Turkish Directorate General of Press-Publication and Tourism (Basın-Yayın ve Turizm Genel Müdürlüğü) used the Korean War to enhance Turkey's global image and stimulate tourism.[30] For example, it collaborated with the New York News Bureau to screen films about Turkish soldiers in Korea in over fifty movie theaters across the United States.[31]

Additional Korean War–themed films were also cataloged by USIS-Turkey during the 1960s, including *Kore'den Aldığımız Ders* (The lessons we learned from Korea) and *Kore'de Türk Askeri* (Turkish soldier in Korea). These films not only highlighted American military prowess but also emphasized narratives of friendship between American and Turkish soldiers. Through this film diplomacy, the United States and Turkey engaged in a reciprocal project to bolster their national images, solidify their alliance, and position themselves as champions of modernization and democratic progress during the Korean War.

The Development of the Educational Film Center

Until the mid-1950s, most of the educational films exhibited in Turkey were produced by the British, French, German, Japanese, and American state agencies to promote their own national images. This phenomenon exemplifies the rationale of film diplomacy, wherein designated agents curated foreign media to serve geopolitical interests. Seeking to construct a modern national image through similar means, the MNET collaborated with the USIS and UNESCO to establish the EFC.[32] The development of the EFC began in 1950 when MNET established ties with UNESCO and began sending teachers abroad to study audiovisual technologies.[33] In a 1951 session of the Grand National Assembly, Istanbul Congresswoman Nazlı Tlabar publicly advocated the integration of communication technologies into education.[34] She criticized the government's use of radio primarily for entertainment and urged the MNET to follow UNESCO's recommendations by adopting radio for mass educational purposes, as countries like Australia, Brazil, and Britain had done. Her intervention prompted Minister of National Education Tevfik İleri to initiate the construction of a workshop for educational films, declaring in the assembly's official magazine, *Tutanak Dergisi*: "We will start a revolution with film in education and teaching."[35]

In parallel, the UNESCO agent Adolphe Hübl, an Austrian film specialist, played a critical role in shaping the early vision of the EFC.[36] In a 1951 interview in *Film ve Öğretim*, Hübl praised Turkey's commitment to educational films and proposed the establishment of a Turkish Film Institute that would oversee both production and pedagogical research.[37] Within two months, he had developed a plan for the creation of the EFC, outlining a £100,000 ($280,000) facility, complete with film production units, staff training programs, and a film archive by the end of 1952.³⁸ Although his recommendations—such as equipping every classroom with a projector—reflected idealized European models largely unattainable in Turkey's economic conditions, they nonetheless shaped the center's early institutional framework.³⁹ The center offered courses to train the directors of regional educational film centers, as well as teachers, to expand its services throughout the country (figure 4.8).

In contrast to Hübl's overly optimistic prescriptions, American involvement through the USIS demonstrated a more methodical, long-term approach to media influence. Beginning in 1949, the USIS film officer Monteagle Stearns and his colleagues worked closely with Turkish ministries to embed American educational films into the national curriculum and "inject" American influence.⁴⁰ This cooperation involved the Ministries of National Education, Health, Public Works, Agriculture and National

FIGURE 4.8 Trainees and teachers attending an EFC course in 1953.

Source: Educational Information Network of Turkey, Photograph Archive of the Ministry of National Education of Turkey, General Directorate of Innovation and Educational Technologies.

Defense; the office of the prime minister, and the Turkish Press Bureau. USIS agents considered this cooperation to be a milestone in the process of building relationships between Americans and Turks through which to develop propaganda and information programming.[41] As Thomas E. Flanagan, a USIS public affairs officer, later noted, this interministerial cooperation was framed as "democracy in action," but in practice, it centralized media production under American strategic oversight. He also viewed the coordination as an initial step toward developing organized channels for disseminating media of all kinds in Turkey under one central authority, the "National Teaching Films Center" or the EFC.[42] By constructing an infrastructure for Turkish media that remained reliant on American models, the USIS advanced Cold War objectives under the guise of supporting Turkish modernization.

This approach to educational film programming, which centralized authority in a Turkish institution subject to American influence, shows how educational technologies are reproducible. American agents created opportunities for Turkish officials to reproduce impact on the public through their work at the EFC. William E. Kugeman, the deputy public affairs officer at the embassy in Ankara, described the nature of the American approach in Turkey as "avant-garde," in the sense that the program was innovative, experimental, and "theoretical." According to Kugeman, "American and Turkish Information Officers theoretically participate[d] in the formulation of a media program designed to support the information objectives." American officers were responsible for creating the groundwork for "indigenous facilities" that would select, adapt, produce, correlate, distribute, and use informational media programs. American agents assumed that Turkish officers would later "do more and more" to design, adapt, and produce media "to ensure the effective perpetuation of information activities."[43] To achieve this goal, the two groups held meetings to develop a joint plan for growing their mutual and individual information activities in Turkey. This approach to educational film programming in Turkey reflects a top-down approach that prioritized American influence and expertise. Privileging American influence worked in service of the Cold War public diplomacy strategy to influence publics through financial incentives and propaganda.[44]

Under the influence of the USIS and UNESCO, the EFC was officially established in 1952 and provided a catalyst for the educational film revolution in Turkey. The goal of the center was to produce and circulate audiovisual materials for educational purposes. Initially, the EFC prepared only film slides (small, transparent pieces of film containing positive images that were projected or viewed through a slide viewer or microscope); scripts were written in collaboration with teachers. The Board of Instruction and Discipline of the Ministry of National Education (Milli Eğitim Vekaleti Talim ve Terbiye Heyeti) controlled the final approval process before copies of the film slides were distributed to schools. Simultaneously, the EFC circulated 350 films that it had acquired from the archives of British, German, Australian, American, and French cultural committees.[45] However, the high cost of foreign media ultimately rendered the program unsustainable, prompting the Turkish government to invest in producing, distributing, and exhibiting its own media.

To address distribution challenges, the USIS and the MNET collaborated to activate a national network of regional film centers. In 1952, thirteen regional hubs were established, supplemented by mobile film units designed to reach rural and underserved areas.[46] The USIS designated nine mobile units to circulate and exhibit films in rural areas. It also cooperated in assigning five centers to help activate these facilities. The EFC's main location was in Ankara, the capital of Turkey, where most of the films were preserved. By 1954, the EFC had established fifty branches across Turkey (figure 4.9). These regional centers (including those is Ankara, Bursa, Diyarbakır, and Istanbul) functioned as redistribution points, supplying educational media to smaller branches in nearby cities. Mobile film units extended the reach of this infrastructure, providing portable screenings in remote villages and areas without electricity.[47] By 1954, this network enabled the wide circulation of educational films, first featuring American cultural content and later expanding to include Turkish productions.

One of the key figures driving this expansion was Şinasi Barutçu, a painter, photographer, teacher, and the director of the EFC's film unit in Ankara (figure 4.10).[48] He became a critical bridge connecting Turkish, American, and UNESCO educational media initiatives. In 1954, he authored *En Modern Ders Vasıtası Film* (The most modern teaching tool film), a government-sponsored booklet promoting educational film as a superior method of instruction. Emphasizing that audiovisual media could stimulate multiple senses simultaneously, Barutçu argued

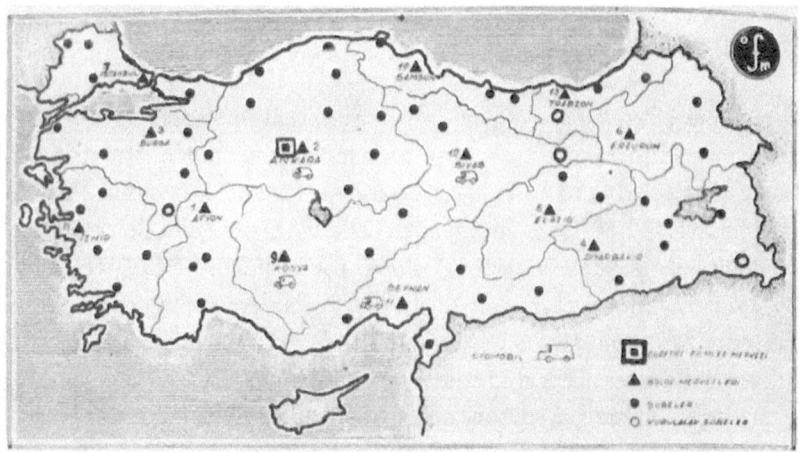

FIGURE 4.9 Map of the EFC facilities in Turkey.

Source: Şinasi Barutçu, *En Modern Ders Vasıtası Film* (Öğretici Filmler Merkezi, Doğuş Matbaası, 1954), 12.

FIGURE 4.10 Şinasi Barutçu holding a camera while seated on a tree branch, circa 1953.

Source: Educational Information Network of Turkey, Photograph Archive of the Ministry of National Education of Turkey, General Directorate of Innovation and Educational Technologies.

that films offered pedagogical advantages that traditional methods—chalkboard drawings, maps, and oral lectures—could not match. He noted that poorly drawn images frustrated students accustomed to the polished visuals of books, newspapers, and magazines and that the inefficiencies of blackboard teaching often caused students to lose attention. By contrast, film screenings, especially in darkened classrooms, were presented as immersive experiences capable of capturing and maintaining even the most distracted student's focus.

Barutçu emphasized sensory engagement and immersion as key principles for modern education. His advocacy of educational film technologies echoed Cold War ideas about media's role in shaping ideologically aligned publics. Mobile projection units and portable audiovisual kits were thus not simply tools for expanding education but also instruments for extending the reach of state influence into rural regions of Turkey.

Despite rapid infrastructural growth, by the late 1950s the EFC had yet to fully achieve its educational ambitions.[49] Audiovisual materials were still mostly considered tools of entertainment rather than serious tools for instruction, and their use in public communication remained limited. In response, Professor İlhan Özdil urged members of the Grand National Assembly to formalize legal frameworks supporting the integration of educational media and collaboration with the USIS.[50] He advocated expanding the EFC's activities to include preparing, translating, publishing, and distributing books, brochures, catalogs, and technical and theoretical materials. He also revealed that Syracuse University was planning to build an audiovisual center in Turkey to further the uses of media for educational purposes. Although Syracuse actually built its audiovisual center in Iran, the university conducted audience reception research in Turkey. Agents from Syracuse measured the effectiveness of educational films in high schools in collaboration with the Ford Foundation, the MNET, and the Education Division of the US Operations Missions.

In 1960, the EFC expanded its scope with the addition of a silk printing workshop to make classroom signboards. In 1962, the center constructed its first film sound studio, enabling the production of magnetic and later optical soundtracks for films and radio broadcasts. These technical advancements allowed the EFC to extend its reach into educational radio programming, with topics ranging from agricultural cooperatives to health and home economics. In recognition of its mission, the center was renamed the Film-Radio-Graphic Center (FRGC, Film-Radyo-Grafik Merkezi) in 1962, and by 1965, following the introduction of educational television programs, it became the Educational Film, Radio, and Television Center (EFRTC, Film-Radyo-Televizyonla Eğitim Merkezi). This period marked an important transition. Turkish-produced films gradually came to outnumber foreign imports, signaling a tentative shift toward national media sovereignty. Between 1952 and 1966, the center produced approximately three thousand educational films and thirty thousand filmstrips on diverse subjects, including agriculture, health, geography, economics, history, arts, and military training.[51] Yet even as Turkish authorities expanded domestic media production, the foundational structures, personnel training, and conceptual frameworks of the EFC remained largely shaped by Cold War transnational networks.

Barutçu's career encapsulates these entanglements. Having worked for the MNET, USIS, and UNESCO, he was at the convergence of national and international agendas. In 1951, he worked in London at the Gaumont-British studios, where he was in charge of dubbing films into Turkish for the MNET.[52] A year later, in 1952, he produced an educational film called *Çay* (Tea), which was written by Kemal Gökaydın and directed by W. Stoitzner. The film, sponsored by the Ministry of Agriculture (Tarım Bakanlığı), informed viewers about tea cultivation and production. That same year Barutçu worked as the director of the film division, and in that capacity, he was invited to represent Turkey at a UNESCO cultural aid meeting about educational films and filmstrips. He also collaborated with Hübl, the Australian film specialist who developed the plan for the EFC. As a diplomatic agent who facilitated communication efforts among the MNET, the USIS, and UNESCO, Barutçu helped construct a media bridge between the West and Turkey.

Alongside his film work, Barutçu wrote a series of instructional books sponsored by the MNET and USIS, including *Görme ve İşitme Yoluyla Eğitim ve Öğretim Hakkında Kısa Notlar* (Short notes on audiovisual education, 1954), *Öğretmenler için Film Kursu* (Film courses for teachers, 1954), and *Yurdun Dört Köşesinde Gezici Ekip* (Mobile units across the nation). These manuals emphasized the technical aspects of audiovisual technologies and sought to equip teachers with the tools to integrate media into modern educational practice. Through publications such as *Bugünün Eğitim ve Öğretiminde DİYA*, Barutçu promoted the vision of an educational system expanded and unified through mobile cinema, slide projectors, and synchronized audiovisual methods. His works indicate not only the state's investment in educational technologies but also the ideological underpinning of modernization: the belief that technology could rationalize learning, unify national identity, and extend the state's pedagogical reach into every corner of society.

Turkey's educational media infrastructure, from the EFC to the EFRTC, emerged through the entangled imperatives of modernization and Cold War agendas. Despite growing domestic production, the structures and ideologies providing the foundation for educational films, radio, and television remained shaped by USIS and UNESCO influence, embedding global struggles over technology, authority, and racialized modernization into Turkey's nation-building project. While educational media projects aimed to position Turkey as a unified and technologically advanced nation, they also masked structural issues beneath the surface of national progress.

Illusion of Progress: Disaster Relief and State Propaganda in the Representation of Black Turks

Depremde Kızılay (Red Crescent in earthquake, Cahit Ünsalan, 1964), produced by the EFC, documents the 1964 earthquake in Manyas, a district in Turkey's Marmara region, and the subsequent relief operations led by the Turkish Red Crescent (Kızılay) and the army.[53] While showing both the destruction and the humanitarian response, the film advances a paternalistic vision of modernization and national unity. It constructs a racialized binary between the secular, urban elite and the rural poor: The Red Crescent is portrayed as the embodiment of modern, white state authority, while the earthquake's victims—devout, economically marginalized Muslim citizens—are metaphorically racialized as "black Turks," positioned as culturally backward subjects in need of control, uplift, and incorporation into the state's civilizing project. Although the film gestures toward collective solidarity, it ultimately reinforces a hierarchical model of care in which modernization is equated with whiteness and administered from above. A male voice-over, speaking in standardized Istanbul Turkish, amplifies this dynamic by positioning the Red Crescent as the humanitarian embodiment of the republic's civilizing mission. As such, the film exemplifies how educational and state-sponsored cinema functioned not merely as an instrument of information or relief but also as an ideological technology of governance—regulating the audiovisual field to consolidate hierarchies and the authority of the modernizing state.

Depremde Kızılay begins with the nondiegetic sound of the *bağlama*, a traditional Turkish folk instrument (like the Western lute), as an opening shot zooms in on a map of the Marmara region. The voice-over describes the region's geography as images show villagers engaging in both traditional and modern farming practices. Idyllic imagery of turning mill wheels and flowing water is followed by scenes of boys and girls playing together in a schoolyard—visual cues that subtly reference the coeducation reforms instituted by Atatürk in 1927. The film takes a dramatic turn when a 6.9 magnitude earthquake strikes Manyas, killing seventy-three people on October 6, 1964.[54] Through a mix of reenactments and documentary footage, the film shows the chaos: Cabinets rattle, tools fall, women clutch their children, and schoolchildren flee in terror. Images of collapsed mosques, damaged homes, and outdoor prayer underscore the severity of the devastation. The haunting sounds of the *bağlama*, now layered with gusting wind, reinforce the emotional weight of these scenes, which culminate with the depiction of children eating stale bread amid the ruins.

The second half of the film focuses on the response effort, showing the rapid mobilization of the Red Crescent teams, Turkish army units, and civilian volunteers. The voice-over, acting as the voice of the state, narrates the coordination of relief as soldiers distribute tents, student volunteers assist in camp construction, veiled women engaged in outdoor cooking, and aid is delivered to the survivors. The film concludes with a medium shot of the Red Crescent flag underscored by the voice-over's tribute: "Selam sana, Kızılay" (Greetings to you, Red Crescent).[55]

What the film shows, however, is not a transformation but a restoration of order. The presence of veiled women reflects a careful negotiation of the state's relationship with rural religious communities—populations historically regarded by the secular elite as culturally peripheral to the nation's modern identity. By integrating these subjects into a controlled vision of unity, the film sustains dominant hierarchies of class, gender, and religion. In doing so, it codifies whiteness as a normative aesthetic and moral order—aligned with secularism, urbanity, and elite authority—while rendering rural piety visible only when it is controlled and made useful within the state's modernization narrative.

As the political sociologist Hande Paker argues, the Red Crescent operated not as an autonomous civil institution but as a semiofficial arm of the state, a tool used to perform state legitimacy both domestically and internationally.[56] Turkish elites strategically aligned the Red Crescent with the language of Western humanitarianism, seeking to project an image of Turkey as modern. Yet this approach also masked persistent problems of accountability, transparency, and unequal representation—within both the state and the organizations it used to extend its reach.

The film crystallizes this contradiction in a brief but telling moment: An elderly male villager, seated at a coffeehouse, moves his mouth but is not allowed to speak. Instead, the voice-over asserts that the state had advised villagers to build their homes on *yamaç yerler* (hilly areas) and proclaims: "Şimdi herkes devlete hak veriyordu" (Now everybody agrees with the state). This silencing technique highlights the film's reproduction of state discourse, replacing authentic public voices with an official narrative that obscures bureaucratic failures—particularly the government's long-standing delay in establishing national construction standards, which would not materialize until 1969.[57] Rather than addressing systemic vulnerabilities, *Depremde Kızılay* stages consent, assigning the black Turks—underprivileged and devout villagers—blame for their own suffering.

In doing so, the film reenacts a familiar trope of developmentalist discourse: Those left most vulnerable by modernization are rendered responsible for their own precarity and need to be educated, while systemic failures remain unacknowledged.[58] This strategy reflects the ideological structures of whiteness within the Turkish modernization project, whereby secular, urban "white Turks" maintain dominance by silencing voices and erasing state culpability. By framing momentary rescue efforts as proof of national progress, the film normalizes elite authority and sustains a modernization narrative grounded in secular, urban, and classed notions of citizenship. As a result, it aestheticizes disaster, renders rural piety and poverty legible only through state intervention, and conceals the asymmetries that modernization failed to resolve. What emerges, then, is that film diplomacy was a mechanism of internal governance—used to manage rural and religious populations, aestheticize state intervention, and mask the structural contradictions embedded in the modernization project.

Depremde Kızılay thus establishes a complex interplay among the state, the public, and the humanitarian network. By centering the Red Crescent as both a logistical and a symbolic agent of recovery, the film aligns disaster relief with the broader goals of modernization and international respectability. This framing is not unique to Turkey. In fact, *Depremde Kızılay* echoes earlier films advertising the Red Crescent that were produced in the 1940s, which similarly employed a male voice-over—often in English—to document the organization's humanitarian labor: building camps, distributing drinking water, and tending to victims.[59] These short films featuring children of different races, ethnicities, and abilities—with images of a Black boy getting food from a mobile kitchen or a disabled girl receiving medical care—not only presented scenes of compassion but also were carefully crafted appeals to donor audiences. Punctuated by commands such as "Don't ever forget the Red Crescent!," these films used strategically curated representations of care and relief to secure financial and moral legitimacy for the organization on a global stage.

Depremde Kızılay belongs to a longer transnational genealogy in which humanitarian film operated not merely as documentary evidence of crisis but also as a visual technology of relief and governance. Originating in the Ottoman Empire in 1868, the Turkish Red Crescent's affiliation with the International Federation of Red Cross and Red Crescent Societies (IFRC) grounded it in a humanitarian framework shaped by Western and Christian traditions.[60] Although the IFRC operates as a secular institution, its foundational values—emerging from the Geneva Convention—retain the marks of Christian universalism. As the historian Julia Irwin has argued, the American Red Cross's twentieth-century shift from Christian universalism to secular humanitarianism did not erase its missionary roots; rather, it reconfigured them into a form of secular governance.[61] This secularism grounded in Christian theology governs difference and regulates religion.[62] Secularism is structured by whiteness, just as whiteness relies on the authority of the secular to appear universal.[63]

Yet unlike its international predecessors, *Depremde Kızılay* targets a domestic audience. It is designed to craft a coherent national narrative. Rather than seeking international goodwill, the film constructs a state-sanctioned vision of national coherence, one that absorbs rural difference without challenging elite authority. It creates a vision of rural Muslims as orderly, obedient, and integrated into the civic body—as long as their piety remains visually useful to the state. In this way, the film aestheticizes internal difference and reaffirms state authority. Film diplomacy here operates not as international projection but as domestic governance—controlling visibility, managing ideological contradictions, and staging unity in the face of crisis.

From Mexican Maracas and Native American Masks to Nasreddin Hoja Tales

Educational films produced in Turkey between 1961 and 1972 offer a window into how state modernization, racialization, and transnational influence coalesced through media. These films excluded Arab, Black, Jewish, Kurdish, Laz, and Tahtacı communities as a structural effect of a whiteness that operated as both an aesthetic norm and an ideological engine of national identity. In this section, I analyze not only what these films represent but also what they erase. Through this lens, I argue that whiteness functioned as a regulatory force in Turkey's modernization project, shaping representation via film diplomacy not only in its international dimensions but also as a domestic strategy of visual and ideological governance.

A group of educational films—especially those featuring the American puppeteer Marjorie Batchelder McPharlin and adaptations of Nasreddin Hoja stories—demonstrates how whiteness operated as a logic of appropriation, authority, and cultural erasure. In *Yaratıcı Oyun I* (Creative game I, Kemal Gökaydın et al., 1961), McPharlin leads Turkish children in puppet-making activities in collaboration with the Ministry of Social Services and the Children's Protection Agency (Sosyal Hizmetler ve Çocuk Esirgeme Kurumu) in Ankara. The film opens with an intertitle thanking McPharlin, followed by a female voice-over in Istanbul Turkish crediting her with the creative design of the activities for the Children's Club of the Anafartalar Children's Protection Agency. Early scenes show puppet shows, collective dancing, and dramatizations of emotional growth.

The camera then focuses on McPharlin's instructional methods. She cuts and assembles puppets from cardboard and thread, guiding children to replicate her steps. She also introduces Mexican maracas and Native American drums, presented not with historical context or cultural significance but as pedagogical props. These performances reframe cultural artifacts as universal tools of child development, stripping them of origin and meaning. What appears as benevolent educational play is, in fact, an act of cultural erasure—authorized by the Turkish state, legitimated by whiteness, and framed as transnational pedagogy.

Such acts of appropriation reflect what the legal theorist Cheryl Harris identifies as the logic of whiteness as property, structured around the power to claim, use, and exclude.[64] McPharlin's performances exemplify how whiteness circulates transnationally, mobilized through institutionalized American cultural capital and embedded within Turkish state media infrastructures. In this context, film diplomacy does not serve external propaganda but rather internal governance: shaping national imaginaries of modernization through Western ideals that center creativity through structured play, civility through discipline, and rationality through modeled cognitive development, each shaped by white pedagogical authority.

As the historian Philip Deloria argues, white Americans appropriated Native American culture through "playing Indian" to construct an identity rooted in freedom and opposition to savagery—a practice that reinforced settler colonial ideologies and informed legal rulings that denied Indigenous land rights.[65] Harris similarly notes that "whiteness and property share" a conceptual foundation grounded in exclusion.[66] A parallel logic unfolded in Turkey through the 1942 Varlık Vergisi (Wealth Tax), which disproportionately targeted non-Muslim citizens—Armenians, Greeks, Jews, and Levantines—to shift economic power into Muslim hands.[67] This punitive policy illustrates how legal and economic structures codify Muslimness as the normative national identity. These same logics of exclusion—codifying who belongs and who does not—are embedded in the pedagogical frameworks of Turkish educational films. In *Yaratıcı Oyun I*, McPharlin's appropriation of Native American and Mexican cultural forms mirrors how the Turkish state managed non-Muslim difference—through the reassertion of whiteness as the aesthetic and ideological standard of national development.

This intersection between cultural representation and systemic dispossession is further present in McPharlin's use of puppetry as both pedagogical method and diplomatic instrument. In *The Puppet Theatre Handbook* (1947), compiled as a manual for the US Army's entertainment and rehabilitation programs, McPharlin frames puppetry as a strategic medium, useful for propaganda, morale-building, and public health campaigns.[68] She claims that puppets can rapidly shift audience emotions, change behaviors, and facilitate mass instruction, citing examples from Mexico's Ministry of Education and hygiene education programs.[69] Her endorsement of puppetry as a modern tool for developmental governance reveals how seemingly innocuous forms of play can become vehicles for ideological influence.

McPharlin's familiarity with Turkey's own shadow puppet traditions—Karagöz and Hacivat—is evident from her writing, where she describes Karagöz as the "vigorous hero" and Hacivat as a "Europeanized Turk."[70] Yet in the *Yaratıcı Oyun* series, she does not build on these local art forms. Instead, she centers Mexican culture and Native American ritual dances, repurposed as instruments of transnational education. That choice, endorsed and circulated by the Turkish state, exposes a key tension: While the government had long used Turkish puppetry to support public health and modernization initiatives,[71] here Western pedagogical authority displaces local traditions in favor of a sanitized, exportable vision of developmental play.

In *Yaratıcı Oyun II* (Creative game II, Kemal Gökaydın et al., 1962), the sequel to the first film, children take center stage.[72] McPharlin introduces them to Native American masks and then leads a puppet-making session assisted by a female teacher who also serves as her translator. The children replicate her steps, and when invited to craft their own story, they choose the folkloric figure Nasreddin Hoja (also known as Nasreddin Hoca, Molla Nasreddin and Hodja Afandi). They build puppets of Hoja and his wife, neighbors, and animals and stage a story about perseverance.

According to the American studies scholar Perin Gürel, Nasreddin Hoja became a "cultural ambassador," strategically reframed by the state as a moral figure to counter orientalist depictions of Turks as backward.[73] Turkish folklorists and ministries edited his bawdier tales, turning him into a folk philosopher whose stories aligned with state pedagogical goals (an instance of what Gürel calls "selective Westernization").[74] The MNET supported this reframing by commissioning a series of Hoja films through the

EFC, including *Biz Bu Eve Taşınmadık mı?* (Haven't we moved to this house?, Cemil Eren, 1962), *Nasreddin Hoca I* (Nebahat Yıldırım, 1972), *Nasreddin Hoca II* (Nebahat Yıldırım, 1972), and *Nasreddin Hoca III* (Nebahat Yıldırım, 1972), which emphasized moral lessons and resilience.

These black-and-white and color films were intended for preschool and elementary school students. They featured Nasreddin Hoja jokes that highlight his cleverness and his ability to respond swiftly with humorous, unexpected answers. For instance, *Biz Bu Eve Taşınmadık mı?* highlights a joke about a thief who enters Hoja's house and steals everything. Hoja follows the thief to his own house, and when the thief questions his presence, Hoja humorously responds by asking if they have not moved into that house. The joke plays on absurdity and highlights Hoja's wit to suggest that the furniture belongs to him. The educational message is to encourage students to maintain a positive attitude, find humor in difficult situations, and be resilient in overcoming challenges.

Whereas *Yaratıcı Oyun II* and *Biz Bu Eve Taşınmadık mı?* emphasize resilience as an educational concept for navigating social interactions and developing problem-solving skills, the films produced a decade later, which showcase Hoja's tricks, place significant emphasis on integrating Islam within the framework of Turkey's national heritage. For instance, *Nasreddin Hoca I* features three non-Muslim foreign scholars asking Hoja questions. The first question is about the center of the world, and in response, Hoja points to his donkey's leg. The second question concerns the number of stars in the sky, and Hoja equates it to the hairs on his donkey. The scholars then ask about the number of hairs in a beard, and Hoja compares it to the hair on his donkey's tail. As the scholars seek evidence for Hoja's answers, he skillfully responds with replies such as "If you don't believe me, you can measure it" and "Can the stars in the sky be counted?" Caught off guard, the scholars find themselves at a loss for words and eventually withdraw. The scholars' admiration for Hoja's astute replies leads them to convert to Islam. While the tale follows Hoja's signature trickster logic, the outcome suggests ideological steering. The scholars' conversion positions Islam as a superior truth validated through wit, a framing likely shaped by the state's shifting discourse on religion.

This shift coincides with the rise of religious cinema in Turkey. As the film scholar Dilek Kaya and the political scientist Umut Azak point out, however, the pioneering fiction film *Birleşen Yollar* (Crossroads, Yücel

Çakmaklı, 1970) played the most significant role in inaugurating the Islamic national cinema movement by presenting Turkish secular modernization as a superficial imitation of the West and emphasizing the Islamic way of life as the exclusive path to genuine happiness.[75] Although secularism remained central to state ideology—positioned as a marker of Western modernization—the media became tightly managed tools for negotiating religion's role in public life. The Hoja films thus exemplify how educational media navigated this tension: reworking Islam into narratives of national unity without ceding control over its representation.[76] While these films demonstrate how film diplomacy operated as a mode of internal governance, the USIS-sponsored Hoja films (analyzed in the previous chapter) mobilized Islam to combat communism abroad. The domestically produced Hoja films repurposed the same figure to enforce morality and conformity at home, marking a shift from transnational projection to domestic regulation.

The Role of Religion in Films Produced by the Educational Film Center

Secularism in Turkey has operated as a dynamic and often contradictory tool of modernization. Drawing on records from the Central Film Control Commission, the film historian Dilek Kaya and the media scholar Zeynep Koçer demonstrate how Turkish censors worked to preserve a distinct form of "Kemalist secularism."[77] This expelled Islam from political life while protecting a state-sanctioned, apolitical Sunni Islam. This ideological balancing act—what scholars call "Turkish Islamic exceptionalism"—set Turkish secularism apart from both Arab-national interpretations of Islam and Anglo-American secular models.[78] Consequently, religion was paradoxically both censored and strategically instrumentalized, suppressed in certain contexts yet utilized in others to bolster national unity or support modernization initiatives. In this setting, Islam emerged as a counterideology, functioning sometimes as an instrument of political dissent and at other times as a partner in state propaganda.[79]

Early radical reforms eliminated Islamic legal codes, banned Ottoman-era attire like the fez, and modernized education through the introduction of the Latin script.[80] However, with the rise of the Demokrat Parti (DP,

Democrat Party) in 1950 and its populist shift toward rural voters, the rigor of secularism softened. DP policies deemphasized cultural modernization and instead prioritized economic development, as seen in the removal of prayer bans and increased public visibility of Islam. Initially, this liberalization occurred without substantially undermining Kemalist principles, but as the DP faced declining popularity amid worsening economic conditions, the party increasingly turned to Islam as a political strategy.[81]

Opponents of the DP grew increasingly concerned by the erosion of secularism resulting from the party's religious liberalization. The escalating tensions ultimately led to the military coup in May 1960, resulting in the ouster and subsequent execution of Prime Minister Adnan Menderes. Military leaders justified their intervention as a necessary reassertion of secular values.[82] Yet when the Adalet Partisi (Justice Party) assumed power in 1965, it continued the religious liberalism and populism established by the DP. This period ended with another military intervention in March 1971.

During these ideological fluctuations, films produced by the EFC became strategic tools for negotiating tensions between Islam and modernization. Films like *Köy Kalkınmasında İmam* (Cleric's role in village development, Nurettin Tancı, 1967) and *Altın Bilezik* (Golden bracelet, Engin Gülen, 1968) foregrounded the imam as both spiritual leader and modernizing agent. *Altın Bilezik*, set in a Turkish village transitioning from an agricultural to a more industrial economy, features an imam who quotes Qur'anic hadiths to encourage the villagers to acquire technical skills and engage in industrial labor. This imam epitomizes the *aydın imam*, an enlightened cleric who promotes rational progress and rejects backwardness in alignment with the state's modernization agenda.[83]

Besides the imam, *Altın Bilezik* features three pivotal characters: Zeki, a diligent villager who is struggling to support himself and his mother through tireless agricultural labor; Dursun, an idle villager consumed by gambling and leisure who is squandering his inherited wealth; and Zeynep, the village's most desirable woman, whom both men aspire to marry. While Zeynep and Zeki participate diligently in government-sponsored sewing and blacksmithing courses, respectively, gaining skills that lead them to entrepreneurial success and mutual fulfillment, Dursun's irresponsible habits lead him to financial ruin. This storyline illustrates the Turkish idiom *kolunda altın bileziği olmak* (to have a golden bracelet on the arm), meaning to have a profitable skill or profession. It contrasts industriousness and moral uprightness, aligned with Islam, to vice and idleness, suggesting religion's compatibility with productivity.

This framing of the imam in *Altın Bilezik* reflects a secularist strategy of redefining Islam as a traditional, apolitical, and culturally contained form of Sunni identity. These representations rarely faced censorship, as they aligned with Kemalist secular norms, in which religion was deployed as cultural heritage without threatening the modern, secular identity of the state. Religion thus served as a resource that was managed carefully to produce civic obedience and national cohesion.

The strategic use of Islam in *Altın Bilezik* exemplifies how film diplomacy operated domestically. Here, film served as a pedagogical instrument to integrate religious sentiment with economic development. By presenting Islamic virtues as compatible with industrial productivity, the film demonstrate how religious discourse was integrated into the state's modernization narrative. The imam's presence—sanctioned by both the state and the Board of Censorship—models how religious discourse was absorbed into the visual grammar of modernization. This form of internal film diplomacy shows how Turkish secularism, while outwardly committed to suppressing religion in public life, in fact relied on carefully curated depictions of Islam to legitimize state authority and mobilize rural populations.

The late 1970s and early 1980s marked a significant shift in public perceptions of the military's role as a guardian of Turkish secularism. Following the military intervention of 1980, the armed forces aimed to mitigate ideological polarization, political violence, and social unrest by strategically mobilizing religion, particularly as a countermeasure to communism. This effort was informed by the Turkish-Islamic synthesis movement, which merged Sunni Islam with Turkish nationalism.[84] Concurrently, film censorship in Turkey underwent regulatory changes with the introduction of the Law of Cinema, Video and Music Works of Art and the Regulation on the Control of Cinema, Video and Music Works of Art in 1986.[85] These changes shifted responsibility for film censorship from the Ministry of the Interior to the Ministry of Culture and Tourism, incorporating members from both the MNET and the General Secretariat of the National Security Council.[86]

In his analysis of Turkey's shift in the 1990s from a Eurocentric model of modernity to an Islamic modernity framework, the political scientist

Alev Çınar offers a critical reframing of the relationship between Islam and modernization. Early modernization efforts positioned secularism as a break from the Ottoman legacy, making Western-oriented modernity central to the Kemalist vision. Çınar challenges scholarly assumptions that cast Islamism as opposed to modernity or the West. After examining political entities such as the Refah Party and the AK Party, he argues that Islamist movements do not fundamentally oppose secularism or Western societies; rather, they critique the state's Western-centric modernization as a betrayal of Turkey's authentic "national culture" and as an unreflective mimicry of Western models.[87] Thus, these parties advanced an "alternative modernization project," mobilizing Islam to reclaim national identity while maintaining secular principles.[88] Films like *Altın Bilezik* exemplify how state-sponsored media negotiated the convergence of Islamic tradition and secular modernization, offering a visual form to Çınar's concept of Islamic modernity as an adaptive framework—one that foregrounds the fluidity of national identity within Turkey's evolving modernization landscape.

Paths to Modernization: Shaping a Nation Through Children's Welfare and Family Planning

Ana Kucağı (Orphanage, or Mom's lap, Nurcan Karagöz, 1977) is an educational film produced under the auspices of the Ministry of Social Services and the Children's Protection Agency, produced to publicize the expanding role of state institutions in Turkey's modernization project—particularly in addressing child welfare.[89] The film opens with a high-angle, panoramic shot of a bustling street, underscored by a melancholy soundtrack. At the center of the frame, a fruit seller pushes a cart with his young daughter, Emine, seated atop it. The camera then zooms into their modest home as a male voice-over (standing in for the father's voice) recounts the recent death of Emine's mother and the father's determination to raise his child under precarious conditions. The narrative shifts back to the father and daughter at work, passing a playground filled with children—a visual juxtaposition of economic struggle and an imagined, orderly future.

They encounter an elderly man who introduces the possibility of institutional care, which they ultimately embrace. At the Children's Protection Agency, the father is greeted with warmth and bureaucratic efficiency. A shot-reverse shot series captures the father and daughter watching children at play, linking the child's emotional vulnerability to the stabilizing promise of state-administered order. Here, modernization is cast as a redemptive force where state institutions reconfigure family breakdown into national coherence.

The film then adopts a didactic tone, offering the institutional history of the Children's Protection Agency, founded in 1921 to support children affected by war.[90] The voice-over describes the society as a beacon of national compassion, attributing its growth to state initiative and public support. A montage of carefully composed close-ups—teachers guiding children during meals, story time, and recreation—reinforces the image of a benevolent institution regulating social order. Scenes of communal dining and sleeping evoke the comfort of routine and surveillance, while the final sequence—children singing patriotic songs outdoors—casts the institution as a cradle of national identity. These audiovisual cues present children as the embodiment of the nation's future and institutional care as a modernizing imperative. The state is not merely a provider of care; it is also a rehabilitative force that transforms vulnerable children into productive, disciplined, and loyal citizens. Poverty, in turn, is rendered as an individual condition, not a structural problem that would be resolved through state intervention.

As the anthropologist and human rights scholar Kathryn Libal notes, the actual operations of the Children's Protection Agency were marked by chronic underfunding and inconsistencies.[91] *Ana Kucağı*, however, offers no such complications. Instead, it stages an idealized fiction in which modernization and the machinery of welfare function efficiently, masking systemic deficiencies with emotionally resonant images of rescue and redemption. In this context, *Ana Kucağı* functions as a domestic instrument of film diplomacy performing the legitimacy of state power for a national audience. It transforms film into a tool of internal governance, using audiovisual affect to frame modernization as not only necessary but also benevolent. The aesthetics of care—warm gazes, shared meals, and patriotic songs—conceal the problematic dimensions of the welfare system and preempt public scrutiny. The film thus becomes a performance of state paternalism that frames modernization as affective common sense.

"We Need Films That Are About Us"

The EFC played a central role in reproducing power asymmetries between the Turkish state and its citizens by promoting a monolithic vision of Turkish identity. Government-sponsored educational films—especially those focused on geography—portrayed Turkey's regions and populations as homogenous, erasing the country's rich religious, linguistic, racial, and ethnic differences. While these films celebrated national pride and developmental progress, they also enacted practices of erasure and standardization.

A key technique in this process was the use of standardized Istanbul Turkish—the accent taught at the Istanbul Municipality Theatre and employed across both domestic and international film dubbing.[92] Although often viewed as a practical industry solution to avoid the costs of synchronized sound, this sonic uniformity carried significant ideological weight. These decisions were auditory strategies of governance that served the state's nation-building project by erasing linguistic differences and reinforcing the dominance of a singular, elite-coded Turkish identity.

The standardization of Istanbul Turkish functioned as an auditory register of modernization, strengthening the authority of a secular, urban, and racialized subjectivity.[93] Voice-over in this context operated as a technique of national pedagogy: It staged who could narrate the nation, who was deemed audible and authoritative and who was silenced, dubbed over, or rendered acoustically invisible. By suppressing regional dialects and non-Turkish languages such as Kurdish, Zaza, and Ladino, these films produced an ideological soundscape in which whiteness, secularism, and linguistic conformity were markers of national belonging.

By privileging Istanbul Turkish, educational films became instruments of sonic and visual pedagogy that not only instructed but also delineated the boundaries of inclusion and exclusion. Those who spoke different languages, practiced non-Sunni religions, or lived outside the urban-industrial ideal were not merely overlooked; they were rendered invisible or backward, or they were framed as deficient subjects to be reformed, managed, or erased in the name of progress. Through such techniques, the EFC's output functioned as a key tool of modernization, constructing citizenship through audiovisual regimes of conformity.

This project of audiovisual standardization did not emerge in a vacuum; rather, it drew on a longer ideological vision that defined Turkish identity through exclusionary norms. At the core of this vision is the work of the sociologist Mehmet Ziya Gökalp, widely regarded as the architect of Turkish nationalism. Despite his Kurdish background, he advocated a homogenous national identity grounded in shared language and cultural affiliation, insisting that speaking Turkish and identifying as Turkish were the primary markers of national belonging;[94] rather than forced displacement, he promoted the assimilation of Kurdish populations into a unified Turkish identity.[95] His assimilationist and racialized discourse laid the groundwork for an ethno-nationalist vision of citizenship that cast linguistic and cultural differences as threats to the coherence of the republic.

The sociologist Barış Ünlü conceptualizes this dynamic through what he terms the "Turkishness contract"—an unspoken set of privileges granted to those who conform to state-defined norms of Turkish identity.[96] This tacit contract mandated that Muslim citizens of diverse ethnic backgrounds backgrounds (e.g., Kurds, Circassians, Bosnians, and Albanians) assimilate Kurds, Circassians, Bosnians, and Albanians—assimilate linguistically and culturally in order to access social and political benefits.[97] In addition to mandating the adoption of Turkish identity, the contract demanded emotional and ideological allegiance to the nation-state and denied legitimacy to any claims of difference. Turkishness, in this framework, became a performative identity, defined by linguistic, cultural, and emotional conformity to state-defined standards.

Educational films served as key instruments in advancing the state's conformist agenda and promoting a singular vision of Turkish identity. Advocates such as Oktay Verel, a contributor to *Film ve Öğretim*, championed educational films as vehicles for cultivating this project of Turkish nationalism. In "Cultural Films and Our Schools," he positioned films as the most effective medium for shaping public culture and enhancing learning, particularly in service of patriotic education. He emphasized that geography films were essential for patriotic education and that schools needed to screen feature films about Turkish culture and identity. "In order to love the nation, we need to know it," he argued, urging the MNET to prioritize domestic-focused educational films rather than international productions.[98]

Similarly, the geography professor Cemal Alagöz recognized educational films as instrumental in nation-building.[99] His perspectives were shaped by international exposure: notably, a 1950 UNESCO geography conference in Canada and an audiovisual training course at McGill University. Exposure to transnational pedagogical networks and modern film technologies convinced him of the ideological and practical utility of film in the classroom. Subsequently, he called for collaboration between geographers and filmmakers, stressing that educational films could significantly promote national unity and modern civic values.

In the 1970s and 1980s, the EFC produced a series of geography films featuring various cities in Turkey (figure 4.11). These films promoted a singular ethnic national identity and neglected the diverse multiethnic and multireligious populations who made up these cities.[100] For example, *Mardin* (Zeki Şahin, 1975) offers a history of this Eastern city and highlights a singular Turkish identity. It opens with a long shot of the cityscape and continues with people working on a farm. The voice-over in Istanbul Turkish explains that civilization began in this territory three thousand years ago and that many nations lived there, including Mesopotamians, Persians, Seljucks, Byzantines, and Ottomans. The voice-over adds that

FIGURE 4.11 Crew from the Educational Film Center filming a panoramic view of a cityscape in 1975.

Source: Educational Information Network of Turkey, Photograph Archive of the Ministry of National Education of Turkey, General Directorate of Innovation and Educational Technologies.

the city's architecture and elaborate use of Yönü stone, which is particular to Mardin, represented the integration of the past with the present. However, it does not mention that this rich architectural history originated from the many religious and ethnic groups who lived in the city. Mardin has been home to Greeks, Armenians, Syrians, Kurds, and Arabs. Presented by a trained voice actor, the film's omission of these diverse groups exemplifies the power asymmetry between dominant and subordinate groups. The film, when critically examined, illuminates the exclusionary nature of the modernization project. The state excluded certain groups based on factors such as language, ethnicity, and religion, which were determiners of and limits to their whiteness.

Turkey's educational film infrastructure was part of a Cold War media ecology in which states deployed documentary and nontheatrical cinema as an instrument of pedagogical governance. Yet what distinguishes the Turkish case is its distinctive fusion of US-sponsored liberal developmentalism, Kemalist secular nationalism, and Islamic exceptionalism. Educational films in Turkey did not merely reflect ideological contradictions; they also worked to manage and aestheticize them. Religious, ethnic, and linguistic heterogeneity was not acknowledged but rather systematically reformed or erased in the service of a modernization project. Instead of resolving ideological tensions, the films produced by the EFC staged coherence, performing care and competence.

Government-sponsored films intended to develop compliant citizens, as one of its exhibition spaces (figure 4.12) shows: the gazes of men and children seated in the foreground, and women gathered at the rear, all around a projector, split between the camera recording them and a screen that goes beyond our view. The photograph complicates this narrative of compliance, however; the mixture of fascination and fatigue on the viewers' faces hints at ambivalence, showing that reception was as much of a negotiation as submission.

In this chapter, I have examined the emergence of Turkey's educational film revolution, culminating in the founding of the EFC in 1952. Drawing on primary archival materials collected in Turkey and the United States (including Turkish government regulations, parliamentary debates, educational periodicals, and records of international collaborations with the USIS and UNESCO), I traced the institutional history of the EFC and the development of an educational film culture shaped by transnational

FIGURE 4.12 EFC audience at an outdoor film screening.

Source: Educational Information Network of Turkey, Photograph Archive of the Ministry of National Education of Turkey, General Directorate of Innovation and Educational Technologies.

alliances and domestic pedagogical agendas. I analyzed how educational films functioned not only as instructional media but also as key instruments of state power, advancing a vision of modernization that was technologically progressive, ideologically conformist, and exclusionary along racial, ethnic, linguistic, and religious lines. From public health campaigns like *Elif'in Çilesi* to geography films such as *Mardin*, these state-sponsored documentaries operationalized a pedagogical regime rooted in modernization and whiteness. Educational film was not just a mirror of national ideology but also a technology for managing citizenship and projecting a homogenized, secular, and racialized modernization. By drawing on Western audiovisual models and Turkish nationalist ideologies, the EFC constructed a media infrastructure that regulated population, influenced public perception, and promoted a national identity aligned with secular, urban, and ethnically Turkish norms. While these films framed modernization as benevolent care, rational development, and national unity, they also erased languages, accents, non-Sunni religious expressions, and non-Turkish ethnic identities—recasting them as elements to be regulated through state intervention. Thus, educational cinema in Turkey was not simply a medium of instruction; it was also a technology of inscription, encoding national myths, hierarchical social orders, and state authority into the audiovisual fabric of everyday life. In this context, film diplomacy—no longer aimed solely at foreign publics but now directed inward—functioned as a mechanism of domestic governance, determining who counts, who belongs, and who is rendered visible and audible within the nation's modernization project.

5
Audience Reception Research

In the early 1950s, agents from the US State Department, the US Information Service (USIS), and the Economic Cooperation Administration (ECA) and researchers from Columbia University collaborated to investigate the media preferences and habits of audiences in Turkey. As part of this effort, they organized screenings of educational films and followed up with interviews. One such film, *Poultry Raising* (Vocational Guidance Films, 1946), screened with a Turkish voice-over, showed modern equipment and techniques for poultry farming, focusing on egg and meat production in the United States.[1] In a follow-up interview, a fifty-six-year-old male villager, who had never previously seen a film, recalled scenes of hens and chickens receiving hygienically maintained food and veterinary care.[2] He further noted that the film emphasized the importance of maintaining clean poultry and allowing them to graze in fields, and he praised the farmers' diligent coop care. When the interviewer asked, "Do you look after your coops in the same way?" the villager answered: "How can we? They [Americans] have nice places. Their [coops] cost much money. Of course, the hens will lay many eggs if they are looked after carefully. We [Turks] cannot do that. They grow corn and give them the kernels. Of course, their country will be better. We cannot do that."[3] His remarks foreground economic disparity as the key barrier to adopting the depicted practices.

In this chapter, I argue that US audience reception research in Cold War Turkey was shaped by a racialized epistemology that positioned whiteness as the invisible standard of modernization. Drawing on archival materials from Columbia University's Bureau of Applied Social Research (BASR), the ECA, and the USIS, I examine how educational films and their reception functioned as tools of ideological production, encoding the economic and racial logics of US-led modernization within narratives of global progress. I introduce the concept of *useful modernization* to describe the ideological work performed by educational films that framed American developmental ideals as universally desirable and pedagogically necessary for progress. Building on the phrase "useful cinema," used by the film historians Charles R. Acland and Haidee Wasson, I examine how nontheatrical films functioned as strategic instruments of governance, shaping perceptions through capitalist logics, racialized hierarchies, and developmentalist assumptions.[4]

Here, I consider whiteness as an ideological and epistemological framework that operates as an unmarked standard for measuring development, rationality, and modernization. It is a normative structure of perception, a "standpoint," as the sociologist Ruth Frankenberg puts it, from which knowledge is produced and difference is evaluated.[5] Whiteness functions by presenting itself as objective and universal while pathologizing those who fall outside its frame as deficient or undeveloped. In the context of Cold War audience research, it structured the interpretation of non-Western subjects using their proximity to the media habits, technological literacy, and capitalist values of the West. Turkish audiences, like others across the Global South, were thus cast as developmental subjects on a civilizational scale defined by their distance from whiteness.

Critically examining categorical labels such as "traditional," "transitional," and "modern Turks" employed in studies by the Columbia University social scientist Daniel Lerner, I demonstrate how these classifications produced a civilizational hierarchy with whiteness as its apex. Lerner's research in Turkey provided the empirical foundation for what was later formalized as modernization theory and helped institutionalize communication studies as an instrument of Cold War governance. I analyze three interrelated dynamics: first, how audience research shaped the selection, circulation, and ideological framing of films shown to Turkish audiences; second, how translation and local adaptation reconfigured the meanings of these films in ways often misread by US agents; and third, how American researchers pathologized Turkish audiences by attributing material constraints to cultural or psychological "deficiencies."

While individual audience responses show the uneven uptake of intended modernization messages, they also point to the institutional logic that aimed to shape such variability. In a catalog that included *Poultry Raising* alongside thousands of other American films, George Allen—director of the USIS from 1957 to 1960—emphasized the pedagogical and developmental utility of motion pictures.[6] He argued that American films could accelerate training by visually demonstrating techniques for improving education, productivity, and living standards. For him, film was a vital instrument in the global dissemination of science, culture, and technical knowledge. He stressed its value to educators, librarians, and school administrators as a tool for cultivating the educational foundations deemed essential for technological progress. What distinguished film was its multisensory immediacy, its capacity to fuse visual demonstration with auditory narration and emotional resonance. In doing so, film translated abstract ideals of progress into concrete and comprehensible practices, positioning cinema as a central tool in the US project of developmental outreach.

Films such as *Poultry Raising* showed the United States as a model of modernization while their use by government agents cast target audiences in countries like Turkey as eager students in need of guidance and transformation. This framing advanced a developmentalist narrative and fostered an orientalist interpretation of research data, as American agents viewed Turkish audiences as "intellectually or psychologically inferior."[7] Such assumptions underscore a core limitation of film diplomacy: While promoting uplift and influence, it reproduced racialized hierarchies and positioned non-Western publics within a civilizational deficit model. However, the impact of film diplomacy was not purely unidirectional. In some instances, translated films reframed messages to match Turkey's domestic political and economic agendas.

The villager's interview after watching *Poultry Raising* provides an example of the limitations of conducting audience reception research to gather and analyze local data to promote transnational interests. The interview shows that the villager not only comprehended and retained the content of *Poultry Raising* but also used it to formulate opinions about the limitations of farming practices in his country. Yet the ECA-USIS team interpreted the responses to mean that the villager did not fully acquire the film's information. It seems more plausible that the villager's answers reflect both an understanding of the film and a preexisting knowledge of poultry care as well as a recognition that the challenges in adopting such practices in Turkey stemmed primarily from resource limitations. Furthermore, it is likely that the villager's comments communicate a knowledge of what was sustainable in a given economic and ecological setting.[8] In either case, the film did not serve its overt educational purpose of teaching him how to raise poultry. Rather, its "educational" label pertains to the ideology of modernization, and it implicitly promises an improved life by learning how to produce goods the American way—that is, by embracing capitalism.

The villager's use of an us-versus-them dichotomy as he compared his situation with that of farmers in the United States highlights the contrasting economic conditions between Turkey and the United States. Moreover, it demonstrates his ability—contrary to the researchers' interpretation of such data—to extrapolate from personal experiences to transnational circumstances. As the villager noted, the problem in his country was primarily due to financial limitations rather than a lack of knowledge about poultry care. The film's educational value resided in its ideological advocacy for modernizing poultry-raising methods. It conveyed that economic progress could be achieved only by adopting modern tools as well as tools adapted to corn production, which flourishes in certain ecological niches. However, acquiring these tools necessitated financial resources, making the Marshall Plan strategically critical for facilitating modernization in Turkey.

The interview with the Turkish villager and its evaluation by American researchers were both parts of larger studies that examined communication and behavioral patterns among Middle Eastern populations.[9] Lerner's analysis categorized the Turkish interviewees into three distinct groups: "traditional Turks," who had little to no engagement with media; "transitional Turks," who showed occasional interest in press, radio, or film; and "modern Turks," who regularly accessed various media channels.[10] This framework of audience categorization, alongside the limited understanding of interview data, exemplifies the racialized logics of whiteness embedded within the research process. Though Lerner refrained from explicit racial language, his classification of Turks as underdeveloped cast them as subjects needing exposure to American media to become modern. These assumptions solidified modernization theory, which positioned media as a tool for uplifting underdeveloped groups by exposing them to the white, modern, American way of life. This framework aligned with Cold War policy goals by casting media as a tool for measuring social advancement.

The US government–sponsored agents like Lerner envisioned Turkey as a strategic testing ground for universalizing modernization theory—framing film as a means of bridging perceived social, economic, cultural, and racial gaps. In this chapter, I demonstrate how US-funded audience studies in Cold War Turkey functioned as mechanisms for shaping public opinion, legitimizing American developmental paradigms, and promoting capitalism and liberal democracy as bulwarks against communism. I address the following questions: How did audience reception research shape the selection, circulation, and interpretation of films shown to Turkish audiences? What do audience responses indicate about the assumptions and structural limitations during the Cold War? How did US-sponsored audience research in Turkey shape the construction of Cold War communication infrastructures and the ideological work they performed?

To reiterate, I contend that the audience reception research conducted by Americans in Turkey operationalized whiteness as an epistemological and ideological framework, enabling researchers to position film as a strategic tool for shaping public opinions and behaviors in the Middle East in alignment with the ideals of US free-market capitalism. This approach not only cast modernization as universally applicable but also obscured the material inequalities—economic, structural, and infrastructural—that constrained the intended effectiveness of these films as tools of transformation. A close analysis of research findings, interviews, films, and translated materials shows how whiteness operated as an ideological lens—one that masked asymmetries of power and rendered US-led media interventions as benevolent and universally applicable.

Educational Films as Tools of Modernization

In a US government–sponsored survey conducted by researchers at Columbia University, a Turkish woman, reflecting on a documentary about American cities, remarked, "What interested me most was life in America and its social significance."[11] Such sentiments, echoed in numerous similar responses, led researchers to conclude that documentary films fostered a "desire to know more about other countries, other social customs and new developments in science."[12] One student, after viewing a film about American schools, commented, "I liked it because I would like to study in an American college, too." For researchers, such reactions affirmed the belief that documentary films possessed the power to nourish dreams, instigate a desire for upward mobility, and sustain hope for a better life.[13] Turkish audiences often described these films as "realistic," "optimistic," and "not superficial"—attributes that contrasted with their expectations of didactic or ideologically rigid state media.[14] A corporate executive who viewed a Walt Disney film about mosquito control praised its "superior use of educational techniques" and added that "it didn't have the attitude of a boring teacher, a now-I'm-going-to-teach-you-something attitude."[15] American researchers interpreted these responses as confirmation of the power of US films to not only inform but also shape desires, influence worldviews, and align foreign publics with the values of free-market capitalism.

In response to audience feedback from Turkey, US-backed researchers launched a comprehensive initiative to develop a film program tailored to local preferences. These carefully selected films spanned a range of topics—including everyday American life, education, social institutions, and scientific innovation—and were framed not as entertainment but as instruments of modernization. As the historian Michael E. Latham puts it, modernization conveyed "an ideology, a conceptual framework that articulated a common collection of assumptions about the nature of American society and its ability to transform a world viewed as both materially and culturally deficient."[16] To maximize institutional uptake and audience engagement, researchers deliberately avoided the term *documentary*, instead classifying the films as educational. This strategic rebranding allowed these films to operate as tools of useful modernization and facilitated their circulation within schools and other civic institutions. In Turkey, the Ministry of National Education (MNET)—through the Educational Film Center (EFC)—adopted this classification, labeling all US-produced films as educational and thereby legitimizing their integration into national pedagogical infrastructures. In doing so, the EFC helped institutionalize educational film as a tool for development, advancing US geopolitical interests by embedding its vision of modernization within Turkish state institutions.

Modernization theory is rooted in the juxtaposition of "the modern" and "the traditional," positioning them as mutually exclusive domains.

The modern is democratic and secular, whereas the traditional is stagnant and antiquated.[17] Proponents of modernization theory understood modernism not merely as "an aesthetic phenomenon" but also as "a social and political practice" that includes the "technical transformation" of "history, society, economy, culture, and [even] nature itself."[18] In the 1950s and 1960s, this framework gained significant traction among American social scientists, including Edward Shils, Harold Lasswell, Talcott Parsons, Walt Whitman Rostow, Gabriel Almond, and Lucian Pye. These figures advanced a developmentalist agenda aimed at restructuring so-called traditional societies through technological progress, urbanization, rising incomes, expanded literacy, and the mass dissemination of media.[19] Framed as a universal model of progress, modernization theory functioned as a key ideological tool of US Cold War strategy, projecting the American way of being as normative and aspirational.

This binary framework found cinematic expression in the genre of educational film, which I conceptualize as advancing *useful modernization*. Recognizing the connections between modernity and cinema, film scholars argue that movies should be understood as central to the cultural formation of modern life.[20] From this perspective, cinema is a site where political, social, economic, and cultural transformations converge. The film historian Miriam Hansen describes classical cinema as vernacular modernism, the quintessential "cultural horizon" that reflects, rejects, disavows, transmutes, or negotiates the effects of modernity.[21] While this formulation captures the multifaceted essence of modern life, it leaves limited space for nonfiction and nontheatrical, or what Acland and Wasson have called "useful cinema," which is identified by "a disposition"—an institutional orientation toward film as a tool for instruction, persuasion, and intervention.[22] By recontextualizing educational films not as peripheral but as central to Cold War media strategy, I examine how their reception shaped and was shaped by national and transnational projects of development, governance, and ideological alignment.

Eager to develop allied nations, promote democracy, and combat poverty, US government–funded researchers formulated modernization as a full-fledged ideology.[23] Education was positioned as a critical lever in this project—especially in Turkey, where social scientists argued that citizens needed to adopt American-style modernization in order to achieve social, economic, and political progress. This vision entailed embracing liberal democracy and a market-based capitalist economy. Supported by policymakers, these experts cast Turkey as both a geopolitical bulwark against Soviet communism and a representative model for the Middle East.

Building on earlier chapters focusing on institutions such as the USIS and the EFC, I turn here to the pivotal role of audience reception reports in shaping Cold War media strategy. These reports laid the foundation not only for the articulation of modernization theory but also for the emergence of communication research as a discipline. By tracing how the EFC labeled and circulated USIS films as educational, I show how audience research operated as both a feedback mechanism and an ideological tool—embedding modernization discourse within the transnational infrastructure of Cold War film diplomacy.

Audience reception research significantly impacted film distribution in Turkey. It quickly became evident that Turks with conservative leanings resisted American fictional films, finding them morally objectionable when viewed through the lens of their Islamic beliefs.[24] Farmers, in particular, shunned these films, deeming them incompatible with their values. A retired fig expert and farmer explained that he prohibited his children from viewing such films because "I want honorable and clean things in the minds of my children, fear of God, love for parents, respect for elders."[25] At the same time, films labeled as documentary failed to resonate with Turkish audiences, and many villagers described them as "boring" or "dull."[26]

Categorizing films about American society as educational, however, addressed the challenges posed by religious beliefs and audience disinterest. Educational films have long been used worldwide to disseminate ideas, facts, skills, morals, and social behaviors across various contexts, both within and beyond the confines of the classroom. In Turkey, American government agents used this label to cultivate the perception that these films served a purpose beyond entertainment, documentaries, or propaganda.[27] The educational label created the expectation that the public would gain something valuable from them.[28] This classification helped mitigate arguments that the films contradicted religious beliefs, and it ensured audience attention, even if the content risked being perceived as dull. By labeling these films as educational, the agents hoped their content related to modernization would appear informative and impartial rather than propagandistic. Moreover, the educational categorization facilitated the integration of these films into school curricula so that they reached younger audiences.

In pursuit of this objective, USIS agents offered training courses for teachers and officials and contributed to establishing "a Turkish documentary film production program," which later became the EFC, as discussed in chapter 4.[29] However, the definition of an educational film remained elusive and left room for interpretation. The USIS categorized films as educational if they disseminated a positive image of the United States and highlighted its modernization efforts. According to an international agreement, audiovisual materials, including films, were deemed educational when their primary purpose or effect was to instruct, inform, develop a subject, increase knowledge, and foster international understanding and goodwill. Additionally, these materials were expected to be representative, authentic, and accurate.[30]

The definition of educational films could potentially justify excluding certain films and thus serve as a form of censorship. As discussed in chapter 3, in the 1980s a group of American filmmakers filed a lawsuit against the USIS after their attempt to have their films labeled educational was rejected. The legal scholar Sharon Esakoff explains that the films were rejected because they presented a "standpoint" and thus conflicted with USIS regulators' belief that educational films should refrain from taking a specific point of view.[31] Yet all films inherently present a viewpoint.[32] As Frankenberg notes, whiteness itself is a "standpoint"—a specific, though often unmarked, "location from which to see selves, others, and national and global orders."[33] This unacknowledged vantage point parallels the framing of USIS-endorsed educational films, which presented viewpoints steeped in whiteness. Just as whiteness claims objectivity, USIS-endorsed educational films claimed objectivity. Films that were granted the "educational" label simply endorsed a standpoint or a kind of whiteness that aligned with the ideology that the US government sought to promote abroad. As a rule, the USIS granted this label to films that communicated a functional ideology of modernization while circumventing problems prevalent within American society.

Columbia University's Research on Turkish Audiences

In 1951, Daniel Lerner joined Columbia University's BASR—a center for media and communication research led by sociologist Paul Lazarsfeld—to analyze data from surveys, including Voice of America (VOA) studies conducted in Turkey and parts of the Middle East. BASR received funds from the US State Department during the Cold War to support studies aligned with American foreign policy goals. The department commissioned the VOA project to evaluate the effectiveness of its broadcasts in countering Soviet influence and promoting American ideology in geopolitically critical regions. Amid growing scrutiny over the impact of such propaganda efforts, Lerner and his colleagues were tasked with providing empirical evidence to justify continued funding while advancing theories on mass media's role in societal transformation.[34]

As part of this initiative, Lerner and the research team created fifteen reports focused on Turkey, Egypt, Iran, Lebanon, Jordan, and Syria.[35] To ensure accuracy, the team enlisted the aid of teachers and advanced students from renowned universities in each country to conduct interviews. These local collaborators, trained and supervised by American researchers, conducted interviews in the native language, which were then translated into English by bilingual interviewers. This research structure reflected a hierarchical division of labor in which local collaborators were positioned primarily as data collectors, while interpretive authority remained concentrated in the hands of American supervisors. This asymmetry reinforced an epistemological framework that privileged Western analytical paradigms and treated local expertise as instrumental rather than intellectual. By embedding these dynamics within the research process, the project reproduced a paternalistic model of knowledge production: one that cast Western observers as objective analysts and non-Western publics as subjects to be studied, categorized, and guided toward modernization. The interview questions aimed to examine how individuals responded to various forms of mass media—including radio, newspapers, films, and current events—to understand the formation of public opinion. Yet the power asymmetries that shaped the research process influenced not only how data were collected but also what kinds of knowledge were produced—classifications of modernization, behavioral prescriptions for media strategy, and "deficit"-based characterizations of local populations—and how such knowledge was framed, interpreted, and ultimately mobilized to serve the Cold War modernization agenda.

The Columbia researchers converted the interview data into statistical datasets to support their claim that modernization could be modeled, replicated, and managed across different cultural contexts. In their report titled "Mass Communications Audiences in Turkey," the team analyzed 259 qualitative interviews conducted in late 1950 with Turkish citizens from both rural and urban areas in Izmir, Istanbul, and Ankara, applying quantitative methods to extract generalizable patterns.[36] While they acknowledged the methodological limitations of their sample and cautioned against interpreting the findings as representative of the entire Turkish population, their analysis nonetheless rested on the assumption that respondents offered candid and sincere answers.[37] This presumption of transparency, coupled with the use of statistical abstraction, lent an air of scientific neutrality to what was ultimately an ideological exercise in mapping cultural difference and prescribing developmental trajectories.

Lerner's categories, grounded in a Eurocentric model of social evolution, reproduced the racialized logic of whiteness by casting Turkish society on a linear axis of development from backwardness to progress.[38] According to these data, transitional Turks emerged as the primary target demographic for US cultural outreach in the Middle East. Though not yet fully integrated into the modern public sphere, they were viewed as malleable and influential—agents capable of disseminating foreign information to less accessible rural populations. The data showed that over half of transitional Turks attended films, eight out of ten engaged with newspapers, six out of ten occasionally listened to the radio, and four out of ten lived in households with radios.[39] They were imagined as the vanguard of Turkey's modernization, a transitional class whose susceptibility to foreign influence made them instrumental to the success of the Cold War agenda. This scheme simplified the complexity of Turkish society, legitimizing a racialized hierarchy based on proximity to Western modernization.

The Columbia team advised the US government to focus its media strategy on transitional Turks, positioning them as intermediaries between the mass-communications sphere of modern Turks and the word-of-mouth communications of traditional Turks. Framed as socially mobile and increasingly receptive to modern forms of communication, the transitional group was seen as uniquely positioned to transmit foreign information into otherwise inaccessible rural areas.[40] The researchers viewed transitional Turks as a malleable and influential demographic: individuals in flux who could facilitate the diffusion of modernization. Described as a "deviant group" or a "heterogeneous collection of deviant types," they were imagined as a communicative conduit linking the poles of tradition and modernity, capable of translating mass-mediated messages into forms legible to less media-integrated publics.[41]

This rigid developmental typology reproduced the ideological operations of whiteness described earlier, framing Turkish audiences through a normative Eurocentric lens. Functioning as an unmarked baseline for evaluating economic, political, and cultural advancement, whiteness established binary hierarchies such as modern versus traditional to normalize the superiority of the American way of life. This logic sustained a paternalistic stance, imagining non-Western subjects as in need of tutelage and intervention. By flattening cultural complexity and forcing heterogeneous populations into reductive typologies, whiteness provided the epistemological justification for using film as a tool of governance—positioning American educational cinema as a developmental aid rather than an ideological instrument of Cold War foreign policy.

These categories were further applied in the Columbia team's report "Movies, Newsreels, and Documentary Films in Turkey," which analyzed patterns of movie attendance and the reception of foreign newsreels and documentaries. Drawing on opinion polls and interviews, the team examined Turkish viewers' recollections of films, their preferences, the traits they valued in films, and whether their opinions or attitudes shifted after viewing.[42] However, the report did not include original language transcripts of the interviews, making it impossible to assess the accuracy or fidelity of the translations. This absence introduces a significant barrier to evaluating the nuances of Turkish audience responses, particularly given the cultural and linguistic inflections that may have been flattened or distorted in translation. Compounding this limitation, the report also failed to identify specific film titles, instead grouping responses under vague thematic headings—such as "Jeeps," "Schools," "Farming," and "The Korean War." To mitigate these gaps, I have drawn on supplementary data, including surveys and reception studies conducted by other entities.

These sources offer additional insight into how Turkish audiences interpreted film content, negotiated meaning, and navigated the structural power asymmetries that shaped Cold War media research and its epistemological claims.

Surveying Turkish Audiences' Response to Films

The ECA played a pivotal role in managing the Marshall Plan initiative, working closely with the USIS in Turkey. In 1951, Basil Rogers, an ECA employee, wrote a report for the US State and Commerce Departments that incorporated surveys conducted by the USIS Film Section in Ankara. These surveys aimed to capture rural audiences' responses to American films, particularly those focused on agriculture.[43] The report also incorporated interviews conducted with Turkish viewers following screenings held in November 1950. Facilitated by the ECA-USIS collaboration, the films' voice-overs were translated from English to Turkish. In contrast to the Columbia research, which anonymized content and segmented the population into developmental categories, the ECA-USIS materials included specific film titles and full transcripts of translated interviews. Rogers, however, referred to participants monolithically as "villagers," eschewing demographic nuance. His narrative employed overtly orientalist language, depicting Turkish rural audiences as "simple country people" with limited cognitive capacity to understand "anything new or unusual."[44] This rhetoric reinforced the civilizational hierarchies already structured by whiteness, casting rural Turks as intellectually marginal and thus legitimizing the ideological function of film diplomacy.

In addition to survey data, the ECA-USIS materials included Rogers's recommendations for developing film programs in Turkey. He emphasized the importance of supplying films to schools, particularly in villages equipped with projectors, and proposed collaborating with Adolphe Hübl, the UNESCO visual aids specialist from Austria, to prepare and acquire films for educational purposes. He further recommended targeting films at both children and adults, producing educational films within Turkey, employing mobile film units to tour the country, and equipping vans with five to ten projectors for showcasing films related to agriculture, economy, industry, and culture. Rogers also included a budget of $54,000 (approximately $673,000 today, or 28.15 million TRY). Costs included building a technical laboratory ($12,000, or approximately $149,500 today, or 6.25 million TRY); buying 150 filmstrip projectors ($6,000, or approximately $74,800 today, or 3.13 million TRY), 100 silent film projectors ($12,000, approximately $149,500 today, or 6.25 million TRY), 600 educational films ($12,000, approximately $149,500 today, or 6.25 million TRY), and 50,000 filmstrips ($8,000, approximately $99,700 today, or 4.17 million TRY); and producing three educational films in Turkey ($4,000, approximately $49,800 today, or 2.09 million TRY).[45] These recommendations were ultimately implemented by 1952, leading to the establishment of the EFC—a Cold War communication hub involving UNESCO, the USIS, and the MNET, as discussed in chapter 4.

Rogers highlighted the significant effort required to convince representatives of the MNET and Hübl that the ECA-USIS team's objective was to provide genuinely educational material rather than propaganda promoting the Marshall Plan.[46] This underscores the concerns among Turkish government agents and international partners who recognized the potentially propagandistic function of US media. In response, Rogers highlighted that the team's objective was the distribution of visual educational materials stripped of overt political messaging.

The archival records of the ECA-USIS surveys and the Columbia University research provide a valuable comparative lens through which to examine audience responses collected by distinct US entities surveying the same population during the early 1950s. Despite differences in method and institutional affiliation, both projects asked Turkish viewers similar questions about their preferences, recollections, and reactions to American films. While the Columbia study offers aggregated statistical data and selective quotations, the ECA-USIS materials go further by preserving full transcripts of interviews between villagers and field agents. These transcripts offer a rare window into the nuances of audience reception and, crucially, show the interpretive assumptions that underpinned the Columbia researchers' characterization of Turkish subjects. These assumptions also reflected in the ECA-USIS materials. What follows is a closer examination of the ideological blind spots embedded in US government–sponsored media research and the ways in which film was strategically deployed to shape public perceptions in Cold War Turkey.

The Nexus of Modernization Theory, Research in Turkey, and US Foreign Policy

The Columbia research was instrumental in shaping the raw data and conceptual models that Lerner would later formalize into modernization theory and development communication research as extensions of US foreign policy. Building on his work on the VOA research, he authored *The Passing of Traditional Society: Modernizing the Middle East* (1958), a book often considered "the bible of the modernization paradigm of development communication research."[47] He received funding to support his work on the book from the BASR at Columbia University and the Center for International Studies (CENIS) at the Massachusetts Institute of Technology, two institutions enmeshed in Cold War projects.[48] Lerner posited that mass media could foster empathy among audiences by allowing them to envision themselves living in a modernized society. He defined empathy as "the capacity to see oneself in the other fellow's situation" and argued that this capacity could be instilled through exposure to media.[49] In his model, modernization was not just a material transformation but also a psychological and cultural shift—one that could be engineered through communication technologies. The West, particularly the United States, was cast as a "useful model" for the Middle East's developmental trajectory.[50]

For Lerner, Turkey stood out as the "most impressive example of modernization" in the region. He described Turkey's steady evolution, which adhered to the guidelines established by Atatürk's "behavioral and institutional innovations," as impressive.[51] Lerner admired Atatürk's ability to transform institutions and individuals through communication revolutions. Atatürk recognized that to change the mindset of the people, he needed to revolutionize the existing communication network. For instance, he introduced the Latin script to replace the Arabic alphabet to increase literacy rates. He also established institutions such as People's Houses and Village Institutes, which played a significant role in promoting literacy and facilitating media growth. People's Houses acted as message centers for transmitting modernization, while Village Institutes provided spaces in which to educate villagers.[52] Lerner viewed Atatürk's objective as reshaping traditional society by transforming the daily lives and aspirations of the masses.

When Lerner attempted to extrapolate from Turkey and apply his theory of modernization to the Middle East, many scholars had negative responses. For example, P. M. Mahar criticized Lerner for not thoroughly examining other countries in the Middle East and for coming up with a "frail theory."[53] Elie Salem and John Gulick likewise were critical of Lerner for generalizing particularities and cultures of the Middle East.[54] Edward Banfield and Samuel Huntington argued that attempts to modernize the Middle East were likely to fail and create instability.[55] The Pakistani economist Inayatullah faulted Lerner's work on modernization for its "ethnocentrism," and the African and Islamic studies scholar Ali Mazrui condemned its "paternalism."[56] The political psychologist Ashis Nandy indicated that modernization caused power asymmetry and justified exploitation.[57]

Hemant Shah, a communication scholar, has offered a historical analysis of the influence of Lerner's research to explain how modernization was produced to justify development communication research and support American foreign policy. He examines how Lerner's institutional affiliations with the US Army's Psychological Warfare Division, the Hoover Institution at Stanford University, the BASR at Columbia University, and the CENIS at MIT affected his research agenda. He notes that Lerner's engagement with the cultural theory of race during his tenure at Stanford likely left an imprint on how he approached the Middle East during his time at Columbia and MIT.[58] Drawing inspiration from Gunnar Myrdal's analysis of race relations in the United States, Lerner embraced the notion that there were no inherent biological differences between races.[59] In line with Myrdal's arguments, Lerner advocated that white people facilitate social, political, and economic transformation among "backward" populations in the Middle East, which he ascribed to an "Oriental mentality." Notably, Lerner asserted that Arabs, Turks, and Persians "were not racially inferior, only psychologically and socially inferior."[60] With the cultural theory of race reinforcing the absence of biological disparities between whites and nonwhites, Lerner championed modernization as a means for Middle Eastern residents to bridge the gap and "*catch up* to whites."[61]

President Harry Truman's containment strategy during the Cold War, which he articulated in his inauguration speech and through his introduction of the Point Four Program in 1949, further supported modernization theory. The Point Four Program aimed to provide technical assistance and economic aid to developing countries and prevent the spread of communism. Truman introduced "the concept of underdevelopment" as an alternative to labeling postcolonial societies as backward or inferior. The concept was intended to shift the "colonizer-colonized dynamic" to an "underdevelopment-development continuum," framing "intervention as a humanitarian mission rather than a new form of colonialism." Truman's foreign policy framework influenced Lerner's language in his book, which presented modernization as a "neutral-sounding process."[62]

Truman's framework with the Point Four Program led other social scientists to produce research about modernization theory, social change, nation-building, and international aid.[63] For example, Edward Shils was a key sociologist who advocated modernization theory and emphasized the superiority of the West without explicitly bringing in theories of race. For him, being modern meant "being Western without the onus of following the West," and a modern state was one that had "democracy, land reform, progressive income taxation, universal suffrage, universal public education, rational technology, scientific knowledge, industrialization, and a high standard of living."[64] He subscribed to the term *modernization* to avoid the implications of words such as *Christianization* and *Westernization*.[65] In this way, he supposedly eliminated terms associated with the biological theories of race as well as with the colonialism of missionaries and Europeans. Consequently, Shils and like-minded scholars used modernization to offer an idealized image of the United States.[66]

Social scientists played a key role in advancing US foreign policy by producing statistical analyses that framed modernization as a solution to Cold War tensions.[67] Funded largely by the US government, these researchers positioned the United States—anchored in capitalism, democracy, and industrial growth—as the ideal model for "traditional" societies. Their production of development communication marginalized "the voices of the raced, classed, [and] gendered subject" to justify "claims of development, modernization, and economic growth."[68] The urgency of responding to the communist threat led policymakers to become heavily invested in modernization in traditional societies through technical and foreign assistance.[69] In this way, the United States could create an American capitalist and democratic way of life in postcolonial and underdeveloped nations and could frame modernization as a universal pathway to progress. Modernization thus became a powerful narrative device.

Turkish Audiences' Interests in American Subjects

The Columbia researchers played a key role in advancing US efforts to promote modernization and counter communism in Turkey by identifying media content likely to resonate with local audiences. Their study revealed that topics related to American ideology—including capitalism, democracy, and modernization—ranked among the most favorably received, alongside themes of economy and society: Of respondents categorized as modern Turks, 47 percent expressed a strong interest in learning about US ideology, compared to 38 percent of transitional Turks and only 15 percent of traditional Turks.[70] These findings provided empirical justification for targeting transitional demographics with films that idealized economic productivity and the American way of life, thereby operationalizing audience research as a tool of ideological alignment.

In collaboration with the MNET, the USIS distributed and exhibited films about American ideology across Turkey. One such film, *Barış Yolu* (*Atoms for Peace*, USIS, 1955), remained in circulation in both USIS and EFC libraries between 1956 and 1986. The film featured President Dwight D. Eisenhower's 1953 speech on peaceful uses of atomic energy, which emphasized the United States' "peaceful intentions and Soviet intransigence."[71] Strategically designed to mitigate international anxiety over nuclear power, the film highlighted its applications in agriculture, medicine, and electricity production.[72] After screenings, USIS officials solicited audience feedback and invited viewers to visit USIS offices to learn more about US nuclear programs. This example of film diplomacy not only demonstrates the US government's strategic use of media to gather feedback from Turkish audiences but also underscores its ongoing efforts to refine propaganda in response to local reception.

The Columbia research equated audience interest with ideological alignment, collapsing curiosity into consent. When asked about their interest in the United States, respondents across all three categories—traditional, transitional, and modern—expressed a strong desire to learn about economic conditions and job opportunities. Notably, 41 percent of traditional Turks were interested in job prospects, surpassing the 27 percent of interested modern Turks, while 40 percent of transitional Turks expressed similar concerns. Rather than treating this interest as a complex response to postwar economic precarity and rural-urban migration patterns, the researchers interpreted it as an endorsement of modernization's ideological promises. This leap—shaped by racialized and paternalistic assumptions—erased the possibility that such interest stemmed from pragmatic need, economic insecurity, or curiosity. In doing so, the study reasserted the ideological fiction that modernization was both desirable and inexorable, echoing the teleological narrative that underwrote Cold War development discourse.

The ideological framework of whiteness shaped the development logic employed by organizations like the USIS and the EFC, whose educational film strategies reproduced racialized and paternalistic assumptions under the guise of technical assistance. Both agencies circulated a substantial number of films extolling American achievements in water management, electricity generation, and infrastructure development—implicitly positioning the United States as the apex of modern civilization. Titles such as *Elektrik ve Toprak* (*Power and the Land*, produced by the US Film Service for the Rural Electrification Administration and directed by Joris Ivens, 1940), *Grand Gülee Barajı* (*Grand Coulee Dam*, the US Department of the Interior's Bureau of Reclamation, 1942), and *Tennessee Vadisi* (*Valley of the Tennessee*, produced by the Office of War Information as part of the "Projections of America" series and directed by Alexander Hammid, 1944), presented idealized narratives of American modernization.[73] *Elektrik ve Toprak* depicted the electrification of a rural American village as a civilizing force, while *Grand Gülee Barajı* and *Tennessee Vadisi* celebrated regional transformation through dam construction. Both agencies promoted these films to position modernization as a universally adaptable solution, reinforcing the notion that Turkey's future lay in emulating the United States' technological advancements and ideological trajectory.

The use of educational films to promote modernization mirrored the paternalistic logic embedded in the Columbia team's research. These films advanced a worldview structured by whiteness, presenting American modernization as a universal ideal while concealing their ideological aims under the label of education. This logic echoed the researchers' reliance on hierarchical binaries—such as modern versus traditional—to classify Turkish society according to proximity to Western norms. Just as audience research imposed developmental frameworks grounded in racialized assumptions, the USIS and the EFC deployed film to normalize the idea that modernization—coded through whiteness—was Turkey's inevitable future. These interventions across both research and media demonstrate how Cold War institutions operationalized whiteness as an invisible standard, embedding modernization within a racialized, ideological project.

Film as a Catalyst for Economic Unity

The Columbia research team surveyed Turkish citizens to assess their personal concerns and perceptions of national challenges. Economic hardship emerged as the most pressing issue for the majority across all groups, as 64 percent of modern Turks, 59 percent of transitional Turks, and 67 percent of traditional Turks identified the local economy as their primary concern. However, responses diverged significantly when participants were asked to name the country's most critical national problem. While 52 percent of modern Turks identified the economy as Turkey's central issue, only 21 percent of transitional Turks and a mere 8 percent of traditional Turks did so. The Columbia team attributed this gap to the purported inability of traditional Turks to abstract from personal hardship to national concerns—a claim that reveals the researchers' paternalistic assumptions about political consciousness and rationality.[74] For Cold War propagandists, this disconnect posed a strategic dilemma: how to mobilize support for national objectives among populations preoccupied with subsistence.[75] The study ultimately framed this challenge as a communication problem, one that required not only tailored messaging but also ideological realignment to render modernization both legible and desirable to the public.

By framing the American economic model as a universal solution to both personal and national challenges, the educational films captured the attention of Turkish audiences and fueled widespread curiosity about American prosperity. A striking majority of Turkish citizens—69 percent of modern Turks, 64 percent of transitional Turks, and 72 percent of traditional Turks—expressed a strong interest in learning about US economic conditions.[76] These films did more than convey economic information; they constructed American capitalism as both aspirational and normative, embedding it within the racialized developmental framework defined earlier. By presenting US economic strategies as solutions to Turkey's structural challenges, the films subtly legitimized a civilizational hierarchy in which American whiteness stood as the symbol of modernity and progress. The Columbia research underscores how cinema served not merely as a medium of communication but also as an ideological instrument—one capable of inciting collective ambition while encoding racialized visions of advancement. Thus, American state-sponsored researchers deployed film as a dual-purpose mechanism to cultivate economic desire and to normalize whiteness as the underlying architecture of modernization itself.

Addressing Turkish Audiences' Interests

Film diplomacy during the Cold War was intertwined with projects of modernization and the racialized ideology of whiteness, as exemplified by the ECA-USIS initiatives in Turkey. In the ECA-USIS report, Rogers stressed the importance of tailoring media to resonate with local audiences.[77] He emphasized producing films within Turkey that featured Turkish individuals to enhance relatability and broaden appeal. This approach echoed the Columbia team's findings, which showed that Turkish audiences were most drawn to films that reflected their own country, particularly those addressing the Marshall Plan and the Korean War. By aligning American ideological content with localized interests, film diplomacy became a vital mechanism for winning government approval and instilling modernization as a desirable trajectory. These efforts encoded whiteness and Western modernity as aspirational norms. Films promoting the American way of life projected a racialized ideal of progress, positioning US economic and social structures as benchmarks of modernization. Over time, Turkish government agents adopted similar strategies, producing similar films that depicted Turkey from 1956 onward, especially once adequate financial and technical infrastructure was in place.

Among these efforts, Marshall Plan films were particularly effective in addressing Turkish viewers' curiosity about the US economy and their aspirations for improved economic conditions. These films not only invited viewers to imagine themselves as beneficiaries of modernization but also prescribed strategies for how to achieve progress. However, a 1950 Columbia study indicated a striking disconnect: Most Turks possessed limited knowledge about the tangible impact of the Marshall Plan, as just

28 percent of modern Turks, 21 percent of transitional Turks, and 9 percent of traditional Turks had a clear understanding of its significance.[78] This gap highlighted the strategic imperative to produce and circulate films that more explicitly framed the Marshall Plan as a catalyst for reimagining the nation and mobilizing public in its transformation.[79]

In this context, both the USIS and the EFC were instrumental in distributing films designed to inform rural populations about the benefits of the Marshall Plan. *Suyun Kontrolü* (*Control of Water*, produced for ECA Turkey by Clarke and Hornby Film Productions, 1951), *Traktör Bakımı* (*Care of Tractors*, Clifford Hornby, 1951), *Köy Traktörü* (*Village Tractor*, Clifford Hornby, 1951 and 1953), and *Yusuf ve Sabanı* (*Yusef and His Plough*, Clifford Hornby, 1951) centered on Turkish villagers and showed pathways toward agricultural modernization. *Suyun Kontrolü*, for instance, illustrated dam construction as a strategy for irrigation and water storage, while *Köy Traktörü* and *Yusuf ve Sabanı* promoted the use of iron plows and tractors to increase yield. These films did more than disseminate technical knowledge through the USIS and the EFC mobile film units; they crafted an ideological narrative that equated agricultural productivity and technological adoption with Western ideals of modernization. By casting Turkish farmers as participants in the larger modernization project, these films sought to bridge the knowledge gap regarding the Marshall Plan by encouraging audiences to see themselves as stakeholders in its implementation and as beneficiaries of its promise.

Virginia Farmers' Cooperative Ventures and the Path to Modernization in Turkey

The Rural Co-Op (Pare Lorentz, 1947) illustrates how translation practices and local political agendas reshaped a film's reception and ideological message. Produced by the Department of the Army's Civil Affairs Division and distributed by the USIS, the film—directed by renowned New Deal documentarian Pare Lorentz—shows how Virginia farmers improved their economic situation by forming agricultural cooperatives.[80] It opens with a cartographic shot of the United States that slowly zooms in on Virginia, situating the local within the national. A male voice-over narrates the region's farming practices, guiding viewers through landscapes of valleys crisscrossed by highways and marked by homes and ruins. Central to the narrative is Fred, a farmer whom the camera follows as he works his fields, tends turkeys, and prepares eggs for sale in the nearby town of Harrisonburg in Rockingham County. This narrative, while grounded in local specificity, was designed to model ideals of cooperation and technocratic progress. Yet when translated and adapted for Turkish audiences, these meanings were neither fixed nor universal. Instead, they became sites of negotiation, refracted through the lens of domestic political priorities, infrastructural disparities, and local reception.

As images of a local store and a milk processing plant appear on screen, the voice-over introduces the concept of cooperatives, emphasizing their practical and economic advantages—particularly in the production and distribution of milk. One domestic scene features a family in their yard: A woman plucks a chicken while a farmer lounges on a bench and a child plays with a toy car. The voice-over states, "If you could make automobiles on a moving line, you could sure clean poultry the same way." This analogy marks a narrative pivot, drawing an explicit connection between Ford Motor Company's assembly-line production and rural agricultural labor. It frames poultry processing within a logic of industrial rationalization, asserting that cooperative infrastructure could replicate the efficiencies of factory-based capitalism in rural settings.

This turning point gives way to a dramatized sequence in which a farmer sketches a plan for the mass production of poultry. He discusses building a co-op with a friend while standing in front of a church on a Sunday. The film then shifts to scenes of a poultry factory and a town meeting, where cooperative logistics are further elaborated. At this juncture, the film's visual style transforms: Animation, paper puppets, and circular wires and coins are used to illustrate the step-by-step establishment of a poultry cooperative. These animated sequences guide viewers through the cooperative's formation—from issuing stock certificates and electing a board of directors to managing distribution, revenue, and taxation. Then the film expands its scope to include additional cooperative models in wool, electricity, and dairy to underscore how these collective efforts facilitate the growth and prosperity of various sectors within the community.

In a series of interviews led by the ECA-USIS team, Turkish villagers shared their opinions about *The Rural Co-Op*. A striking pattern emerges in their responses: The villagers gravitated toward the film's portrayal of hen care, particularly the poultry-cleaning process. This pattern highlights a disjuncture between the film's intended pedagogical aims—centered on the virtues of cooperative capitalism—and the aspects of the film that resonated with local viewers. While advocates of educational film framed such productions as tools for increasing economic productivity, villagers instead gravitated toward practical, personally relatable details grounded in their everyday experience. One farmer recalled the voice-over's discussion of hens, the act of cleaning poultry, and a group of men making decisions and pushing for progress. His account, reflected a coherent engagement with the film's content on his own terms. Given *The Rural Co-Op* had a complex and lengthy storyline, the villager's description offered an accurate reflection of what he comprehended from the film. Rather than acknowledging this form of reception as contextually grounded, American researchers interpreted such responses as evidence of a cognitive or cultural "deficit"—what they characterized as an "inferior" capacity to understand film. This interpretive stance reflects an orientalist and racist logic that pathologized local viewers and dismissed the legitimacy of their perspectives. As the political scientist Begüm Adalet notes, villagers often felt too intimidated to articulate their ideas during such interviews,[81] a dynamic the researchers failed to recognize. Instead, they instrumentalized the transcripts to justify prescriptive interventions aligned with US foreign policy objectives, flattening complex local interpretations into data that confirmed their own ideological assumptions.

A comparison between the original English-language version of *The Rural Co-Op* and the responses from Turkish interviewees suggests that the version shown to Turkish villagers differed substantially in content. This divergence likely resulted from both the translation process and efforts to align the film with the Turkish government's domestic political agenda. In one interview, one villager claimed that the factory belonged to the "government." However, the original English narration states, "It belonged to all of us," referring to the collective farmer ownership.[82] Such a shift in meaning reframes the cooperative not as a grassroots economic model but as a state-led enterprise—realigning the film's message with statist narratives of development.

Further discrepancies emerge in the interpretation of the animation segment. When asked about the scenes involving puppets, one villager recalled the narrator saying "Open your eyes. Do everything with electricity. Your work will be faster."[83] Yet no such phrasing appears in the accessible English-language versions of the film. The original voice-over instead offers a step-by-step explanation of cooperative formation without any direct reference to electricity or exhortative slogans. These altered elements point not to a failure of comprehension but to the layered effects of dubbing, localization, and audience expectations. Translation, in this context, not only mediated access to the film but also reshaped its ideological contours.

These changes reflect the Turkish state's developmental priorities in the 1950s. At the time, most Turkish villages lacked access to electricity, and the government's push for infrastructural development—particularly dam construction and rural electrification—was central to its modernization agenda. By modifying the voice-over to emphasize electricity and technological efficiency, the translated version of The Rural Co-Op was tailored to resonate with Turkish villagers and reinforce the state's emphasis on industrial modernization as a path to national progress.

This retranslation also mirrors shifts in Turkey's economic policy following the rise of the Democrat Party in 1950. While the government under Prime Minister Adnan Menderes initially embraced liberal economic principles, it gradually adopted a modified form of statism that prioritized the cultivation of an entrepreneurial middle class over collective labor initiatives, promoting individual enterprise and minimizing the role of unionization and cooperatives. Investments focused on industries such as cement, sugar, power generation, and construction, coupled with policies promoting private investment through generous credits for farmers, tax exemptions, and favorable treatment of foreign capital.[84] Within this context, Turkish state agents likely adapted The Rural Co-Op to promote a vision of modernization rooted in state-led development and private enterprise.

The adaptation of the voice-over demonstrates two key aspects of film diplomacy. First, it highlights the malleability of film diplomacy; state agents could reinterpret and repurpose films to serve their political and economic objectives. Second, it exposes a critical flaw in audience reception research. Rather than acknowledging how translation and localization altered the narrative and shaped audience perceptions, American researchers continued to mischaracterize Turkish villagers' responses as evidence of cognitive or cultural "inadequacies," concluding simplistically that "farm people" found the film "challenging."[85] This interpretation exemplifies the persistent racialized assumptions embedded within Cold War modernization projects, where whiteness functioned as the normative standard against which not-yet-Western audiences were evaluated and pathologized. Indeed, the recurrence of this ideological framing across multiple studies—including Lerner's research—highlights a systemic pattern rather than an isolated misreading, demonstrating how racial epistemologies consistently informed interpretations of Turkish audience responses.

From Battlefield to Screen: Turkish Audiences' Reception of the Korean War Media

American-led training of the Turkish military played a crucial role in mediating US-Turkey relations, particularly during the Korean War. For Turkish leaders, participation in the war served as a strategic opportunity to end post-Ottoman diplomatic isolation and to reposition Turkey within the Western bloc.[86] It offered not only access to foreign investment and military aid but also a powerful media platform where Turkey could perform its alignment with Western modernization. As a result of its involvement, Turkey secured NATO membership—signaling a formal US commitment to its security and a symbolic entry into the Euro-Atlantic order.[87]

As discussed in previous chapters, the Korean War became a site where Turkey enacted a performance of whiteness—a racialized and ideological framework through which it sought to be recognized as modern, democratic, and Western. Turkish soldiers were represented as heroic and disciplined, embodying anticommunist values. The "Terrible Turk" stereotype, historically a symbol of Western fear, was reimagined as a narrative of martial bravery, positioning Turkey as a protector of Western civilization against communist forces. The vilification of China in Turkish media constructed the communist Other, further asserting Turkey's aspirational whiteness. Military participation secured Turkey's acceptance into NATO and validation from Western leaders, marking it as worthy of belonging to the West. Media representations glorified Turkish soldiers, emphasizing heroism and nationalism while avoiding critiques of war, further entrenching Turkey's place in the racial and geopolitical hierarchies of the Cold War.

Audience reception studies reveal how this performance of modernization—framed through military valor and Western alignment—resonated with domestic viewers. Columbia researchers found that both traditional and transitional Turks paid greater attention to war coverage when it emphasized Turkish military involvement: Among transitional Turks, 35 percent reported interest in the Korean War overall, while 40 percent expressed interest specifically in Turkish troops in Korea. Among traditional Turks, 37 percent expressed interest in news specifically about Turkish troops, compared to only 12 percent who followed general coverage of the war.[88] This focus on Turkish troops in Korea deepened audiences' emotional engagement and fostered pro-American sentiment. One businessman's remark—"US movies give every detail about the war news. I saw last week the actions of South Koreans with US troops. . . . I felt like going over there to fight"—illustrates how US films mobilized Turkish audiences through emotional identification and militarized nationalism.[89]

This reception pattern underscores the importance of personalizing film subjects to engage viewers effectively. Korean War films played a central role in advancing narratives of Turkey's military, tourism, and modernization. From the early 1950s onward, films such as *Kore'den Aldığımız Ders* (The lessons we learned from Korea), *Kore'de Türk Askeri* (Turkish soldier in Korea), *Kore Gazilerimiz İstanbul'da* (Our Korea veterans in Istanbul), and *Mehmetçik Kore'de* (Mehmetçik in Korea, Kenan Erginsoy, 1951) were widely circulated by the USIS and the EFC, as discussed in chapters 3 and 4.[90] These productions framed the Turkish military as modernized through American training, linking martial strength to national development. *Kore'den Geliyorum* (I am coming from Korea, Nurullah Tilgen, 1951), for example, followed a returning veteran touring historical sites, tying military valor to cultural pride and the promotion of tourism.

Circuits of Access and Hierarchies of Vision: Racialized Logics in Cold War Film Reception

According to the Columbia team, traditional Turks had low movie attendance rates, which the researchers attributed to a lack of interest in or openness to information.[91] However, a closer examination of the interviews shows that both traditional Turks and transitional Turks had limited movie attendance because of geographical and economic constraints. Living in or near villages, both groups had limited access to movie theaters and exhibition spaces, which were primarily located in distant cities or institutions such as universities, libraries, consulates, and cultural centers. Most documentary and educational films were exhibited at universities, the American library in Ankara, the USIS theater, the American Pavilion of the Izmir International Fair, the British Council, the National Library in Ankara, the Democratic Party building, the Medical Society, and commercial movie houses.[92]

As villagers reported in interviews, travel to these venues was not only time consuming but also economically unviable. One farmer stated, "My village is too distant from Ankara, and I am so busy in the village that I have no time."[93] A grocer similarly said, "To go to the movies means to lose a whole day. That is why we cannot go. There is no movie nearby."[94] These responses underscore how class and geography—not cultural apathy—shaped movie going and access. Moreover, many villages lacked electricity,[95] further limiting the infrastructure necessary for film exhibition. Despite this, American researchers framed these logistical barriers as evidence of cultural backwardness or cognitive deficiency. In doing so, they pathologized rural Turkish audiences through a racialized lens of modernization that equated curiosity, openness, and media consumption with whiteness.

To address these disparities in media access, mobile cinema units were deployed to rural regions, reversing the direction of film circulation: Rather than villagers traveling to films, films were brought to them. USIS-sponsored "cinema buses," equipped with projectors, screens, and generators, were provided to Turkey's EFC in 1954 to reach audiences in previously inaccessible locations. These units played a central role in disseminating documentary and educational films, as the partnership between the USIS and the EFC marked a significant institutional collaboration. A photograph of a USIS mobile unit donated to the EFC captures the visual rhetoric of this effort. Bearing the flags of both Turkey and the United States, the vehicle is labeled Sinema Otomobili (Cinema Bus), with a subtext reading "From the people of the United States to the Turkish public"—an example of film diplomacy.[96] According to an ECA-USIS report, at least five vans operated as mobile film units, reaching an estimated 300,000 to 350,000 viewers monthly across key regions, including Erzurum, Istanbul, Adana, and Diyarbakır. These units screened films on economic development, health, agriculture, and democratic values, advancing the modernization agenda under the guise of audiovisual education. The USIS film officer Monteagle Stearns emphasized the importance of contextualizing these American films for Turkish audiences by producing translated pamphlets and instructional booklets.[97] The success of the program was attributed to the efforts of the USIS film officer, Monteagle Stearns.[98] These supplementary materials aimed to clarify the social context of the films and address potential "questions that foreign audiences might have."[99]

This interplay of structural barriers, mobile cinema technologies, and racialized audience research highlights how whiteness operated as both a methodological assumption and a normative ideal in Cold War media research. By attributing limited film attendance to psychological or cultural deficiencies, American researchers disregarded the conditions—geographic isolation, inadequate infrastructure, and class-based limitations—that shaped the patterns of media access. As the interviews make clear, these barriers were products not of cultural disinterest but of persistent regional disparities in access to public services and educational resources. The deployment of mobile cinema units sought to compensate for these limitations, but it also reinforced a hierarchical model of modernization in which film functioned not only as a medium of instruction but also as an instrument of governance. Rural Turkish audiences were positioned not merely as viewers but also as developmental subjects—measured, managed, and interpreted through a racialized framework that equated curiosity, access, and media literacy with proximity to whiteness.

Films Spark Interest in American Schools

Films played a pivotal role in promoting modernization in Turkey by idealizing the role of education. According to the historian Frederick W. Frey, education helped foster an ideological commitment to democratic principles in Turkey,[100] and American documentary films became key instruments in advancing this agenda. These films depicted education not only as a means of individual achievement but also as a cornerstone of democratic and technological development. In doing so, they reinforced the modernization thesis, positioning American education as both exemplary and exportable.

Analyzing the audience reception reports validates this strategy, documenting Turkish enthusiasm for American education. As mentioned at the beginning of this chapter, a Turkish student expressed her admiration for American schools and her desire to attend college in the United States after viewing a film on the subject.[101] However, this admiration did not emerge in a vacuum. As discussed in chapter 2, American missionary schools had long cultivated the perception of American education as desirable, even among non-Christian families. By the 1950s, this religious mission had shifted: Missionaries, in coordination with US agencies, began promoting democracy rather than Christianity through educational programs, and USIS films about American schools became a central tool in this effort.

These films were distributed free of charge to Turkey's EFC, expanding their reach. Once the EFC incorporated these films into its catalogs, the MNET began circulating them through the national school system, thereby institutionalizing their ideological content. The 1956 EFC catalog, developed in collaboration with the USIS, featured numerous films showing American schools in cities such as Philadelphia, New York, and Los Angeles. For example, *Teknik Ticaret Okulu* (Technical commerce school), *Öğrenme, Hürriyet* (Education, freedom), and *Ziraat Koleji* (Agriculture college) highlighted how American students contributed to national development through vocational training and civic participation.[102] Their label as educational facilitated classroom screenings, reduced suspicion of propaganda, and helped position American democracy as a model for Turkish modernization.

The audience reception research operated within a racialized framework that equated whiteness with progress. American education was framed as universally superior—a benchmark for development. Audience research, in turn, reproduced this assumption by interpreting Turkish interest in American education as evidence that modernization theory held universal validity. This validation was circular: Audience responses were read through a lens already structured by whiteness, in which American norms were treated as globally applicable. Education, in this context, was merely promoted as a social good; it became a tool for spreading ideological narratives that positioned American democracy, capitalism, and modernization as the ultimate standard for progress. It is this imposition of a universal standard that reflects and sustains whiteness as an ideology and an invisible norm against which all progress is measured. By framing American education as both superior and universally applicable, these films and their accompanying audience research upheld a racialized hierarchy.

The Racial Epistemologies of Cold War Audience Reception Studies

In this chapter, I have traced how Cold War audience reception research in Turkey produced and legitimized a racialized vision of modernization through the medium of educational film. These research studies cast Turkish audiences as developmental subjects to be measured, guided, and ultimately transformed. What these research projects shared was not merely an interest in assessing media impact but also a deeper investment in epistemological control—rendering American-style capitalism, liberal democracy, and industrial development universally desirable through the lens of whiteness.

By examining the translation, circulation, and reception of films such as *Poultry Raising* and *The Rural Co-Op*, I have shown how educational cinema functioned as more than an instructional device; it was also a vehicle for embedding ideological assumptions into everyday life. Turkish viewers, far from being passive recipients of these messages, often engaged with the films critically, filtering them through material constraints, local cultural knowledge, and national political agendas. Yet their responses were repeatedly misread or dismissed by American researchers, who pathologized these audiences as deficient or incapable of abstraction. This interpretive violence was not incidental but constitutive of how whiteness operated as an epistemic frame—conflating economic scarcity with cultural subordination and reducing pragmatic critiques to signs of cognitive underdevelopment.

The use of categories such as traditional, transitional, and modern Turks exemplified this framework, reifying developmental hierarchies that aligned with US Cold War strategy. These typologies reduced complex social formations to legible subjects of intervention, justifying propaganda and audience segmentation. Meanwhile, the strategic labeling of American films as educational allowed ideological content to circulate with the veneer of neutrality, bypassing religious, cultural, and political objections. In both method and message, the research projects and films advanced a techno-rationalist model of uplift that relied on visual pedagogy to install the American way of life as a model.

Yet I also foregrounded the unevenness of this process. Turkish audiences expressed clear interest in economic advancement, education, and national development, but they did so on terms shaped by their own lived experiences, not necessarily those scripted by American developmental ideology. The villager who noted the impossibility of adopting US poultry techniques without access to corn offers a telling example. His statement challenged the prescriptive logic of the film, pointing instead to structural inequality as the real barrier to progress. Similarly, the reinterpretation of *The Rural Co-Op*'s message to emphasize state-led modernization over cooperative capitalism reveals how films could be localized and repurposed, even as American researchers failed to register these shifts. In emphasizing these disjunctures—between intention and interpretation, ideology and materiality—I considered the limits of Cold War audience research by showing how educational films served as instruments of useful modernization—as tools that projected ideological visions of American development—while local responses were misread or dismissed. I have argued that such research functioned as a racialized epistemic tool—one that aimed to measure, influence, and reorient not-yet-Western publics in accordance with a vision of whiteness. Film diplomacy in this context functioned not only as a racialized mechanism for producing developmental legibility in foreign publics but also as a feedback system for extracting audience responses and evaluating them through epistemologies that reinforced whiteness as the normative measure of progress.

Epilogue

I have shown in this book that film functions not merely as a tool of mediation but also as a technology of organization, structuring international and public relations by way of infrastructure and ideology. Through the infrastructures of film production, exhibition, distribution and reception, film diplomacy demonstrates how networks of individuals and institutions build power structures, encode developmental ideologies, and enact institutional mandates. Far from operating at the periphery, cinema has functioned as a central tool through which geopolitical alignments are visualized, enacted, and rendered intelligible to disparate publics. Film diplomacy unfolds in classrooms and churches, in prisons and public squares, where its work goes beyond the screen and enters the domain of governance.

Film diplomacy is potent due to its dual operation: It relies on affect as much as infrastructure and on pedagogy as much as persuasion. It does not act alone but rather through a transnational network of missionaries, state bureaucrats, military liaisons, educators, and international organizations. These actors mobilize film to shape public perceptions, align domestic audiences with foreign agendas, and render geopolitical objectives legible through stories, images, and institutional aesthetics. As I have demonstrated, film diplomacy manages ideological contradictions, and cultivates a shared aspirational order grounded in Western ideals and, crucially, in whiteness.

Whiteness operated in Cold War Turkey not as an explicit objective but as a structuring logic—an index of progress, a civilizational metric, and a prerequisite for global legibility. It was inscribed in the authority of voice-overs, the elevation of secular aesthetics, and the systematic erasure of linguistic and religious differences. Whiteness did not declare itself; it sedimented norms—determining who was visible, who was audible, and who was rendered absent. In Turkey, it functioned as both aspiration and alibi—as an index of progress and a mechanism of exclusion embedded in state pedagogy, policy, and the aesthetic codes of national belonging. Its force was legible in the voice-over used for narration, the suppression of minority languages and dialects, and the visual codes of modernity. It was enacted in the timbre of a voice, the composition of a shot, the vilification of Chinese soldiers, the othering of Arab Muslims, and the calculated invisibility of Afro-Turkish, Alevi, Azeri, Kurdish, Arab, Crimean Tatar, Roma and Jewish communities.

At the heart of this book are the educational films produced, circulated, and received in the context of US-Turkey relations. These films operated not as conveyors of knowledge but as techniques of governance—teaching audiences not just what to know but also how to be: how to speak, labor, and belong. They recoded citizenship through developmental scripts, aligning rural villagers, students, and urban citizens with the values of modernity. Whether promoting agricultural reform or population control, hygiene or civic duty, these films visualized development as both moral imperative and aesthetic order.

To dismiss educational films as obsolete or culturally insignificant is to ignore their function as tools of governance—mobilized to secure institutional legitimacy, regulate political imaginaries, and discipline social difference across both domestic and international contexts. Educational films reconfigured publics, reshaped behavior, and constructed authority through visual codes that prized compliance, and a Western-aligned national subject. They linked local governance to transnational agendas while embedding whiteness into the visual and auditory systems of modern Turkish identity.

Yet these films are not just ideological objects; they are also material ones, vulnerable to economic and institutional pressures. In Turkey, educational films were sometimes burned for their silver content—an act of repurposing that transformed state media into raw commodity. This destruction came at the cost of historical memory. Each reel lost was not only a casualty of time or neglect but also the victim of value judgments about which narratives warranted preservation. A reel discarded was a narrative erased, a pedagogical trace extinguished. This material fragility exposes a structural condition: Archives are not passive storage sites but rather institutional mechanisms that govern access to the past. This dynamic is evident in the case of the Turkish educational films whose online versions exist only as low-quality telecine transfers, projected and recorded from reels. Their digitization was recently deferred to another government institution under a protocol that stalled, leaving the films in a state of bureaucratic limbo. The compromised quality of their digital surrogates, exemplify how archival conditions and institutional negotiations materially shape what survives as historical evidence. What survives in the archive is not an accidental record but a curated residue of power, structured by decisions about what a nation or institution considers worth remembering.

The metamorphosis of these films into digital objects on Facebook, YouTube, and government platforms further indicates the continued power of film diplomacy. In 2016, a repurposed version of *Turkey: The Land of "In-Between"* (Armed Forces, 1952) went viral on Facebook after being stripped of its original framing and recontextualized as evidence of US imperialism. This transformation testifies to archival film's malleability, to its susceptibility to nationalist critique and ideological repurposing. The pedagogical ambitions of Cold War media have not vanished; they have migrated into digital infrastructures where they are reshaped by algorithms and platform politics.[1] Digital infrastructures spread these ambitions through algorithmic amplification, recommendation engines, and affective polarization.

The practice of producing educational films continues into the present, as the controversy over *Adnan Menderes* (Kilometre Taşları, 2012) illustrates. *Adnan Menderes* is an animated educational film about the political life of the first democratically elected prime minister of Turkey.[2] Narrated in Istanbul Turkish by a male voice-over, the film traces Menderes's life from his early education to his political career. It begins with his formative years at the American Collegiate Institute (ACI, Özel İzmir Amerikan Koleji), a Protestant missionary–founded school known for its liberal learning environment and its promotion of the American way of life.[3] The narrative highlights that Menderes fought in the Turkish War of Independence (Kurtuluş Savaşı, 1919–1923), met Mustafa Kemal Atatürk in 1930, and within a year joined the Republican People's Party (Cumhuriyet Halk Partisi, CHP) and secured a seat in the parliament. Menderes, along with his ACI schoolmate Celâl Bayar and their supporters, established the Democrat Party (DP) in 1946.

Both the voice-over and the intertitles of *Adnan Menderes* indicate that Menderes participated in the 1950 elections with "the most effective slogan in the history of Turkish politics; *Enough, the power is with the people.*"[4] Following a wave of populist support, Bayar became the president and Menderes the prime minister of Turkey. Their electoral success marked a new era in Turkey's political history. The film shows animated footage of soldiers with guns marching as the voice-over states: "Despite the objections to send soldiers to the Korean War, Turkey received its reward by becoming a member of NATO. This membership allowed Turkish farmers to make profits from selling produce to the West." These were key events in the evolution of US-Turkey relations in the 1950s. The film cuts to a map of Turkey filled with images of tractors, a port, and an oil refinery, noting that Menderes and other members of the DP were supportive of a liberal free-market economy and agriculture-based modernization.[5] Indeed, the DP's policies embraced aid from the American Marshall Plan to boost the Turkish economy. However, Menderes's political life declined beginning in the mid-1950s, largely due to struggles in the Turkish economy that led to widespread protests and a military coup. The film ends with an animated shot of an executioner's foot pushing the stool out from under Menderes during his execution by hanging.

Adnan Menderes, a film primarily aimed at middle school students, gained national attention during the COVID-19 pandemic in 2020 when it sparked controversy over its inclusion of the execution scene. Critics accused the government of using the film as "propaganda," given that President Recep Tayyip Erdoğan's frequently referred to Menderes as his political inspiration and even adopted his election slogan, "Enough, the power is with the people."[6] Erdoğan's parallels with Menderes—including appealing to conservative Muslims (often framing himself and this group as black Turks),[7] enacting similar economic policies, and facing a coup—intensified the ideological debates.[8] Erdoğan's main opposition, the Republican People's Party, criticized the film for serving "ideological" purposes,[9] while progovernment media outlets, such as the television channel ATV and the newspaper *Sabah*, defended it as fostering "democratic culture."[10] The pro-Kurdish and left liberal Halkların Demokratik Partisi (HDP, Peoples' Democratic Party)[11] and concerned parents flagged the execution scene as inappropriate for children, prompting Education Minister Ziya Selçuk to acknowledge its unsuitability while citing pandemic-related priorities.[12] Amid mounting public and political pressure, the Ministry of National Education of Turkey (MNET) removed the film from the digital platform of its Educational Information Network (EIN, Eğitim Bilişim Ağı or EBA). The story of *Adnan Menderes*—from its production to its politicized reception and eventual censorship—illustrates how educational films continue to operate as hybrid instruments of pedagogy and ideological influence.

The film's male Istanbul Turkish voice-over, maps, marching soldiers, and scenes of modern infrastructure reactivate the Cold War audiovisual grammar traced throughout this book. Its eventual removal from the MNET's digital archive following public outcry illustrates the precarious position educational films occupy within state efforts to manage historical memory and political legitimacy. As this controversy shows, educational cinema remains a hybrid object at once instructional, ideological, and institutional. Its production and circulation are shaped by a dynamic feedback loop between the state and its publics, where the legitimacy of national identity is constructed through narrative content and continually tested—not only through institutional deployment but also through audience interpretation and political backlash.

The *Adnan Menderes* case is not an isolated anomaly but rather part of a shift in how film diplomacy operates through digital infrastructures today. TikTok explainers, YouTube retrospectives, PragerU videos, multilingual subtitling tools, and branded interface designs now reproduce the pedagogies of Cold War media, filtering ideological content through algorithms that shape visibility and engagement. Whiteness remains the unmarked standard of legitimacy—silent yet structurally dominant in determining which narratives attain visibility, value, and institutional traction. These insights demand that we understand educational film as a central tool in shaping governance and managing difference.

In this book, I traced the emergence of educational films as tools that facilitated alliances, controlled difference, and staged national belonging in the context of US-Turkey relations. Rather than simply transmitting information, these films enacted a system of useful modernization, merging aspirational citizenship with developmental discourse. While the infrastructures have changed, the stakes remain. Educational film has multiplied across screens and temporalities, governing not only through what it shows but also through what it enables publics to imagine as possible. To study film diplomacy, then, is to confront the infrastructures through which governance is rendered ordinary—whether racialized, religious, commercial, or algorithmic. While grounded in US-Turkey relations, the dynamics I traced here resonate beyond this bilateral frame. They offer a comparative lens for understanding Cold War media strategies across nations like China, Iran, and South Korea, where US-sponsored educational films circulated. These formations demand that we approach educational films not as ephemeral propaganda but as enduring technologies of governance, calibrated to hierarchies and racialized imaginaries. As contemporary entities increasingly mobilize media to consolidate power and narrate legitimacy, the logic of film diplomacy persists—retooled but no less potent. Film diplomacy is no relic of the Cold War; it is a recursive formation, reanimated across platforms and political systems, continually recalibrated to manage social difference, manufacture legitimacy, and govern through image and sound. It remains durable not in spite its transformations but precisely because it evolves with them. Looking forward, film diplomacy offers a critical framework through which to understand how communication infrastructures are mobilized to shape collective imaginaries, mediate geopolitical tensions, and organize power in a world increasingly governed by audiovisual media.

Acknowledgments

Film Diplomacy represents the culmination of years of research, writing, and reflection. It would not have been possible without the support, encouragement, and guidance of many individuals and institutions, to whom I owe profound gratitude.

First, I extend my deepest thanks to my mentors and colleagues, whose intellectual generosity and critical insights have profoundly shaped this project. I am most grateful to Joshua Malitsky, Greg Waller, Elizabeth Ellcessor, Terri Francis, and Stephanie DeBoer. Their mentorship, feedback, and encouragement sustained me throughout my academic career. I am also forever grateful to my brain trust—Perin Gürel, Kaveh Askari, Dilek Kaya Mutlu, Nick Cull, Camilla Fojas, Hemant Shah, Emily Conroy-Krutz, and Maria Fritsche—who engaged with my ideas, read drafts, and provided crucial feedback. Many conversations were instrumental in my process for completing this book. My heartfelt thanks go to Ross Melnick, Şebnem Baran, Joseph Ho, Sarah O'Brien, Laura Partain, John Brooks, and Taylor M. Moore for their insights. I am equally fortunate to have colleagues at the University of Virginia who provided support at different stages: Chris Gratien, Robin Means Coleman, Aynne Kokas, Kevin Driscoll, Lana Swartz, Barış Ünlü, Sean Duncan, Samitha Sunya, Anikó Bodroghkozy, Andrea Press, Paul Dobryden, David Nemer, Kevin Everson, Jennie S. Knight, Jennifer Bair, and Claudrena Harold.

This work benefited immensely from the resources and expertise of numerous archivists and librarians. My gratitude goes to Rachael Stoeltje, Madeline Webb-Mitchel, Andy Uhrich, and Carmel Curtis at the Indiana University Moving Image Archive for their generous assistance. I am also thankful to the American Board of Commissioners for Foreign Missions Archives in Houghton Library at Harvard University, the American Research Institute in Turkey, the National Library in Ankara, and the National Archives and Records Administration in College Park, Maryland, where I spent countless hours finding materials that brought the story of film diplomacy to life. Additionally, I am grateful to the General Directorate of Cinema of the Ministry of Culture at the Ministry of Culture and Tourism in Turkey, the Media History Digital Library, and the Audio-Visual Archives of the International Federation of Red Cross and Red Crescent Societies, with thanks to Sarah-Joy Maddeaux. I am likewise indebted to Fikret Özkaplan who connected me with Ihsan Akşehirli of the Yenilik ve Eğitim Teknolojileri Genel Müdürlüğü (Innovation and Educational Technologies General Directorate), whose generosity in sharing higher resolution visual archival resources on the Educational Film Center of Turkey enriched this project.

This book would not have been possible without the support of internal and external grants that provided the time and resources for archival research and writing. I am sincerely thankful to Indiana University's Center for Research on Race and Ethnicity in Society, the College of Arts and Sciences Dissertation Fellowship, the Center for Documentary Research and Practice, the Louise Hess Miller Fund, the Ogan Fund, and the Media School Graduate Association. I also thank the Walsh School of Foreign Service at Georgetown University for its support. At the University of Virginia, I am deeply grateful for the Center for Global Inquiry and Innovation Grant; the Arts, Humanities, and Social Sciences Research Support; the Buckner W. Clay Dean of Arts and Sciences Fund; and the Arts, Humanities, and Social Sciences Summer Research Fellowship.

This book also grew out of scholarly conversations at conferences, workshops, and invited talks. I am particularly grateful to participants I met through the European Network for Cinema and Media Studies, Society for Cinema and Media Studies, International Communication Association, the Buffett Institute for Global Affairs, A Century of 16mm Conference, Radio Preservation Task Force of the Library of Congress, International Studies

Association, HoMER (History of Moviegoing, Exhibition, and Reception), Middle East Studies Association, and Visible Evidence Conference. Special thanks to organizers Dave Park, Jeff Pooley, Pete Simonson, Özen Baş, Hadi Gharabaghi, Bret Vukoder, Thorn Hongwei, and Wunpini Mohammed, as well as to audiences at Smith College, the University of Georgia, Bentley University, Kadir Has University, and the History of Media Studies Group at the Consortium for History of Science, Technology, and Medicine for their feedback on my work.

My sincere thanks go to my students, whose curiosity and insight sharpened my thinking over the years. Special gratitude is owed to Aisha Hinds, a brilliant research assistant whose rigor and diligence in organizing materials were essential. Teaching courses such as the Cinema of Türkiye, Nontheatrical Films, Introduction to Film, History of Media Arts, and International Cinema at the University of Virginia, Emerson College, and Clark University has greatly enriched this book. I am grateful to my students for the stimulating discussions that focused my thinking and refined the arguments presented in these pages.

I am extremely grateful to Columbia University Press, and especially to my editor, Philip Leventhal, whose belief in this project and thoughtful guidance have been invaluable. Philip's keen insights and his careful selection of outstanding anonymous reviewers have greatly enriched this book. Working with this exceptionally strong team at CUP, particularly Emily Elizabeth Simon, Michael Haskell and Ben Kolstad, has been truly a delight. Many thanks to Sherry Goldbecker for the amazing copyediting.

To my family, thank you for your unwavering support and love. To Alex Gates—your love, presence, and belief in me made this possible. To Maya Su and Ryan Leo; you fill my life with joy, brilliance, and purpose. To my mother Beyhan, father Yücel, and sister Melike, thank you for your unconditional love and encouragement. And to my mother- and father-in-law, Lauren and Steve, thank you for your kindness and curiosity.

Finally, this book is dedicated to the many educators, archivists, diplomats, filmmakers, and audiences whose labor and imagination remain central to the story of film diplomacy.

While my name appears on the cover, this book is the product of collective effort. For all the kindness I have received along the way, I remain profoundly grateful.

Notes

Introduction

1. Aysehan Jülide Etem, "A Transnational Communication Network Promoting Film Diplomacy: The Case of Turkey and the USA, 1950–86," *Historical Journal of Film, Radio and Television* 41, no. 2 (2020): 292.
2. Joseph Nye, "Soft Power: The Origins and Political Progress of a Concept," *Palgrave Communications* 3, no. 1 (2017): 1–3.
3. Lisa Parks, "'Stuff You Can Kick': Toward a Theory of Media Infrastructures," in *Between Humanities and the Digital*, ed. David Theo Goldberg and Patrik Svensson (MIT Press, 2015), 355.
4. See Michel Foucault, *"Society Must Be Defended": Lectures at the Collège de France, 1975-76*, ed. Mauro Bertani and Alessandro Fontana (Palgrave Macmillan, 2003); Michel Foucault, *Security, Territory, Population: Lectures at the Collège de France, 1977-1978*, ed. Michel Senellart (Palgrave Macmillan, 2007). Also see Lee Grieveson, "Discipline and Publish: The Birth of Cinematology," *Cinema Journal* 49, no. 1 (2009).
5. For whiteness, see Ruth Frankenberg, "The Mirage of an Unmarked Whiteness," in *The Making and Unmaking of Whiteness*, ed. Birgit Brander Rasmussen et al. (Duke University Press, 2001), 73.
6. See Lorenz M. Lüthi, "The Non-Aligned Movement and the Cold War, 1961–1973," *Journal of Cold War Studies* 18, no. 4 (2016); Diane Fujino, "Political Asian America: Afro-Asian Solidarity, Third World Internationalism, and the Origins of the Asian American Movement," *Ethnic Studies Review* 47, no. 1 (2024).
7. Devin Orgeron et al., introduction to *Learning with the Lights Off: Educational Film in the United States*, ed. Devin Orgeron et al. (Oxford University Press, 2011), 10. For educational film and technologies, also see Brian Goldfarb, *Visual Pedagogy: Media*

Cultures of Education in and Beyond the Classroom (Duke University Press, 2002); Geoff Alexander, *Academic Films for the Classroom: A History* (McFarland, 2010); Eef Masson, *Watch and Learn: Rhetorical Devices in Classroom Films After 1940* (Amsterdam University Press, 2012); Marina Dahlquist and Joel Frykholm, eds., *The Institutionalization of Educational Cinema: North America and Europe in the 1910s and 1920s* (Indiana University Press, 2019); Katie Day Good, *Bringing the World to the Child: Technologies of Global Citizenship in American Education* (MIT Press, 2020).
8. Feroz Ahmad, *Turkey: The Quest for Identity* (Oneworld, 2003), 109.
9. For instance, the young Turks, influenced by Western racial theories, merged the concept of civilization with an elitist view of the general population, intertwining it with Ottoman-Muslim identity, Turkish nationalism, and Darwinist notions. See M. Şükrü Hanioğlu, *The Young Turks in Opposition* (Oxford University Press, 1995), 22, 208–209.
10. For Halk Evleri, see Kemal H. Karpat, "The Impact of the People's Houses on the Development of Communication in Turkey: 1931–1951," *Die Welt des Islams* 15, no. 1/4 (1974).
11. Eugene Hinkle, "The Motion Picture in Modern Turkey" (1933), in *The Turkish Cinema in the Early Republican Years*," by Rifat N. Bali (Isis Press and Gorgias Press, 2010), 33.
12. Hinkle, "The Motion Picture in Modern Turkey," 40, 54.
13. Hinkle, "The Motion Picture in Modern Turkey," 56, 179. See Paul E. Nilson, "Report on the Use of the 16mm. Movie Machine in Central Anatolia, from April 1931 to October 1932," app. 3.
14. Naoko Shibusawa, "Ideology, Culture, and the Cold War," in *The Oxford Handbook of the Cold War*, ed. Richard H. Immerman and Petra Goedde (Oxford University Press, 2013), 38.
15. See Edward W. Said, *Orientalism* (Vintage, 1979), 6–7.
16. Sedef Arat-Koç, "(Some) Turkish Transnationalism(s) in an Age of Capitalist Globalization and Empire: 'White Turk' Discourse, the New Geopolitics, and Implications for Feminist Transnationalism," *Journal of Middle East Women's Studies* 3, no. 1 (2007): 40.
17. Nancy Snow and Nicholas J. Cull, eds., *Routledge Handbook of Public Diplomacy*, 2nd ed. (Routledge, 2020); Ien Ang et al., "Cultural Diplomacy: Beyond the National Interest?," *International Journal of Cultural Policy* 21, no. 4 (2015); Andrew F. Cooper et al., eds., *The Oxford Handbook of Modern Diplomacy* (Oxford University Press, 2013); Lisa E. Davenport, *Jazz Diplomacy: Promoting America in the Cold War Era* (University Press of Mississippi, 2010); Naima Prevots, *Dance for Export: Cultural Diplomacy and the Cold War* (Wesleyan University Press, 1999).
18. Kenneth Alan Osgood, *Total Cold War: Eisenhower's Secret Propaganda Battle at Home and Abroad* (University Press of Kansas, 2006), 3–4.
19. Andrei Kozovoi, "A Foot in the Door: The Lacy-Zarubin Agreement and Soviet-American Film Diplomacy During the Khrushchev Era, 1953–1963," *Historical Journal of Film, Radio and Television* 36, no. 1 (2016). The italics are mine.
20. Hadi Parandeh Gharabaghi, "'American Mice Grow Big!' The Syracuse Audiovisual Mission in Iran and the Rise of Documentary Diplomacy" (PhD diss., New York

University, 2018), viii–ix. Also see Hadi Parandeh Gharabaghi, "The Syracuse Mission to Iran During the 1950s and the Rise of Documentary Diplomacy," *JCMS: Journal of Cinema and Media Studies* 60, no. 4 (2021).
21. Sangjoon Lee, *Cinema and the Cultural Cold War: US Diplomacy and the Origins of the Asian Cinema Network* (Cornell University Press, 2020).
22. Mila Turajlić, "Filmske Novosti: Filmed Diplomacy," *Nationalities Papers* 49, no. 3 (2021).
23. Mark Williams and Bret Vukoder, "Local Insights, Global Networked Scholarship: The Media Ecology Project USIA Pilot," in *Nuevas aproximaciones al cine documental. Un estado de la cuestión contemporáneo*, ed. Javier Campo, Tomás Crowder-Taraborrelli, Clara Garavelli, Pablo Piedras and Kristi Wilson (Prometeo, 2020).
24. For film and diplomacy, also see Jens Ulff-Mǿller, *Hollywood's Film Wars with France: Film-Trade Diplomacy and the Emergence of the French Film Quota Policy* (University of Rochester Press, 2001); Michael Baskett, "Japan's Film Festival Diplomacy in Cold War Asia," *Velvet Light Trap* 73 (2014); Hye Seung Chung, *Hollywood Diplomacy: Film Regulation, Foreign Relations, and East Asian Representations* (Rutgers University Press, 2020); Lanjun Xu, "The Southern Film Corporation, Opera Films and the PRC's Cultural Diplomacy in Cold War Asia, 1950s–1960s," in *Chineseness and the Cold War: Contested Cultures and Diaspora in Southeast Asia and Hong Kong*, ed. Jeremy E. Taylor and Lanjun Xu (Routledge, 2021); Ross Melnick, *Hollywood's Embassies: How Movie Theaters Projected American Power Around the World* (Columbia University Press, 2022); Masha Salazkina, *World Socialist Cinema: Alliances, Affinities, and Solidarities in the Global Cold War* (University of California Press, 2023); Rielle Navitski, *Transatlantic Cinephilia: Film Culture Between Latin America and France, 1945-1965* (University of California Press, 2023).
25. For the connection between film studies and the shaping of behavior, see Lee Grieveson, "Cinema Studies and the Conduct of Conduct," in *Inventing Film Studies*, ed. Lee Grieveson and Haidee Wasson (Duke University Press, 2008).
26. For public diplomacy, see Benno H. Signitzer and Timothy Coombs, "Public Relations and Public Diplomacy: Conceptual Convergence," *Public Relations Review* 18, no. 2 (1992).
27. R. S. Zaharna, "Communication Logics of Global Public Diplomacy," in Snow and Cull, *Routledge Handbook of Public Diplomacy*, 102.
28. Nancy Snow, "Rethinking Public Diplomacy in the 2020s," in Snow and Cull, *Routledge Handbook of Public Diplomacy*, 8.
29. Nicholas J. Cull, "Film as Public Diplomacy: The USIA's Cold War at Twenty-Four Frames per Second," in *The United States and Public Diplomacy*, ed. Kenneth A. Osgood (Brill, 2010), 258. Also see Nicholas J. Cull, "Public Diplomacy: Taxonomies and Histories," *Annals of the American Academy of Political and Social Science* 616, no. 1 (2008).
30. Snow, "Rethinking Public Diplomacy," 10.
31. Anthologies include Vinzenz Hediger and Patrick Vonderau, eds., *Films That Work: Industrial Film and the Productivity of Media* (Amsterdam University Press, 2009); Charles R. Acland and Haidee Wasson, *Useful Cinema* (Duke University Press, 2011); Orgeron et al., *Learning with the Lights Off*; Bo Florin et al., *Films That Sell: Moving*

Pictures and Advertising (Palgrave, 2016); Haidee Wasson and Lee Grieveson, eds., *Cinema's Military Industrial Complex* (University of California Press, 2018); Allyson Nadia Field and Marsha Gordon, eds., *Screening Race in American Nontheatrical Film* (Duke University Press, 2019); and Vinzenz Hedinger et al., *Films That Work Harder: The Circulation of Industrial Film* (Amsterdam University Press, 2023).

32. Some monographs include Allyson Nadia Field's *Uplift Cinema: The Emergence of African American Film and The Possibility of Black Modernity* (Duke University Press, 2015); Florian Hoof's *Angels of Efficiency: A Media History of Consulting*, trans. Daniel Fairfax (Oxford University Press, 2020); Victoria Cain's *Schools and Screens: A Watchful History* (MIT Press, 2021); Denise Khor's *Transpacific Convergences: Race, Migration and Japanese American Film Culture Before World War II* (University of North Carolina Press, 2022); Han Sang Kim's *Cine-Mobility: Twentieth-Century Transformations in Korea's Film and Transportation* (Harvard University Asia Center, 2022); Haidee Wasson's *Everyday Movies: Portable Film Projectors and the Transformation of American Culture* (University of California Press, 2020); and Gregory A. Waller's *Beyond the Movie Theater: Sites, Sponsors, Uses, Audiences* (University of California Press, 2023).
33. See Nijat Özön, *Türk Sinema Tarihi* (Artist Yayinevi, 1962); Giovanni Scognamillo, *Türk Sinema Tarihi* (Kabalcı Yayınevi, 1998); Rekin Teksoy, *Rekin Teksoy'un Türk Sineması* (Oğlak Yayıncılık, 2007); Gonul Donmez-Colin, *Turkish Cinema* (Reaktion Books, 2008); Savas Arslan, *Cinema in Turkey: A New Critical History* (Oxford University Press, 2011).
34. Dan Streible et al., "Introduction: Nontheatrical Film," *Film History* 19, no. 4 (2007): 342.
35. Streible et al., "Introduction: Nontheatrical Film," 339. Also see Rick Prelinger, *The Field Guide to Sponsored Films* (National Film Preservation Foundation, 2006).
36. Haidee Wasson, *Museum Movies: The Museum of Modern Art and the Birth of Art Cinema* (University of California Press, 2005), 36.
37. Ögretici ve Teknik Filimler Hakkında Kanun, *T. C. [Türkiye Cumhuriyeti] Resmi Gazete*, Sayi 3537, Sayıfa 7698, Subat 1937 [Law on Educational and Technical Films, Republic of Turkey official gazette, Number 3537, p. 7698, February 1937].
38. Jacqueline Najuma Stewart, "Giving Voice, Taking Voice: Nonwhite and Nontheatrical," foreword to Field and Gordon, *Screening Race in American Nontheatrical Film*, xiii.
39. Stewart, "Giving Voice, Taking Voice," xiv.
40. Stewart, "Giving Voice, Taking Voice," xiv, xv, xxii.
41. Stewart, "Giving Voice, Taking Voice," xix.
42. These questions include "What value do you think the people of this Turkish community place upon the traditional teaching of their religion? Do you think that this community would be eager for rapid changes in their way of life? From what you have seen, do you think that women hold the same position in this Turkish village as they do in a small American town? What is the position of both the mother and father in this family? Are their roles similar to that which you find in your home? What have you seen to explain whether or not Turkey will progress in the future to assume a more prominent role in the community of nations?"

43. Doris A. Santoro and Charles Dorn, "A Vital, Free, Independent, and Lay Republic: John Dewey and the Role of Education in Establishing the Turkish State," in *Teaching America to the World and the World to America: Education and Foreign Relations Since 1870*, ed. Richard Garlitz and Lisa Jarvinen (Palgrave Macmillan, 2012): 93–94.
44. Richard Dyer MacCann, *The People's Films: A Political History of U.S. Government Motion Pictures* (Hastings House, 1973), xiii.
45. MacCann, *The People's Films*, 14–15.
46. Maria Fritsche, *The American Marshall Plan Film Campaign and the Europeans: A Captivated Audience?* (Bloomsbury, 2018), 11.
47. Fritsche, *The American Marshall Plan Film Campaign*, 11.
48. Ndinawe Byekwaso, "The Politics of Modernization and the Misleading Approaches to Development," *World Review of Political Economy* 7, no. 2 (2016): 288.
49. Barın Kayaoğlu, review of *Malleable Modernity: Rethinking the Role of Ideology in American Policy, Aid Programs, and Propaganda in Fifties' Turkey*, by Nicholas Danforth, *Diplomatic History* 39, no. 3 (2015): 3.
50. Ayse Kadıoğlu, "The Paradox of Turkish Nationalism and the Construction of Official Identity," *Middle Eastern Studies* 32, no. 2 (1996): 181.
51. Kadıoğlu, "The Paradox of Turkish Nationalism," 183.
52. Kadıoğlu, "The Paradox of Turkish Nationalism," 186.
53. Nathan J. Citino, "The Ottoman Legacy in Cold War Modernization," *International Journal of Middle East Studies* 40, no. 4 (2008).
54. For an analysis of the reforms, see Hale Yilmaz, *Becoming Turkish: Nationalist Reforms and Cultural Negotiations in Early Republican Turkey 1923–1945* (Syracuse University Press, 2013).
55. Nils Gilman, *Mandarins of the Future: Modernization Theory in Cold War America* (Johns Hopkins University Press, 2007), 30–31.
56. Begüm Adalet, *Hotels and Highways: The Construction of Modernization Theory in Cold War Turkey* (Stanford University Press, 2018), 7.
57. Erik Jan Zürcher, *Turkey: A Modern History* (Tauris, 2017), 226.
58. For more on Menderes, see Reşat Kasaba, "Populism and Democracy in Turkey, 1946–1961," in *Rules and Rights in the Middle East: Democracy, Law, and Society*, ed. Ellis Goldberg et al. (University of Washington Press, 1993).
59. Perin E. Gürel, *The Limits of Westernization: A Cultural History of America in Turkey* (Columbia University Press, 2017), 76–79.
60. Nicholas Danforth, "Malleable Modernity: Rethinking the Role of Ideology in American Policy, Aid Programs, and Propaganda in Fifties' Turkey," *Diplomatic History* 39, no. 3 (2015): 478. See also Michael Hunt, *Ideology and U.S. Foreign Policy* (Yale University Press, 2009), 12.
61. Daniel Lerner, *The Passing of Traditional Society: Modernizing the Middle East* (Free Press, 1958), 50.
62. Gunnar Myrdal, *An American Dilemma: The Negro Problem and Modern Democracy* (Harper & Bros., 1944).

63. Hemant Shah, *The Production of Modernization: Daniel Lerner, Mass Media, and the Passing of Traditional Society* (Temple University Press, 2011), 89.
64. Lerner, *The Passing of Traditional Society*, 105.
65. Lerner, *The Passing of Traditional Society*, 117.
66. Sibel Bozdoğan and Reşat Kasaba, eds., *Rethinking Modernity and National Identity in Turkey* (University of Washington Press, 1997), 3.
67. Adalet, *Hotels and Highways*, 7–8.
68. Adalet, *Hotels and Highways*, 8.
69. Adalet, *Hotels and Highways*, 8.
70. Bozdoğan, and Kasaba, *Rethinking Modernity and National Identity in Turkey*, 4.
71. Kadıoğlu, "The Paradox of Turkish Nationalism," 190.
72. For the national identity discourse, see Kadıoğlu, "The Paradox of Turkish Nationalism," 177.
73. Kadıoğlu, "The Paradox of Turkish Nationalism," 185.
74. Nell Irvin Painter, *The History of White People* (W. W. Norton, 2010), 2.
75. Painter, *The History of White People*, 72–77.
76. Painter, *The History of White People*, 80.
77. Matthew Frye Jacobson, *Whiteness of a Different Color* (Harvard University Press, 1999), 4.
78. Murat Ergin, *"Is the Turk a White Man?" Race and Modernity in the Making of Turkish Identity* (Brill, 2016), 1.
79. "Is the Turk a White Man?," *New York Times*, September 30, 1909, https://www.nytimes.com/1909/09/30/archives/is-the-turk-a-white-man.html.
80. *Sacramento Daily Union*, September 25, 1909, "Turks Are Beyond the Pale of the Law."
81. *In re Halladjian (1909)*, Circuit Court, District of Massachusetts, December 24, 1909, in Teaching Legal History, University of Nebraska–Lincoln, https://teachinglegalhistory.unl.edu/s/oer/item/2048.
82. Ergin, *"Is the Turk a White Man?,"* 1.
83. Elise K. Burton, *Genetic Crossroads: The Middle East and the Science of Human Heredity* (Stanford University Press, 2021), 47.
84. Burton, *Genetic Crossroads*, 48.
85. Ergin, *"Is the Turk a White Man?,"* 194.
86. Burton, *Genetic Crossroads*, 50.
87. For more on the West's influence on shaping racial theories and policies in Turkey, see Nazan Maksudyan, *Türklüğü Ölçmek: Bilimkurgusal Antropoloji ve Türk Milliyetçiliginin Irkçı Çehresi: 1925-1939* (Metis Yayınları, 2005); Nazan Maksudyan, "The Turkish Review of Anthropology and the Racist Face of Turkish Nationalism," *Cultural Dynamics* 17, no. 3 (2005).
88. Arat-Koç, "(Some) Turkish Transnationalism(s) in an Age of Capitalist Globalization and Empire," 47.
89. Barnor Hesse, "Racialized Modernity: An Analytics of White Mythologies," *Ethnic and Racial Studies* 30, no. 4 (2007): 643, 646.

90. Patricia L. Price, "At the Crossroads: Critical Race Theory and Critical Geographies of Race," *Progress in Human Geography* 34, no. 2 (2010).
91. Arslan, *Cinema in Turkey*, 5.
92. Iain Robert Smith, "'Beam Me Up, Ömer': Transnational Media Flow and the Cultural Politics of the Turkish Star Trek Remake," *Velvet Light Trap*, no. 61 (2008): 5, 12. Also see Marwan M. Kraidy, *Hybridity, or the Cultural Logic of Globalization* (Temple University Press, 2005).
93. Aileen Moreton-Robinson et al., eds., *Transnational Whiteness Matters* (Rowman & Littlefield, 2008), x.
94. Richard Dyer, *White* (Routledge, 2017), 45.
95. Ergin, *"Is the Turk a White Man?,"* 106.
96. Barış Ünlü, "The Turkishness Contract and the Formation of Turkishness," in *Kurds in Dark Times: New Perspectives on Violence and Resistance in Turkey*, ed. Ayça Alemdaroğlu and Fatma Müge Göçek (Syracuse University Press, 2023), 90. Also see Barış Ünlü, "The Kurdish Struggle and the Crisis of the Turkishness Contract," *Philosophy & Social Criticism* 42, no. 4–5 (2016).
97. For the intersection of race and secularism, see Jonathon S. Kahn and Vincent W. Lloyd, eds., *Race and Secularism in America* (Columbia University Press, 2016).
98. For both historical and contemporary debates on race, see Michael Ferguson, "The African Presence in Late Ottoman Izmir and Beyond" (PhD diss., McGill University, 2014); Christoph Ramm, "Beyond 'Black Turks' and 'White Turks'—The Turkish Elites' Ongoing Mission to Civilize a Colourful Society," *Asiatische Studien—Études Asiatiques* 70, no. 4 (2016).
99. Here, I draw on Wendy Hui Kyong Chun's insight that "race as technology shifts the focus from the *what* of race to the *how* of race, from *knowing* race to *doing* race by emphasizing the similarities between race and technology." See Wendy Hui Kyong Chun, "Introduction: Race and/as Technology; or, How to Do Things to Race," *Camera Obscura* 24, no. 1 (2009): 8.
100. See Henry Giroux, "Post-Colonial Ruptures and Democratic Possibilities: Multiculturalism as Anti-Racist Pedagogy," *Cultural Critique*, no. 21 (1992): 15; Henry Giroux, "White Squall: Resistance and the Pedagogy of Whiteness," *Cultural Studies* 11, no. 3 (1997): 382–384.
101. Bam Willoughby, "Opposing a Spectacle of Blackness: *Arap Baci, Baci Kalfa, Dadi*, and the Invention of African Presence in Turkey," *Lateral* 10, no. 1 (2021).
102. Müslüm Elibol, "Türkiye'de Yaşayan Afro-Türkler Hakkında Bilmeniz Gerekenler," *Onedio*, 2015; Ozlem Yurtcu, "Çikolata renkli Türkler," *Sabah*, 2005, cited in Mehmet Özkan, "Emergence of Afro-Turks in Turkish Politics," *Turkish Journal of Diaspora Studies* 1, no. 1 (2021): 14.
103. Ed Guerrero, *Framing Blackness: The African American Image in Film* (Temple University Press, 1993), 2.
104. Tunay Altay, "Is There Really No Anti-Black Racism in Turkey?," Bianet, November 17, 2020, https://bianet.org/yazi/is-there-really-no-anti-black-racism-in-turkey-226799.

105. Lee Grieveson, *Cinema and the Wealth of Nations: Media, Capital, and the Liberal World System* (University of California Press, 2018), 158.
106. Hatim El-Hibri, *Visions of Beirut: The Urban Life of Media Infrastructure*. (Duke University Press, 2021), 3–4.
107. Ussama Samir Makdisi, *Artillery of Heaven: American Missionaries and the Failed Conversion of the Middle East* (Cornell University Press, 2008), 2.
108. David Hollinger, *Protestants Abroad: How Missionaries Tried to Change the World but Changed America* (Princeton University Press, 2018), 5.
109. Khyati Y. Joshi, *White Christian Privilege: The Illusion of Religious Equality in America* (NYU Press, 2021), 71.
110. Joshi, *White Christian Privilege*, 70.
111. Hillary Kaell, *Christian Globalism at Home: Child Sponsorship in the United States* (Princeton University Press, 2020), 111. Also see Jasbir K. Puar, *Terrorist Assemblages: Homonationalism in Queer Times* (Duke University Press, 2018): 34–35.
112. The catalogue description of Washington'da İslam Etüdleri Merkezinin Açılışı corresponds to the Hearst Metrotone News segment *Ike Opens Muslim Mosque* (1957), which documents President Eisenhower's inauguration of the Islamic Center of Washington. The newsreel was produced by Hearst Metrotone News. See *Ike Opens Muslim Mosque*, Hearst Metrotone News, 1957, https://newsreels.net/v/pqkf02.
113. Miriam Hansen, "The Mass Production of the Senses: Classical Cinema as Vernacular Modernism," *Modernism/Modernity* 6, no. 2 (1999): 69.
114. Acland and Wasson, *Useful Cinema*, 3–6.

1. From Ottoman Shadows to Global Stage: Rise of Film in Turkey

1. Nazım Hikmet, "Who Invented Cinema?," *Sinema Postası*, December 1923, trans. Jason Vivrette and reprinted in *Early Popular Visual Culture* 6, no. 2 (2008).
2. The practice of Karagöz involves intricately crafted puppets, made from leather or other materials, manipulated by performers from behind a screen to tell stories or act out plays that convey moral lessons to the audience. The Karagöz tradition has played a significant role in Turkish culture, serving as a form of entertainment, education, and social commentary. The puppet performances often satirize political and social issues, providing a form of comedic relief for the audience.
3. Fan Pen Chen, "Shadow Theaters of the World," *Asian Folklore Studies* 62, no. 1 (2003): 48.
4. Asuman Suner, *New Turkish Cinema: Belonging, Identity and Memory* (Tauris, 2010), 2. See also Özde Çeliktemel-Thomen, "Prime Ministry Ottoman Archives: Inventory of Written Archival Sources for Ottoman Cinema History," *Tarih Graduate History Journal* 2, no. 3 (2013).
5. Nijat Özön, *Türk Sineması Tarihi (Dünden Bugüne) 1896-1960* (İstanbul: Artist Yayınları, 1962).
6. Nezih Erdoğan and Deniz Göktürk, "Turkish Cinema," in *Companion Encyclopedia of Middle Eastern and North African Film*, ed. Oliver Leaman (Routledge, 2001).

1. FROM OTTOMAN SHADOWS TO GLOBAL STAGE 229

7. Dilek Kaya Mutlu, "The Russian Monument at Ayastefanos (San Stefano): Between Defeat and Revenge, Remembering and Forgetting," *Middle Eastern Studies* 43, no. 1 (2007): 76.
8. Kaya Mutlu, "The Russian Monument at Ayastefanos," 75.
9. Kaya Mutlu, "The Russian Monument at Ayastefanos." 82. *Fuad Bey* means "Mr. Fuad." The variations in the Turkish spelling of the name Fuad as *Fuad* and *Fuat* are a result of historical changes in transliteration conventions and pronunciation shifts between Arabic and Turkish, as well as the modernization of the Turkish language.
10. Kaya Mutlu, "The Russian Monument at Ayastefanos," 81.
11. Kaya Mutlu, "The Russian Monument at Ayastefanos," 82.
12. Suner, *New Turkish Cinema*, 2.
13. Özde Çeliktemel-Thomen, "The Curtain of Dreams: Early Cinema in Istanbul" (master's thesis, Central European University, 2009), 63. For more, see Savaş Arslan, *Cinema in Turkey: A New Critical History* (Oxford University Press, 2011), 53. Arslan notes that Kemal Film was a distributor in 1919 and initially imported films.
14. Rekin Teksoy, *Turkish Cinema* (Oğlak Yayıncılık, 2008), 25.
15. Gonul Donmez-Colin, *The Routledge Dictionary of Turkish Cinema* (Routledge, 2013).
16. Tekerek Meltem, "Cinema in Turkish-Soviet Relations in the Ataturk Period," История и современное мировоззрение 1 (2020): 33.
17. Eugene Hinkle, "The Motion Picture in Modern Turkey," in *The Turkish Cinema in the Early Republican Years*, by Rifat N. Bali (Isis Press and Gorgias Press, 2010), 68.
18. Hinkle, "The Motion Picture in Modern Turkey," 74.
19. Hinkle, "The Motion Picture in Modern Turkey," 76.
20. Hinkle, "The Motion Picture in Modern Turkey," 27–28.
21. Priscilla Peña Ovalle, *Dance and the Hollywood Latina: Race, Sex, and Stardom* (Rutgers University Press, 2010), 24.
22. Ovalle, *Dance and the Hollywood Latina*, 33.
23. Ebru Boyar and Kate Fleet, "Mak[ing] Turkey and the Turkish Revolution Known to Foreign Nations Without any Expense: Propaganda Films in the Early Turkish Republic," *Oriente Moderno* 24, no. 1 (2005): 125.
24. The censorship system that governed Turkey under the Regulation About the Control of Films and Film Screenplays date back to 1934. Issued under the Police Duty and Authorization Law, this regulation set out ten criteria that films were required to avoid: promoting state propaganda, degrading ethnic and racial communities, offending other nations or states, promoting religion, supporting ideologies that contradict the national regime, violating national and moral values, insulting the military, harming national discipline and security, inciting criminal activity, and attacking the state. These laws remained largely unchanged until 1977. For more, see Nezih Erdoğan and Dilek Kaya, "Institutional Intervention in the Distribution and Exhibition of Hollywood Films in Turkey," *Historical Journal of Film, Radio and Television* 22, no. 1 (2002): 54.
25. Cumhurbaşkanlığı Devlet Arşivleri Başkanlığı, Cumhuriyet Arşivi (BCA) [Directorate of State Archives of the Presidency of the Republic of Türkiye, Ankara], Fon

Kodu 30.10.0.0; Yer No. 86.567.1, 1926-02-01. See also Fatma Samime İnceoğlu, "Erken Dönem Türk Sinemasının Arşiv Kaynakları," *Türkiye Araştırmaları Literatür Dergisi (TALİD)* 19, no. 37 (2021): 272; Mustafa Türkan, "Yakub'un Kuyusu (Le Puits de Jacob) Ne Kadar Derindir?," in *Yarının Kültürü I*, ed. Nazlı Esen Albayrak (Ankara: Yarının Kültürü Kitaplığı, 2023), 42–43.

26. Boyar and Fleet, "Mak[ing] Turkey and the Turkish Revolution Known," 122.
27. Boyar and Fleet, "Mak[ing] Turkey and the Turkish Revolution Known," 123.
28. Boyar and Fleet, "Mak[ing] Turkey and the Turkish Revolution Known," 125.
29. Boyar and Fleet, "Mak[ing] Turkey and the Turkish Revolution Known," 124.
30. Boyar and Fleet, "Mak[ing] Turkey and the Turkish Revolution Known," 124–125.
31. For Shub, see Joshua Malitsky, *Post-Revolution Nonfiction Film: Building the Soviet and Cuban Nations* (Indiana University Press, 2013); Anastasia Kostina, "The Mother of Soviet Documentary: Esfir Shub in Compilation Film and Beyond, 1927–1937" (PhD diss., Yale University, 2022); Ilana Shub Sharp, *Esfir Shub: Pioneer of Documentary Filmmaking* (Bloomsbury, 2021).
32. Samuel J. Hirst, "Soviet Orientalism Across Borders: Documentary Film for the Turkish Republic," *Kritika: Explorations in Russian and Eurasian History* 18, no. 1 (2017): 38–40.
33. Hirst, "Soviet Orientalism Across Borders," 47.
34. Elise K. Burton, *Genetic Crossroads: The Middle East and the Science of Human Heredity* (Stanford University Press, 2021), 53.
35. John M. Vander Lippe, "The 'Terrible Turk': The Formulation and Perpetuation of a Stereotype in American Foreign Policy," *New Perspectives on Turkey* 17 (1997): 41.
36. Vander Lippe, "The 'Terrible Turk,'" 42.
37. Vander Lippe, "The 'Terrible Turk,'" 41.
38. Vander Lippe, "The 'Terrible Turk,'" 41, 53.
39. Albert Bushnell, "Reservations as to the Near Eastern Question," *Annals of the Academy of Political and Social Science* 108 (1923): 120–122.
40. For an analysis of this film, see Dilek Kaya Mutlu, "*The Midnight Express* (1978) Phenomenon and the Image of Turkey," *Historical Journal of Film, Radio and Television* 25, no. 3 (2005).
41. RG 59, General Records of the Department of State Relating to Internal Affairs of Turkey 1930–1944, Microfilm 1224, Roll 11, Document 864.4061/Movietone/I, in US Diplomatic Documents on Turkey II: The Turkish Cinema in the Early Republican Years, ed. Rıfat N. Bali (Istanbul: The Isis Press and Gorgias Press, 2010), 13. In archival sources, the film is referred to as the "Atatürk movie" or *Atatürk's Reception of US Ambassador Joseph C. Grew at the Forest Farm*. A part of the film is available online: T. C. Kültür ve Turizm Bakanlığı, *Atatürk's Reception of US Ambassador Joseph C. Grew at the Forest Farm*, November 11, 1930, https://filmmirasim.ktb.gov.tr/en/film/atatrks-reception-of-us-ambassador-joseph-c-grew-at-the-forest-farm.
42. Enis Dinç, "Performing Modernity: The Film of Mustafa Kemal Atatürk on His Forest Farm," *Historical Journal of Film, Radio and Television* 39, no. 1 (2019): 19.

43. Enis Dinç, "Performing Modernity: The Film of Mustafa Kemal Atatürk on His Forest Farm," *Historical Journal of Film, Radio and Television* 39, no. 1 (2019): 22. For more, see Enis Dinç, *Atatürk on Screen: Documentary Film and the Making of a Leader* (Bloomsbury, 2020).
44. Julia Emberley, *The Cultural Politics of Fur* (Cornell University Press, 1997), 182.
45. *Cumhuriyet*, Bilim ve Kültür, "Afet Inan/Atatürk'ün Tarihe Verdiği Önem ve Medeniyet Anlayışı (1981)," April 7, 2017, https://www.youtube.com/watch?v=AJMhT4hjYkQ. For more on Inan, see Murat Ergin, *"Is the Turk a White Man?" Race and Modernity in the Making of Turkish Identity* (Brill, 2016).
46. Charles Hitchcock Sherrill, *A Year's Embassy to Mustafa Kemal* (Charles Scribner's Sons, 1934).
47. Sherrill, *A Year's Embassy to Mustafa Kemal*, vii, 18, 68, 138, quoted in Turgay Akbaba, "From the Terrible Turk to the Incredible Turk: Reimagining Turkey as an American Ally, 1919–1960" (PhD diss., University of North Carolina at Chapel Hill, 2020): 60–61.
48. Another government leader who praised Atatürk's progress in Turkey while constructing a racial discourse was Édouard Herriot, a leading politician in the French Radical Party. In *Orient* (1934), he wrote about Atatürk's reforms and applauded the president's efforts to detach Turkey from the Muslim world and adopt Western principles. According to Herriot, the Turks' "mistake" was joining Eastern civilization and adopting "oriental" religion and culture. He considered Turks to be Aryan and European, like French and Germans. See Édouard Herriot, *Orient* (Hachette, 1934). For more, see Akbaba, "From the Terrible Turk to the Incredible Turk," 64. Praising Atatürk's leadership is linked to giving up Islam, adopting principles like democracy, and sharing a racial sameness with dominant groups in Western nations.
49. Nan A. Lee, "Korean War Records and Research Trends in Turkey," *Seoul Journal of Korean Studies* 31, no. 2 (2018).
50. Tülay Gül, "Decision of Turkey Sending Soldiers to Korea in National Press," *Belgi* 7 (2014): 871.
51. For whiteness and anticommunism, see Cheris Brewer Current, "Normalizing Cuban Refugees: Representations of Whiteness and Anti-Communism in the USA During the Cold War," *Ethnicities* 8, no. 1 (2008); Richard Seymour, "The Cold War, American Anticommunism and the Global 'Colour Line,'" in *Race and Racism in International Relations: Confronting the Global Colour Line*, ed. A. Anievas et al. (Routledge, 2015).
52. Sam Williams, *Letter from General Sam Williams to Sergeant Nejdet Ayhan*, December 4, 1952, Williams Papers, Box 4, Folder 4, Hoover Institution Library & Archives, Stanford University, quoted in Vander Lippe, "The 'Terrible Turk,'" 54.
53. George C. McGhee, *The US-Turkish-NATO Middle East Connection: How the Truman Doctrine and Turkey's NATO Entry Contained the Soviets* (Springer, 2016).
54. Nadav Solomonovich, *The Korean War in Turkish Culture and Society* (Palgrave Macmillan, 2021), 137.

55. *Hürriyet*, October 30, 1953, cited in Solomonovich, *The Korean War in Turkish Culture and Society*, 150.
56. This performance is different from Eurasianness, the combination of European and Asian. For a counterexample, see Michael Kunichika, *"Our Native Antiquity": Archaeology and Aesthetics in the Culture of Russian Modernism* (Academic Studies Press, 2015).
57. Gavin D. Brockett, "The Legend of 'The Turk' in Korea: Popular Perceptions of the Korean War and Their Importance to a Turkish National Identity," *War & Society* 22, no. 2 (2004).
58. *Cumhuriyet*, December 7, 1950, cited in Solomonovich, *The Korean War in Turkish Culture and Society*, 155.
59. *Hürriyet*, April 29, 1951–June 4, 1951, cited in Solomonovich, *The Korean War in Turkish Culture and Society*, 150.
60. George C. McGhee, "Turkey Joins the West," *Foreign Affairs* 32, no. 4 (1954). *The Incredible Turk* is a TV documentary presented by the Prudential Insurance Company of America. It repurposes some of the footage from *Atatürk'ün Amerikan Büyükelçisi Joseph C. Grew'u Orman Çiftliginde Kabulü* (1930), probably without any permission. *The Incredible Turk*, produced by Burton Benjamin, narrated by Walter Cronkite (CBS News, 1958), https://archive.org/details/gov.archives.arc.651784. See Dinç, "Performing Modernity."
61. Perin E. Gürel, *The Limits of Westernization: A Cultural History of America in Turkey* (Columbia University Press, 2017), 86.
62. Gürel, *The Limits of Westernization*, 78–88.
63. Gürel, *The Limits of Westernization*, 86–89.
64. Encyclopaedia Britannica, *The Middle East: Change—Turkey and Saudi Arabia*, 1984, https://archive.org/details/themiddleeastchangeturkeyandsaudiarabia.
65. Ergin, *"Is the Turk a White Man?,"* 106.
66. Ülkü Ülküsal Bates, "The Anatolian Mausoleum of the Twelfth, Thirteenth, and Fourteenth Centuries" (PhD diss., University of Michigan, 1970).
67. The networks of hotels functioned as a form of modernizing technology that contributed to building tourism infrastructures with the American capitalist enterprise. For more on hotels and modernization, see Begüm Adalet, *Hotels and Highways: The Construction of Modernization Theory in Cold War Turkey* (Stanford University Press, 2018).
68. Al-Shanbary was in the process of completing a doctoral degree in early Islamic history at Columbia University, but this piece of information is absent from the film. See "News of Fellows and Scholars," *Middle East Studies Association Bulletin* 19, no. 1 (1985), http://www.jstor.org/stable/23057860.
69. Both Arabs and Turks are considered to be white according to the US consensus, yet debates around the necessity of their racial categorization under the label Middle Eastern or North African (MESA) continue, in large part because their social experiences suggest their brownness.
70. Ergin, *"Is the Turk a White Man?,"* 161.

2. Beyond the Contract: How Missionaries Forged Nontheatrical Havens

1. Biography of Paul E. Nilson, American Board of Commissioners for Foreign Missions (ABCFM) Archives, 1810–1961 (ABC 1–91), ABCFM 77.1, Box 53, Houghton Library, Harvard University.
2. This film could be *Donald Gets Drafted* (Jack King, 1942).
3. Letter written by Paul Nilson, February 16, 1953, ABCFM Archives, 1810–1961 (ABC 1–91), ABCFM 77.1, Box 53, Houghton Library, Harvard University.
4. The part of Nilson's quotation in Turkish translates as "God loves me, loves me, Allah loves me, Allah loves flowers, Even loves me, . . . Loves YOU, God loves you." *Allah* is the Turkish word for "God." Interestingly, he does not use the word *Tanrı*.
5. Letter written by Paul Nilson, February 16, 1953.
6. Joseph W. Ho, *Developing Mission: Photography, Filmmaking, and American Missionaries in Modern China* (Cornell University Press, 2022).
7. Pamela E. Klassen, *The Story of Radio Mind: A Missionary's Journey on Indigenous Land* (University of Chicago Press, 2019).
8. Lauren Frances Turek, *To Bring the Good News to All Nations: Evangelical Influence on Human Rights and US Foreign Relations* (Cornell University Press, 2020).
9. Clyde E. Fant and Mitchell G. Reddish, *A Guide to Biblical Sites in Greece and Turkey*. (Oxford University Press, 2003), 227.
10. See Ussama Samir Makdisi, *Artillery of Heaven: American Missionaries and the Failed Conversion of the Middle East* (Cornell University Press, 2008), 3, 7. Also see Eleanor Harvey Tejirian and Reeva Spector Simon, *Conflict, Conquest, and Conversion: Two Thousand Years of Christian Missions in the Middle East* (Columbia University Press, 2012).
11. Barış Ünlü, *Türklük Sözleşmesi: Oluşumu, İşleyişi ve Krizi* (Dipnot Yayınları, 2018), 119, 149. Also see Charles W. Mills, *The Racial Contract* (Cornell University Press, 1997).
12. "Ankarada Misyoner Faaliyeti," *İslâm-Türk Ansiklopedisi/Muhitülmaarif Mecmuası*, 2, no. 76 (Agustos 1947): 16, https://katalog.idp.org.tr/yazilar/60980/ankarada-misyoner-faaliyeti.
13. Ömer Rıza Doğrul, "Misyonerliğin Yeni Şekli," *Sebilürreşad*, 1, no. 18 (1948): 277, https://katalog.idp.org.tr/yazilar/92267/misyonerligin-yeni-sekli.
14. Filmlerin ve Film Senaryolarının Kontrolüne Dair Nizamname, *T. C. Resmi Gazete*, 4272, July 31, 1939, 12375–12377. The Board of Censorship—which included members from the Ministry of Interior, the General Staff of the Army, the Ministry of Tourism, the Ministry of National Education, and the police—regulated films. Moreover, to control foreign films, there were additional steps that involved the Film Control Committee in Ankara or in Istanbul and the City Film Control Committee.
15. Nezih Erdoğan and Dilek Kaya, "Institutional Intervention in the Distribution and Exhibition of Hollywood Films in Turkey," *Historical Journal of Film, Radio and Television* 22, no. 1 (2002): 55–56.
16. Letter written by Paul Nilson, February 16, 1953, ABCFM Archives, 1810–1961 (ABC 1–91), ABCFM 77.1, Box 53, Houghton Library, Harvard University.

17. Letter written by Paul Nilson, February 23, 1953, ABCFM Archives, 1810–1961 (ABC 1–91), ABCFM 77.1, Box 53, Houghton Library, Harvard University.
18. Barış Ünlü, "The Kurdish Struggle and the Crisis of the Turkishness Contract," *Philosophy & Social Criticism* 42, no. 4–5 (2016): 399. Also see Barış Ünlü, *Türklük Sözleşmesi*.
19. In 1949, Stearns was the film officer for the US International Information and Educational Exchange Program (USIE), later renamed the US Information Service/US Information Agency. For more, see Monteagle Stearns, "Report of USIE Activities in Turkey," Section 4: Motion Pictures, November 1949, RG 59 General Records of the Department of State, Office of the Assistant Secretary for Public Affairs, Office of International Information/Division of International Motion Pictures, Country Reports, 1949–1950, Box 23, ARC ID 4751078, Entry 239, National Archives at College Park, MD.
20. See Glenn Reynolds, *Movies on a Mission: American Protestants and the Foreign Missionary Film, 1906-1956* (McFarland, 2023), 3–5.
21. Paul E. Nilson, "Report of Rural Work Turkey," June 25, 1936, Near East Mission in Turkey, Annual Station Reports, 1931–1937, Salt Araştırma, https://archives.saltresearch.org/handle/123456789/42832.
22. Ögretici ve Teknik Filimler Hakkında Kanun, *T. C. Resmi Gazete*, Sayi 3537, Sayıfa 7698, Subat 1937 [Law on Educational and Technical Films, Republic of Turkey official gazette, Number 3537, p. 7698, February 1937], https://www.ogm.gov.tr/ekutuphane/Kanunlar/3116%20Sayılı%20Orman%20Kanunu%20(Orjinal%20Metin).pdf.
23. Emily Conroy-Krutz, *Christian Imperialism: Converting the World in the Early American Republic* (Cornell University Press, 2015), 2.
24. Conroy-Krutz, *Christian Imperialism*, 7–9. Kaveh Askari noted that the Presbyterian archives related to the Iran missions, shows that they largely gave up on converting Shia Iranians and instead focused on converting non-Muslim Armenian Iranians to Protestantism.
25. Conroy-Krutz, *Christian Imperialism*, 20–21.
26. Conroy-Krutz, *Christian Imperialism*, 41.
27. "Survey of the Near East Mission," 1951, prepared by Margaret R. Blemker, the secretary of Europe and the Near East, ABCFM Archives, HOU GEN ABC 85.2.2–85.2.4. Houghton Library, Harvard University.
28. Emrah Sahin, *Faithful Encounters: Authorities and American Missionaries in the Ottoman Empire* (McGill-Queen's University Press, 2018), 38.
29. Harlan P. Beach, *A Geography and Atlas of Protestant Missions*, vol. 1 (Student Volunteer Movement for Foreign Missions, 1901), 421.
30. Michael Oren, *Power, Faith, and Fantasy: America in the Middle East, 1776 to the Present* (W. W. Norton, 2007), 131, 291.
31. Oren, *Power, Faith, and Fantasy*, 292.
32. Jaffa Panken, "'Lest They Perish': The Armenian Genocide and the Making of Modern Humanitarian Media in the US, 1915–1925" (PhD diss., University of Pennsylvania, 2014), 16.

33. Panken, "'Lest They Perish,'" 16.
34. Anthony Slide, *Ravished Armenia and the Story of Aurora Mardiganian* (University Press of Mississippi, 2014). Although the initial intention was to raise awareness and garner support for the Armenian cause, Hollywood's treatment of Mardiganian highlights the ethical complexities that arise when attempting to capture historical atrocities through the medium of film.
35. Ünlü, "The Kurdish Struggle," 400.
36. Meeting of the W.T.M., Constantinople, January 9, 1923, ABCFM Archives, 1810–1961 (ABC 1-91), Houghton Library, Harvard University.
37. For John Dewey's progressive reforms to the American educational system in the context of film studies, see Kaveh Askari, *Making Movies Into Art: Picture Craft from the Magic Lantern to Early Hollywood* (Bloomsbury, 2019).
38. Bahri Ata, "The Influence of an American Educator John Dewey on the Turkish Educational System," *Turkish Yearbook of International Relations* 31 (2000): 121.
39. Selahattin Turan, "John Dewey's Report of 1924 and His Recommendations on the Turkish Educational System Revisited," *History of Education* 29, no. 6 (2000).
40. Committee on Education, August 1, 1921, ABCFM Archives, 1810–1961 (ABC 1-91), Houghton Library, Harvard University.
41. ViewLex projectörü, Talas Amerikan Koleji, 1930. Sağlık ve Eğitim Vakfı (SEV), Sanal Müze, https://www.sev.org.tr.
42. Letter written by Paul Nilsen, May 16, 1949, ABCFM Archives, 181–1961 (ABC 1-91), Houghton Library, Harvard University.
43. Tom Gunning, "An Aesthetics of Astonishment: Early Film and the (In)Credulous Spectator," in *Viewing Positions: Ways of Seeing Film*, ed. Linda Williams (Rutgers University Press, 1995), 119.
44. Ercüment Ekrem Talu, "İstanbulda İlk Sinema ve İlk Gramofon," *Perde ve Sahne* 7 (1943): 5.
45. Talu, "İstanbulda İlk Sinema ve İlk Gramofon," 14.
46. Talu, "İstanbulda İlk Sinema ve İlk Gramofon," 14.
47. Yasemin Alptekin, "Can Progressive Education Be Translated Into a Progressive Idea? Dewey's Report on Turkish," *International Journal of Progressive Education* 2, no. 2 (2006): 12.
48. John Dewey, *Experience and Education* (Macmillan, 1938); Morgan K. Williams, "John Dewey in the 21st Century," *Journal of Inquiry and Action in Education* 9, no. 1 (2017): 91–92.
49. Alptekin, "Can Progressive Education Be Translated Into a Progressive Idea?," 13–14.
50. Alptekin, "Can Progressive Education Be Translated Into a Progressive Idea?," 14. Also see H. Bal, John *Dewey'in Egitim Felsefesi* (Kor, 1991).
51. Charles Dorn and Doris A. Santoro, "Political Goals and Social Ideals: Dewey, Democracy, and the Emergence of the Turkish Republic," *Education and Culture* 27, no. 2 (2011): 3.
52. Dorn and Santoro, "Political Goals and Social Ideals," 15.

53. Paul E. Nilson, "Moral Education in American Schools in Turkey" (master's thesis, University of Chicago, 1926), 24.
54. Talas American College was established in 1871, when Talas, a district of Kayseri, was mostly populated by Armenians. It was initially established by the missionary James L. Fowle as a girls' school. In 1889, the missionary Henry K. Wingate added a boys' campus. During the war, the girls' school was closed and used as a hospital. Nilson became the school principal when the college reopened in 1928. See also Amerikan Bord Heyeti, Personnel Records for Henry K. Wingate, Istanbul Center Library, American Research Institute in Turkey, accessed October 20, 2017, http://www.dlir.org/archive/items/show/15841.
55. Letter written by Paul E. Nilson to Messers. Riggs, Goodsell, and Fowle, November 16, 1928, Near East Mission Archives, Istanbul.
56. For historical context, see Şahin, *Faithful Encounters*. For genocide, see Charlie Laderman, *Sharing the Burden: The Armenian Question, Humanitarian Intervention, and Anglo-American Visions of Global Order* (Oxford University Press, 2019).
57. Viewing images from *Beneath the Snows of Mount Argeaus* alongside an archival document from Houghton Library at Harvard University allowed me to estimate the film's year of production. Images from the film show Nilson with his wife, Harriet, and their four children. A report about the Nilson family prepared by the ABCFM in 1937 includes a photograph and notes the ages of the four children: in 1937, Mary Emily was twelve, Paul Herman was ten, Sylvia Elan was nine, and Dorothy Grace was seven. It also notes that Sylvia Elan was born in 1928 and Dorothy Grace in 1930. Thus, the film must have been made after 1930, two years after the college's opening. In the images, Dorothy Grace appears to be about one year old and Sylvia Elan about three; thus, the film was most likely made in 1931. The film is available at https://www.youtube.com/watch?v=jVotJRrHXKo.
58. Gridley aimed to test the assertion by the Greek geographer Strabon that he could see both the Mediterranean and the Black Sea from the top of Mount Argeaus. See Ayhan Öztürk and S. Tunay Kamer, "Activities of American Missionaries in Kayseri," *Cumhuriyet Uluslararası Eğitim Dergisi* 2, no. 2 (2013).
59. This association between religion and mountains is present in other films, such as *The Epic of Everest* (John Baptist Lucius Noel, 1924), that missionaries in Turkey carried in their libraries. See Peter H. Hansen, "The Dancing Lamas of Everest: Cinema, Orientalism, and Anglo-Tibetan Relations in the 1920s," *American Historical Review* 101, no. 3 (1996): 724; Charles Acland, "Mapping the Serious and the Dangerous: Film and the National Council of Education, 1920–1939," *Cinémas: Revue d'études cinématographiques/Journal of Film Studies* 6, no. 1 (1995): 103.
60. Sports diplomacy unites communities through a mutual appreciation for physical activities and facilitates the pursuit of development objectives. See Stuart Murray, "Sports Diplomacy: History, Theory, and Practice," *Oxford Research Encyclopedia of International Studies* (Oxford University Press, 2020).
61. Dodd was the medical director for the Near East Foundation, and in 1943, he set up a medical program for twenty-five thousand Yugoslav refugees at a camp on

Egypt's Sinai Peninsula across the Suez Canal. To protect the camp from epidemics, he started a campaign to vaccinate against smallpox and inoculated every refugee in the camp against typhus and typhoid fevers. From 1945 to 1953, he worked for the Mount Hermon School in Massachusetts. The Turkish government changed its regulations about medical services, making it difficult for American doctors to practice in Turkey. According to the new regulations, American doctors had to become Turkish citizens and pass an examination in all medical subjects in the Turkish language to practice medicine in Turkey. Dodd returned to Turkey after Mark H. Ward of the United Church Board for World Ministries Libraries officially requested that Dodd serve three more years for the ABCFM in the Talas area. Dodd retained his license to practice medicine in Turkey because of a Turkish-American Treaty signed in 1927, and he went back to Talas to provide medical services for the board for three more years.

62. For medical diplomacy, see Michael L. Gross, "Medical Diplomacy and the Battle for Hearts and Minds," in *Military Medical Ethics in Contemporary Armed Conflict: Mobilizing Medicine in the Pursuit of Just War* (Oxford University Press, 2021), 204.
63. Barbara Reeves-Ellington, "American Women Missionaries on Trial in Turkey: Religion, Diplomacy, and Public Perceptions in the 1920s," *Diplomatic History* 43, no. 2 (2018).
64. Although the exact date of the film was not recorded in the archives, an analysis of the holiday dates mentioned in the film and the historical alignment of the Islamic calendar indicates that it was likely produced in 1933. The film marked the end of Ramadan as "26 Thursday" to indicate the beginning of the Muslim holiday. The Muslim holiday happens after the end of the Ramadan, and the only year in which the 26th fell on a Thursday and the next day was the Sugar Feast was 1933 (when considering calendars between 1921 and 1938). To check the years and days in the calendar, I used the website https://takvim.ihya.org/1933-yili-dini-gunler-takvimi.html.
65. "About UAA—History," Üsküdar American Academy, http://www.uaa.k12.tr/en/Icerik/okulumuzun-tarihcesi/256/. Halide Edib Adıvar, an alumna of the school in the same period and a famous feminist writer and leader, shared experiences similar to Malatyalıoğlu's.
66. Memorandum from Melvin A. Wittler to Miss Margaret Blomker, "Death of Herman Harold Kreider," 1967, ABCFM Archives, 1810–1961 (ABC 1–91) / ABC 77.1, Box 966, Houghton Library, Harvard University.
67. Letter written by Luther Fowle to E. W. Riggs, July 23, 1927, Turkish Mission of the American Board, ABCFM Archives, 1810–1961 (ABC 1–91), Houghton Library, Harvard University.
68. *The Work of Mr. Kreider*, 1939, ABCFM Archives, 1810–1961 (ABC 1–91) / ABC 77.1, Box 966, Houghton Library, Harvard University.
69. Paul E. Nilson, "Report of the Rural Work Committee," 1932, Near East Mission in Turkey Annual Station Reports, 1931–1937, Salt Araştırma, https://archives.saltresearch.org/handle/123456789/45733.

2. BEYOND THE CONTRACT

70. Nilson, "Report of the Rural Work Committee," 1932. Other films included *Irrigation, Cotton Growing, In Florence Nightingale's Footsteps, Waste Disposal in Cities, By Their Fruits, Mosquitoes, Fly Danger, Getting Acquainted with Bacteria, The Spider Web, The Evolution of a Butterfly, Mrs. Fly, Wisconsin Diaries, Sun Babies, Parade of Comic Balloons, Tales of Two Cities, Epic of Everest, The Forest & Water, Sniffles Snuffles,* and *Planting & Care of Trees*. The years and directors of these films are unknown. Either Nilson or a Turkish teacher named Faruk Caner often translated these films to Turkish audiences. It is essential to note that translation does not always convey every aspect, and translators possess the authority to emphasize certain elements, omit others, or alter the meaning of the written text.
71. Robert College, *Annual Report of the President, 1900-01*, 14–15, cited in Robert L. Daniel, *American Philanthropy in the Near East, 1820-1960* (Ohio University Press, 1970), 76.
72. Robert College, *Annual Report of the President, 1926-27*, 14–17, cited in Daniel, *American Philanthropy in the Near East*, 70, 180.
73. Frank A. Ross et al., *The Near East and American Philanthropy*, passim, cited in Robert College, *Annual Report of the President, 1926-27*, 14–17.
74. *Highlights of Village Life* (Near East Mission of the ABCFM, 1920s), https://www.travelfilmarchive.com/item.php?id=12017&country_id=83&startrow=0&keywords=Turkey+Turkey.
75. Salomé Aguilera Skvirsky, *The Process Genre: Cinema and the Aesthetic of Labor*. (Duke University Press, 2020), 2.
76. *Quality Milk*, in *Educational Film Catalog* (H. W. Wilson, 1939), 637–639, https://archive.org/stream/educationalfilmc00hwwirich#page/192/mode/2up/search/Quality+Milk.
77. Skvirsky, *The Process Genre*, 56.
78. An extract of a letter written by John G. A. Leishman, US minister to Turkey, to Thomas Spees Carrington is included in American Hospital and Training School for Nurses, *American Medical Work in Turkey* (American Hospital and Training School for Nurses, 1905), 9, https://archive.org/details/americanmedicalw00unse.
79. Paul E. Nilson, "Report of the Rural Work Committee," 1937, ABCFM/Annual Station Reports, Near East Mission in Turkey Annual Station Reports, 1931–1937, Talas (Turkey), https://www.archives.saltresearch.org/R/-?func=dbin-jump-full&object_id=4005966&silo_library=GEN01.
80. William E. Winn, "Tom Brown's Schooldays and the Development of 'Muscular Christianity,'" *Church History* 29, no. 1 (1960): 70.
81. For discussions of science and religion, see Jacques Derrida and Gil Anidjar, *Acts of Religion* (Routledge, 2002); Gary B. Ferngren, *Science and Religion: A Historical Introduction* (Johns Hopkins University Press, 2002); Holmes Rolston, *Science and Religion: A Critical Survey* (Templeton Foundation Press, 2006).
82. *Personal Hygiene for Young Men* (Bray Studios, 1924), Internet Archive, https://archive.org/details/rppersonalhygieneforyoungmen001.
83. Clifford Putney, *Muscular Christianity: Manhood and Sports in Protestant America, 1880–1920* (Harvard University Press, 2001), 2.

84. Aslı Cırakman, *From the "Terror of the World" to the "Sick Man of Europe": European Images of Ottoman Empire and Society from the Sixteenth Century to the Nineteenth* (Lang, 2002).
85. "Report of Rural Work Committee," June 29, 1937, ABCFM Archives, 1810-1961 (ABC 1-91), Houghton Library, Harvard University.
86. Letter written by Paul E. Nilson, May 16, 1949
87. "Mrs. Mary Louise Lee Winkler," Confidential Letter of Recommendation, March 1956, ABCFM Archives, 1810-1961 (ABC 1-91), ABCFM 78.4, Vol. 11, Box 21, Houghton Library, Harvard University.
88. For the use of white lab coat, see Gonzalo Bearman et al., "Healthcare Personnel Attire in Non-Operating-Room Settings," *Infection Control & Hospital Epidemiology* 35, no. 2 (2014).
89. See Alison Griffiths, *Wondrous Difference: Cinema, Anthropology and Turn-of-the-Century Visual Culture* (Columbia University Press, 2002); John Harvey, *Photography and Spirit* (Reaktion Books, 2007); Eric H. Cline, *Biblical Archaeology: A Very Short Introduction* (Oxford University Press), 2009.
90. Terry Lindvall and Andrew Quicke, *Celluloid Sermons: The Emergence of the Christian Film Industry, 1930-1986* (NYU Press, 2011), 1.
91. Heather Hendershot, *Shaking the World for Jesus: Media and Conservative Evangelical Culture* (University of Chicago Press, 2010), 13.
92. Hendershot, *Shaking the World for Jesus*, 13, 151-153. For Hendershot, "soft-sell" evangelism is about "asking questions that would get people thinking about the logic of science and then, by extension, the logic of God's plan for salvation" (151).
93. Marsha Orgeron and Skip Elsheimer, "'Something Different in Science Films': The Moody Institute of Science and the Canned Missionary Movement," *Moving Image* 7, no. 1 (2007): 2.
94. Orgeron and Elsheimer, "'Something Different in Science Films,'" 2.
95. James Gilbert, *Redeeming Culture: American Religion in an Age of Science* (University of Chicago Press, 1997), 135.
96. Orgeron and Elsheimer, "'Something Different in Science Films,'" 2.
97. Gilbert, *Redeeming Culture*, 95, 142.
98. Gilbert, *Redeeming Culture*, 99.
99. Orgeron and Elsheimer, "'Something Different in Science Films,'" 22.
100. Letter written by Paul Nilson, February 16, 1953.
101. American Board of Commissioners for Foreign Missions Archives, 1810-1961 (ABC 1-91) Houghton Library, Harvard University. Biography of Paul E. Nilson. ABCFM 77.1, Box 53. A letter written by Paul Nilson. July 20, 1951.
102. Lindvall and Quicke, *Celluloid Sermons*, 15.
103. Letter written by Paul Nilson, February 16, 1953.
104. Letter written by Paul Nilson, February 16, 1953.
105. Letter written by Paul Nilson, February 23, 1953.
106. Letter written by Paul Nilson, January 13, 1953, ABCFM Archives, 1810-1961 (ABC 1-91), ABCFM 77.1, Box 53, Houghton Library, Harvard University.

107. Letter written by Paul Nilson, January 13, 1953.
108. Letter written by Paul Nilson, February 7, 1951, ABCFM Archives, 1810–1961 (ABC 1–91), ABCFM 77.1, Box 53, Houghton Library, Harvard University. In the letter, Nilson quotes a letter by White dated January 23, 1951. Luther R. Fowle, Istanbul, February 15, 1951, Post Box 142, no. 266, American Research Institute in Turkey, Istanbul Center Library, http://www.dlir.org/archive/archive/files/96dfa90f7585c96aa351e17be51517fb.pdf. The films' production years and directors are unknown.
109. Letter written by Paul Nilson, February 7, 1951, quoting a letter by White dated January 23, 1951.
110. Paul E. Nilson, "Report of Rural Work Turkey," 1936, ABCFM/Annual Station Reports, Near East Mission in Turkey Annual Station Reports, 1931–1937, Talas, Turkey.
111. Ögretici ve Teknik Filimler Hakkinda Kanun, *T. C. Resmi Gazete*, Sayi 3537.Eight days later *T. C. Resmi Gazete*, the official newspaper of the Republic of Turkey, published the six articles of this law. The first article stated that no taxes are to be imposed on imported technical and educational films. The tax-free regulation applied to any audiovisual materials for filmmaking and screening including mobile units and projectors. The Turkish government's tax-free approach aimed to attract importers and create businesses around educational films. The second article established a group from the Film Audit Commission to evaluate educational and technical films and exempt the agencies that brought them to the customs offices in Istanbul and Ankara. The Film Audit Commission consisted of five associates who conducted investigations on behalf of the Delegates and Chief of General Staff of Economics and Agriculture Mandates. This indicates that the Turkish government established a system in which specific roles are assigned to the agencies in its associated organizations to control the process of bringing in imported films and inspecting their content. The third article made it mandatory that movie theaters screen technical and educational films, whether made inside or outside Turkey, before they exhibit regular movies. It was the government's responsibility to provide technical and educational films to the exhibitors. The fourth article noted that those who did not obey article three would pay a penalty based on a municipal decision. The other three articles explained the technical aspects of these regulations, including the surveillance method and period. The government's incentives for importation, circulation, and exhibition were clearly on the positive side of the spectrum. However, the government failed to regulate the application of the law.

3. US Government Film Programming in Turkey

1. *Turkey*, Motion Picture 111-OF-49 (Orientation Film No. 49), Records of the Office of the Chief Signal Officer, Record Group (RG) 111, National Archives and Records Administration, College Park, MD, https://catalog.archives.gov/id/36095.
2. Nicholas Cull noted that to promote the New Deal, the Roosevelt administration established the USIS as a department within the National Executive Council in 1934.

See Nicholas J. Cull, *The Cold War and the United States Information Agency: American Propaganda and Public Diplomacy, 1945–1989* (Cambridge University Press, 2010), 11.
3. For the USIS and film, see Richard Dyer MacCann, "Film and Foreign Policy: The USIA, 1962–67," *Cinema Journal* 9, no. 1 (1969); Nicholas J. Cull, "Auteurs of Ideology: USIA Documentary Film Propaganda in the Kennedy Era As Seen in Bruce Herschensohn's *The Five Cities of June* (1963) and James Blue's *The March* (1964)," *Film History* 10, no. 3 (1998); Seth Fein, "New Empire Into Old: Making Mexican Newsreels the Cold War Way," *Diplomatic History* 28, no. 5 (2004); Jennifer Horne, "Experiments in Propaganda: Reintroducing James Blue's Colombia Trilogy," *Moving Image* 9, no. 1 (2009); Tony Shaw and Denise J. Youngblood, *Cinematic Cold War: The American and Soviet Struggle for Hearts and Minds* (University Press of Kansas, 2010); Hamid Naficy, *A Social History of Iranian Cinema*, vol. 2, *The Industrializing Years, 1941–1978* (Duke University Press, 2011), xxiii; Burcu Sari Karademir, "Turkey as a 'Willing Receiver' of American Soft Power: Hollywood Movies in Turkey During the Cold War," *Turkish Studies* 13, no. 4 (2012); Han Sang Kim, "Cold War and the Contested Identity Formation of Korean Filmmakers: On *Boxes of Death* and Kim Ki-yong's USIS Films," *Inter-Asia Cultural Studies* 14, no. 4 (2013); Sangjoon Lee, "Creating an Anti-Communist Motion Picture Producers' Network in Asia: The Asia Foundation, Asia Pictures, and the Korean Motion Picture Cultural Association," *Historical Journal of Film, Radio and Television* 37, no. 3 (2017); Hongwei Thorn Chen, "Moving Pictures, Empty Words: Cinema as Developmental Interface in the Chinese Reconstruction, 1932–1952" (PhD diss., University of Minnesota, 2017); Hadi Paraydeh Gharabaghi, "'American Mice Grow Big!' The Syracuse Audiovisual Mission in Iran and the Rise of Documentary Diplomacy" (PhD diss., New York University, 2018); Brian Real, "Private Life, Public Diplomacy: Tibor Hirsch and Documentary Filmmaking for the Cold War USIA," *Historical Journal of Film, Radio and Television* 40, no. 2 (2020); Bret Vukoder, "Filmic Aesthetics and Technologies of War, Policy, and 'Truth' in the Motion Pictures of the United States Information Agency" (PhD diss., Carnegie Mellon University, 2020); Sangjoon Lee, *Cinema and the Cultural Cold War: US Diplomacy and the Origins of the Asian Cinema Network* (Cornell University Press, 2020); Bret Vukoder and Mark Williams, "The Great War at Scale," in *Provenance and Early Cinema*, ed. Joanne Bernardi et al. (Indiana University Press, 2021).
4. The Overseas Film Program, U.S. Information Agency, 1959, RG 306 General Records of the USIA, Historical Collection to the Overseas Film Program, Box 155, Subject Files, 1953–2000, Motion Pictures, 1983–2000.
5. Laura Belmonte, *Selling the American Way: U.S. Propaganda and the Cold War* (University of Pennsylvania Press, 2011), 4–7.
6. The Overseas Film Program, U.S. Information Agency, 1959.
7. Mikael Nilsson, *The Battle for Hearts and Minds in the High North: The USIA and American Cold War Propaganda in Sweden, 1952–1969* (Brill, 2016), 197.
8. USIS Amerikan Haberler Merkezi Türkiye, *16mm-35mm Film Kataloğu, 1960* (Yeni Desen Matbaası, 1960), 1.
9. I am grateful to Charles Acland for drawing my attention to this film and to the archival materials housed at Ohio State University.

10. Robert W. Wagner, interview, February 5, 2001 (edited by R.W.W. February 1, 2002). Ohio State University Archives.
11. Wagner's involvement extended well beyond *Sadiye*. Under his supervision, a number of films were produced throughout the Middle East, covering topics such as public health, agriculture, and military training. In Turkey, these included films on hygiene and rural development as well as documentaries of joint US-Turkish army maneuvers during periods of geopolitical tension with the USSR.
12. USIS Amerikan Haberler Merkezi, *Film Kataloğu, 1965* (Ayyıldız Matbaası, 1965), 53, 54, 55, 79. Based on accessible catalogs, the film directors and years are unknown.
13. USIS Amerikan Haberler Merkezi Türkiye, *16mm-35mm Film Kataloğu, 1960*, 1, 9, 10, 14. Based on accessible catalogs, the film directors and years are unknown.
14. USIS Amerikan Haberler Merkezi, *"USIS" Film Kataloğu, 1962* (Yeni Desen Matbaası, 1962), 7, 33, 53. Based on accessible catalogs, the film directors and years are unknown.
15. USIS Amerikan Haberler Merkezi Türkiye, *16mm-35mm Film Kataloğu, 1960*, 2, 4, 16. Based on accessible catalogs, the film directors and years are unknown.
16. USIS Amerikan Haberler Merkezi Türkiye, *16mm-35mm Film Kataloğu, 1960*, 7, 12, 14. Based on accessible catalogs, the film directors and years are unknown.
17. Cull, *The Cold War and the United States Information Agency*, 206–218, 248, 249, 283, 284.
18. In an early guide from the 1950s, USIA/USIS is also abbreviated as USIE. The USIS also operated under the name Amerikan Haberler Merkezi/Bürosu (American News Center/Bureau).
19. Burcu Feyzullahoğlu, "*Ufuk*: How the US Information Agency Molded Turkish Elite Opinion, 1960–1980" (PhD diss., Bilkent University, 2014).
20. Wilson P. Dizard, *Inventing Public Diplomacy: The Story of the US Information Agency* (Lynne Rienner, 2004), 6.
21. For how the USIS collaborated with commercial media companies and produced media in exchange for access to markets, see Herbert I. Schiller, *Mass Communications and American Empire* (A. M. Kelley, 1969).
22. Nezih Erdoğan and Dilek Kaya, "Institutional Intervention in the Distribution and Exhibition of Hollywood Films in Turkey," *Historical Journal of Film, Radio and Television* 22, no. 1 (2002): 51.
23. Erdoğan and Kaya, "Institutional Intervention," 52.
24. Erdoğan and Kaya, "Institutional Intervention," 52–53.
25. Erdoğan and Kaya, "Institutional Intervention," 53.
26. Aysehan Jülide Etem, "Media Infrastructure as Smart Power in the Case of the Educational Film, Radio and Television Center of Turkey, 1949–1973," *Journal of E-Media Studies* 6, no. 1 (2022): 3.
27. Erdoğan and Kaya, "Institutional Intervention," 52.
28. Semih Tugrul, "Türkiye'de Amerikan Sansürü," *Hür Vatan*, May 10, 1962, 3.
29. Erdoğan and Kaya, "Institutional Intervention," 52.
30. Nijat Özön, "Türkiye'de Amerikan Sansürü," *Yön*, no. 18 (April 18, 1962): 18.
31. Erdoğan and Kaya, "Institutional Intervention," 53.
32. USIS Amerikan Haberler Merkezi, *Film Kataloğu, 1965*. While these films were made available in both Turkish and English, the film titles in the USIS-Turkey catalogs

are exclusively in Turkish; the English titles are my translations. The film directors and years are inaccessible.
33. For race and democracy, see Mary L. Dudziak, *Cold War Civil Rights: Race and the Image of American Democracy* (Princeton University Press, 2011). For race and integration, see Anna McCarthy, *The Citizen Machine: Governing by Television in 1950s America* (New Press, 2010).
34. Belmonte, *Selling the American Way*, 173.
35. Melinda M. Schwenk, "Reforming the Negative Through History: The U.S. Information Agency and the 1957 Little Rock Integration Crisis," *Journal of Communication Inquiry* 23, no. 3 (1999): 289.
36. USIS Amerikan Haberler Merkezi, *Film Kataloğu, 1965*.
37. USIS-Country Program Memorandum for FY 1972, RG 0306 US Information Agency, Office of the Assistant Director for Europe, Country Files for Turkey 1953–1972, Entry #P403, Robert Lincoln, National Archives and Records Administration, College Park. MD.
38. USIS Amerikan Haberler Merkezi, *"USIS" Film Kataloğu, 1962*. The production dates of these films are inaccessible.
39. USIS Amerikan Haberler Merkezi Türkiye, *16mm-35mm Film Kataloğu, 1960*.
40. "Cami Gezdiler," *Milliyet Gazete Arşivi*, March 7, 1957, http://gazetearsivi.milliyet.com.tr/GununYayinlari/7xqvl0v_x2F_LjKtQMDHByA5wg_x3D__x3D_. On the other hand, the religion scholar Michael Graziano noted that when intelligence operations like those of the CIA were influenced by American religious ideals, global religious dynamics were often misinterpreted, leading to significant international consequences. See Michael Graziano, *Errand Into the Wilderness of Mirrors: Religion and the History of the CIA* (University of Chicago Press, 2021).
41. Ögretici ve Teknik Filimler Hakkında Kanun, *T. C. Resmi Gazete*, Sayi 3537, Sayifa 7698, Subat 1937 [Law on Educational and Technical Films, Republic of Turkey official gazette, Number 3537, p. 7698, February 1937], https://www.ogm.gov.tr/ekutuphane/Kanunlar/3116%20Sayılı%20Orman%20Kanunu%20(Orjinal%20Metin).pdf.
42. World-Wide Free Flow (Export-Import) of Audio-Visual Materials, 22 C.F.R. § 502.7(B) (1984).
43. Sharon Esakoff, "USIA Censorship of Education Films for Distribution Abroad," *Cardozo Arts & Entertainment Law Journal* 3, no. 2 (1984): 403.
44. Nancy Snow, *Propaganda, Inc.: Selling America's Culture to the World* (Seven Stories Press, 2010), 57. See also Weston R. Sager, "Apple Pie Propaganda: The Smith-Mundt Act Before and After the Repeal of the Domestic Dissemination Ban," *Northwestern University Law Review* 109 (2014).
45. Esakoff, "USIA Censorship of Education Films for Distribution Abroad," 403.
46. Esakoff, "USIA Censorship of Education Films for Distribution Abroad," 420.
47. Under Secretary of State Acheson to Secretary of War Patterson, in *Foreign Relations of the United States*, vol. 3, *The British Commonwealth; Europe*, ed. Ralph E. Goodwin et al. (GPO, 1947), 197–198.
48. Sebnem Üstün, "Turkey and the Marshall Plan: Strive for Aid," *Turkish Yearbook of International Relations* 27 (1997): 39–40.

49. Economic Cooperation Act of 1948, George C. Marshall Foundation, https://www.marshallfoundation.org/library/documents/economic-cooperation-act-1948/.
50. Central Intelligence Agency, *Turkey (Situation Report SR 1/1)*, December 22, 1948, CIA FOIA Electronic Reading Room, Document ID: CIA-RDP78-01617A001400020001-3, https://www.cia.gov/readingroom/document/cia-rdp78-01617a001400020001-3.
51. Aysehan Jülide Etem, review of *The American Marshall Plan Film Campaign and the Europeans: A Captivated Audience?*, by Maria Fritsche, *Alphaville: Journal of Film and Screen Media*, no. 17 (2019): 230–231.
52. I use the terms *propaganda* and *information* interchangeably.
53. Maria Fritsche, *The American Marshall Plan Film Campaign and the Europeans: A Captivated Audience?* (Bloomsbury Academic, 2018), 69.
54. Fritsche, *The American Marshall Plan Film Campaign*, 70.
55. Aysehan Jülide Etem, "A Transnational Communication Network Promoting Film Diplomacy: The Case of Turkey and the USA, 1950–86," *Historical Journal of Film, Radio and Television* 41, no. 2 (2020).
56. Joint American Military Mission for Aid to Turkey, "General Information About Turkey," March 1954, 15, Headquarters Commandant Section, R G 334, National Archives and Records Administration, College Park, MD.
57. "Incirlik Air Base History," Incirlik Air Base, accessed June 13, 2023, https://www.incirlik.af.mil/About-Us/Fact-Sheets/Display/Article/300814/incirlik-air-base-history/.
58. Howard Adelbert Munson IV, "The Joint American Military Mission to Aid Turkey: Implementing the Truman Doctrine and Transforming US Foreign Policy, 1947–1954" (PhD diss., Washington State University, 2012.
59. Clifford H. Bernath, "JUSMMAT and Turkey: History and Overview," *DISAM Journal of International Security Assistance Management* 7, no. 4 (1985): 5.
60. Douglas A. Howard, *The History of Turkey* (Greenwood, 2001), 128.
61. *Turkey: The Land of "In-Between"* (Armed Forces, 1952), https://archive.org/details/gov.archives.arc.654133#reviews.
62. US Department of Defense, Office of Armed Forces Information and Education, *A Pocket Guide to Turkey* (Department of the Army, 1953).
63. US Department of Defense, *A Pocket Guide to Turkey*, 4.
64. US Department of Defense, *A Pocket Guide to Turkey*, 2.
65. Monteagle Stearns, "Report of USIE Activities in Turkey," Section IV: Motion Pictures, November 1949, RG 59 General Records of the Department of State, Office of the Assistant Secretary for Public Affairs, Office of International Information/Division of International Motion Pictures, Country Reports, 1949–1950, Box 23, ARC ID 4751078, Entry 239, US National Archives, College Park, MD.
66. William E. Kugeman, Memorandum, "From Embassy, Ankara—To the Department of State, Washington, October 1, 1952, Subject: Motion Pictures—Cooperation with Turkish Ministries," RG 306 US Information Agency, Office of the Assistant Director for Europe, Entry P403: COU, Country Files for Turkey 1953–1972, US National Archives, College Park, MD.

67. Thomas E. Flanagan, Memorandum, "From Embassy Ankara to the Department of State, Washington, February 5, 1953, Subject: Motion Pictures—Cooperation with Turkish Ministries, Inter-Ministerial Committee—Evidence of Effectiveness." US National Archives, College Park, MD.
68. Etem, "A Transnational Communication Network," 295.
69. Kugeman, Memorandum, "From Embassy, Ankara . . . October 1, 1952."
70. Hugh A. Crumpler, Memorandum, "Motion Pictures—Establishment of Film Production Facilities in Turkey," February 4, 1953, RG 59 General Records of the Department of State, Office of the Assistant Secretary for Public Affairs, Office of International Information/Division of International Motion Pictures, Country Reports, 1949–1950, Box 23, ARC ID 4751078, Entry 239, US National Archives, College Park, MD.
71. Crumpler, Memorandum, "Motion Pictures."
72. Ögretici Filmler Merkezi, *Film Kataloğu* (M. K. B. Matbaasi, 1956).
73. Crumpler, Memorandum, "Motion Pictures."
74. Crumpler, Memorandum, "Motion Pictures."
75. Crumpler, Memorandum, "Motion Pictures."
76. Crumpler, Memorandum, "Motion Pictures."
77. Crumpler, Memorandum, "Motion Pictures."
78. Crumpler, Memorandum, "Motion Pictures."
79. Ögretici Filmler Merkezi, *Film Kataloğu*.
80. USIA, Memorandum, "From USIS Ankara to USIA Washington," September 5, 1956, RG 306 US Information Agency, Office of the Assistant Director for Europe, Entry #P403: Country Files for Turkey 1953–1972, US National Archives, College Park, MD.
81. USIA, Secret Document, June 27, 1956, RG 306 US Information Agency, Office of the Assistant Director for Europe, Entry P403: Country Files for Turkey 1953–1972, US National Archives, College Park, MD.
82. USIA, Memorandum, "From USIS Ankara to USIA Washington."
83. USIA, Memorandum, "From USIS Ankara to USIA Washington."
84. "Amerikan Haberler Bürosu Film Servisi Nasıl Çalışıyor?," *Film ve Öğretim*, no. 1 (1950): 8.
85. "Amerikan Haberler Merkezinin Seyyar Sinemasinda Bir Saat," *Film ve Öğretim*, no. 6–7 (1951): 6.
86. "Amerikan Haberler Merkezinin Seyyar Sinemasinda Bir Saat," 6.
87. Other spellings of Hoja include *Hodja* and *Hoca*.
88. Nebi Özdemir, *Nasreddin Hodja: The Philosopher's Philosopher*, Handbook Series, vol. 14; Ministry of Culture and Tourism General Directorate of Libraries and Publications, no. 3311 (Ankara: Ministry of Culture and Tourism, 2011), 89. 14. Also see Mustafa Duman, *Nasreddin Hoca ve 1555 Fıkrası* (Istanbul: Heyamola Yayınları, 2008), 146–148. These scholars discuss the influence of the Hoja films on the Turkish film industry, but as I note in this book, there were also American and Russian films based on this folklore figure.
89. *Educational Film Guide*, ed. Frederic A. Krahn, 11th ed. (H. W. Wilson, 1953), 330, 434, 658, https://archive.org/details/11theducationalfilm00wilsrich/page/434/mode/2up.

Additionally, the Office of the US Commissioner General commissioned Trident Films to create documentary films aimed at promoting the United States overseas. See "Films at Brussels," *Business Screen Magazine*, 1958, https://lantern.mediahist.org/catalog/1958businessscreenmav19rich_0386.

90. Motion Picture Films from the "Hoja" Program Series, 1952–1974, RG 306 Records of the US Information Agency, NAID: 56717, Local ID: 306-HA, National Archives and Records Administration, College Park, MD, https://catalog.archives.gov/id/56717.
91. *United States Embassy (Iraq)*, Despatch from Philip W. Ireland to the Department of State, "Evaluation of 'Hoja' Films," July 18, 1953, National Archives, Record Group 59, *Records of the Department of State: Decimal Files, 1950–1954*, reprinted in National Security Archive Electronic Briefing Book No. 78.
92. *The Heart of a Tyrant*, Motion Picture Films from the "Hoja" Program Series, 1952–1974, RG 306: Records of the US Information Agency, NAID: 140135766, Local ID: 306-HA-4, National Archives and Records Administration, College Park, MD, https://catalog.archives.gov/id/140135766.
93. In 1954, Istanbul Film produced *Nasreddin Hoca ve Timurlenk* (Nasreddin Hoja and Tamburlaine), a film directed by Faruk Genc, covering the emperor's tale.
94. R. D. Bisbee, Memorandum, "Screening of Hoja Films," October 10, 1961, RG 306 US Information Agency, Office of the Assistant Director for Near East and South Asia, Entry P246, Policy Files: 1956–1964, Box 2 US National Archives, College Park, MD.
95. For Hoja films in the context of Tajikistan, see Sharofat Arabova, "Dystopia and Utopia: Soviet Politics and the Musicals of Tajikistan," *East European Film Bulletin* 110 (2020), https://eefb.org/retrospectives/soviet-politics-and-the-musicals-of-tajikistan/.
96. For context on Soviet whiteness, see Yuri Slezkine, *Arctic Mirrors: Russia and the Small Peoples of the North* (Cornell University Press, 1994); Hilary Lynd and Thom Loyd, "Histories of Color: Blackness and Africanness in the Soviet Union," *Slavic Review* 81, no. 2 (2022): 404–406; Katherine Anne Baldwin, *Beyond the Color Line and the Iron Curtain: Reading Encounters Between Black and Red, 1922–1963* (Duke University Press, 2002).
97. Elvira Kulieva, "'The East Is a Delicate Matter' or Soviet Orientalism in Films About Central Asia 1955–1970" (master's thesis, Ibn Khaldun University, 2018), 59.
98. Kulieva, "'The East Is a Delicate Matter,'" 61.
99. Kulieva, "'The East Is a Delicate Matter,'" 60.
100. JoAnn Conrad, "'This Is Not Our Hoca!' Repurposing, Repackaging, and Reappropriating Nasreddin Hoca," in *Terra Ridens, Terra Narrans: Festschrift Zum 65. Geburtstag Von Ulrich Marzolph*, vol. 45, ed. Regina Bendix and Dorothy Noyes (Dortmund, 2008).
101. For his work in international relations, see Monteagle Stearns, *Entangled Allies: US Policy Toward Greece, Turkey, and Cyprus* (Council on Foreign Relations, 1992); Monteagle Stearns, *Talking to Strangers: Improving American Diplomacy at Home and Abroad* (Princeton University Press, 1999).
102. Stearns's first assignment was in Iran as the motion picture officer; when this position was eliminated, he started working in Turkey. For more, see Monteagle Stearns, "Ambassador Monteagle Stearns," interview by Charles Stuart Kennedy,

Association for Diplomatic Studies and Training Foreign Affairs Oral History Project, April 30, 2013, https://adst.org/wp-content/uploads/2013/12/Stearns-Monteagle.pdf.

103. Monteagle Stearns—People—Department History—Office of the Historian, U.S. Department of State, last updated March 14, 2024, https://history.state.gov/departmenthistory/people/stearns-monteagle. His extensive experience also included postings in Zaire, the United Kingdom, Laos, and Turkey.

104. Turkish-American University Association - Katipoglu, Sadun, 1958-1960; Rockefeller Foundation records; Rockefeller Foundation records, Projects (Grants), RG 1; Rockefeller Foundation records, Projects, SG 1.2; Rockefeller Foundation records, Projects, SG 1.2, Series 300-833, Latin America, Europe, Africa, Asia, Oceania; Turkey, Series 805; Turkey - Humanities and Arts, Subseries 805.R; Rockefeller Archive Center; https://dimes.rockarch.org/objects/HSdyLDCj488Non35Sb2pWn.

105. "Sadun Katipoglu ACG," *RC Quarterly* (Robert College Alumni Magazine) 40 (Spring/Summer 2011): 34, 52.

106. Betûl Mardin, another graduate of Robert College, Istanbul, also contributed to the USIS's efforts to promote its media and public relations in Turkey. In an interview, Mardin acknowledged that her tenure with the USIS laid the groundwork for her eventual role as one of the country's first public relations experts. See Türkiye'nin İlk Kadın Halkla İlişkiler Danışmanı Betül Mardin'in Unutamadığı Jest: Dormen'in Pembeli Gülleri, Taha Toros Arşivi, Istanbul.

107. The film is available at https://www.youtube.com/watch?v=Zj47Nd3G3fg.

108. "Suha Arın," Filmler, http://www.mtvfilm.com/tr/film/.

109. Ilhan Özdil, "A Causative-Diagnostic Analysis of Turkey's Major Problems and a Communicative Approach to Their Solution (Democratic Planning and Mass Communication)" (PhD diss., Ohio State University, 1954), 194–195.

4. The Educational Film Center of Turkey

1. There are different views on abortion in Islam. See Gilla K Shapiro, "Abortion Law in Muslim-Majority Countries: an Overview of the Islamic Discourse with Policy Implications," *Health Policy and Planning* 29, no. 4, (2014): 483–494; Gilla K. Shapiro, and Jonathan K. Crane, "Islamic Bioethics: Abortion," *Oxford Research Encyclopedia of Religion*, April 17, 2024.

2. For scholarship on educational health films, see Kirsten Ostherr, *Cinematic Prophylaxis: Globalization and Contagion in the Discourse of World Health* (Duke University Press, 2005); Christian Bonah et al., eds., *Health Education Films in the Twentieth Century* (University of Rochester Press, 2018); Lisa Cartwright and Brian Goldfarb, "Cultural Contagion: On Disney's Health Education Films for Latin America," in *Disney Discourse: Producing the Magic Kingdom*, ed. Eric Smoodin (Routledge, 1994). For biopolitics and governmentality see Michel Foucault, *The Birth of Biopolitics: Lectures at the Collège de France, 1978–79*, ed. Michel Senellart (Palgrave Macmillan, 2008);

Benjamin J. Muller, "Governmentality and Biopolitics," *Oxford Research Encyclopedia of International Studies* (Oxford University Press, 2011).
3. Emre Yanikkerem et al., "Withdrawal Users' Perceptions of and Experience with Contraceptive Methods in Manisa, Turkey," *Midwifery* 22, no. 3 (2006): 274.
4. Ayça Alemdaroğlu, "Politics of the Body and Eugenic Discourse in Early Republican Turkey," *Body & Society* 11, no. 3 (2005): 69.
5. Alemdaroğlu, "Politics of the Body," 69.
6. B. Ö. Akalın, *Türk Cocugunu Nasıl Yasatmalı?* [How should one make the Turkish child live?] (Ahmet Ihsan, 1938); F. K. Gökay, *Kısırlastırmanın Rolü* [The role of sterilization] (Kader, 1938); Server Kamil Tokgöz, *Öjenism: Irk Islahı* [Eugenics: Racial correction] (Sümer Basımevi, 1938).
7. Alemdaroğlu, "Politics of the Body," 70.
8. For racial hygiene films as tools of propaganda and modernity in Germany, see Paul Dobryden, *The Hygienic Apparatus: Weimar Cinema and Environmental Disorder* (Northwestern University Press, 2022).
9. Alemdaroğlu, "Politics of the Body," 73; Akalın, "Türk Cocugunu Nasıl Yasatmalı?"; Gökay, "Kısırlastırmanın Rolü."
10. I use the names EFRTC and EFC interchangeably.
11. Esin Örücü, "Conseil d'Etat: The French Layer of Turkish Administrative Law," *International and Comparative Law Quarterly* 49, no. 3 (2000).
12. For example, the Law on Surnames (Soyadı Kanunu) required all citizens, regardless of their ethnic, religious, or linguistic background, to adopt Turkish names. This led to the creation of a homogenous Turkish identity (sometimes referred to as Turkification) by promoting nationalism and suppressing minority identities within the country.
13. "Niçin Çıkıyoruz?," *Film ve Öğretim*, no. 1 (1950): 1.
14. Suha Arın, *Suha Arın: Yaşam Öyküsü*, accessed December 18, 2004, https://www.youtube.com/watch?v=Qm46nh_O-SA. This is in reference to Arın's first educational film about traffic safety in 1964.
15. "Sinemaların Öğretici Film Gösterme Mecburiyeti," *Film ve Öğretim*, no. 3 (1951): 1.
16. Öğretici ve Teknik Filimler Hakkinda Kanun, *T. C. Resmi Gazete*, Sayi 3537, Safiya 7698, Subat 1937 [Law on Educational and Technical Films, Republic of Turkey official gazette, Number 3537, p. 7698, February 1937], https://www.ogm.gov.tr/ekutuphane/Kanunlar/3116%20Sayılı%20Orman%20Kanunu%20(Orjinal%20Metin).pdf.
17. "Sinemaların Öğretici Film Gösterme Mecburiyeti."
18. Bell & Howell–Gaumont was a collaboration that allowed Gaumont British Equipments to produce film equipment under license from the US company Bell & Howell. The advertisements and articles in the magazine also referred to this company as G.B.–Bell and Howell.
19. Mahmut Özdeniz, "Avrupa'nin En Büyük Film Kütüphanesi olan G.B. Library'de Neler Gördum?," *Film ve Öğretim*, no. 1 (1950): 10–15.
20. Mahmut Özdeniz, "Gaumont-British'in Istanbul'a Gelen Mümessili Mr. Allen ile Bir Konusma," *Film ve Öğretim*, no. 4–5 (1951): 13–14.

4. THE EDUCATIONAL FILM CENTER OF TURKEY 249

21. Özdeniz, "Avrupa'nin En Büyük Film Kütüphanesi olan G.B. Library'de Neler Gördum?"
22. Esra Elmas and Dilek Kurban, *Background Information Report: Media Policies and Regulatory Practices in a Selected Set of European Countries, the EU and the Council of Europe: The Case of Turkey* (TESEV, 2010), 415.
23. Elmas and Kurban, *Background Information Report*. Also see E. Bilgic, "The Role of the Press in the Construction of National Identity 1934–1937" (PhD thesis, University of Bosphorus, 2010), 35.
24. Yaşar Karayalçın, "Film Dernekleri," *Film ve Öğretim*, no. 4–5 (1951): 8–11.
25. Baha Gelenbevi, "Filmciliğimizin Dertleri: Sinema Umum Müdürlüğü," *Film ve Öğretim*, no. 3 (1951): 4. Also see Yaşar Karayalçın, "Türk Film Enstitüsü," *Film ve Öğretim*, no. 3 (1951): 8–9.
26. *Film ve Öğretim*, no. 1 (1950).
27. *Film ve Öğretim*, no. 3 (1951). There is a typographical error on the cover of some issues of the magazine, including numbers 3 and 6–7. The Turkish title of the magazine is written there as *Filim and Öğretim*, yet the correct spelling should be *Film ve Öğretim*. The misspelling *filim* for *film* in the Turkish language is likely due to phonetic spelling or typographical error. In Turkish, the word *film* is pronounced as "filim," and some individuals might mistakenly write it that way.
28. *Film ve Öğretim*, no. 6–7 (1951).
29. "16mm Mevzulu Bir Film Cekiliyor," *Film ve Ogretim*, no. 10–11 (1951–1952): 7.
30. Erol Evcin, "Turkiye Cumhuriyeti'nin Ilk Yıllarında Turizm ve Tanıtma Faaliyetleri," *Ankara Universitesi Turk Inkılap Tarihi Enstitusu Ataturk Yolu Dergisi* 14, S no. 55 (2014): 68–69.
31. Evcin, "Turkiye Cumhuriyeti'nin Ilk Yıllarında Turizm ve Tanıtma Faaliyetleri," 124. The scholar does not identify the title of the film.
32. Aysehan Jülide Etem, "A Transnational Communication Network Promoting Film Diplomacy: The Case of Turkey and the USA, 1950–86," *Historical Journal of Film, Radio and Television* 41, no. 2 (2020).
33. "Film, Radyo, Televizyon ile Eğitim Merkezi/III. Akşam Sanat Okulu," in *M. E. B. Eğitim Araçları ve Teknik İşbirliği Genel Müdürlüğü* (Doğuş Matbaacılık, 1967).
34. "Kültür Filmleri Davasi Büyük Millet Meclisinde," *Film ve Öğretim*, no. 6–7 (1951): 5–6.
35. "Kültür Filmleri Davasi Büyük Millet Meclisinde." Ileri's sentence, quoted in *Tutanak Dergisi*, was requoted in this article in *Film and Education*.
36. He was also the director of the Bundesstaatliche Hauptshelle fur Lichtbuild und Bildungfilm at Vienna. For more on Hübl, see G. Buckland-Smith, "Hofrat Dr. Adolf Hübl," *Audiovisual Media* 1, no. 2 (June 1967).
37. "UNESCO Tarafindan Memleketimize Gönderilen Avusturyali Okul Filmleri Mütehassisi Prof. Hübl ile Bir Konusma," *Film ve Öğretim*, no. 2 (1951): 8–9.
38. United Nations Educational, Scientific, and Cultural Organization, International Bureau of Education, "Turkey: Educational Developments in 1950–1951, Out-of-School Activities, Educational Films," in *International Yearbook of Education, 1951* (UNESCO/

IBE, 1951), 245, http://unesdoc.unesco.org/images/0013/001329/132912eo.pdf. Also see United Nations Educational Scientific, and Cultural Organization, International Bureau of Education, "United Nations Film Board," in *International Yearbook of Education*, 1953, 334. United Nations Educational, Scientific, and Cultural Organization, International Bureau of Education, "Turkey: Educational Developments in 1952–1953, Miscellaneous, Educational Film Centre," in *International Yearbook of Education, 1953* (UNESCO/IBE, 1953), 334.

39. The illiteracy rate in Turkey was very high during this period; in 1949, only 20 percent of the population was literate. To fight illiteracy, the government established People's Houses to train teachers in trades, including carpentry, agriculture, breeding, weaving, bricklaying, and smithery. The public could attend these institutes and learn new skills from teachers and then contribute to the nation's economy. Newly trained teachers worked in approximately forty thousand villages, reaching both young students and adult learners. For the 1951–1952 period, the MNET budget was ₤175,931,990 ($492,242,772, considering the exchange rate for ₤1 was roughly $2.80 through 1951 and 1953). Then it increased to ₤239,469,389 ($670,370,907.20) for the 1952–1953 period, which facilitated the construction of the EFC. This also allowed the MNET to use its resources to offer education, declaring that it followed principles based on modern sciences, nationalism, solidarity, freedom of thought and religion, hard work, and family values. Also see United Nations Educational, Scientific, and Cultural Organization, International Bureau of Education, "Turkey: Educational Developments 1948–1949," *International Yearbook of Education, 1949* (UNESCO/IBE, 1949), 268, http://unesdoc.unesco.org/images/0013/001329/132908eo.pdf; UNESCO/IBE, "Turkey: Educational Developments in 1950–1951," 242, 243;UNESCO/IBE, "Turkey: Educational Developments in 1952–1953," 331.

40. Monteagle Stearns, "Report of USIE Activities in Turkey," Section IV: Motion Pictures, November 1949, RG 59 General Records of the Department of State, Office of the Assistant Secretary for Public Affairs, Office of International Information/Division of International Motion Pictures, Country Reports, 1949–1950, Box 23, ARC ID 4751078, Entry 239, US National Archives, College Park, MD.

41. William E. Kugeman, Memorandum, "From Embassy, Ankara—To the Department of State, Washington, October 1, 1952, Subject: Motion Pictures—Cooperation with Turkish Ministries," RG 0306 US Information Agency, Office of the Assistant Director for Europe, Entry #P403: COU, Country Files for Turkey 1953–1972, US National Archives and Records Administration (NARA), College Park, MD.

42. Thomas E. Flanagan, Memorandum, "From Embassy Ankara to the Department of State, Washington, February 5, 1953, Subject: Motion Pictures—Cooperation with Turkish Ministries, Inter-Ministerial Committee—Evidence of Effectiveness."

43. Kugeman, Memorandum, "From Embassy Ankara—To the Department of State."

44. For Cold War public diplomacy, see Nicholas J. Cull, *The Cold War and the United States Information Agency: American Propaganda and Public Diplomacy, 1945–1989* (Cambridge University Press, 2010), xv.

45. "Film, Radyo, Televizyon ile Eğitim Merkezi/III. Akşam Sanat Okulu."

4. THE EDUCATIONAL FILM CENTER OF TURKEY 251

46. Etem, "Media Infrastructure as Smart Power," 8.
47. Şinasi Barutçu, *En Modern Ders Vasıtası Film* (Öğretici Filmler Merkezi, Doğuş Matbaası, 1954), 12.
48. Under the sponsorship of the Turkish government, Barutçu studied painting and photography in Germany from 1928 to 1932. He then worked as a painter, graphic designer, writer, and photography teacher at Gazi Education Institute in Ankara, where he established Turkey's Amateur Photo Club (Türkiye Amatör Foto Kulübü). In collaboration with his friend Safder Sürel, he published a journal of photography titled *Amatör ve Profesyonelin Foto Dergisi* (The amateur and professional photography magazine) for both amateurs and professionals. Barutçu's photographic artistry was internationally praised; he received many awards from Germany and Turkey as well as first, second, and third prizes at the Marshall Photography Competition organized by USIS. Seyit Ali Ak, *Erken Cumhuriyet Dönemi Türk Fotoğrafı 1923-1960* (Remzi Kitabevi, 2001), 21, 199, 322.
49. "Film, Radyo, Televizyon ile Eğitim Merkezi/III. Akşam Sanat Okulu."
50. İlhan Özdil, *Öğretici Filmler Merkezi Hakkında Rapordur* (Maarif Vekâleti, 1957).
51. "Film, Radyo, Televizyon ile Eğitim Merkezi/III. Akşam Sanat Okulu."
52. "Filim Enstitüsünün İnşaatı Yakında Bitiyor," *Film ve Öğretim*, no. 6-7 (1951), 1.
53. Güler Eryasar, *Film ve Şeritleri Kataloğu* (M. E. B. Eğitim Teknolojisi Dairesi, 1979). The film has an educational purpose: to inform the public about the earthquake; it also celebrates of the work of the Red Crescent. Educational film catalogs list *Depremde Kızılay* under the category of Belirli Günler ve Haftalar (Certain days and weeks) to celebrate and commemorate special days and weeks selected by the MNET to regulate social activities in primary and secondary schools. Red Crescent Week (October 29–November 4) fosters an understanding of how students can engage in its activities and contribute to its efforts in assisting those in need.
54. Akın Kürçer et al., "The Manyas Fault Zone (Southern Marmara Region, NW Turkey): Active Tectonics and Paleoseismology," *Geodinamica Acta* 29, no. 1 (2017): 42.
55. *Depremde Kızılay* [Red Crescent in earthquake] (Cahit Ünsalan, 1964), YouTube, https://www.youtube.com/watch?v=NFTjbY-S99w.
56. Hande Paker, "Reflection of the State in the Turkish Red Crescent: From Modernization to Corruption to Reform?," *Middle Eastern Studies* 43, no. 4 (2007): 649–650.
57. Polat Gülkan and Oktay Ergünay, "Earthquake Engineering in Turkey: A Brief History," In *Proceedings of the 14th World Conference on Earthquake Engineering* (International Association for Earthquake Engineering, 2008), 6.
58. For more on how states, regardless of their ideological orientations, sought to modernize fellahs, peasants, villagers, and other groups through media initiatives, see Lila Abu-Lughod, *Dramas of Nationhood: The Politics of Television in Egypt* (University of Chicago Press, 2005).
59. *Turkish Red Crescent Ingilize Reklilize Reklam* (Turkish Red Crescent Society, 1940), Red Cross Red Crescent Historic Film Collection, Turkey Earthquakes, https://youtu.be/ztyP9gpnJuA.
60. Paker, "Reflection of the State in the Turkish Red Crescent," 649.

61. Julia Irwin, *Making the World Safe: The American Red Cross and a Nation's Humanitarian Awakening* (Oxford University Press, 2013), 9.
62. Willie James Jennings, "Binding Landscapes: Secularism, Race, and the Spatial Modern," in *Race and Secularism in America*, ed. Jonathon Samuel Kahn and Vincent W. Lloyd (Columbia University Press, 2016), 207.
63. Vincent W. Lloyd, "Managing Race, Managing Religion," in Kahn and Lloyd, *Race and Secularism in America*, 5.
64. Cheryl I. Harris, "Whiteness as Property," *Harvard Law Review* 106, no. 8 (1993): 1714.
65. Philip Joseph Deloria, *Playing Indian* (Yale University Press, 1998), 4.
66. Harris, "Whiteness as Property," 1714.
67. For context, see Seven Ağır and Cihan Artunç, "The Wealth Tax of 1942 and the Disappearance of Non-Muslim Enterprises in Turkey," *Journal of Economic History* 79, no. 1 (2019).
68. Marjorie Batchelder McPharlin, *The Puppet Theatre Handbook* (Harper & Bros., 1947), 8.
69. McPharlin, *The Puppet Theatre Handbook*, 2.
70. McPharlin, *The Puppet Theatre Handbook*, xviii–xx.
71. The communication scholar Serdar Öztürk noted that the Turkish government strategically employed the characters of Karagöz and Hacivat to support modernization initiatives and to promote language reform, public health, and various socioeconomic policies. Karagöz, originally known for his role as a critic of the powerful, was a political weapon used to denounce corruption in the Ottoman era. Indeed, during the nineteenth century, visitors from Europe remarked on the freedom enjoyed by puppeteers in their critiques, emphasizing Karagöz's role as an uncensored "newspaper" of the people (Joseph Méry, *Constantinople et la mer Noire* [Belin-Leprieur et Morizot, 1855]). However, as the modernization movement gained momentum, the shadow theater lost its appeal and came to be considered outdated as well as being limited by bans. The emergence of cinema as the dominant art form further marginalized Karagöz, leading puppeteers to introduce technical innovations and modify content in an attempt to adapt to the changing times. Karagöz underwent a significant transformation from an anarchistic figure to a supporter of the state, symbolizing the shift in societal roles during the period of Turkish modernization. Originally a venue for political satire and criticism in Ottoman coffeehouses, the Karagöz and Hacivat performances shifted to government cultural centers (People's Houses, or Halkevleri), where the political messages were aligned with the ruling ideology (and sexual content was removed). See Serdar Öztürk, "Karagöz Co-Opted: Turkish Shadow Theatre of the Early Republic (1923–1945)," *Asian Theatre Journal* 23, no. 2 (2006): 293.
72. To watch the film, visit https://www.youtube.com/watch?v=B_QxG_lXQ_k&t=8s. The second film, despite being listed as made a year later, is a clear continuation of the first film, as it features the same setting, teachers, and orphans.
73. Perin E. Gürel, *The Limits of Westernization: A Cultural History of America in Turkey* (Columbia University Press, 2017), 127.
74. Gürel, *The Limits of Westernization*, 126–127.

75. Dilek Kaya and Umut Azak, "*Crossroads* (1970) and the Origin of Islamic Cinema in Turkey," *Historical Journal of Film, Radio and Television* 35, no. 2 (2015): 257.
76. For secularism and religion, see Michael Allan, "Reading Secularism: Religion, Literature, Aesthetics," *Comparative Literature* 65, no. 3 (2013).
77. Dilek Kaya and Zeynep Koçer, "A Different Story of Secularism: The Censorship of Religion in Turkish Films of the 1960s and Early 1970s," *European Journal of Cultural Studies* 15, no. 1 (2012): 70–71.
78. Kaya and Koçer, "A Different Story of Secularism," 71.
79. Kaya and Koçer, "A Different Story of Secularism," 72.
80. Kaya and Koçer, "A Different Story of Secularism," 72.
81. Kaya and Koçer, "A Different Story of Secularism," 73.
82. Kaya and Koçer, "A Different Story of Secularism," 73.
83. For enlightenment and religion in Turkey, see Haldun Gülalp, "Enlightenment by Fiat: Secularization and Democracy in Turkey," *Middle Eastern Studies* 41, no. 3 (2005): 361–362.
84. Kaya and Koçer, "A Different Story of Secularism," 82.
85. Kaya and Koçer, "A Different Story of Secularism," 75.
86. *Sinema, Video ve Müzik Eserleri Kanunu ile Yönetmelikler* (Kültür ve Turzim Bakanlığı, 1989); As Onaran, "Yeni Film Sansür Düzeni," *Istanbul Üniversitesi İletişim Fakültesi Dergisi*, no. 1–2 (1992–1993).
87. Alev Çinar, *Modernity, Islam, and Secularism in Turkey: Bodies, Places, and Time* (University of Minnesota Press, 2005), 12.
88. Çinar, *Modernity, Islam, and Secularism in Turkey*, 30.
89. To watch the film, visit https://www.youtube.com/watch?v=KBVw1dP0FxM. Nurcan Karagöz is one of the few woman film directors who worked at the EFC. She began her career in television production, specializing in documentaries and children's programs. She later transitioned to the advertising industry, working in advertising and public relations while also teaching courses in public relations and advertising at universities. She held various positions in advertising agencies, associations, and educational institutions. See Nurcan Karagöz Herischi, accessed November 5, 2023, http://www.kameraarkasi.org/yonetmenler/nurcankaragoz.html.
90. The first national Children's Protection Society (Himaye-i Etfal Cemiyeti) was founded in Ankara in 1917 and reorganized as a national institution under Atatürk in 1921, later adopted the name *Çocuk Esirgeme Kurumu* ("Child Protection Institution/Agency") in 1935. See Alemdaroğlu, "Politics of the Body," 74. Also see Taner Bilgin, "*Himâye-yi Etfâl Cemiyeti (1921-1935)*," *Türk Maarif Ansiklopedisi*, December 18, 2022, accessed October 26, 2024, https://turkmaarifansiklopedisi.org.tr/himaye-yi-etfal-cemiyeti.
91. Kathryn Libal, "The Children's Protection Society: Nationalizing Child Welfare in Early Republican Turkey," *New Perspectives on Turkey* 23 (2000): 72–76.
92. Ahmet Gürata, "Hollywood in Vernacular: Translation and Cross-Cultural Reception of American Films in Turkey," in *Going to the Movies: Hollywood and the Social Experience of Cinema*, ed. Richard Maltby et al. (University of Exeter Press, 2007), 342.

93. For sonic representation and its relation to race, see Kaja Silverman, *The Acoustic Mirror: The Female Voice in Psychoanalysis and Cinema* (Indiana University Press, 1988); Jennifer Lynn Stoever, *The Sonic Color Line: Race and the Cultural Politics of Listening* (NYU Press, 2016); Dylan Robinson, *Hungry Listening: Resonant Theory for Indigenous Sound Studies* (University of Minnesota Press, 2020).
94. Barbara Celarent, review of *Turkish Nationalism and Western Civilization*. By Ziya Gökalp, *American Journal of Sociology* 117, no. 5 (2012), 1557.
95. Fuat Dündar, *Modern Turkiye'nin Sifresi: Ittihat ve Terakki'nin Etnisite Mühendisligi (1913-1918)* (Iletisim, 2008), 403.
96. Barış Ünlü, "The Kurdish Struggle and the Crisis of the Turkishness Contract," *Philosophy & Social Criticism* 42, no. 4-5 (2016): 399-400.
97. Ünlü, "The Kurdish Struggle," 399.
98. Oktay Verel, "Kültür Filmleri ve Okullarimiz," *Film ve Öğretim*, no. 6-7 (1951): 7.
99. "Coğrafya Öğretiminde Filim," *Film ve Öğretim*, no. 6-7 (1951): 8-9.
100. Some of these geography films include *Sivas* (1972), *Ankara* (1973), *Konya* (1973), *Hakkari* (1974), *Mardin* (1975), *Diyarbakır* (1975), *Urfa* (1975), *Ordu* (1975), *Artvin* (1976), *Kars* (1976), *Erzincan* (1976), *Amasya* (1977), *Çatalhöyük* (1977), *Tokat* (1977), *Kastamonu* (1977), *Bolu* (1977), *Çankırı* (1977), *Elazığ* (1979), *Aydın* (1980), and *Edirne* (1986). To watch some of these films, visit https://www.julideetem.com/gallery-1.

5. Audience Reception Research

1. US Information Agency, *United States Educational, Scientific, and Cultural Motion Pictures and Filmstrips: Education Section 1958, Selected and Available for Use Abroad* (USIA, 1959), 106.
2. Basil Rogers, "Report on Uses, Possible Uses and Requirements for Visual Aids Program in Turkey," March 1951, 3-4, Technical Aids Unit, ECA/OSR, National Archives and Records Administration.
3. Rogers, "Report on Uses," 4.
4. Charles R. Acland and Haidee Wasson, *Useful Cinema* (Duke University Press, 2011), 3-6.
5. Ruth Frankenberg, "The Mirage of an Unmarked Whiteness," in *The Making and Unmaking of Whiteness*, ed. Birgit Brander Rasmussen et al. (Duke University Press, 2001), 75-76. Also see Ruth Frankenberg, *White Women, Race Matters: The Social Construction of Whiteness* (University of Minnesota Press, 1993).
6. US Information Agency, *United States Educational, Scientific, and Cultural Motion Pictures and Filmstrips*, iii.
7. Hemant Shah, *The Production of Modernization: Daniel Lerner, Mass Media, and the Passing of Traditional Society* (Temple University Press, 2011), 89.
8. See Harun Tanrivermis, "Agricultural Land Use Change and Sustainable Use of Land Resources in the Mediterranean Region of Turkey," *Journal of Arid Environments* 54,

no. 3 (2003); Chris Gratien, *The Unsettled Plain: An Environmental History of the Late Ottoman Frontier* (Stanford University Press, 2022).

9. For peasants in the Middle East in a different context, see Timothy Mitchell, *Rule of Experts: Egypt, Techno-Politics, Modernity* (University of California Press, 2002).
10. Daniel Lerner et al., "Movies, Newsreels, and Documentary Films in Turkey: A Comparison of the Reactions of Four Key Groups in Turkish Society," August 1952, vi, Bureau of Applied Social Research Papers, Box 117, Folder B-0370-8, Rare Book and Manuscript Library, Columbia University.
11. Lerner et al., "Movies, Newsreels, and Documentary Films in Turkey," 16.
12. Lerner et al., "Movies, Newsreels, and Documentary Films in Turkey," 15.
13. Lerner et al., "Movies, Newsreels, and Documentary Films in Turkey," 16.
14. Lerner et al., "Movies, Newsreels, and Documentary Films in Turkey," 4–5.
15. Lerner et al., "Movies, Newsreels, and Documentary Films in Turkey," 17.
16. Michael E. Latham, *Modernization as Ideology: American Social Science and "Nation Building" in the Kennedy Era* (University of North Carolina Press, 2000), 5.
17. Nils Gilman, *Mandarins of the Future: Modernization Theory in Cold War America* (Johns Hopkins University Press, 2003), 4–5.
18. Gilman, *Mandarins of the Future*, 7.
19. Gilman, *Mandarins of the Future*, 5.
20. Eileen Bowser and Vanessa Schwartz, *Cinema and the Invention of Modern Life* (University of California Press, 1995), 2, 10.
21. Miriam Hansen, "The Mass Production of the Senses: Classical Cinema as Vernacular Modernism," *Modernism/Modernity* 6, no. 2 (1999): 69.
22. Charles R. Acland and Haidee Wasson, *Useful Cinema* (Duke University Press, 2011): 3–6.
23. Michael E. Latham, *The Right Kind of Revolution: Modernization, Development, and US Foreign Policy from the Cold War to the Present* (Cornell University Press, 2011), 3–6.
24. Lerner et al., "Movies, Newsreels, and Documentary Films in Turkey," 5.
25. Lerner et al., "Movies, Newsreels, and Documentary Films in Turkey," 6.
26. Lerner et al., "Movies, Newsreels, and Documentary Films in Turkey," 18.
27. Monteagle Stearns, "Report of USIE Activities in Turkey," Section 4: Motion Pictures, 13, November 1949, RG 59 General Records of the Department of State, Office of the Assistant Secretary for Public Affairs, Office of International Information/Division of International Motion Pictures, Country Reports, 1949–1950, Box 23, ARC ID 4751078, Entry 239.
28. Devin Orgeron et al., eds., introduction to *Learning with the Lights Off: Educational Film in the United States* (Oxford University Press, 2011), 10.
29. Monteagle Stearns, "Report of USIE Activities in Turkey.".
30. Agreement for Facilitating the International Circulation of Visual and Auditory Materials of an Educational, Scientific and Cultural Character, opened for signature July 15, 1949, 17 U.S.T. 1578, art. II at 1581, T.I.A.S. No. 6116, 197 U.N.T.S. 3.
31. Sharon Esakoff, "USIA Censorship of Education Films for Distribution Abroad," *Cardozo Arts & Entertainment Law Journal* 3, no. 2 (1984): 420.

32. For discussion of film and subjectivity, see Noël Carroll, "From Real to Reel: Entangled in Nonfiction Film," *Philosophic Exchange* 14, no. 1 (1983); Bill Nichols, *Blurred Boundaries: Questions of Meaning in Contemporary Culture* (Indiana University Press, 1994).
33. Frankenberg, "The Mirage of an Unmarked Whiteness," 75–76.
34. Shah, *The Production of Modernization*, 79–82.
35. Daniel Lerner, *The Passing of Traditional Society: Modernizing the Middle East* (Free Press, 1958), 79–80.
36. Daniel Lerner et al., "Mass Communications Audiences in Turkey," 1951, Bureau of Applied Social Research Papers, Box 117, Folder B-0370-5, Rare Book and Manuscript Library, Columbia University.
37. Lerner et al., "Mass Communications Audiences in Turkey."
38. Lerner et al., "Mass Communications Audiences in Turkey," vi. According to Shah, Lerner and his team's grouping of the Turks in the initial Cold War era was similar to the grouping of the Germans during World War II that Lerner had proposed in his 1948 dissertation analyzing the propaganda efforts of the Psychological Warfare Division (PWD) of the Supreme Headquarters Allied Expeditionary Force. As Shah notes, the mission of the PWD was to disseminate propaganda in Germany "to undermine the enemy's will to resist, demoralize his forces and sustain the morale of [American] supporters." Lerner categorized Germans as "anti-Nazis," "nonpoliticals," and "hard-core Nazis." He concluded that the nonpoliticals, who were ambivalent types, would be the most effective target of the PWD. Shah, *The Production of Modernization*, 33–34, 90. See also Daniel Lerner, "Sykewar, ETO: An Account of the Psychological Warfare Campaign Against Germany, Conducted in the European Theater of Operation from D-Day to V-E Day by PWD/SHAEF (Psychological Warfare Division, Supreme Headquarters Allied Expeditionary Force), 6 June 1944–8 May 1945" (PhD diss., New York University, 1948), 4, 8, 10.
39. Lerner et al., "Mass Communications Audiences in Turkey," 34.
40. Lerner et al., "Mass Communications Audiences in Turkey," vi.
41. Lerner et al., "Mass Communications Audiences in Turkey," 34.
42. Lerner et al., "Movies, Newsreels and Documentary Films in Turkey."
43. Rogers, "Report on Uses." Based on the identified documents and literature review, it is unclear who Basil Rogers was and what his role was, beyond writing this report.
44. Rogers, "Report on Uses," 15.
45. Rogers, "Report on Uses," 15. Dollar/lira quivalents were calculated using US Consumer Price Index (CPI) inflation from 1951 to 2025 (CPI 26.0 → 323.98; multiplier approximately 12.46), yielding a 2025 value of about $673,000. Turkish lira (TRY) equivalents were estimated by converting 2025 USD amounts at the mid-October 2025 exchange rate of approximately ₺41.83 per USD.
46. Rogers, "Report on Uses," 17. This report misspells the UNESCO agent's name as Hubl (it is Hübl).
47. Umaru Bah, "Rereading *The Passing of Traditional Society*: Empathy, Orthodoxy and the Americanization of the Middle East," *Cultural Studies* 22, no. 6 (2008): 795.

48. Lerner, *The Passing of Traditional Society*, 79.
49. Lerner, *The Passing of Traditional Society*, 50.
50. Lerner, *The Passing of Traditional Society*, 45–46, 47.
51. Lerner, *The Passing of Traditional Society*, 105.
52. Lerner, *The Passing of Traditional Society*, 117.
53. Shah, *The Production of Modernization*, 5. See also P. M. Mahar, review of *The Passing of Traditional Society*, by Daniel Lerner, Lucille W. Pevsner, *American Journal of Sociology* 65, no. 1 (1959).
54. Elie A. Salem, review of *The Passing of Traditional Society: Modernizing the Middle East*, Daniel Lerner and Lucille W. Pevsner, *Political Science Quarterly* 74, no. 1 (1959): 129; John Gulick, review of *The Passing of Traditional Society*, Daniel Lerner, *American Anthropologist* 61, no. 1 (1959): 136.
55. Edward Banfield, "American Foreign Aid Doctrines," in *Why Foreign Aid: Two Messages by President Kennedy and Essays*, ed. Robert A. Gordon (Rand McNally, 1959), 13, 16; Samuel Huntington, "Political Development and Political Decay," *World Politics* 17, no. 3 (1965): 391–393.
56. Inayatullah, "Toward a Non-Western Model of Development," in *Communication and Change in the Developing Countries*, ed. Daniel Lerner and Wilbur Schramm (East-West Center Press, 1967), 100; Ali Mazrui, "From Social Darwinism to Current Theories of Modernization," *World Politics* 21, no. 1 (1968): 76, 82.
57. Ashis Nandy, ed., "Introduction: Science as a Reason of State," in *Science, Hegemony, and Violence: A Requiem for Modernity* (Oxford University Press, 1990), 10.
58. Shah, *The Production of Modernization*, 78.
59. Myrdal was a Swedish social economist who was commissioned by the Carnegie Corporation to write about Black people in the United States. See Gunnar Myrdal, *An American Dilemma: The Negro Problem and Modern Democracy* (Harper & Bros., 1944).
60. Shah, *The Production of Modernization*, 89.
61. Shah, *The Production of Modernization*, 22.
62. Shah, *The Production of Modernization*, 12.
63. Shah, *The Production of Modernization*, 12.
64. Shah, *The Production of Modernization*, 22. See also Gilman, *Mandarins of the Future*, 1–2.
65. Shah, *The Production of Modernization*, 23.
66. Gilman, *Mandarins of the Future*, 142.
67. Latham, *The Right Kind of Revolution*, 4.
68. Mohan J. Dutta, "Decolonizing Communication for Social Change: A Culture-Centered Approach." *Communication Theory* 25, no. 2 (2015): 131–132. Also see Mohan J. Dutta, *Communicating Social Change: Structure, Culture, and Agency* (Routledge, 2011); Mohan J. Dutta, *Voices of Resistance: Communication and Social Change* (Purdue University Press, 2012).
69. Latham, *The Right Kind of Revolution*, 3.

5. AUDIENCE RECEPTION RESEARCH

70. Lerner et al., "Mass Communications Audiences in Turkey," 17.
71. Wilson P. Dizard, *Inventing Public Diplomacy: The Story of the US Information Agency* (Lynne Rienner, 2004), 70.
72. Dizard, *Inventing Public Diplomacy*, 70–118.
73. Ögretici Filmler Merkezi, *Film Kataloğu* (M. K. B. Matbaasi, 1956).
74. Lerner et al., "Mass Communications Audiences in Turkey," 18.
75. Lerner et al., "Mass Communications Audiences in Turkey," 19.
76. Lerner et al., "Mass Communications Audiences in Turkey," 19.
77. Rogers, "Report on Uses," 15.
78. Rogers, "Report on Uses," 38.
79. For nations as imagined communities, see Benedict Anderson, *Imagined Communities: Reflections on the Origin and Spread of Nationalism*, rev. ed. (Verso, 2006).
80. Pare Lorentz, *The Rural Co-Op* (US Information Service, 1947), https://www.worldcat.org/title/rural-co-op/oclc/37822933.
81. Begüm Adalet, "Mirrors of Modernization: The American Reflection in Turkey" (PhD diss., University of Pennsylvania, 2014), 20.
82. Rogers, "Report on Uses," 7.
83. Rogers, "Report on Uses," 7. The USIS made a series of puppet films in which Nasreddin Hoja communicates messages using the same expression—"Open your eyes"—and offers a supportive view of the government.
84. Kemal H. Karpat, "Political Developments in Turkey, 1950–70," *Middle Eastern Studies* 8, no. 3 (1972): 353–354.
85. Rogers, "Report on Uses," 26.
86. John M. Vander Lippe, "Forgotten Brigade of the Forgotten War: Turkey's Participation in the Korean War," *Middle Eastern Studies* 36, no. 1 (2000): 93.
87. Vander Lippe, "Forgotten Brigade of the Forgotten War," 95.
88. Rogers, "Report on Uses," 26.
89. Rogers, "Report on Uses," 9.
90. USIS Amerikan Haberler Merkezi, *Film Kataloğu 16mm ve 35mm* (Yeni Desen Matbaası, 1960); USIS Amerikan Haberler Merkezi, *Film Kataloğu 16 mm ve 35 mm* (Yeni Desen Matbaası, 1962); USIS Amerikan Haberler Merkezi, *Film Kataloğu 16 mm ve 35 mm* (Yeni Desen Matbaası, 1965). The production years and names of directors are unlisted.
91. Rogers, "Report on Uses," 90.
92. Rogers, "Report on Uses," 13.
93. Rogers, "Report on Uses," 2.
94. Rogers, "Report on Uses," 90.
95. Erik Jan Zürcher, *Turkey: A Modern History* (Tauris, 2017), 209.
96. This photograph was retrieved in 1920 from the "nostalgia" section of Eğitim Bilişim Ağı (Educational Information Network of Turkey), https://www.eba.gov.tr.
97. Rogers, "Report on Uses," 34.
98. Rogers, "Report on Uses," 34.

99. Monteagle Stearns, "Report of USIE Activities in Turkey," with added notes by Assistant Public Affairs Officer Bracken, 122.
100. Frederick W. Frey, *Political Modernization in Turkey and Japan* (Princeton University Press, 1964), 224, 225, 230.
101. Lerner et al., "Movies, Newsreels, and Documentary Films in Turkey," 16.
102. Öğretici Filmler Merkezi, *Film Kataloğu*. Some of the films were *Okul* (School), *Bryn Mavr Koleji* (Bryn Mawr College), *Girard Koleji* (Girard College), and *Halk Okulu* (Public school).

Epilogue

1. For contemporary context in Turkey, see Bilge Yesil, *Talking Back to the West: How Turkey Uses Counter-Hegemony to Reshape the Global Communication Order* (University of Illinois Press, 2024).
2. *Adnan Menderes* (Kilometre Taşları, 2012), https://www.dailymotion.com/video/x4x85oy.
3. See Sabri Sayari, "Adnan Menderes: Between Democratic and Authoritarian Populism," in *Political Leaders and Democracy in Turkey*, ed. Metin Heper and Sabri Sayari (Lexington Books, 2002).
4. The slogan in Turkish is *Yeter, söz milletindir!*
5. See Erik Jan Zürcher, *Turkey: A Modern History* (Tauris, 2017), 226.
6. See Ayla Jean Yackley, "Turkish President Casts Self as Heir to Reformer Who Died on Gallows," Reuters, August 28, 2014, https://www.reuters.com/article/us-turkey-erdogan-vision/turkish-president-casts-self-as-heir-to-reformer-who-died-on-gallows-idUSKBN0GS1ZP20140828; Ishaan Tharoor, "The Execution of a Former Turkish Leader That Still Haunts Erdogan," *Washington Post*, July 30, 2016, https://www.washingtonpost.com/world/the-execution-of-a-former-turkish-leader-that-still-haunts-erdogan/2016/07/29/4772c256-54b4-11e6-994c-4e3140414f34_story.html.
7. See Deborah Sontag, "The Erdogan Experiment," *New York Times*, May 11, 2003, https://www.nytimes.com/2003/05/11/magazine/the-erdogan-experiment.html; Michael Ferguson, "White Turks, Black Turks, and Negroes: The Politics of Polarization," *Jadaliyya*, July 10, 2017, https://www.jadaliyya.com/Details/28868.
8. For this comparison, see Nicholas Danforth, "Erdogan's Unsung Victory," *Foreign Policy*, 2014, https://foreignpolicy.com/2014/11/05/erdogans-unsung-victory/; Mikayel Zolyan, "From Menderes to Erdogan, the Complicated History of the Relationship Between Military and the Civilian Leadership in Turkey," Regional Post, May 1, 2017, https://regionalpost.org/en/articles/from-menderes-to-erdogan.html.
9. Tuvan Gumrukcu, "Turkey Investigates Why School Pupils Were Shown Footage of Ex-PM's Hanging," *New York Times*, March 24, 2020, https://www.nytimes.com/reuters/2020/03/24/world/europe/24reuters-health-coronavirus-turkey-schools.html.

10. "MEB'nın Adnan Menderes videosu ile ilgili Melih Altınok'tan 'Demokrasi kültürünün gelişmesi için bunlar çok önemli,'" *Sabah*, March 24, 2020, https://www.sabah.com.tr/video/haber/mebnin-adnan-menderes-videosu-ile-ilgili-melih-altinoktan-demokrasi-kulturunun-gelismesi-icin-bunlar-cok-onemli-video.
11. Gumrukcu, "Turkey Investigates Why School Pupils Were Shown Footage of Ex-PM's Hanging."
12. Selçuk indicated that he experienced extreme discomfort from the talks about how missing a few minutes of a film created damage over the system. He noted that he did not feel the need to control its content, as he trusted the team members. He also wrote, "We established three new channels and determined their content in one week." Yet the film was produced eight years ago. See Ziya Selcuk, Twitter (now X), March 23, 2020, https://twitter.com/ziyaselcuk/status/1242082498588413955.

Bibliography

Abu-Lughod, Lila. *Dramas of Nationhood: The Politics of Television in Egypt*. University of Chicago Press, 2005.
Acland, Charles. "Mapping the Serious and the Dangerous: Film and the National Council of Education, 1920–1939." *Cinémas: Revue d'études cinématographiques/Journal of Film Studies* 6, no. 1 (1995): 101–118.
Acland, Charles R., and Haidee Wasson. *Useful Cinema*. Duke University Press, 2011.
Adalet, Begüm. *Hotels and Highways: The Construction of Modernization Theory in Cold War Turkey*. Stanford University Press, 2018.
Adalet, Begüm. "Mirrors of Modernization: The American Reflection in Turkey." PhD diss., University of Pennsylvania, 2014.
Adnan Menderes. Kilometre Taşları, 2012. https://www.dailymotion.com/video/x4x85oy.
Ağır, Seven, and Cihan Artunç. "The Wealth Tax of 1942 and the Disappearance of Non-Muslim Enterprises in Turkey." *Journal of Economic History* 79, no. 1 (2019): 201–243.
Ahmad, Feroz. *Turkey: The Quest for Identity*. Oneworld, 2003.
Ahmed, Sara. "A Phenomenology of Whiteness." *Feminist Theory* 8, no. 2 (2007): 149–168.
Akalın, B. Ö. *Türk Cocugunu Nasıl Yasatmalı?* Ahmet Ihsan, 1938.
Akbaba, Turgay. "From the Terrible Turk to the Incredible Turk: Reimagining Turkey as an American Ally, 1919–1960." PhD diss., University of North Carolina at Chapel Hill, 2020.
Akdemir, Orhan, Photo Paris, and Kayseri. "Mary Louise Winkler, Talas." American Research Institute in Turkey, United Church of Christ, SALT Research. https://www.archives.saltresearch.org/R/-?func=dbin-jump-full&object_id=4329086&silo_library=GEN01.
Alemdaroğlu, Ayça. "Politics of the Body and Eugenic Discourse in Early Republican Turkey." *Body & Society* 11, no. 3 (2005): 61–76.

Alexander, Geoff. *Academic Films for the Classroom: A History*. McFarland, 2010.

Allan, Michael. "Reading Secularism: Religion, Literature, Aesthetics." *Comparative Literature* 65, no. 3 (2013): 257–264.

Alptekin, Yasemin. "Can Progressive Education Be Translated Into a Progressive Idea? Dewey's Report on Turkish." *International Journal of Progressive Education* 2, no. 2 (2006): 9–21.

Altay, Tunay. "Is There Really No Anti-Black Racism in Turkey?" Bianet, November 17, 2020. https://bianet.org/yazi/is-there-really-no-anti-black-racism-in-turkey-226799.

Amerikan Bord Heyeti. Personnel Records for Henry K. Wingate. Istanbul Center Library, American Research Institute in Turkey. Accessed October 20, 2017. http://www.dlir.org/archive/items/show/15841.

Anderson, Benedict. *Imagined Communities: Reflections on the Origin and Spread of Nationalism*. Rev. ed. Verso, 2006.

Ang, Ien, Yudhishthir Raj Isar, and Phillip Mar. "Cultural Diplomacy: Beyond the National Interest?" *International Journal of Cultural Policy* 21, no. 4 (2015): 365–381.

"Ankarada Misyoner Faaliyeti." *İslâm-Türk Ansiklopedisi/Muhitülmaarif Mecmuası*, Sayi 2, Cilt 76 (Agustos 1947). https://katalog.idp.org.tr/yazilar/60980/ankarada-misyoner-faaliyeti.

Arabova, Sharofat. "Dystopia and Utopia: Soviet Politics and the Musicals of Tajikistan." *East European Film Bulletin* 110 (2020). https://eefb.org/retrospectives/soviet-politics-and-the-musicals-of-tajikistan/.

Arat-Koç, Sedef. "(Some) Turkish Transnationalism(s) in an Age of Capitalist Globalization and Empire: 'White Turk' Discourse, the New Geopolitics, and Implications for Feminist Transnationalism." *Journal of Middle East Women's Studies* 3, no. 1 (2007): 35–57.

Arın, Suha. *Suha Arın: Yaşam Öyküsü*. Accessed December 18, 2024. https://www.youtube.com/watch?v=Qm46nh_O-SA.

Arslan, Savas. *Cinema in Turkey: A New Critical History*. Oxford University Press, 2011.

Askari, Kaveh. *Making Movies Into Art: Picture Craft from the Magic Lantern to Early Hollywood*. Bloomsbury, 2019.

Ata, Bahri. "The Influence of an American Educator John Dewey on the Turkish Educational System." *Turkish Yearbook of International Relations* 31 (2000): 119–130.

Auerbach, Jonathan, and Russ Castronovo. *The Oxford Handbook of Propaganda Studies*. Oxford University Press, 2013.

Aufderheide, Patricia. *Documentary Film: A Very Short Introduction*. Oxford University Press, 2007.

Bah, Umaru. "Rereading *The Passing of Traditional Society*: Empathy, Orthodoxy and the Americanization of the Middle East." *Cultural Studies* 22, no. 6 (2008): 795–819.

Bal, H. *John Dewey'in Egitim Felsefesi*. Kor, 1991.

Baldwin, Katherine Anne. *Beyond the Color Line and the Iron Curtain: Reading Encounters Between Black and Red, 1922–1963*. Duke University Press, 2002.

Bali, Rifat N. *The Turkish Cinema in the Early Republican Years.* Isis Press and Gorgias Press, 2010.

Banfield, Edward. "American Foreign Aid Doctrines." In *Why Foreign Aid: Two Messages by President Kennedy and Essays,* ed. Robert A. Gordon. Rand McNally, 1959.

Barutçu, Şinasi. *En Modern Ders Vasıtası Film.* Öğretici Filmler Merkezi, Doğuş Matbaası, 1954.

Baskett, Michael. "Japan's Film Festival Diplomacy in Cold War Asia." *The Velvet Light Trap* 73 (2014): 4–18.

Bates, Ülkü Ülküsal. "The Anatolian Mausoleum of the Twelfth, Thirteenth, and Fourteenth Centuries." PhD diss., University of Michigan, 1970.

Beach, Harlan P. *A Geography and Atlas of Protestant Missions.* Vol. 1. Student Volunteer Movement for Foreign Missions, 1901.

Bearman, Gonzalo, Kristina Bryant, Surbhi Leekha et al. "Healthcare Personnel Attire in Non-Operating-Room Settings." *Infection Control & Hospital Epidemiology* 35, no. 2 (2014): 107–121.

Belmonte, Laura. *Selling the American Way: U.S. Propaganda and the Cold War.* University of Pennsylvania Press, 2011.

Benjamin, Burton, and Walter Cronkite. *The Incredible Turk.* Produced by Burton Benjamin. CBS News, 1958.

Bernath, Clifford H. "JUSMMAT and Turkey: History and Overview." *DISAM Journal of International Security Assistance Management* 7, no. 4 (1985).

Bernays, Edward. *Propaganda.* Liveright, 1928; repr., IG Publishing, 2005.

Bilgic, E. "The Role of the Press in the Construction of National Identity 1934–1937." PhD thesis, University of Bosphorus, 2010.

Biography of Paul E. Nilson. American Board of Commissioners for Foreign Missions (ABCFM) Archives, 1810–1961 (ABC 1–91), ABCFM 77.1, Box 53. Houghton Library, Harvard University.

Bonah, Christian, David Cantor, and Anja Laukötter, eds. *Health Education Films in the Twentieth Century.* University of Rochester Press, 2018.

Bowser, Eileen, and Vanessa Schwartz. *Cinema and the Invention of Modern Life.* University of California Press, 1995.

Boyar, Ebru, and Kate Fleet. "Mak[ing] Turkey and the Turkish Revolution Known to Foreign Nations Without Any Expense: Propaganda Films in the Early Turkish Republic." *Oriente Moderno* 24, no. 1 (2005): 117–132.

Bozdoğan, Sibel, and Reşat Kasaba, eds. *Rethinking Modernity and National Identity in Turkey.* University of Washington Press, 1997.

Brockett, Gavin D. "The Legend of 'The Turk' in Korea: Popular Perceptions of the Korean War and Their Importance to a Turkish National Identity." *War & Society* 22, no. 2 (2004): 109–142.

Buckland-Smith, G. "Hofrat Dr. Adolf Hübl." *Audiovisual Media* 1, no. 2 (1967): 3–4.

Burton, Elise K. *Genetic Crossroads: The Middle East and the Science of Human Heredity.* Stanford University Press, 2021.

Bushnell, Albert. "Reservations as to the Near Eastern Question." *Annals of the Academy of Political and Social Science* 108 (1923): 120–124.

Byekwaso, Ndinawe. "The Politics of Modernization and the Misleading Approaches to Development." *World Review of Political Economy* 7, no. 2 (2016): 285–312.

Cain, Victoria. *Schools and Screens: A Watchful History*. MIT Press, 2021.

Carpenter, Kristen A., and Angela R. Riley. "Owning Red: A Theory of Indian (Cultural) Appropriation." *Texas Law Review* 94, no. 5 (2015): 861–931.

Carroll, Noël. "From Real to Reel: Entangled in Nonfiction Film." *Philosophic Exchange* 14, no. 1 (1983): 1–45.

Cartwright, Lisa, and Brian Goldfarb. "Cultural Contagion: On Disney's Health Education Films for Latin America." In *Disney Discourse: Producing the Magic Kingdom*, ed. Eric Smoodin. Routledge, 1994.

Celarent, Barbara. Review of *Turkish Nationalism and Western Civilization*. By Ziya Gökalp. *American Journal of Sociology* 117, no. 5 (2012): 1556–1563.

Çeliktemel-Thomen, Özde. "The Curtain of Dreams: Early Cinema in Istanbul." Master's thesis, Central European University, 2009.

Çeliktemel-Thomen, Özde. "Prime Ministry Ottoman Archives: Inventory of Written Archival Sources for Ottoman Cinema History." *Tarih Graduate History Journal* 2, no. 3 (2013): 17–48.

Chen, Fan Pen. "Shadow Theaters of the World." *Asian Folklore Studies* 62, no. 1 (2003): 25–64.

Chen, Hongwei Thorn. "Acting Out Industrial 'Knowhow': Cinema and Tacit Knowledge in Republican China." *Configurations of the Film*, Goethe University.

Chen, Hongwei Thorn. "Building the Nation on 16mm: Film Formats and the Institutionalization of Cinematic Portability in 1930s China." *Journal of Chinese Cinemas* 16, no. 1 (2022): 40–57.

Chen, Hongwei Thorn. "Cinemas, Highways, and the Making of Provincial Space: Mobile Screenings in Jiangsu, China, 1933–1937." *Wide Screen* 7, no. 1 (2018): 1–34.

Chen, Hongwei Thorn. "Moving Pictures, Empty Words: Cinema As Developmental Interface in the Chinese Reconstruction, 1932–1952." PhD diss., University of Minnesota, 2017.

Christian, Michelle. "A Global Critical Race and Racism Framework: Racial Entanglements and Deep and Malleable Whiteness." *Sociology of Race and Ethnicity* 5, no. 2 (2019): 169–185.

Chun, Wendy Hui Kyong. "Introduction: Race and/as Technology; or, How to Do Things to Race." *Camera Obscura* 24, no. 1 (2009): 7–35.

Chung, Hye Seung. *Hollywood Diplomacy: Film Regulation, Foreign Relations, and East Asian Representations*. Rutgers University Press, 2020.

Çinar, Alev. *Modernity, Islam, and Secularism in Turkey: Bodies, Places, and Time*. University of Minnesota Press, 2005.

Cırakman, Aslı. *From the "Terror of the World" to the "Sick Man of Europe": European Images of Ottoman Empire and Society from the Sixteenth Century to the Nineteenth*. Lang, 2002.

Citino, Nathan J. "The Ottoman Legacy in Cold War Modernization." *International Journal of Middle East Studies* 40, no. 4 (2008): 579–597.

Cline, Eric H. *Biblical Archaeology: A Very Short Introduction*. Oxford University Press, 2009.

Conrad, JoAnn. "'This Is Not Our Hoca!' Repurposing, Repackaging, and Reappropriating Nasreddin Hoca." In *Terra Ridens, Terra Narrans: Festschrift Zum 65. Geburtstag Von Ulrich Marzolph*. Vol. 45, ed. Regina Bendix and Dorothy Noyes. Dortmund, 2018.

Conroy-Krutz, Emily. *Christian Imperialism: Converting the World in the Early American Republic*. Cornell University Press, 2015.

Cooper, Andrew F., Jorge Heine, and Ramesh Thakur, eds. *The Oxford Handbook of Modern Diplomacy*. Oxford University Press, 2013.

Coppen, Helen E. "What Can School Films Do for Peace?" *Educational Screen* 30, no. 3 (1951). Reprinted from *Look and Listen*, November 1950.

Crumpler, Hugh A. Memorandum. "Motion Pictures—Establishment of Film Production Facilities in Turkey," February 4, 1953. RG 59 General Records of the Department of State, Office of the Assistant Secretary for Public Affairs, Office of International Information/Division of International Motion Pictures, Country Reports, 1949–1950, Box 23, ARC ID 4751078, Entry 239, National Archives and Records Administration (NARA), College Park, MD.

Cull, Nicholas J. "Auteurs of Ideology: USIA Documentary Film Propaganda in the Kennedy Era as Seen in Bruce Herschensohn's *The Five Cities of June* (1963) and James Blue's *The March* (1964)." *Film History* 10, no. 3 (1998): 295–310.

Cull, Nicholas J. *The Cold War and the United States Information Agency: American Propaganda and Public Diplomacy, 1945–1989*. Cambridge University Press, 2010.

Cull, Nicholas J. "Film as Public Diplomacy: The USIA's Cold War at Twenty-Four Frames per Second." In *The United States and Public Diplomacy*, ed. Kenneth A. Osgood. Brill, 2010.

Cull, Nicholas J. "Public Diplomacy: Taxonomies and Histories." *Annals of the American Academy of Political and Social Science* 616, no. 1 (2008): 31–54.

Cumhuriyet, Bilim ve Kültür. "Afet Inan/Atatürk'ün Tarihe Verdiği Önem ve Medeniyet Anlayışı (1981)." April 7, 2017. https://www.youtube.com/watch?v=AJMhT4hjYkQ.

Current, Cheris Brewer. "Normalizing Cuban Refugees: Representations of Whiteness and Anti-Communism in the USA During the Cold War." *Ethnicities* 8, no. 1 (2008): 42–66.

Dahlquist, Marina, and Joel Frykholm, eds. *The Institutionalization of Educational Cinema: North America and Europe in the 1910s and 1920s*. Indiana University Press, 2019.

Danforth, Nicholas. "Erdogan's Unsung Victory." *Foreign Policy*, November 15, 2014. https://foreignpolicy.com/2014/11/05/erdogans-unsung-victory/.

Danforth, Nicholas. "Malleable Modernity: Rethinking the Role of Ideology in American Policy, Aid Programs, and Propaganda in Fifties' Turkey." *Diplomatic History* 39, no. 3 (2015): 477–503.

Daniel, Robert L. *American Philanthropy in the Near East, 1820–1960*. Ohio University Press, 1970.

Davenport, Lisa E. *Jazz Diplomacy: Promoting America in the Cold War Era*. University Press of Mississippi, 2010.

Deloria, Philip Joseph. *Playing Indian*. Yale University Press, 1998.

Depremde Kızılay. Cahit Unsalan, 1964. https://www.youtube.com/watch?v=NFTjbY-S99w.

Derrida, Jacques, and Gil Anidjar. *Acts of Religion*. Routledge, 2002.

Dewey, John. *Experience and Education*. Macmillan, 1938.

Dinç, Enis. *Atatürk on Screen: Documentary Film and the Making of a Leader*. Bloomsbury, 2020.

Dinç, Enis. "Performing Modernity: The Film of Mustafa Kemal Atatürk on His Forest Farm." *Historical Journal of Film, Radio and Television* 39, no. 1 (2019): 18–35.

Dizard, Wilson P. *Inventing Public Diplomacy: The Story of the US Information Agency*. Lynne Rienner, 2004.

Dobryden, Paul. *The Hygienic Apparatus: Weimar Cinema and Environmental Disorder*. Northwestern University Press, 2022.

Doğrul, Ömer Rıza. "Misyonerliğin Yeni Şekli." *Sebilürreşad*, 1, Cilt 18, Sayı (1948). https://katalog.idp.org.tr/yazilar/92267/misyonerligin-yeni-sekli.

Donmez-Colin, Gonul. *The Routledge Dictionary of Turkish Cinema*. Routledge, 2013.

Donmez-Colin, Gonul. *Turkish Cinema*. Reaktion Books, 2008.

Dorn, Charles, and Doris A. Santoro. "Political Goals and Social Ideals: Dewey, Democracy, and the Emergence of the Turkish Republic." *Education and Culture* 27, no. 2 (2011): 3–27.

Dudziak, Mary L. *Cold War Civil Rights: Race and the Image of American Democracy*. Princeton University Press, 2011.

Duman, Mustafa. *Nasreddin Hoca ve 1555 Fikrasi*. Heyamola, 2008.

Dündar, Fuat. *Modern Turkiye'nin Sifresi: Ittihat ve Terakki'nin Etnisite Mühendisligi (1913–1918)*. Iletisim, 2008.

Dutta, Mohan J. *Communicating Social Change: Structure, Culture, and Agency*. Routledge, 2011.

Dutta, Mohan J. "Decolonizing Communication for Social Change: A Culture-Centered Approach." *Communication Theory* 25, no. 2 (2015): 123–143.

Dutta, Mohan J. *Voices of Resistance: Communication and Social Change*. Purdue University Press, 2012.

Dyer, Richard. *White*. Routledge, 2017.

Economic Cooperation Act of 1948. George C. Marshall Foundation. https://www.marshallfoundation.org/library/documents/economic-cooperation-act-1948/.

Educational Film Guide, ed. Frederic A. Krahn. 11th ed. H. W. Wilson, 1953. https://archive.org/details/11theducationalfilm00wilsrich/page/434/mode/2up.

El-Hibri, Hatim. *Visions of Beirut: The Urban Life of Media Infrastructure*. Duke University Press, 2021.

Elibol, Müslüm. "Türkiye'de Yaşayan Afro-Türkler Hakkında Bilmeniz Gerekenler." *Onedio*, 2015. https://onedio.com/haber/turkiye-de-yasayan-afro-turkler-hakkinda-bilmeniz-gerekenler-508140.

Elmas, Esra, and Dilek Kurban. *Background Information Report: Media Policies and Regulatory Practices in a Selected Set of European Countries, the EU and the Council of Europe: The Case of Turkey*. TESEV, 2010.

Emberley, Julia. *The Cultural Politics of Fur*. Cornell University Press, 1997.

Encyclopaedia Britannica. *The Middle East: Change—Turkey and Saudi Arabia*. 1984. https://archive.org/details/themiddleeastchangeturkeyandsaudiarabia.

Erdoğan, Nezih, and Deniz Göktürk. "Turkish Cinema." In *Companion Encyclopedia of Middle Eastern and North African Film*, ed. Oliver Leaman. Routledge, 2001.

Erdoğan, Nezih, and Dilek Kaya, "Institutional Intervention in the Distribution and Exhibition of Hollywood Films in Turkey." *Historical Journal of Film, Radio and Television* 22, no. 1 (2002): 47–59.

Ergin, Murat. *"Is the Turk a White Man?" Race and Modernity in the Making of Turkish Identity*. Brill, 2016.

Eryasar, Güler. *Film ve Şeritleri Kataloğu*. M. E. B. Eğitim Teknolojisi Dairesi, 1979.

Esakoff, Sharon. "USIA Censorship of Education Films for Distribution Abroad." *Cardozo Arts & Entertainment Law Journal* 3, no. 2 (1984): 403–425.

Etem, Aysehan Jülide. "Media Infrastructure as Smart Power in the Case of the Educational Film, Radio and Television Center of Turkey, 1949-1973," *Journal of E-Media Studies* 6, no. 1 (2022): 1–21.

Etem, Aysehan Jülide. Review of *The American Marshall Plan Film Campaign and the Europeans: A Captivated Audience?*, by Maria Fritsche. *Alphaville: Journal of Film and Screen Media*, no. 17 (2019): 229–233.

Etem, Aysehan Jülide. "A Transnational Communication Network Promoting Film Diplomacy: The Case of Turkey and the USA, 1950-86." *Historical Journal of Film, Radio and Television* 41, no. 2 (2020): 292–316.

Evcin, Erol. "Turkiye Cumhuriyeti'nin Ilk Yıllarında Turizm ve Tanıtma Faaliyetleri." *Ankara Universitesi Turk Inkılap Tarihi Enstitusu Ataturk Yolu Dergisi, Atatürk Yolu Dergisi* 14, no. 55 (March 2014): 23–82.

Fant, Clyde E., and Mitchell G. Reddish. *A Guide to Biblical Sites in Greece and Turkey*. Oxford University Press, 2003.

Fein, Seth. "New Empire Into Old: Making Mexican Newsreels the Cold War Way." *Diplomatic History* 28, no. 5 (2004): 703–748.

Feldman, Keith P. *A Shadow Over Palestine: The Imperial Life of Race in America*. University of Minnesota Press, 2015.

Ferguson, Michael. "The African Presence in Late Ottoman Izmir and Beyond." PhD diss., McGill University, 2014.

Ferguson, Michael. "White Turks, Black Turks, and Negroes: The Politics of Polarization." *Jadaliyya*, July 10, 2017. https://www.jadaliyya.com/Details/28868.

Ferngren, Gary B. *Science and Religion: A Historical Introduction*. Johns Hopkins University Press, 2002.

Feyzullahoğlu, Burcu. "*Ufuk*: How the US Information Agency Molded Turkish Elite Opinion, 1960–1980." PhD diss., Bilkent University, 2014.

Field, Allyson Nadia. *Uplift Cinema: The Emergence of African American Film and the Possibility of Black Modernity*. Duke University Press, 2015.

Field, Allyson Nadia, and Marsha Gordon, eds. *Screening Race in American Nontheatrical Film*. Duke University Press, 2019.

"Film, Radyo, Televizyon ile Eğitim Merkezi/III. Akşam Sanat Okulu." In *M. E. B. Eğitim Araçları ve Teknik İşbirliği Genel Müdürlüğü*. Doğuş Matbaacılık, 1967.

Film ve Öğretim, nos. 1–11 (1950–1952).

Filmler. Accessed December 18, 2024. http://www.mtvfilm.com/tr/film/.

Filmlerin ve Film Senaryolarının Kontrolüne Dair Nizamname. *T. C. [Türkiye Cumhuriyeti] Resmi Gazete*, 4272, July 31, 1939.

Flanagan, Thomas E. Memorandum. "From Embassy Ankara to the Department of State, Washington, February 5, 1953, Subject: Motion Pictures—Cooperation with Turkish Ministries, Inter-Ministerial Committee—Evidence of Effectiveness."

Florin, Bo, Nico De Klerk, and Patrick Vonderau, eds. *Films That Sell: Moving Pictures and Advertising*. Palgrave, 2016.

Foucault, Michel. *The Birth of Biopolitics: Lectures at the Collège de France, 1978-79*, ed. Michel Senellart. Palgrave Macmillan, 2008.

Foucault, Michel. *Security, Territory, Population: Lectures at the Collège de France, 1977-1978*, ed. Michel Senellart. Palgrave Macmillan, 2007.

Foucault, Michel. *Society Must Be Defended: Lectures at the Collège de France, 1975-76*. Palgrave Macmillan, 2003.

Fowle, Luther. Letter to E. W. Riggs, July 23, 1927. Turkish Mission of the American Board, ABCFM Archives, 1810–1961 (ABC 1–91). Houghton Library, Harvard University.

Frankenberg, Ruth. "The Mirage of an Unmarked Whiteness." In *The Making and Unmaking of Whiteness*, ed. Birgit Brander Rasmussen, Eric Klinenberg, Irene J. Nexica, and Matt Wray. Duke University Press, 2001.

Frankenberg, Ruth. *White Women, Race Matters: The Social Construction of Whiteness*. University of Minnesota Press, 1993.

Frey, Frederick W. *Political Modernization in Turkey and Japan*. Princeton University Press, 1964.

Fritsche, Maria. *The American Marshall Plan Film Campaign and the Europeans: A Captivated Audience?* Bloomsbury, 2018.

Fujino, Diane. "Political Asian America: Afro-Asian Solidarity, Third World Internationalism, and the Origins of the Asian American Movement." *Ethnic Studies Review* 47, no. 1 (2024): 60–97.

Fukuyama, Yoshio. "The American Board in Turkey." BD thesis, Chicago Theological Seminary, 1950.

Gharabaghi, Hadi Parandeh. "'American Mice Grow Big!' The Syracuse Audiovisual Mission in Iran and the Rise of Documentary Diplomacy." PhD diss. New York University, 2018.

Gharabaghi, Hadi Parandeh. "The Syracuse Mission to Iran During the 1950s and the Rise of Documentary Diplomacy." *JCMS: Journal of Cinema and Media Studies* 60, no. 4 (2021): 9–36.
Gilbert, James. *Redeeming Culture: American Religion in an Age of Science.* University of Chicago Press, 1997.
Gilman, Nils. *Mandarins of the Future: Modernization Theory in Cold War America.* Johns Hopkins University Press, 2007.
Giroux, Henry. "Post-Colonial Ruptures and Democratic Possibilities: Multiculturalism as Anti-Racist Pedagogy." *Cultural Critique*, no. 21 (1992): 5–39.
Giroux, Henry. "White Squall: Resistance and the Pedagogy of Whiteness." *Cultural Studies* 11, no. 3 (1997): 376–389.
Gökay, F. K. "Kısırlastırmanın Rolü." *Kader*, 1938.
Göknar, Erdağ. "The Limits of 'Whiteness' in Orhan Pamuk's Fiction." In *Texts, Contexts, Intertexts*, ed. Julian Tentzsch and Petr Kučera. Ergon Verlag, 2022.
Goldberg, David Theo. *Racist Culture: Philosophy and the Politics of Meaning.* Wiley-Blackwell, 1993.
Goldfarb, Brian. *Visual Pedagogy: Media Cultures of Education in and Beyond the Classroom.* Duke University Press, 2002.
Good, Katie Day. *Bringing the World to the Child: Technologies of Global Citizenship in American Education.* MIT Press, 2020.
Gratien, Chris. *The Unsettled Plain: An Environmental History of the Late Ottoman Frontier.* Stanford University Press, 2022.
Graziano, Michael. *Errand Into the Wilderness of Mirrors: Religion and the History of the CIA.* University of Chicago Press, 2021.
Grieveson, Lee. *Cinema and the Wealth of Nations: Media, Capital, and the Liberal World System.* University of California Press, 2018.
Grieveson, Lee. "Cinema Studies and the Conduct of Conduct." In *Inventing Film Studies*, ed. Lee Grieveson and Haidee Wasson. Duke University Press, 2008.
Grieveson, Lee. "Discipline and Publish: The Birth of Cinematology." *Cinema Journal* 49, no. 1 (2009): 168–175.
Griffiths, Alison. *Wondrous Difference: Cinema, Anthropology and Turn-of-the-Century Visual Culture.* Columbia University Press, 2002.
Gross, Michael L. "Medical Diplomacy and the Battle for Hearts and Minds." In *Military Medical Ethics in Contemporary Armed Conflict: Mobilizing Medicine in the Pursuit of Just War.* Oxford University Press, 2021.
Guerrero, Ed. *Framing Blackness: The African American Image in Film.* Temple University Press, 1993.
Gül, Tülay. "Decision of Turkey Sending Soldiers to Korea in National Press." *Belgi* 7 (2014): 871–879.
Gülalp, Haldun. "Enlightenment by Fiat: Secularization and Democracy in Turkey." *Middle Eastern Studies* 41, no. 3 (2005): 351–372.

Gulick, John. Review of *The Passing of Traditional Society*, Daniel Lerner. *American Anthropologist* 61, no. 1 (1959): 135–138.

Gülkan, Polat, and Oktay Ergünay. "Earthquake Engineering in Turkey: A Brief History." In *Proceedings of the 14th World Conference on Earthquake Engineering*. International Association for Earthquake Engineering, 2008.

Gumrukcu, Tuvan. "Turkey Investigates Why School Pupils Were Shown Footage of Ex-PM's Hanging." *New York Times*, March 24, 2020. https://www.nytimes.com/reuters/2020/03/24/world/europe/24reuters-health-coronavirus-turkey-schools.html.

Gunning, Tom. "An Aesthetics of Astonishment: Early Film and the (In)Credulous Spectator." In *Viewing Positions: Ways of Seeing Film*, ed. Linda Williams. Rutgers University Press, 1995.

Gürata, Ahmet. "Hollywood in Vernacular: Translation and Cross-Cultural Reception of American Films in Turkey." In *Going to the Movies: Hollywood and the Social Experience of Cinema*, ed. Richard Maltby, Melvyn Stokes, and Robert C. Allen. University of Exeter Press, 2007.

Gürata, Ahmet. "Translating Modernity: Remakes in Turkish Cinema." In *Asian Cinemas: A Reader and Guide*, ed. Dimitris Eleftheriotis and Gary Needham. Edinburgh University Press, 2006.

Gürel, Perin E. The *Limits of Westernization: A Cultural History of America in Turkey*. Columbia University Press, 2017.

Hanioğlu, M. Şükrü. *The Young Turks in Opposition*. Oxford University Press, 1995.

Hansen, Miriam. "The Mass Production of the Senses: Classical Cinema as Vernacular Modernism." *Modernism/Modernity* 6, no. 2 (1999): 59–77.

Hansen, Peter H. "The Dancing Lamas of Everest: Cinema, Orientalism, and Anglo-Tibetan Relations in the 1920s." *American Historical Review* 101, no. 3 (1996): 712–747.

Harris, Cheryl I. "Whiteness as Property." *Harvard Law Review* 106, no. 8 (1993): 1707–1791.

Harvey, John. *Photography and Spirit*. Reaktion Books, 2007.

Hediger, Vinzenz, Florian Hoof, and Yvonne Zimmermann, eds. *Films That Work Harder: The Circulation of Industrial Film*. With Scott Anthony. Amsterdam University Press, 2023.

Hediger, Vinzenz, and Patrick Vonderau, eds. *Films That Work: Industrial Film and the Productivity of Media*. Amsterdam University Press, 2009.

Hendershot, Heather. *Shaking the World for Jesus: Media and Conservative Evangelical Culture*. University of Chicago Press, 2010.

Herriot, Édouard. *Orient*. Hachette, 1934.

Hesse, Barnor. "Racialized Modernity: An Analytics of White Mythologies." *Ethnic and Racial Studies* 30, no. 4 (2007): 643–663.

Highlights of Village Life. Near East Mission of the American Board, 1920s. https://www.travelfilmarchive.com/item.php?id=12017&country_id=83&startrow=0&keywords=Turkey+Turkey.

Hikmet, Nazım. "Who Invented Cinema?" *Sinema Postası*, December 1923, trans. Jason Vivrette and reprinted in *Early Popular Visual Culture* 6, no. 2 (2008): 189–193.

Hinkle, Eugene. "Motion Picture in Modern Turkey." In *The Turkish Cinema in the Early Republican Years*, by Rifat N. Bali. Isis Press and Gorgias Press, 2010.
Hirst, Samuel J. "Soviet Orientalism Across Borders: Documentary Film for the Turkish Republic." *Kritika: Explorations in Russian and Eurasian History* 18, no. 1 (2017): 35–61.
Ho, Joseph W. *Developing Mission: Photography, Filmmaking, and American Missionaries in Modern China*. Cornell University Press, 2022.
Hollinger, David. *Protestants Abroad: How Missionaries Tried to Change the World but Changed America*. Princeton University Press, 2018.
Hoof, Florian. *Angels of Efficiency: A Media History of Consulting*, trans. Daniel Fairfax. Oxford University Press, 2020.
Horne, Jennifer. "Experiments in Propaganda: Reintroducing James Blue's Colombia Trilogy," *Moving Image* 9, no. 1 (2009): 183–200.
Howard, Douglas A. *The History of Turkey*. Greenwood, 2001.
Hunt, Michael. *Ideology and U.S. Foreign Policy*. Yale University Press, 2009.
Huntington, Samuel. "Political Development and Political Decay." *World Politics* 17, no. 3 (1965): 386–430.
Inayatullah. "Toward a Non-Western Model of Development." In *Communication and Change in the Developing Countries*, ed. Daniel Lerner and Wilbur Schramm. East-West Center Press, 1967.
"Incirlik Air Base History." Incirlik Air Base. Accessed June 13, 2023. https://www.incirlik.af.mil/About-Us/Fact-Sheets/Display/Article/300814/incirlik-air-base-history/.
International Federation of the Red Cross and Red Crescent Societies. *Turkish Red Crescent Ingilize Reklilize Reklam* (1940, English), Red Cross Red Crescent Historic Film Collection, Turkey Earthquakes. https://youtu.be/ztyP9gpnJuA.
Irwin, Julia. *Making the World Safe: The American Red Cross and a Nation's Humanitarian Awakening*. Oxford University Press, 2013.
Jacobson, Matthew Frye. *Whiteness of a Different Color*. Harvard University Press, 1999.
Jennings, Willie James. "Binding Landscapes: Secularism, Race, and the Spatial Modern." In *Race and Secularism in America*, ed. Jonathon Samuel Kahn and Vincent W. Lloyd. Columbia University Press, 2016.
Joint American Military Mission for Aid to Turkey. "General Information About Turkey," March 1954. Headquarters Commandant Section, Record Group 334. National Archives and Records Administration, College Park, MD.
Joshi, Khyati Y. *White Christian Privilege: The Illusion of Religious Equality in America*. NYU Press, 2021.
Jowett, Garth S., and Victoria O'Donnell. *Propaganda and Persuasion*. Sage, 2018.
Kadıoğlu, Ayse. "The Paradox of Turkish Nationalism and the Construction of Official Identity." *Middle Eastern Studies* 32, no. 2 (1996): 177–193.
Kaell, Hillary. *Christian Globalism at Home: Child Sponsorship in the United States*. Princeton University Press, 2020.
Kahn, Jonathon S., and Vincent W. Lloyd, eds. *Race and Secularism in America*. Columbia University Press, 2016.

Karademir, Burcu Sari. "Turkey as a 'Willing Receiver' of American Soft Power: Hollywood Movies in Turkey During the Cold War." *Turkish Studies* 13, no. 4 (2012): 633–645.

Karpat, Kemal H. "The Impact of the People's Houses on the Development of Communication in Turkey: 1931–1951." *Die Welt des Islams* 15, no. 1/4 (1974): 69–84.

Karpat, Kemal H. "Political Developments in Turkey, 1950–70." *Middle Eastern Studies* 8, no. 3 (1972): 349–375.

Kasaba, Reşat. "Populism and Democracy in Turkey, 1946–1961." In *Rules and Rights in the Middle East: Democracy, Law, and Society*, ed. Ellis Goldberg, Reşat Kasaba, and Joel Migdal. University of Washington Press, 1993.

Kaya, Dilek, and Umut Azak. "*Crossroads* (1970) and the Origin of Islamic Cinema in Turkey." *Historical Journal of Film, Radio and Television* 35, no. 2 (2015): 257–276.

Kaya, Dilek, and Zeynep Koçer. "A Different Story of Secularism: The Censorship of Religion in Turkish Films of the 1960s and Early 1970s." *European Journal of Cultural Studies* 15, no. 1 (2012): 70–88.

Kayaoğlu, Barın. Review of *Malleable Modernity: Rethinking the Role of Ideology in American Policy, Aid Programs, and Propaganda in Fifties' Turkey*, by Nicholas Danforth. *Diplomatic History* 39, no. 3 (2015).

Keating, AnnLouise. "Interrogating 'Whiteness,' (De)Constructing 'Race.'" *College English* 57, no. 8 (1995): 901–918.

Khor, Denise. *Transpacific Convergences: Race, Migration and Japanese American Film Culture Before World War II*. University of North Carolina Press, 2022.

Kim, Han Sang. *Cine-Mobility: Twentieth-Century Transformations in Korea's Film and Transportation*. Harvard University Asia Center, 2022.

Kim, Han Sang. "Cold War and the Contested Identity Formation of Korean Filmmakers: On *Boxes of Death* and Kim Ki-yong's USIS Films." *Inter-Asia Cultural Studies* 14, no. 4 (2013): 551–563.

Kim, Nadia Y. *Imperial Citizens: Koreans and Race from Seoul to LA*. Stanford University Press, 2008.

Klassen, Pamela E. *The Story of Radio Mind: A Missionary's Journey on Indigenous Land*. University of Chicago Press, 2019.

Kostina, Anastasia. "The Mother of Soviet Documentary: Esfir Shub in Compilation Film and Beyond, 1927–1937." PhD diss., Yale University, 2022.

Kozovoi, Andrei. "A Foot in the Door: The Lacy-Zarubin Agreement and Soviet-American Film Diplomacy During the Khrushchev Era, 1953–1963." *Historical Journal of Film, Radio and Television* 36, no. 1 (2016): 21–39.

Kraidy, Marwan M. *Hybridity, or the Cultural Logic of Globalization*. Temple University Press, 2005.

Kugeman, William E. Memorandum. "From Embassy, Ankara—To the Department of State, Washington, October 1, 1952, Subject: Motion Pictures—Cooperation with Turkish Ministries." RG 306 US Information Agency, Office of the Assistant Director for Europe, Entry P403: COU, Country Files for Turkey 1953–1972.

Kunichika, Michael. *"Our Native Antiquity": Archaeology and Aesthetics in the Culture of Russian Modernism.* Academic Studies Press, 2015.

Kürçer, Akın, Volkan Özaksoy, Selim Özalp, Çağıl Uygun Güldoğan, Ersin Özdemir, and Tamer Y. Duman. "The Manyas Fault Zone (Southern Marmara Region, NW Turkey): Active Tectonics and Paleoseismology." *Geodinamica Acta* 29, no. 1 (2017): 42–61.

Laderman, Charlie. *Sharing the Burden: The Armenian Question, Humanitarian Intervention, and Anglo-American Visions of Global Order.* Oxford University Press, 2019.

Lasswell, Harold D. "The Person: Subject and Object of Propaganda." *Annals of the American Academy of Political and Social Science* 179, no. 1 (1935): 187–193.

Lasswell, Harold D. "The Theory of Political Propaganda." *American Political Science Review* 21, no. 3 (1927): 627–631.

Latham, Michael E. *Modernization as Ideology: American Social Science and "Nation Building" in the Kennedy Era.* University of North Carolina Press, 2000.

Latham, Michael E. *The Right Kind of Revolution: Modernization, Development, and US Foreign Policy from the Cold War to the Present.* Cornell University Press, 2011.

Lee, Nan A. "Korean War Records and Research Trends in Turkey." *Seoul Journal of Korean Studies* 31, no. 2 (2018): 197–218.

Lee, Sangjoon. *Cinema and the Cultural Cold War: US Diplomacy and the Origins of the Asian Cinema Network.* Cornell University Press, 2020.

Lee, Sangjoon. "Creating an Anti-Communist Motion Picture Producers' Network in Asia: The Asia Foundation, Asia Pictures, and the Korean Motion Picture Cultural Association." *Historical Journal of Film, Radio and Television* 37, no. 3 (2017): 517–538.

Lerner, Daniel. *The Passing of Traditional Society: Modernizing the Middle East.* Free Press, 1958.

Lerner, Daniel. "Sykewar, ETO: An Account of the Psychological Warfare Campaign Against Germany, Conducted in the European Theater of Operation from D-Day to V-E Day by PWD/SHAEF (Psychological Warfare Division, Supreme Headquarters Allied Expeditionary Force), 6 June 1944–8 May 1945." PhD diss., New York University, 1948.

Lerner, Daniel, George Schueller, and Mary Stycos. "Mass Communications Audiences in Turkey," 1951. Bureau of Applied Social Research Papers, Box 117, Folder B-0370-5. Rare Book and Manuscript Library, Columbia University.

Lerner, Daniel, George Schueller, and Mary Stycos. "Movies, Newsreels, and Documentary Films in Turkey: A Comparison of the Reactions of Four Key Groups in Turkish Society," August 1952. Bureau of Applied Social Research Papers, Box 117, Folder B-0370-8. Rare Book and Manuscript Library, Columbia University.

Libal, Kathryn. "The Children's Protection Society: Nationalizing Child Welfare in Early Republican Turkey." *New Perspectives on Turkey* 23 (2000): 53–78.

Lindvall, Terry, and Andrew Quicke. *Celluloid Sermons: The Emergence of the Christian Film Industry, 1930–1986.* NYU Press, 2011.

Lippmann, Walter. *Public Opinion.* Macmillan, 1922; repr., Free Press, 1997.

Lloyd, Vincent W. "Managing Race, Managing Religion." In Kahn and Lloyd, *Race and Secularism in America.*

Lorentz, Pare. *The Rural Co-Op*. US Information Service, 1947. https://www.worldcat.org/title/rural-co-op/oclc/37822933.

Lüthi, Lorenz M. "The Non-Aligned Movement and the Cold War, 1961–1973." *Journal of Cold War Studies* 18, no. 4 (2016): 98–147.

Lynd, Hilary, and Thom Loyd. "Histories of Color: Blackness and Africanness in the Soviet Union." *Slavic Review* 81, no. 2 (2022): 394–417.

MacCann, Richard Dyer. "Film and Foreign Policy: The USIA, 1962–67." *Cinema Journal* 9, no. 1 (1969): 23–42.

MacCann, Richard Dyer. *The People's Films: A Political History of U.S. Government Motion Pictures*. Hastings House, 1973.

Maghbouleh, Neda. *The Limits of Whiteness*. Stanford University Press, 2017.

Mahar, P. M. Review of *The Passing of Traditional Society*, by Daniel Lerner, Lucille W. Pevsner. *American Journal of Sociology* 65, no. 1 (1959): 110.

Makdisi, Ussama Samir. *Artillery of Heaven: American Missionaries and the Failed Conversion of the Middle East*. Cornell University Press, 2008.

Maksudyan, Nazan. "The Turkish Review of Anthropology and the Racist Face of Turkish Nationalism." *Cultural Dynamics* 17, no. 3 (2005): 291–322.

Maksudyan, Nazan. *Türklüğü Ölçmek: Bilimkurgusal Antropoloji ve Türk Milliyetçiliğinin Irkçı Çehresi: 1925–1939*. Metis Yayınları, 2005.

Malitsky, Joshua. *Post-Revolution Nonfiction Film: Building the Soviet and Cuban Nations*. Indiana University Press, 2013.

Mardin, Şerif. *The Genesis of Young Ottoman Thought: A Study in the Modernization of Turkish Political Ideas*. Princeton University Press, 1962.

Markham, R. F. "Report of the Sub-Committee of the Educational Committee on Extracurricular Activities and Physical Education and Hygiene," June 17, 1924. ABCFM Archives, 1810–1961 (ABC 1–91). Houghton Library, Harvard University.

Masson, Eef. *Watch and Learn: Rhetorical Devices in Classroom Films After 1940*. Amsterdam University Press, 2012.

Mazrui, Ali. "From Social Darwinism to Current Theories of Modernization." *World Politics* 21, no. 1 (1968): 69–83.

Mbembe, Achille. *Critique of Black Reason*, trans. Laurent Dubois. Duke University Press, 2017.

McCarthy, Anna. *The Citizen Machine: Governing by Television in 1950s America*. New Press, 2010.

McGhee, George C. "Turkey Joins the West." *Foreign Affairs* 32, no. 4 (1954): 617–630.

McGhee, George C. *The US-Turkish-NATO Middle East Connection: How the Truman Doctrine and Turkey's NATO Entry Contained the Soviets*. Springer, 2016.

McPharlin, Marjorie Batchelder. *The Puppet Theatre Handbook*. Harper & Brothers, 1947.

MEB. "EBA, EBATV, Mesleki Gelişim, Eğitim Bilişim Ağı." EBA. Accessed 3AD. https://www.eba.gov.tr/.

Mei-Shih, Shu. "Comparative Racialization: An Introduction." *PMLA* 123, no. 5 (2008): 1347–1362.

Melnick, Ross. *Hollywood's Embassies: How Movie Theaters Projected American Power Around the World*. Columbia University Press, 2022.

Meltem, Tekerek. "Cinema in Turkish-Soviet Relations in the Ataturk Period." *История и современное мировоззрение* 1 (2020).

Milliyet Gazete. "Cami Gezdiler," March 7, 1957.

Mills, Charles W. *The Racial Contract*. Cornell University Press, 1997.

Moreton-Robinson, Aileen, Maryrose Casey, and Fiona Nicoll, eds. *Transnational Whiteness Matters*. Rowman & Littlefield, 2008.

Motion Picture Films from the "Hoja" Program Series, 1952–1974. RG 306 Records of the US Information Agency, NAID: 56717, Local ID: 306-HA. National Archives and Records Administration, College Park, MD. https://catalog.archives.gov/id/56717.

"Mrs. Mary Louise Lee Winkler," Confidential Letter of Recommendation, March 1956. ABCFM Archives, 1810–1961 (ABC 1–91), ABCFM 78.4, Vol. 11, Box 21. Houghton Library, Harvard University.

Muller, Benjamin J. "Governmentality and Biopolitics." *Oxford Research Encyclopedia of International Studies*. Oxford University Press, 2011.

Munson, Howard Adelbert, IV. "The Joint American Military Mission to Aid Turkey: Implementing the Truman Doctrine and Transforming US Foreign Policy, 1947–1954." PhD diss., Washington State University, 2012.

Murray, Stuart. "Sports Diplomacy: History, Theory, and Practice." *Oxford Research Encyclopedia of International Studies*. Oxford University Press, 2020.

Mutlu, Dilek Kaya. "*The Midnight Express* (1978) Phenomenon and the Image of Turkey." *Historical Journal of Film, Radio and Television* 25, no. 3 (2005): 475–496.

Mutlu, Dilek Kaya. "The Russian Monument at Ayastefanos (San Stefano): Between Defeat and Revenge, Remembering and Forgetting." *Middle Eastern Studies* 43, no. 1 (2007): 75–86.

Myrdal, Gunnar. *An American Dilemma: The Negro Problem and Modern Democracy*. Harper & Bros., 1944.

Naficy, Hamid. *A Social History of Iranian Cinema*. Vol. 2, *The Industrializing Years, 1941-1978*. Duke University Press, 2011.

Nandy, Ashis, ed. "Introduction: Science as a Reason of State." In *Science, Hegemony, and Violence: A Requiem for Modernity*. Oxford University Press, 1990.

Navitski, Rielle. *Transatlantic Cinephilia: Film Culture Between Latin America and France, 1945-1965*. University of California Press, 2023.

"News of Fellows and Scholars." *Middle East Studies Association Bulletin* 19, no. 1 (1985): 147–152. http://www.jstor.org/stable/23057860.

Nichols, Bill. *Blurred Boundaries: Questions of Meaning in Contemporary Culture*. Indiana University Press, 1994.

Nilson, Paul E. "Moral Education in American Schools in Turkey." Master's thesis, University of Chicago, 1926.

Nilson, Paul E. "Report of Rural Work Turkey," 1936. Near East Mission in Turkey Annual Station Reports, 1931-1937, Salt Araştırma, https://archives.saltresearch.org/handle/123456789/42832.

Nilson, Paul E. "Report on the Rural Work Committee, 1932. Near East Mission in Turkey Annual Station Reports, 1931-1937, Salt Araştırma, https://archives.saltresearch.org/handle/123456789/45733.

Nilsson, Mikael. *The Battle for Hearts and Minds in the High North: The USIA and American Cold War Propaganda in Sweden, 1952-1969*. Brill, 2016.

Nye, Joseph. "Soft Power: The Origins and Political Progress of a Concept." *Palgrave Communications* 3, no. 1 (2017): 1-3.

Ögretici Filmler Merkezi. *Film Kataloğu*. Milli Kütüphane. M. K. B. Matbaasi, 1956.

Ögretici ve Teknik Filimler Hakkında Kanun. *T. C. Resmi Gazete*, Sayi 3537, Sayıfa 7698, Subat 1937 [Law on Educational and Technical Films. Republic of Turkey official gazette, no. 3537, p. 7698, February 1937]. https://www.ogm.gov.tr/ekutuphane/Kanunlar/3116%20Sayılı%20Orman%20Kanunu%20(Orjinal%20Metin).pdf.

Omi, Michael, and Howard Winant. *Racial Formation in the United States*. Routledge, 2015.

Onaran, As. "Yeni Film Sansür Düzeni." *Istanbul Üniversitesi İletişim Fakültesi Dergisi*, no. 1-2 (1992-1993): 139-146.

Oren, Michael. *Power, Faith, and Fantasy: America in the Middle East, 1776 to the Present*. W. W. Norton, 2007.

Orgeron, Devin, Marsha Orgeron, and Dan Streible, eds. *Learning with the Lights Off: Educational Film in the United States*. Oxford University Press, 2011.

Orgeron, Marsha, and Skip Elsheimer. "'Something Different in Science Films': The Moody Institute of Science and the Canned Missionary Movement." *Moving Image* 7, no. 1 (2007): 1-26.

Örücü, Esin. "Conseil d'Etat: The French Layer of Turkish Administrative Law." *International and Comparative Law Quarterly* 49, no. 3 (2000): 679-700.

Osgood, Kenneth Alan. *Total Cold War: Eisenhower's Secret Propaganda Battle at Home and Abroad*. University Press of Kansas, 2006.

Ostherr, Kirsten. *Cinematic Prophylaxis: Globalization and Contagion in the Discourse of World Health*. Duke University Press, 2005.

Ostherr, Kirsten. *Medical Visions: Producing the Patient Through Film, Television, and Imaging Technologies*. Oxford University Press, 2013.

Ovalle, Priscilla Peña. *Dance and the Hollywood Latina: Race, Sex, and Stardom*. Rutgers University Press, 2010.

The Overseas Film Program, U.S. Information Agency, 1959. RG 306 General Records of the USIA, Historical Collection to the Overseas Film Program, Box 155, Subject Files, 1953-2000, Motion Pictures, 1983-2000.

Özdemir, Nebi. "The Philosopher's Philosopher Nasreddin Hodja." In vol. 14. Republic of Turkey, Ministry of Culture and Tourism, General Directorate of Libraries and Publications, 2011.

Özdil, İlhan. "A Causative-Diagnostic Analysis of Turkey's Major Problems and a Communicative Approach to Their Solution (Democratic Planning and Mass Communication)." PhD diss., Ohio State University, 1954.

Özdil, İlhan. *Öğretici Filmler Merkezi Hakkında Rapordur.* Maarif Vekâleti, 1957.

Özkan, Mehmet. "Emergence of Afro-Turks in Turkish Politics." *Turkish Journal of Diaspora Studies* 1, no. 1 (2021): 7–19.

Özön, Nijat. *Türk Sinema Tarihi.* Artist Yayinevi, 1962.

Özön, Nijat. "Türkiye'de Amerikan Sansürü." *Yön* 18 (1962).

Öztürk, Ayhan, and S. Tunay Kamer. "Activities of American Missionaries in Kayseri." *Cumhuriyet Uluslararası Eğitim Dergisi* 2, no. 2 (2013): 106–122.

Öztürk, Serdar. "Karagöz Co-Opted: Turkish Shadow Theatre of the Early Republic (1923–1945)." *Asian Theatre Journal* 23, no. 2 (2006): 292–313.

Painter, Nell Irvin. *The History of White People.* W. W. Norton, 2010.

Paker, Hande. "Reflection of the State in the Turkish Red Crescent: From Modernization to Corruption to Reform?" *Middle Eastern Studies* 43, no. 4 (2007): 647–660.

Panken, Jaffa. "'Lest They Perish': The Armenian Genocide and the Making of Modern Humanitarian Media in the US, 1915–1925." PhD diss., University of Pennsylvania, 2014.

Personal Hygiene for Young Men. Bray Studios, 1924. https://archive.org/details/rppersonalhygieneforyoungmen001.

Plummer, Brenda Gayle. "Race and the Cold War." In *The Oxford Handbook of the Cold War*, ed. Richard H. Immerman and Petra Goedde. Oxford Academic, 2013.

Prelinger, Rick. *The Field Guide to Sponsored Films.* National Film Preservation Foundation, 2006.

Prevots, Naima. *Dance for Export: Cultural Diplomacy and the Cold War.* Wesleyan University Press, 1999.

Price, Patricia L. "At the Crossroads: Critical Race Theory and Critical Geographies of Race." *Progress in Human Geography* 34, no. 2 (2010): 147–174.

Puar, Jasbir K. *Terrorist Assemblages: Homonationalism in Queer Times.* Duke University Press, 2018.

Putney, Clifford. *Muscular Christianity: Manhood and Sports in Protestant America, 1880–1920.* Harvard University Press, 2001.

"Putting the Generator Into Work for Exhibiting a Film About Childcare," x. American Board of Commissioners for Foreign Missions. https://www.archives.saltresearch.org/R/-?func=dbin-jump-full&object_id=4329156&silo_library=GEN01.

Quality Milk. In *Educational Film Catalog.* H. W. Wilson, 1939. https://archive.org/stream/educationalfilmc00hwwirich#page/192/mode/2up/search/Quality+Milk.

Ramm, Christoph. "Beyond 'Black Turks' and 'White Turks'—The Turkish Elites' Ongoing Mission to Civilize a Colourful Society." *Asiatische Studien-Études Asiatiques* 70, no. 4 (2016): 1355–1385.

Real, Brian. "Private Life, Public Diplomacy: Tibor Hirsch and Documentary Filmmaking for the Cold War USIA." *Historical Journal of Film, Radio and Television* 40, no. 2 (2020): 297–324.

Reeves-Ellington, Barbara. "American Women Missionaries on Trial in Turkey: Religion, Diplomacy, and Public Perceptions in the 1920s." *Diplomatic History* 43, no. 2 (2018): 246–264.

Reynolds, Glenn. *Movies on a Mission: American Protestants and the Foreign Missionary Film, 1906–1956*. McFarland, 2023.

Robert College. *Annual Report of the President, 1926–27*.

Rogers, Basil. "Report on Uses, Possible Uses and Requirements for Visual Aids Program in Turkey," March 1951. Technical Aids Unit, ECA/OSR. National Archives and Records Administration.

Rolston, Holmes. *Science and Religion: A Critical Survey*. Templeton Foundation Press, 2006.

Ross, Frank A., C. Luther Fry, and Elbridge Sibley. *The Near East and American Philanthropy*. Annual Report of the President, 1926–27.

Sabah. "MEB'nın Adnan Menderes videosu ile ilgili Melih Altınok'tan 'Demokrasi kültürünün gelişmesi için bunlar çok önemli.'" March 24, 2020. https://www.sabah.com.tr/video/haber/mebnin-adnan-menderes-videosu-ile-ilgili-melih-altinoktan-demokrasi-kulturunun-gelismesi-icin-bunlar-cok-onemli-video.

Sager, Weston R. "Apple Pie Propaganda: The Smith-Mundt Act Before and After the Repeal of the Domestic Dissemination Ban." *Northwestern University Law Review* 109 (2014): 511–546.

Sahin, Emrah. *Faithful Encounters: Authorities and American Missionaries in the Ottoman Empire*. McGill-Queen's University Press, 2018.

Said, Edward W. *Orientalism*. Vintage, 1979.

Salazkina, Masha. *World Socialist Cinema: Alliances, Affinities, and Solidarities in the Global Cold War*. University of California Press, 2023.

Salem, Elie A. Review of *The Passing of Traditional Society: Modernizing the Middle East*, Daniel Lerner and Lucille W. Pevsner. *Political Science Quarterly* 74, no. 1 (1959): 127–129.

Santoro, Doris A., and Charles Dorn. "A Vital, Free, Independent, and Lay Republic: John Dewey and the Role of Education in Establishing the Turkish State." In *Teaching America to the World and the World to America: Education and Foreign Relations Since 1870*, ed. Richard Garlitz and Lisa Jarvinen. Palgrave Macmillan, 2012.

Sayari, Sabri. "Adnan Menderes: Between Democratic and Authoritarian Populism." In *Political Leaders and Democracy in Turkey*, ed. Metin Heper and Sabri Sayari. Lexington Books, 2002.

Schiller, Herbert I. *Mass Communications and American Empire*. A. M. Kelley, 1969.

Schwenk, Melinda M. "Reforming the Negative Through History: The U.S. Information Agency and the 1957 Little Rock Integration Crisis." *Journal of Communication Inquiry* 23, no. 3 (1999): 288–306.

Scognamillo, Giovanni. *Türk Sinema Tarihi*. Kabalcı Yayınevi, 1998.

Seymour, Richard. "The Cold War, American Anticommunism and the Global 'Colour Line.'" In *Race and Racism in International Relations: Confronting the Global Colour Line*, ed. A. Anievas, N. Manchanda, and R. Shilliam. Routledge, 2015.

Shah, Hemant. *The Production of Modernization: Daniel Lerner, Mass Media, and the Passing of Traditional Society*. Temple University Press, 2011.

Sharp, Ilana Shub. *Esfir Shub: Pioneer of Documentary Filmmaking*. Bloomsbury, 2021.

Shaw, Tony, and Denise J. Youngblood. *Cinematic Cold War: The American and Soviet Struggle for Hearts and Minds*. University Press of Kansas, 2010.

Sherrill, Charles Hitchcock. *A Year's Embassy to Mustafa Kemal*. Charles Scribner's Sons, 1934.

Shibusawa, Naoko. "Ideology, Culture, and the Cold War." In *The Oxford Handbook of the Cold War*, ed. Richard H. Immerman and Petra Goedde. Oxford University Press, 2013.

Signitzer, Benno H., and Timothy Coombs. "Public Relations and Public Diplomacy: Conceptual Convergence." *Public Relations Review* 18, no. 2 (1992): 137–147.

Sinema, Video ve Müzik Eserleri Kanunu ile Yönetmelikler. Kültür ve Turzim Bakanlığı, 1989.

Skvirsky, Salomé Aguilera. *The Process Genre: Cinema and the Aesthetic of Labor*. Duke University Press, 2020.

Slezkine, Yuri. *Arctic Mirrors: Russia and the Small Peoples of the North*. Cornell University Press, 1994.

Slide, Anthony. *Ravished Armenia and the Story of Aurora Mardiganian*. University Press of Mississippi, 2014.

Smith, Iain Robert. "'Beam Me Up, Ömer': Transnational Media Flow and the Cultural Politics of the Turkish Star Trek Remake." *Velvet Light Trap*, no. 61 (2008): 3–13.

Snow, Nancy. *Propaganda, Inc.: Selling America's Culture to the World*. Seven Stories Press, 2010.

Snow, Nancy. "Rethinking Public Diplomacy in the 2020s." In Snow and Cull, *Routledge Handbook of Public Diplomacy*.

Snow, Nancy, and Nicholas J. Cull, eds. *Routledge Handbook of Public Diplomacy*. 2nd ed. Routledge, 2020.

Solomonovich, Nadav. *The Korean War in Turkish Culture and Society*. Palgrave Macmillan, 2021.

Sontag, Deborah. "The Erdogan Experiment." *New York Times*, May 11, 2003. https://www.nytimes.com/2003/05/11/magazine/the-erdogan-experiment.html.

Stearns, Monteagle. *Entangled Allies: US Policy Toward Greece, Turkey, and Cyprus*. Council on Foreign Relations, 1992.

Stearns, Monteagle. "Report of USIE Activities in Turkey," Section 4: Motion Pictures, November 1949. RG 59 General Records of the Department of State, Office of the

Assistant Secretary for Public Affairs, Office of International Information/Division of International Motion Pictures, Country Reports, 1949–1950, Box 23, ARC ID 4751078, Entry 239.

Stearns, Monteagle. *Talking to Strangers: Improving American Diplomacy at Home and Abroad.* Princeton University Press, 1999.

Stewart, Jacqueline Najuma. "Giving Voice, Taking Voice: Nonwhite and Nontheatrical." Foreword to Field and Gordon, *Screening Race in American Nontheatrical Film.*

Streible, Dan, Martina Roepke, and Anke Mebold. "Introduction: Nontheatrical Film." *Film History* 19, no. 4 (2007): 339–343.

Suner, Asuman. *New Turkish Cinema: Belonging, Identity and Memory.* Tauris, 2010.

Sünnet, Ehli. "Tövbe Zamanı Gelmedi mi?" *Ehli Sünnet* Cilt 76, Sayı 4 (1950).

Talu, Ercüment Ekrem. "İstanbulda İlk Sinema ve İlk Gramofon." *Perde ve Sahne* 7 (1943).

Tanrivermis, Harun. "Agricultural Land Use Change and Sustainable Use of Land Resources in the Mediterranean Region of Turkey." *Journal of Arid Environments* 54, no. 3 (2003): 553–564.

Tejirian, Eleanor H., and Reeva Spector Simon. *Conflict, Conquest, and Conversion: Two Thousand Years of Christian Missions in the Middle East.* Columbia University Press, 2012.

Teksoy, Rekin. *Rekin Teksoy'un Türk Sineması.* Oğlak Yayıncılık, 2007.

Teksoy, Rekin. *Turkish Cinema.* Oğlak Yayıncılık, 2008.

Tharoor, Ishaan. "The Execution of a Former Turkish Leader That Still Haunts Erdogan." *Washington Post*, July 30, 2016. https://www.washingtonpost.com/world/the-execution-of-a-former-turkish-leader-that-still-haunts-erdogan/2016/07/29/4772c256-54b4-11e6-994c-4e3140414f34_story.html.

Tokgöz, Server Kamil. *Öjenism: Irk Islahı.* Sümer Basımevi, 1938.

Tugrul, Semih. "Türkiye'de Amerikan Sansürü." *Hür Vatan*, May 10, 1962.

Turajlić, Mila. "Filmske Novosti: Filmed Diplomacy." *Nationalities Papers* 49, no. 3 (2021): 483–503.

Turan, Selahattin. "John Dewey's Report of 1924 and His Recommendations on the Turkish Educational System Revisited." *History of Education* 29, no. 6 (2000): 543–555.

Turek, Lauren Frances. *To Bring the Good News to All Nations: Evangelical Influence on Human Rights and US Foreign Relations.* Cornell University Press, 2020.

Turkey: The Land of "In-Between." Armed Forces, 1952. https://archive.org/details/gov.archives.arc.654133#reviews.

Ulff-Møller, Jens. *Hollywood's Film Wars with France: Film-Trade Diplomacy and the Emergence of the French Film Quota Policy.* University of Rochester Press, 2001.

Ünlü, Barış. "The Kurdish Struggle and the Crisis of the Turkishness Contract." *Philosophy & Social Criticism* 42, no. 4–5 (2016): 397–405.

Ünlü, Barış. "The Turkishness Contract and the Formation of Turkishness." In *Kurds in Dark Times: New Perspectives on Violence and Resistance in Turkey*, ed. Ayça Alemdaroğlu and Fatma Müge Göçek. Syracuse University Press, 2023.

Ünlü, Barış. *Türklük Sözleşmesi: Oluşumu, İşleyişi ve Krizi.* Dipnot Yayınları, 2018.

United Nations Educational, Scientific, and Cultural Organization, International Bureau of Education. "Turkey: Educational Developments in 1950-1951, Out-of-School Activities, Educational Films." In *International Yearbook of Education, 1951*. UNESCO/IBE, 1951. http://unesdoc.unesco.org/images/0013/001329/132912eo.pdf.

United Nations Educational, Scientific, and Cultural Organization International Bureau of Education. "United Nations Film Board." In International Yearbook of Education, 1953. http://unesdoc.unesco.org/images/0017/001787/178798eb.pdf.

US Department of Defense, Office of Armed Forces Information and Education. *A Pocket Guide to Turkey*. Department of the Army, 1953.

USIA. Memorandum. "From USIS Ankara to USIA Washington," September 5, 1956. RG 306 US Information Agency, Office of the Assistant Director for Europe, Country Files for Turkey 1953-1972, Entry P403.

USIA. Secret Document, June 27, 1956. RG 306 US Information Agency, Office of the Assistant Director for Europe, Country Files for Turkey 1953-1972, Entry P403.

USIA. *United States Educational, Scientific, and Cultural Motion Pictures and Filmstrips: Education Section 1958, Selected and Available for Use Abroad*. USIA, 1959.

USIS Amerikan Haberler Merkezi. *Film Kataloğu, 1965*. Ayyıldız Matbaası, 1965.

USIS Amerikan Haberler Merkezi. *"USIS" Film Kataloğu, 1962*. Yeni Desen Matbaası, 1962.

USIS Amerikan Haberler Merkezi Türkiye. *16mm-35mm Film Kataloğu, 1960*. Yeni Desen Matbaası, 1960.

USIS-Country Program Memorandum for FY 1972. RG 306 US Information Agency, Office of the Assistant Director for Europe, Country Files for Turkey 1953-1972, Entry P403. Robert Lincoln. National Archives and Records Administration, College Park, MD.

Üsküdar American Academy. "About Us, History." http://www.uaa.k12.tr/en/Icerik/okulumuzun-tarihcesi/256/.

Üstün, Sebnem. "Turkey and the Marshall Plan: Strive for Aid." *Turkish Yearbook of International Relations* 27 (1997): 31-52.

Vander Lippe, John M. "Forgotten Brigade of the Forgotten War: Turkey's Participation in the Korean War." *Middle Eastern Studies* 36, no. 1 (2000): 92-102.

Vander Lippe, John M. "The 'Terrible Turk': The Formulation and Perpetuation of a Stereotype in American Foreign Policy." *New Perspectives on Turkey* 17 (1997): 39-57.

Vukoder, Bret. "Filmic Aesthetics and Technologies of War, Policy, and 'Truth' in the Motion Pictures of the United States Information Agency." PhD diss., Carnegie Mellon University, 2020.

Vukoder, Bret, and Mark Williams. "The Great War at Scale." In *Provenance and Early Cinema*, ed. Joanne Bernardi, Paolo Cherchi Usai, Tami Williams, and Joshua Yumibe. Indiana University Press, 2021.

Wagner, Robert W. Interview, February 5, 2001 (edited by R.W.W. February 1, 2002). Ohio State University Archives.

Waller, Gregory A. *Beyond the Movie Theater: Sites, Sponsors, Uses, Audiences*. University of California Press, 2023.

Wasson, Haidee. *Everyday Movies: Portable Film Projectors and the Transformation of American Culture*. University of California Press, 2021.

Wasson, Haidee. *Museum Movies: The Museum of Modern Art and the Birth of Art Cinema*. University of California Press, 2005.

Wasson, Haidee, and Lee Grieveson. *Cinema's Military Industrial Complex*. University of California Press, 2018.

Williams, Morgan K. "John Dewey in the 21st Century." *Journal of Inquiry and Action in Education* 9, no. 1 (2017): 91–102.

Willoughby, Bam. "Opposing a Spectacle of Blackness: *Arap Baci, Baci Kalfa, Dadi*, and the Invention of African Presence in Turkey." *Lateral* 10, no. 1 (2021): 1–11.

Winn, William E. "Tom Brown's Schooldays and the Development of 'Muscular Christianity.'" *Church History* 29, no. 1 (1960): 64–73.

Wittler, Melvin A. Memorandum to Miss Margaret Blomker. "Death of Herman Harold Kreider," 1967. ABCFM Archives, 1810–1961 (ABC 1–91) / ABC 77.1, Box 966. Houghton Library, Harvard University.

The Work of Mr. Kreider, written by an unknown associate in Istanbul, 1939. ABCFM Archives, 1810–1961 (ABC 1–91) / ABC 77.1, Box 966. Houghton Library, Harvard University.

Xu, Lanjun. "The Southern Film Corporation, Opera Films and the PRC's Cultural Diplomacy in Cold War Asia, 1950s–1960s." In *Chineseness and the Cold War: Contested Cultures and Diaspora in Southeast Asia and Hong Kong*, ed. Jeremy E. Taylor and Lanjun Xu. Routledge, 2021.

Yackley, Ayla Jean. "Turkish President Casts Self as Heir to Reformer Who Died on Gallows." Reuters, August 28, 2014. https://www.reuters.com/article/us-turkey-erdogan-vision/turkish-president-casts-self-as-heir-to-reformer-who-died-on-gallows-idUSKBN0GS1ZP20140828.

Yanikkerem, Emre, Hatice Acar, and Emel Elem. "Withdrawal Users' Perceptions of and Experience with Contraceptive Methods in Manisa, Turkey." *Midwifery* 22, no. 3 (2006): 274–284.

Yesil, Bilge. *Talking Back to the West: How Turkey Uses Counter-Hegemony to Reshape the Global Communication Order*. University of Illinois Press, 2024.

Yilmaz, Hale. *Becoming Turkish: Nationalist Reforms and Cultural Negotiations in Early Republican Turkey 1923–1945*. Syracuse University Press, 2013.

Yorukoglu, Ilgin. "Whiteness as an Act of Belonging: White Turks Phenomenon in the Post 9/11 World." *Glocalism: Journal of Culture, Politics and Innovation*, no. 2 (2017): 1–22.

Yurtcu, Ozlem. "Çikolata renkli Türkler." *Sabah*, 2005.

Zaharna, R. S. "Communication Logics of Global Public Diplomacy." In Snow and Cull, *Routledge Handbook of Public Diplomacy*.

Zolyan, Mikayel. "From Menderes to Erdogan, the Complicated History of the Relationship Between Military and the Civilian Leadership in Turkey." Regional Post, May 1, 2017. https://regionalpost.org/en/articles/from-menderes-to-erdogan.html.

Zürcher, Erik Jan. *Turkey: A Modern History*. Tauris, 2017.

Index

ABCFM. *See* American Board of Commissioners for Foreign Missions
abortion, 138–139, 140, 247n1
Abraham Lincoln (film), 106
Acland, Charles R., 37, 180, 185, 241n9
Adalet Partisi (Justice Party), 169
Adnan Menderes (educational films), 213, 214, 215–216
aesthetic, of films, 27, 164
Afro-Asian Peoples Solidarity Group, 7
Afro-Turks, 28–29, 212
agriculture, 21, 33, 117, 191, 242n11, 250n39; development of, 50, 86, 96; Ministry of, 114, 159; missionaries and, 86; modernization and, 83–84, 102, 200–204; *Poultry Raising* and, 38, 179, 181–182, 209; *Quality Milk* and, 83, 86–87, 100; *The Rural Co-Op*, 38, 200–203, 209, 210; US Department of, 87, 105
Ahmet Yılmaz (fictional character), 1, *2*, *3*, *4*, 17
Air Force, US, 94, 115–116
Akdemir, Orhan, 90
Alagöz, Cemal, 174–175
Ali (fictional character), 75, 76
Allen, George, 181

Altın Bilezik (Golden bracelet), 23, 169–171
amateur films, 17
America. *See* United States
American Academy for Girls, 80, *92*
American Board of Commissioners for Foreign Missions (ABCFM), 9, 33, 74, *92*; Bursa American College for Girls trial, 79–80; Christian values and, 10, 32, 34, 59–60, 65–66, 69, 80–81, 88; films sponsored by, 34, 66, 75; Kreider and, 81–82; Near East Mission of, 84; propaganda, 10
American Collegiate Institute, 213
American dream, the, 148, 183–184
American Research Institute in Turkey, 30, 218
Amerikan Birleşik Devletleri Haberler Servisi. *See* US Information Service
Ana Kucağı (Orphanage) (documentary film), 36, 171–172
Ankara (documentary film), 47
anticommunism, 20, 27, 123, 128, 136, 231n51
appropriation, 165
Arat-Koç, Sedef, 27
Arın, Suha, 36, 104, 132, 133–135, 144, 248n14

Armenian genocide (1915-1916), 48, 49, 68
Arrival of a Train, The (silent film), 71
Arslan, Savas, 16, 26
artistic heritage, 134
Atatürk, Mustafa Kemal, 21-22, 25, 43, 49, 89, 116; educational reform and, 18-19, 61, 70, 73, 143, 145, 231n48; Lerner on, 193; Reception on, 33, 50-51, 54, 58; Sherrill on, 51
Ateşten Gömlek (Shirt of Flame) (film), 43
atheism, 23, 35, 129, 131
Atoms for Peace (Barış Yolu) (film), 196
Auction of Souls (biographical film), 68
audiences, 196-200; Cold War research, 180, 210; global, 104-107; Korean War media and, 204-205; for "Mass Communications Audiences in Turkey," 188-191; racialized, 207, 208; reception of, 8, 10, 14, 37, 158, 180, 181, 183, 186, 192, 204-205, 207-210; research on, 37-38, 180, 181, 183, 186, 208, 210; response to films, 112, 191-192, 207; target, 5, 14, 181
audiovisual center, 158
audiovisual education, 10, 147, 158-159, 192, 206-207
audiovisual technology, 5, 6, 112, 151, 153, 159-160
Ayastefanos'taki Rus Abidesi'nin Yıkılışı (Demolition of the Russian monument at San Stefano, The) (documentary film), 41-42, 48, 229n9
Azak, Umut, 167-168

Baby's Bath and Toilet (health film), 83, 89
Balkan War, The (military film), 46
Banfield, Edward, 194
Barış Yolu (Atoms for Peace) (film), 196
Barton, James L., 69
Barutçu, Şinasi, 9, 142, 144, 156, 157, 158-159, 251n48
BASR. *See* Bureau of Applied Social Research
Bell and Howell-Gaumont (British licensed manufacturer and distributor), 9, 142, 145-146, 248n18
Beneath the Snows of Mount Argeaus and *Schoolmates at Scutare* (silent films), 66, 75-76, 77, 78, 79, 92, 100, 236n57

Bey, Ismail Safa, 72
Bible, 64, 66, 67-68, 91, 94, 95-96, 193
biblical archaeology, 93
Birleşen Yollar (Crossroads), 167-168
Bir Millet Uyanıyor (Nation is awakening, A) (film), 43
Biz Bu Eve Taşınmadık mı? (Haven't we moved to this house?) (Hoja film), 167
blackface, 29
Blackness, 28, 29, 45
black-skinned (*zenci*), 28
black Turks, 11-12, 160-162, 214, 215
Blumenbach, Johann Friedrich, 24
Board of Censorship, 63, 98, 110, 170, 233n14
Bosphorus mystery, The (Nur Baba) (silent film), 42-43
Boyar, Ebru, 45
Bridgeland. *See* Turkey: Middle East Bridgeland
Bugünün Eğitim ve Öğretiminde DİYA (Barutçu), 160
Buntat na Robite (Slaves' revolt, The) (Bulgarian film), 46
Bureau of Applied Social Research (BASR), 37, 180, 188-191, 193, 194
Burhan (puppet character), 124, 125, 126, 128
Bursa American College for Girls trial, 79-80
Burton, Elise K., 25

caliphate, 21, 72, 143
Caner, Faruk, 238n70
capitalism, 23, 104, 132, 182, 196, 201; cooperative, 202, 210; free-market, 183, 184; US style, 20, 37, 195, 198, 208, 209
Carrington, Thomas Spees, 87
caucasian, 24
Çay (Tea) (educational film), 159
censorship, 34, 45, 48-49, 109, 170, 229n24; Board of, 63, 98, 110, 170, 233n14; film diplomacy and, 46; in Ottoman Empire, 46-47; regulations for, 33, 35, 63, 64
Chase, Mary, 124
Chen, Fan Pen, 40

Children's Protection Agency (*Sosyal Hizmetler ve Çocuk Esirgeme Kurumu*), 164, 171–172, 253n90
child welfare, 171–172
Christian imperialism, 67, 79
Christianity, 61–64, 163; medical services for, 34, 87–89, 236n61; muscular, 88; Muslims and, 33, 34; Nilson on, 73–74, 94–96; principles of, 70, 88; theology in, 27, 163; values of, 10, 32, 34, 59–60, 65–66, 69, 80–81, 88. *See also* missionaries
Christianization, 21, 79, 100, 195
Chun, Wendy Hui Kyong, 227n99
cinema, 211; classical, 37, 185; early republican, 40–42; as ideological instrument, 28, 190, 199; Law of, 170; mobile, 6, 36, 37, 121–123, 159, 206, 207; national, 42, 48–49, 168; shadow theater, 40–41, 252n71; traditional, 16; in Turkey, 16–18, 31–32, 57–58, 167–168, 178; useful, 37, 180, 185; USIS, 121, *122*, 123–132
Cinema Bus (*Sinema Otomobili*), 206
civilizational hierarchy, 37, 180, 199
civilized society, 9, 29, 49, 51
Çınar, Alev, 170–171
classical cinema, 37, 185
Cold War, 7, 8, 35, 39, 101, 183; audience research on, 180, 210; BASR, 188; film diplomacy, 132, 186; films on, 104, 205–207, 209–210; Korean War and, 52–54; media, 5, 17, 54–55, 133, 176, 185, 186, 191, 207, 213, 216; modernization and, 20–23, 37, 199; propaganda, 32–33, 40, 54, 109, 129, 198; public diplomacy during, 12, 155, 250n44; USIS and, 15, 19–20, 108–111; US strategy for, 113, 185, 209; whiteness and, 38, 212
collaborative models, of film diplomacy, 15–16
commercial enterprises, 8, 144
communication network, for US-Turkey, 98, 132, 133, 135
communication technologies, 61, 153, 193
communism, 11, 94, 110, 124, 132; anti-, 20, 27, 123, 128, 136, 231n51; counter to, 53, 54, 108, 116, 168, 170, 183, 186, 196; films about, 106–107; Nasreddin Hoja and, 23; public opinion in favor of, 47; religion and, 111, 129; spread of, 54, 113–114, 194–195
Conference of Lausanne, 69
Conroy-Krutz, Emily, 67
contraception, 138–140
Control of Water (*Suyun Kontrolü*) (educational film), 200
Coppen, Helen E., 39
Creative game I (*Yaratıcı Oyun I*), 164, 165
Creative game II (*Yaratıcı Oyun II*), 166, 167
critical race theory, 6
Cronkite, Walter, 53–54
Crossroads (film). *See Birleşen Yollar*
Crumpler, Hugh A., 118, 120
Cull, Nicholas, 14, 217, 240n2
cultural contexts, 8, 73, 83, 112, 189
cultural diplomacy, 12, 14
Cultural Films and Our Schools (educational film), 174
cultural heritage, 1, 130, 170
culture, of educational films, 9, 10, 13, 46, 97, 142, 147, 176–177
Cumhuriyet Halk Partisi (Republican People's Party), 74, 213, 214
Cumhuriyet (newspaper), 53, 102

Darwinism, 93–94, 222n9
Daughter of Israel, A (*Yakub'un Kuyusu*) (French film), 45–46
Deloria, Philip, 165
Del Rio, Dolores, 44–45
Democratic Party (*Demokrat Parti*) (DP), 21, 168–169, 203, 206, 214
Demolition of the Russian monument at San Stefano, The (*Ayastefanos'taki Rus Abidesi'nin Yıkılışı*) (documentary film), 41–42, 48, 229n9
Department of Agriculture, US, 87, 105
Department of Defense, US, 94, 101, 116
Depremde Kızılay (*Red Crescent in earthquake*) (documentary film), 36, 160–164, 251n53
Dewey, John, 18, 19, 69–70, 72–73, 235n37
diplomatic intervention, 4
disaster relief, 160–164

distribution, of educational films, 6, 7, 8, 14, 31, 38, 117, 140, 201
documentary films, 19, 183–184, 207
Dodd, Wilson F., 75, 76, *77*, *78*, *92*, 236n61
DP. *See* Democratic Party
Dulles, John Foster, 110

earthquake, disaster relief for, 160–164, 251n53
Economic Cooperation Administration (ECA), 37, 179; BASR and, 180; propaganda and, 114; USIS and, 181–182, 191–192, 199–200, 201–202, 206
economic hardships, 198
economic prosperity, 9, 33, 107
economic unity, 198–199
education: missionary schools, 70, 81, 208; reform for, 18–20, 70, 73, 143, 145, 231n48; technology for, 143, 150, 151, 155, 159–160; Turkey school systems, 10, 18–20, 70, 74, 208; US schools, 70, 75, 76, 79, 81, 184, 207–208
Educational Film, Radio, and Television Center of Turkey (EFRTC), 36, 117, *141*, 159
Educational Film Catalog, 87, 251n53
Educational Film Center (EFC), 5–6, 9, 36, 98, 103; categorization for, 186–187; crew from, *175*; development of, 153–160; Flanagan and, 117; mobile film, 156, 200; modernization and, 10–11; outdoor film screening, *177*; trainees and teachers, *154*
Educational Film Library Association (EFLA), 117
educational films, 82–83, 137, 174, 208, 212–216; Barutçu on, 158; classifications for, 184, 186–187; commercial enterprise for, 8, 144; culture of, 9, 10, 13, 46, 97, 142, 147, 176–177; discursive strategies in, 8, 57; distribution of, 6, 7, 8, 14, 31, 38, 117, 140, 201; infrastructure of, 35–36, 147, 176; Law of Educational and Technical Films, 17, 66–67, 112, 144–145, 240n111; as modernization initiative, 6–7, 32, 183–187, 197–198; national ideology as reflection of, 12, 177; national unity and, 6, 73, 129, 142, 160, 168, 175; for public relations, 19; religion in, 23; revolution of, 9, 36, 155–156, 176; scholarships and, 13, 16, 32, 247n2; Verel on, 174; whiteness and, 140–141. *See also* nontheatrical films
Educational Information Network (EIN), 30–31, 215
educational media, 29, 36, 54, 143; Barutçu and, 158–159; infrastructure for, 117–120; production of, 156
educational reform, 18–20, 70, 73, 143, 145, 231n48
educational technologies, 143, 150, 151, 155, 159–160
EFC. *See* Educational Film Center
Effendi (puppet sheik character), 124–125, *126*, 127–130
EFLA. *See* Educational Film Library Association
EIN. *See* Educational Information Network
Eisenhower, Dwight D., 35, 107, 111, 120, 196, 228n112
Elan, Sylvia, 236n57
Elektrik ve Toprak (*Power and the Land*) (educational film), 197
Elif'in Çilesi (*Suffering of Elif, The*) (Turkish film), 23, 137, *138*, *139*, 140–141, 177
Emperor's Elephant, The (educational films), 124, 129–130
Erciyes Dağı (Mount Argeaus), 75, 236n58
Erdoğan, Nezih, 41, 229n24
Erdoğan, Recep Tayyip, 214, 215
ERFTC. *See* Educational Film, Radio, and Television Center of Turkey
Ergin, Murat, 25, 27
Ertuğrul, Muhsin, 42–43, 123
Esakoff, Sharon, 187
eugenics, 25–26, 28, 51, 140
Europeanness, 26, 50
exceptionalism, 11, 168, 176
exhibitions, for films, 6, 7, 8, 14; Cold War, 205–206; for nontheatrical films, 33–34, 63–65, 66, 71, 89–93, 132, 206; Stearns organizing, 132–133

faith, 25, 33, 39, 69, 87–88, 94, 128
"faithful training," 88
Families of the World (Journal Film), 18
family planning, 11, 137–140, 171–172
Film Audit Commission, 240n111
film diplomacy. *See specific topics*
film education, 134
Film-Radio-Graphic Center (FRGC), 159
films: ABCFM sponsored, 34, 66, 75; aesthetic of, 27, 164; amateur, 17; banned, 98, 109–110; as catalyst for economic unity, 198–199; Cold War, 104, 205–207, 209–210; communism, 106–107; distribution of, 116, 186; documentary, 19, 183–184, 207; emphasis on wealth in, 44, 50, 140; Ertuğrul influence on, 42–43; foreign, 10, 33, 37, 41, 43–44, 58, 109, 233n14; geography, 175, 177, 254n100; government-sponsored, 5, 19, 37, 156, 158, 170, 173, 176, 183, 192; as harbinger of civilization, 71; international relations and, 4, 5, 6, 31, 39, 135, 246n101; interpretation by foreign audiences, 112, 207; Korean War, 53, 152, 205; libraries for, 9, 14, 29, 95, 104, 117, 121, 145–146; marionette, 124–125, *126*, *127*, 128–129, 131; Marshall Plan, 36, 113–115, 199–200; military, 10, 52, 94, 101, 115–117, 121, 211; mobile, 14, 29, 65, 97, 121, *122*, 123, 156, 191, 200, 206; moral influence of, 45; national image rebranded through, 46–47; in prisons, 59–60; production of, 116–117, 118–119, 144, 158–159, 164, 168–171, 211; programs for, 34–35, 82, 98, 104–105, 108, 133, 184, 191; projectors for, 6, 14, 34, 70, 96, 97, 108, 121, 147–151, 191–192, 240n111; propaganda, 105, 124; public opinion shaped by, 39; screening of, 15, 59, 63, 65, 71, 97, 145, 158, 176, *177*; small-gauge, 17; sound, 43. *See also* educational films; exhibitions; silent films; sponsored films
film technologies, 66, 70, 82, 91, 93, 98, 158–159, 175

Film ve Öğretim (film and education magazine), 9, 10, 36, 121, *122*, 142; covers of, *48*, *149*, *150*; role of, 143–147, 151–153, 249n27; Verel on, 174
First Lessons in Modern Turkish (Krieder), 82
Flanagan, Thomas E., 117, 155
Fleet, Kate, 45
foreign films, 10, 33, 37, 41, 43–44, 58, 109, 233n14
foreign policy, US, 15, 38, 54, 61, 98, 101, 108, 121, 193–195
Foucault, Michel, 5
Fowle, James L., 236n54
Frankenberg, Ruth, 180, 187
freedom of speech, 110, 113, 250n39
Frey, Frederick W., 207
FRGC. *See* Film-Radio-Graphic Center
Fritsche, Maria, 19
Fuad Bey. *See* Uzkınay, Fuat

G. B. Film Library, 146
Gaumont-British (G. B.), 145–146, 159, 248n18
geography films, 175, 177, 254n100
Gharabaghi, Hadi, 12, 219
global audiences, of USIS, 104–107
global hierarchies, 28, 48
God, 59, 61, 94, 129
God of Creation (film), 27, 59–61, 63–64, 93–95, 100, 239n92
Gökalp, Mehmet Ziya, 174
Golden bracelet (*Altın Bilezik*), 23, 169–171
governmentality, 5
Grace, Dorothy, 236n57
Grand Coulee Dam (*Grand Gülee Barajı*) (educational film), 197
Graziano, Michael, 243
Grew, Joseph C., 33, 49–50, 51, 54, 230n41
Gridley, Elnathan, 75, 236n58
Grieveson, Lee, 32
Guerrero, Ed, 29
Gulick, John, 194
Gunning, Tom, 71
Gürbüz Çocuk Yarışmaları (Sturdy Child Competitions), 140
Gürel, Perin, 54, 166

Hacivat, 125, 167, 252n71
Halk Evleri (People's Houses), 9, 22, 82, 97, 193, 250n39, 252n71
Hamid (puppet character), 124–125, 127, 128–129
Hansen, Miriam, 37, 185
Harris, Cheryl, 165
Haven't we moved to this house? (Biz Bu Eve Taşınmadık mı?) (Hoja film), 167
Hays Code (Motion Picture Production Code), 45
health education, 87–89, 138–139, 247n2
Heart of a Tyrant, The (educational film), 124, 125, 126, 127, 128
heritage: artistic, 134; cultural, 1, 130, 170; national, 167
Hibri, Hatim El-, 32
hierarchies: civilizational, 37, 180, 199; global, 28, 48; modernization, 207; racialized, 11–12, 24, 31, 49, 57–58; social, 27
Highlights of Village Life (silent film), 65, 84, 85, 86
Hikmet, Nâzım, 40–41
Hinkle, Eugene M., 10
historiography, 5, 16, 32
Ho, Joseph W., 61
Hollywood, 8, 50, 68; educational films contrasted to, 10–11; Ovalle on, 45; Yeşilçam and, 16, 26, 29
Hübl, Adolphe, 9, 142, 153–154, 159, 191–192, 249n36, 256n46
Huntington, Samuel, 194
Hürriyet (newspaper), 53

I am coming from Korea (Kore'den Geliyorum) (Turkish film), 53, 151, 152, 205
identity: black Turks, 11–12, 160–162, 214, 215; educational films exploration of, 6; monolithic vision of, 11–12, 173; of Muslims, 80, 111; national, 11–12, 16, 26, 27, 28, 33, 38, 40, 46, 55, 64, 164; Sunni Muslim, 11, 12, 36, 141; of Turkey, 5, 11–12, 23, 28–29, 40, 46–47, 53–54, 64, 173–175, 212; of Turkification, 68–69, 248n12; of US, 107; white Turks, 11–12, 26, 162

ideological narratives, 5, 38, 110, 200, 208
ideological production, 40, 180
Idet novaia Turtsiia (New Turkey on the move, The) (documentary film), 47
IFRC. See International Federation of Red Cross and Red Crescent Societies
İleri, Tevfik, 153
illiteracy, 10, 250n39
IMG. See Information Media Guaranty
immigration, 96
Inan, Afet, 25–26, 50–51, 57
Incredible Turk, The (documentary film), 53–54
Information Media Guaranty (IMG) Program, 108, 109, 110
Inshallah (educational film), 124, 128–129
institutional agents, 6, 8, 9–10, 32, 50, 82, 132, 142
International Federation of Red Cross and Red Crescent Societies (IFRC), 30, 163, 218
international recognition, 39–40, 51, 106
international relations, 4, 5, 6, 31, 39, 135, 246n101
Irwin, Julia, 163
Islam, 22–23, 27, 28; compatibility with US, 35, 111; Inshallah and, 124, 128–129; mosque, 35, 75, 79, 80, 111, 161
Istanbul Turkish, standardized, 11, 36, 138, 161, 173

Jacobson, Matthew Frye, 24
JAMMAT. See Joint American Military Mission for Aid to Turkey
Jesus (biblical figure), 60, 63, 95
Jets over Turkey (Tepkili Uçaklar Türk Semalarında) (military film), 115
Jewish communities, 33, 42, 45–46, 164, 212
Joint American Military Mission for Aid to Turkey (JAMMAT), 115–116
Justice Party (Adalet Partisi), 169

Kadıoğlu, Ayşe, 20–21
Karagöz, Nurcan, 36, 40, 125, 166, 252n71, 253n89
Karagöz puppetry, 40, 125, 166, 228n2, 252n71, 253n89

INDEX 289

Katipoğlu, Sadun, 10, 36, 104, 121, *122*, 132–133, 135, 247n104
Kaya, Dilek, 167–168
Kemalists, 23, 88–89, 168–169, 170, 176
Kershner, Irvin, 106
key actors, 7
King of Kings, The (silent film), 63, 93–94, 95, 100
Klassen, Pamela E., 61
Koçer, Zeynep, 168
Korean War (1950–1953), 33, 52–54, 118, 151–153, 199, 204–205, 214
Kore'den Geliyorum (*I am coming from Korea*) (Turkish film), 53, 151, *152*, 205
Köy Enstitüleri (Village Institutes), 22, 72, 102, 193
Köy Traktörü (*Village Tractor*) (Marshall Plan film), 36, 113, 114–115, 200
Kozovoi, Andrei, 12
Kreider, Herman Harold, 81–83, 84, *92*
Kugeman, William E., 120, 155

Latham, Michael E., 184
Law 3122. *See* Law of Educational and Technical Films
Law for the Unification of Instruction (*Tevhid-i Tedrisat*), 72
Law of Cinema, Video and Music Works of Art, 170
Law of Educational and Technical Films (Öğretici ve Teknik Filmler Hakkında Kanun), 17, 66–67, 98, 112, 144–145, 240n111
Law on Surnames (*Soyadı Kanunu*), 248n12
Lazarsfeld, Paul, 188
Lean Years (educational film), 59
Lee, Sangjoon, 13
Lerner, Daniel, 10, 23, 26, 180, 182–183; audience research by, 37; "Mass Communications Audiences in Turkey" and, 188–191; *The Passing of Traditional Society*, 22, 193; PWD and, 256n38
Libal, Kathryn, 172
liberalism, 17–18, 135, 143, 169
libraries, for films, 9, 14, 29, 95, 104, 117, 121, 145–146

Lincoln, Abraham, 88, 106
Lindvall, Terry, 93
Lippmann, Walter, 19
Little Rock Crisis, 110
Little Rock"dan Dokuz Kişi (*Nine from Little Rock*), 35, 110–111
Lorentz, Pare, 200

MacCann, Richard Dyer, 19, 27
Mahar, P. M., 194
Malatyalıoğlu, Semiha, 81, *92*
malleable whiteness, 34, 60
Manaki, Milton, 42
Manaki, Yanaki, 42
manual labor, 84, *85*, 86
Mardiganian, Aurora, 68, 235n34
Mardin, BetÛl, 247n106
Mardin (documentary film), 36, 175–176, *177*
marginalization, 28, 29, 33, 54
marionette films, 124–125, *126*, *127*, 128–129, 131
Marshall, George C., 114
Marshall Plan, 21, 36, 113–115, 199–200, 214
"Mass Communications Audiences in Turkey" (report), 188–191
Mataş (distributor of media equipment), 9, 142, 146
Mazrui, Ali, 194
McGhee, George C., 52
McPharlin, Marjorie Batchelder, 164–166
media companies, 108–109, 242n21
media initiatives, 133, 143, 158, 251n58
medical services, 34, 87–89, 236n61
Mehmet (fictional character), 75, 79
Menderes, Adnan, 21, 169, 203, 213–216
MESA. *See* Middle Eastern or North African
Middle East: Change—Turkey and Saudi Arabia, The (foreign film), 33, 54–55, 56, 57–58
Middle Eastern or North African (MESA), 232n69
Midnight Express, The (film), 49
Mike Adams (fictional character), 1, *2*, *3*, *4*
military films, 10, 52, 94, 101, 115–117, 121, 211

290   INDEX

Milli Kütüphane (National Library), 30
Mills, Charles, 62
Ministry of Agriculture, 114, 159
Ministry of National Education of Turkey (MNET), 9, 30, 32, 70, 72, 82, 98; educational media and, 118; films produced by, 119; UNESO and, 153
MIS. *See* Moody Institute of Science
missionaries, 45, 48; agriculture and, 86; communication networks and, 67–69; criticism of, 62; doctors for, 88; film diplomacy and, 15, 34, 79–81; film programs of, 34–35, 98; film utilized by, 59–60, 62–63, 70–71, 91, 93, 100; malleable whiteness of, 34, 60; Protestant, 9, 59, 61, 63, 65, 69–70, 97, 99–100, 132–133, 213; schools in, 70, 81, 208; technologies used by, 61; USIS and, 97–100; whiteness and, 34, 60; Winkler work in, 65, 89, *90, 91, 92,* 93. *See also* American Board of Commissioners for Foreign Missions
MNET. *See* Ministry of National Education of Turkey
mobile cinema, 6, 36, 37, 121–123, 159, 206, 207
mobile film, 14, 29, 65, 97, 121, 123, 206; EFC, 156, 200; Hübl and, 191–192; people gathering at, *122*
modernization, 1, 4, 12, 55, 104, 116, 140, 143; agriculture and, 83–84, 102, 200–204; campaign for, 142–143; Christianization and, 100, 195; Cold War and, 20–23, 37, 199; educational films as initiatives for, 6–7, 32, 183–187, 197–198; educational reform and, 18–20, 70, 73, 145; EFC role in, 10–11; hierarchical model of, 207; hotels and, 232n67; Karagöz and, 252n71; Lerner on, 22; "Mass Communications Audiences in Turkey" and, 188–191; missionaries and, 34; nationalism and, 32, 45; *Poultry Raising* and, 180, 181, 182; project for, 6–7, 10, 20, 23, 25, 26, 43; secularism and, 3, 5; theory of, 11, 21–22, 38, 54, 180, 182–186, 193–195, 208; useful, 37, 180, 184–185, 210, 216;

USIS and, 155; visions of, 11, 63, 132, 141, 160, 177, 178, 184–185, 203, 209; whiteness and, 5, 6–7, 8, 9, 11, 16, 33, 81, 151, 162, 164, 165
Mongolian, 24, 25
Moody Bible Institute, 94
Moody Institute of Science (MIS), 27, 59, 93, 94
Moon, Irwin A., 94
mosque, 35, 75, 79, 80, 111, 161
Mount Argeaus (*Erciyes Dağı*), 75, 236n58
"Movies, Newsreels, and Documentary Films in Turkey" (report), 190
Muslimness contract, 62, 64
Muslims, 22, 28, 35, 61; Christianity and, 33, 34; converting of, 79–80; identity, 80, 111; non-, 32, 41–42, 48, 62, 68–69, 81, 165, 167, 234n24; in Ottoman Empire, 62; Ramadan holiday for, 80, 237n64; Sunni, 11, 12, 36, 141, 170
Mutena (fictional character), 80
Mutlu, Dilek Kaya, 41–42, 217, 229n9, 230n40
Myrdal, Gunnar, 22, 194, 257n59

Nandy, Ashis, 194
NARA. *See* National Archives and Records Administration
Nasreddin Hoja (folktale figure), 31, 123–124, 129–132, 136, 164–168, 245n88, 258n83; communism and, 23; propaganda and, 35; whiteness and, 27
National Archives and Records Administration (NARA), 30, 31
National Geographic (magazine), 82
national heritage, 167
national identity, 11–12, 16, 27, 40, 46; modernization of Turkey and, 26, 38; religion and, 23; Westernization and, 28, 33, 55
national ideology, educational film as reflection of, 12, 177
national image, 46–47, 48, 153
nationalism, 10; modernization and, 32, 45; secular, 18, 20, 176; Turkish, 23, 57, 81, 170, 174, 222n9; unitary, 26
National Library (*Milli Kütüphane*), 30

INDEX   291

National Teaching Films Center, 117, 118, 155
national unity, 177–178; educational films and, 6, 73, 129, 142, 160, 168, 175; religious devotion and, 129
nation-building projects, 70, 73, 89, 160, 173, 174–175, 195
Nation is awakening, A (*Bir Millet Uyanıyor*) (film), 43
Native American masks, 166
NATO, 52, 107, 115–116, 120, 204, 214
Nazis, 22, 256n38
Near East Mission, of ABCFM, 84
Near East Relief (NER), 68–69, 84
New Turkey on the move, The (*Idet novaia Turtsiia*) (documentary film), 47
New York Times (newspaper), 24
Nilson, Harriet, 236n57
Nilson, Paul, 10, 27, 59–61, 63–65, 71, 72, 233n4; *Beneath the Snows of Mount Argeaus* and, 75–76; Caner and, 238n70; on Christianity, 73–74, 94–96; on film technologies, 66, 98; *God of Creation* shared by, 94–95
Nine from Little Rock (documentary film), 35, 110–111
Non-Aligned Movement, 7
non-Muslims, 32, 41–42, 68–69, 81, 167, 234n24; targeted, 165; treatment of, 48, 62
nontheatrical films, 5–6, 8, 16–18, 35, 98–100; exhibitions for, 33–34, 63–65, 66, 71, 89–93, 132, 206; as instrument of governance, 176, 180
nuclear power, 196
Nur Baba (*Bosphorus mystery, The*) (silent film), 42–43

Öğretici ve Teknik Filmler Hakkında Kanun (Law of Educational and Technical Films), 17, 66–67, 112, 144–145, 240n11
Opening of the Islamic Center of Washington, The (*Washington'da İslam Etüdleri Merkezinin Açılışı*), 35, 111, 228n112
Orphanage (*Ana Kucağı*) (documentary film), 36, 171–172

Ottoman Empire, 20, 40–42, 48, 49, 65, 252n71; censorship and, 46–47; Muslims in, 62; NER and, 68
Ovalle, Priscilla Peña, 45
Özdeniz, Mahmut, 10, 142, 145–146
Özdil, İlhan, 135, 158
Özön, Nijat, 16, 41, 110
Öztürk, Serdar, 252n71

Painter, Nell Irvin, 24
Paker, Hande, 162
Parks, Lisa, 5
Passing of Traditional Society, The (Lerner), 22, 193
Paul (saint), 61, 72
People's Houses (*Halk Evleri*), 9, 22, 82, 97, 193, 250n39, 252n71
perceptions, of Turkey: geopolitical, 39, 48; shaped through film, 5, 108–111, 130, 180; United States, 50, 136
Pergamum, Turkey, 1, 3
Personal Hygiene for Young Men (silent film), 83, 88–89, 100
Pittard, Eugène, 25
Pocket Guide to Turkey, A (military pamphlet), 116
Point Four Program, 194–195
policy objectives, 4, 6, 12, 101, 202
Polimnia (fictional character), 80
Poultry Raising (educational film), 38, 179, 181–182, 209
Power and the Land (*Elektrik ve Toprak*) (educational film), 197
prisons, films in, 59–60
private commercial interests, 143, 144, 145, 146
privilege: of missionaries, 33; Muslims and, 62; socioeconomic, 12; structures of, 54; Turkishness and, 64
production: of educational films, 6, 7, 8, 13, 14; of educational media, 156; of films, 116–117, 118–119, 144, 158–159, 164, 168–171, 211; ideological, 40, 180
progressive education, 72–73
projects, for modernization, 6–7, 10, 20, 23, 25, 26, 43

292 INDEX

propaganda, 4, 13, 27; ABCFM, 10; Cold War, 32–33, 40, 54, 109, 129, 198; ECA and, 114; education and, 18–20; film democracy and, 45; films as, 105, 124; Jewish, 45–46; Nasreddin Hoja and, 35; religious, 63–64, 98; state, 160–164, 168, 229n24; state-sponsored films and, 45, 145; Stearns on, 117; US, 20, 130; USIS and, 19–20, 35, 36

Protestant missionaries, 9, 59, 65, 69–70, 97, 99–100, 132–133; American Collegiate Institute founded by, 213; radio programs and, 61; whiteness and, 63

Psalms, book of, 27, 59–60

Psychological Warfare Division (PWD), 194, 256n38

public diplomacy, 13–14, 19, 223n26; Cold War, 12, 155, 250n44; women in, 133

public opinion: in favor of communism, 47; film diplomacy and, 4, 5; film shaping, 39; Snow on, 13–14; Turkishness influence on, 36–37; US influence on, 20

public relations, 14, 49, 94, 211, 247n106, 253n89; educational film as tool for, 19; IMG Program for, 108, 109, 110; between Turkey and United States, 5; women in, 132–133, 135

public welfare, 98

puppetry, 201, 202–203, 258n83; *The Heart of a Tyrant*, 124, *125*, *126*, *127*, *128*; Karagöz, 40, 125, 166, 228n2, 252n71, 253n89; McPharlin and, 164–166; shadow, 32, 40, 124

Putney, Cliff, 88

PWD. *See* Psychological Warfare Division

Quality Milk (agricultural silent film), 83, 86–87, 100

Quicke, Andrew, 93

race, 47–49, 243n33; black Turks, 11–12, 160–162, 214, 215; Chun on, 227n99; as conceptual tool, 24–26; *Depremde Kızılay* and, 160–164; in educational films, 6, 17; films related to, 110–111; Gürel on, 54; secularism and, 227n97; technology of, 28, 81; Western racial theories, 222n9, 226n87; white Turks, 11–12, 26, 162; yellow, 24, 25. *See also* whiteness

racial categorization, 24–25, 26

Racial Contract, The (Mills), 62

racial differentiation, 57

racial epistemologies, 204, 209–210

racialized diplomacy, 35

racialized hierarchies, 11–12, 24, 31, 49, 57–58

radio programs, 61, 108, 133–134, 158–159

Ramadan (Muslim holiday), 80, 237n64

Reception of the US Ambassador Joseph C. Grew by Atatürk on the Forest Farm, The (foreign film), 33, 50–51, 54, 58

Red Crescent in earthquake (*Depremde Kızılay*) (documentary film), 36, 160–164, 251n53

relationships, between United States and Turkey, 3–4, 5, 6, 22, 76, 117, 204; educational films and, 16, 212, 216; film diplomacy and, 31–32, 51; transnational context of, 19–20; whiteness and, 27

religious conversions, 34, 62, 67, 72–75, 79–80, 167

religious devotion, 129

religious propaganda, 63–64, 98

Republican People's Party (*Cumhuriyet Halk Partisi*), 74, 213, 214

Republic of Turkey, 8, 18, 42, 65, 69, 72, 83, 240n111

revolution, of educational films, 9, 36, 155–156, 176

Rogers, Basil, 191–192, 199

Roosevelt, Theodore, 88, 240n2

Rural Co-Op, The (agriculture film), 38, 200–203, 209, 210

Russo-Turkish War, 41

Sadiye (Turkish film), 106, 242n11

Salem, Elie, 194

Saudi Arabia, 54–55, *56*, 57

scholarships, 13, 16, 32, 247n2

INDEX 293

Schoolmates at Scutare (silent film), 66, 75, 80–81, 82, 92, 100
school systems, in Turkey, 10, 18–20, 70, 74, 208
secular classrooms, 1, 3, 70
secular education, 66, 69–70, 79–80
secularism, 55; Kemalist, 168, 176; modernization and, 3, 5; race and, 227n97; role of, 28; Turkish, 168, 170; whiteness and, 163
secular nationalism, 18, 20, 176
Şeker Bayramı (Sugar Feast), 80
Selçuk, Ziya, 215, 260n12
shadow puppetry, 32, 40, 124
shadow theater, 40–41, 252n71
Shah, Hemant, 194
Shanbary, Ahmad Al-, 57, 232n68
Sherrill, Charles H., 51
Shibusawa, Naoko, 11
Shils, Edward, 185, 195
Shipping, Communications, and National Defense (booklets), 101
Shirt of Flame (Ateşten Gömlek) (film), 43
silent films, 192; The Arrival of a Train, 71; Beneath the Snows of Mount Argeaus and Schoolmates at Scutare, 66, 75–76, 77, 78, 79, 92, 100, 236n57; Highlights of Village Life, 65, 84, 85, 86; The King of Kings, 63, 93–94, 95, 100; Nur Baba, 42–43; Personal Hygiene for Young Men, 83, 88–89, 100; Quality Milk (agricultural silent film), 83, 86–87, 100; Schoolmates at Scutare, 66, 75, 80–81, 82, 92, 100
silver screens, 43–44
Sinema Otomobili (Cinema Bus), 206
Sinema Postası (film magazine), 40
Skvirsky, Salomé Aguilera, 86, 87
Slaves' revolt, The (Buntat na Robite) (Bulgarian film), 46
small-gauge films, 17
Smith-Mundt Act of 1948, 31, 36, 112–113
Smyrna, 67–69
Snow, Nancy, 13–14
social hierarchies, 27
social welfare, 45
socioeconomic privilege, 12
soft power, 4–5, 13

Sosyal Hizmetler ve Çocuk Esirgeme Kurumu (Children's Protection Agency), 164, 171–172, 253n90
sound films, 43
Soviet Union, 5, 23, 43, 48, 52, 54, 116, 120; films, 47, 131–132; values of, 131
Soyadı Kanunu (Law on Surnames), 248n12
Sözde Kızlar (Would-be girls, The) (film), 43
sponsored films, 17; ABCFM-, 34, 66, 75; government-, 5, 19, 37, 156, 158, 170, 173, 176, 183, 192; Marshall Plan and, 114; NER-, 68–69; state-, 36–37, 45, 47, 58, 106, 145, 160–161, 171; US-, 133, 199
Standardized Istanbul Turkish, 11, 36, 138, 161, 173
state propaganda, 160–164, 168, 229n24
state-sponsored films, 36–37, 58, 106, 160–161, 171; national image rebranded through, 47; propaganda and, 45, 145; whiteness and, 199
Stearns, Monteagle, 9, 34, 36, 65, 97, 98, 154, 246n102; film diplomacy and, 104; film exhibitions organized by, 132–133; on propaganda, 117; USIE, 234
Stewart, Jacqueline Najuma, 17–18
Sturdy Child Competitions (Gürbüz Çocuk Yarışmaları), 140
Suffering of Elif, the (Elif"in Çilesi) (Turkish film), 23, 137, 138, 139, 140–141, 177
Sugar Feast (Şeker Bayramı), 80
Suner, Asuman, 41
Sunni Muslim, 11, 12, 36, 141, 170
Sürel, Safder, 251n48
Suyun Kontrolü (Control of Water) (educational film), 200
Syracuse University, 106, 158

T. C. Resmi Gazete (newspaper), 233n14, 240n111
Talas American College (TAC), 74, 75–76, 236n54
Talas Nute Clinic, 89–90, 99
Talu, Ercüment Ekrem, 71
Tamerlane (emperor), 127, 129, 130
target audiences, 5, 14, 181

294 INDEX

Tea (*Çay*) (educational film), 159
Technical Bookstore (*Teknik Kitabevi*), 9, 142, 145–146
Tennessee Vadisi (*Valley of the Tennessee*) (educational film), 197
Tepkili Uçaklar Türk Semalarında (*Jets over Turkey*) (military film), 115
"Terrible Turk" stereotype, 33, 48–50, 52, 53–54, 58, 152, 204, 231n48
Tevhid-i Tedrisat (Law for the Unification of Instruction), 72
theory of modernization, 11, 21–22, 38, 54, 180, 182–186, 193–195, 208
Third World nations, 7
TPB. *See* Turkish Press Bureau
traditional cinema, 16
Traffic safety for pedestrians (*Yayalar için Trafik Emniyeti*) (educational film), 134
transnational networks, 66, 99, 132, 159, 211; film diplomacy and, 4, 49, 115, 130; between United States and Turkey, 38; whiteness in, 7
transnational racialization, 26, 27–29, 54, 81
TRT. *See* Turkish Radio and Television
Truman, Harry S., 113–114, 194–195
Truman Doctrine, 101, 113–114
Turajlić, Mila, 13
Turek, Lauren, 61
Turkey: American Research Institute in, 30, 218; as a bridge, 23; cinema in, 16–18, 31–32, 57–58, 167–168, 178; communication network US-, 98, 132, 133, 135; early republican, 55, 87–89; eugenics in, 25–26, 28, 51, 140; film production facilities in, 119–120; *Film ve Öğretim* influence on, 146–153; government interventions of, 45–46; identity of, 5, 11–12, 23, 28–29, 40, 46–47, 53–54, 64, 173–175, 212; ideological production in, 40, 180; illiteracy in, 10, 250n39; image of, 29, 162; JAMMAT, 115–116; Korean War and, 52–54; landscapes of, 1, 3; as little America, 9; map of, 1, *2, 56, 102, 157*; Marshall Plan in, 21, 36, 113–115, 199–200, 214; military of, 52–53, 115, 204–205; mixed ancestry of, 24–25; MNET, 9, 30, 32, 70, 72, 82, 98, 118; National Teaching Films Center in, 117, 118, 155; *Öğretici ve Teknik Filmler Hakkında Kanun*, 17, 66–67, 112, 144–145, 240n11; perceptions of, 5, 39, 48, 50, 108–111, 130, 136, 180; Pergamum, 1, 3; Republic of, 8, 18, 42, 65, 69, 72, 83, 240n111; school systems in, 10, 18–20, 70, 74, 208; silver screens of, 43–44; stereotypes of, 33, 47–50, 52–54, 58, 152, 204; Truman Doctrine influence on, 101, 113–114; villages in, 65, 75, 91, 169, 182–183, 200–204, 224n42; Western powers and, 7, 9, 11, 48, 108. *See also* identity; modernization; perceptions; relationships, between United States and Turkey
Turkey: Middle East Bridgeland (American educational film), 1–5, 11, 17–18
Turkey: The Land of "In-Between" (military film), 116, 213
Turkey (film), 101–103
Turkey's Amateur Photo Club (*Turkiye Amator Foto Kulubu*), 251n48
Turkification, 68–69, 248n12
Turkish Anthropometric Survey, 25
Turkish nationalism, 23, 57, 81, 170, 174, 222n9
Turkishness, 26; public opinion influenced by, 36–37; Ünlü on, 64; whiteness and, 7, 25, 27–29, 34, 36, 53
Turkishness contract, 34, 64, 68–69, 174
Turkish Press Bureau (TPB), 117, 119, 155
Turkish Radio and Television (TRT), 133–134
Turkish society, 18, 20, 34, 80, 189, 197
Turkish Troops in Korea (training film), 52, 118
Turkish War of Independence, 43, 69, 72, 213
Turkiye Amator Foto Kulubu (Turkey's Amateur Photo Club), 251n48
Tutanak Dergisi (magazine), 153

Ufuk (magazine), 108
UNESCO. *See* United Nations Educational, Scientific, and Cultural Organization

Union of Soviet Socialist Republics (USSR), 12, 43, 45, 97, 113–114, 242n11
unitary nationalism, 26
United Nations Educational, Scientific, and Cultural Organization (UNESCO), 9–10, 30, 36, 153
United States (US): Air Force, 94, 115–116; Cold War strategy, 113, 185, 209; communication network Turkey-, 98, 132, 133, 135; Department of Agriculture, 87, 105; Department of Defense, 94, 101, 116; exceptionalism of, 11; film programming of, 35, 108, 155; foreign policy, 15, 38, 54, 61, 98, 101, 108, 121, 193–195; ideals of, 28, 58, 103, 104–107, 148; identity of, 107; ideology from, 188, 196–197; interests of, 50, 112, 130; Islam compatibility with, 35, 111; Nasreddin Hoja films from, 132; perceptions of Turkey, 50, 136; policy objectives of, 202; propaganda, 20, 130; public opinion influenced by, 20; reputation of, 35; schools in, 70, 75, 76, 79, 81, 184, 207–208; sponsored films by, 133, 199; State Department of, 9, 10, 49, 98, 106, 118, 179, 188; style of capitalism, 20, 37, 195, 198, 208, 209; values in, 18, 35, 99–100, 109, 121; Westernization from, 20–22, 28, 43, 55, 166, 195. *See also* relationships, between United States and Turkey
United World Films, 3, 145
Ünlü, Barış, 27–28, 34, 62, 64, 174
Ünsalan, Cahit, 144, 160
US. *See* United States
useful modernization, 37, 180, 184–185, 210, 216
USIE. *See* US International Information and Educational Exchange Program
US Information Agency (USIA), 13, 65, 108, 114, 234n19, 242n18
US Information Service (USIS), 9, 242n18, 242n21; cinema course, 121, *122*, 123–132; Cold War and, 15, 19–20, 108–111; ECA and, 181–182, 191–192, 199–200, 201–202, 206; educational media and, 117–120; film diplomacy and, 15, 36; films, 31, 34, 36, 98, 104–107, 112–113; global audiences of, 104–107; Marshall Plan films and, 36, 113–115, 199–200; missionaries and, 97–100; Nasreddin Hoja, 23, 27, 31, 35, 123–124, 129–131, 136, 164–168, 245n88, 258n83; propaganda and, 19–20, 35, 36; in Turkey, *103*; Turkish Troops in Korea, 52, 118
US International Information and Educational Exchange Program (USIE), 234n19, 242n18
USSR. *See* Union of Soviet Socialist Republics
Uzkınay, Fuat, 41, 42, 229n9

Valley of the Tennessee (*Tennessee Vadisi*) (educational film), 197
values: of Christianity, 10, 32, 34, 59–60, 65–66, 69, 80–81, 88; Soviet Union, 131; US, 18, 35, 99–100, 109, 121; Western, 18, 20, 27, 123
Verel, Oktay, 174
Village Institutes (*Köy Enstitüleri*), 22, 72, 102, 193
villages, in Turkey, 65, 75, 91, 169, 182–183, 200–204, 224n42
Village Tractor (*Köy Traktörü*) (Marshall Plan film), 36, 113, 114–115, 200

Wagner, Robert W., 106, 242n11
Washington Cami (film), 35, 111
Washington'da İslam Etüdleri Merkezinin Açılışı (*Opening of the Islamic Center of Washington, The*), 35, 111, 228n112
Wasson, Haidee, 37, 180, 185
wealth, films emphasis on, 44, 50, 140
Weinberg, Sigmund, 42
welfare: child, 171–172; public, 98; social, 45
Western bloc, 35, 54, 204
Westernization, 20–22, 23, 28, 43, 55, 166, 195
Western modernity, 49, 199
Western powers, 7, 9, 11, 48, 108
Western racial theories, 222n9, 226n87
Western values, 18, 20, 27, 123

What Is Disease? (tuberculosis film), 90
White, Raymond, 65, 97
whiteness, 57, 91, 197–198, 210, 211; anticommunism and, 231n51; civilizational hierarchy grounded in, 37, 180, 199; Cold War and, 38, 212; economic prosperity achieved through, 33; educational films and, 140–141; as form of power, 51; Frankenberg on, 180, 187; ideology of, 60, 199; lens of, 5, 91, 209; liberalism and, 18; malleable, 34, 60; missionaries and, 34, 60; modernization and, 5, 6–7, 8, 9, 11, 16, 33, 81, 151, 162, 164, 165; Nasreddin Hoja and, 27; as property, 165; Protestant missionaries and, 63; secularism and, 163; as selective filter, 112, 113; state-sponsored films and, 199; in transnational networks, 7; transnational racialization of, 26–29, 81; Turkishness and, 7, 25, 27–29, 34, 36, 53
white Turks, 11–12, 26, 162
Williams, Mark, 13

Wilson, Edwin C., 101
Wingate, Henry K., 236
Winkler, Mary Louise Lee, 65, 89, *90*, *91*, *92*, 93
women, in public relations, 132–133, 135
World War I, 69–70
World War II, 26, 94, 114, 256n38
Would-be girls, The (*Sözde Kizlar*) (film), 43

Yakub'un Kuyusu (*Daughter of Israel, A*) (French film), 45–46
Yaratıcı Oyun I (Creative game I), 164, 165
Yaratıcı Oyun II (Creative game II), 166, 167
Yayalar için Trafik Emniyeti (*Traffic safety for pedestrians*) (educational film), 134
yellow race, 24, 25
Yeşilçam (Turkey's counterpart to classical Hollywood), 16, 26, 29
young Turks, 103, 222n9
yufka (bread), 84, *85*
Yusef and His Plough (*Yusuf ve Sabanı*) (Marshall Plan film), 113, 114, 200

Zaharna, R. S., 13
zenci (black-skinned), 28

GPSR Authorized Representative: Easy Access System Europe, Mustamäe tee 50, 10621 Tallinn, Estonia, gpsr.requests@easproject.com